W9-AXI-417

Sharing space: Soldiers, family, and the mission-first premise.

Army of Hope, Army of Alienation

Culture and Contradiction in the American Army Communities of Cold War Germany

John P. Hawkins

Foreword by Faris R. Kirkland

Westport, Connecticut
London

Library of Congress Cataloging-in-Publication Data

Hawkins, John Palmer, 1946–
    Army of hope, army of alienation : culture and contradiction in the American Army
communities of Cold War Germany / John P. Hawkins ; foreword by Faris Kirkland.
     p. cm.
    Includes bibliographical references and index.
    ISBN 0–275–96738–7 (alk. paper)
     1. Sociology, Military—United States. 2. Sociology, Military—Germany. 3. United
States. Army—Germany. 4. Military bases, American—Germany. I. Title.
UA26.G3H39   2001
306.2′7′0973—dc21   00–061111

British Library Cataloguing in Publication Data is available.

Library of Congress Catalog Card Number: 00–061111
ISBN: 0–275–96738–7

First published in 2001

Praeger Publishers, 88 Post Road West, Westport, CT 06881
An imprint of Greenwood Publishing Group, Inc.
www.praeger.com

Printed in the United States of America

The paper used in this book complies with the
Permanent Paper Standard issued by the National
Information Standards Organization (Z39.48–1984).

10 9 8 7 6 5 4 3 2 1

To the soldiers and spouses
who opened their hearts and minds and lives to me.

And to those like them, in all services,
whose sacrifices have made democracy secure
during a half century of Cold War.

*****

In Memoriam

Faris R. Kirkland, 1932–2000,
who helped me make this a better book even though he knew
his remaining time was ever so short.

Contents

A photo essay follows Chapter 6.

Foreword

Lieutenant Colonel John Hawkins's anthropological field study of American soldiers and their families serving and living in Germany between 1986 and 1988 is remarkable in three respects. It presents for the first time the story of families facing the constant threat of imminent and proximate nuclear war while coping with the special stresses of living and raising children in a foreign country. Second, it is the only examination of the culture of the U.S. Army in Germany by an anthropologist who also is a field grade officer in the U.S. Army Reserve.[1] Finally, Hawkins integrates cultural, social, and psychological data to go beyond ethnographic description to analyze the processes through which soldiers, families, and the military hierarchy interact for the good or ill of each group.

It is important to place the Hawkins study in context. In the wake of the Vietnam War, the Army was in psychological and moral disarray.[2] Among the few organizations keeping a professional watch over the mental health of the institution as a whole during the post-Vietnam era were the Army War College and the Department of Military Psychiatry in the Division of Neuropsychiatry of the Walter Reed Army Institute of Research (WRAIR). In 1970, at the War College, a group of students led by Lieutenant Colonel Walter F. Ulmer Jr. conducted the *Study on Military Professionalism*. They documented officers' perceptions that to achieve promotion they had to please their superiors at whatever cost to their own integrity, the legitimate needs of their subordinates, or the mission capability of their units.[3] In 1973 and 1974, Captains Larry H. Ingraham and Frederick J. Manning of the Department of Military Psychiatry of WRAIR conducted an investigation of drug use among enlisted personnel in the Washington, D.C., area. Their findings complemented the *Study on Military Professionalism* by showing that soldiers used drugs primarily to bring a sense of identity and purpose to lives rendered meaningless and barren by the incompetence of officers and their indifference to the welfare of their subordinates or the capabilities of their units.[4]

These two studies, which might have served as a call for self-examination in the Army, antagonized senior officers. The Chief of Staff of the Army who had commissioned the *Study on Military Professionalism,* General William C. Westmoreland, had it placed under close hold for thirteen years.[5] Though not suppressed, Ingraham's book, *The Boys in the Barracks,* was not published until 1984. Dissatisfaction with the military culture, although not universal, was widespread, and eventually officers who believed the military culture had to be changed reached senior rank.

Constructive reform of the military culture began in 1979 with the appointment of General Edward C. Meyer as Chief of Staff of the Army. Meyer was the first officer to serve as Chief of Staff who had not served in World War II. He had not experienced directly the fear-driven authoritarianism and intimidation that characterized much of the leadership behavior during that conflict.[6] General Meyer initiated several measures to change the human dimensions of the Army. One of these was a new unit manning system designed to keep soldiers together in the same unit from their enlistments through initial entry training and throughout their first three years of service. Called COHORT (Cohesion, Operational Readiness, Training), this program offered the possibilities of building stronger unit cohesion and allowing accretive training to build unit competence far superior to that attainable in units that experienced the rapid turnover of personnel caused by a manning system based on individual replacements.[7] Another of Meyer's initiatives was to assign Major General Maxwell R. Thurman to command the Army recruiting program.

When General Thurman took over Recruiting Command, it was a scandal-ridden organization that could not meet the Army's needs for manpower even by recruiting principally among high school dropouts—men with limited ability to learn and often with maladaptive attitudes toward work. He transformed its ways of doing business and refused to accept recruits who did not have the potential to be effective soldiers in a complex Army. By 1990, Recruiting Command met Army manpower requirements with personnel 97 percent of whom had high school diplomas.[8] By making Recruiting Command a system for bringing capable people into the Army, Thurman laid the foundation for self-paced training, empowering leadership, and a truly professional brotherhood of arms.

General Thurman went on to serve as Deputy Chief of Staff for Personnel (1981–1983), Vice Chief of Staff of the Army (1983–1987), and commanding general, Training and Doctrine Command (1987–1989). His fingerprints as initiator or executor are on almost every innovation in recruiting, training, organization, and family support of the 1980s. Collectively, those reforms produced the superb Army that took down Manuel Noriega's military regime in Panama in forty-eight hours in 1989, and drove the Iraqi army from Kuwait in 100 hours in 1991.

Throughout General Thurman's decade of senior service, he relied on Dr. David H. Marlowe, chief of the Department of Military Psychiatry at WRAIR, for information on how his reforms were working out and for advice on how to improve them. Prominent among the tasks Thurman assigned Marlowe was to find out what mattered to soldiers' spouses and children, how well the Army was meeting their needs, and what the Army could do better. Lieutenant Colonel John Hawkins, a professor of anthropology at Brigham Young University and an Army Reservist, did his annual training with the Department of Military Psychiatry. He took a leave of absence from Brigham Young and, with Dr. Marlowe, worked out a plan that was to become a centerpiece of the Army family studies—an ethnographic study of Army communities in Germany.

John Hawkins is an experienced field anthropologist who received his doctorate from the University of Chicago and has conducted ethnographic research in Guatemala and Mexico. With his family, he moved to a U.S. Army community in Germany in 1986 and used the military family support system to secure housing in a German village, as would any military family just arriving. Hawkins did his fieldwork as a civilian. Having long been a reserve officer, however, Lieutenant Colonel Hawkins understood enough of military language and hierarchical relationships to begin at once to observe the details of military family life in Germany. Having never served on extended active duty, his eye was fresh and keenly observant of the interpersonal and organizational dynamics unique to the culture of the U.S. Army there. He identified and tracked the unintended second- and third-order consequences of orders and policies enacted to alleviate the anxiety of an insecure commander or placate an exigent superior. His "outsider status" as a civilian anthropologist worked with his "insider status" as a reserve officer to make such military commonplaces as mission creep and chronic demand overload stand out in sharp relief. He has described the origins, effects on personnel, and impact on operational efficiency of these processes with a clarity never before achieved by any commentator on military affairs. Having his own family with him gave him additional sources of information on the social processes within military communities.

As you read *Army of Hope, Army of Alienation*, you will feel the idealism of soldiers as they sought to prepare themselves for war. You will sense the dedication of their spouses as they struggled to have family lives in military communities that in the event of war would have been the initial targets of Soviet nuclear strikes. Their lives were constrained by a complex mix of military regulations, American civil laws, and German laws to which they were subject. Most did not have the time to learn the language and customs of Germany, much less the legal complexities. As they struggled to make sense of the stressful situation in which they lived, they discovered that their most severe problems came not from the threat of Soviet forces or from German customs and laws but from the culture of the U.S. Army.

The War College *Study on Military Professionalism* and Ingraham's *Boys in the Barracks* both describe a dysfunctional military culture that existed in the 1970s. By the mid-1980s, the Army was well into the cultural renaissance that began with General Meyer's appointment as Chief of Staff. But U.S. forces in Germany were a fiefdom in which the older culture of fear, intimidation, and indifference to the welfare of junior personnel was intensified because of its cultural isolation and the proximity of a lethal threat. There was more resistance in Germany to the winds of change sweeping the Army. John Hawkins makes his readers feel as if they were living in that culture. You will read about institutional and interpersonal processes that wreaked havoc with relationships among leaders, subordinates, and spouses and undermined combat efficiency, including:

- Forces that pushed insecure commanders, wanting their units to appear competent, to micromanage details of unit operations. In the process their subordinates' skills withered, and their units became progressively less capable of performing their missions.
- International economic trends that impoverished U.S. soldiers with respect to the German economy. In an effort to cope, spouses sought to find jobs, but mutually contradictory regulations drastically limited their access to child-care facilities.
- Contradictions between command-trumpeted slogans that claimed "The Army takes care of its own" and medical clinic practices allowing only a four-hour period each week during which family members could try to arrange appointments for the following week. As a result, phone lines were consistently overwhelmed during those periods. To complete the "Catch-22," some clinics refused to honor requests for appointments made in person, whereas others gave priority to walk-ins, thereby greatly handicapping the families living away from post.
- Commanders' demands that soldiers put accomplishment of the mission ahead of all other considerations, whereas some included in "the mission" such activities as putting on elaborately rehearsed demonstrations for visiting dignitaries or painting all the vehicles prior to a command inspection. The resulting perception of waste and misdirection of effort alienated many soldiers and spouses.
- Pressure on commanders and staff functionaries to put first priority on any program sponsored by a higher commander, no matter how irrelevant or trivial. Thus, they downgraded the programs and tasks essential to troop welfare and undermined morale and readiness.
- Evaluation of professional soldiers based not only on their own performance of duty but also on the conduct and attitudes of their wives and children. As a result, soldiers intimidated their families, families could blackmail soldiers by threatening to get in trouble, and everyone was afraid of being reported for some offense by a neighbor.
- The desire of soldiers and their families to escape from the surveillance and pressures of life in a military community, though many feared living among or even going on vacation among Germans because they did not know the language or customs and could too easily create problems for the command as a result. The consequent isolation "boiled over" into hostile interpersonal relationships within the densely interconnected military community.

Dr. Hawkins documents these and other processes, using the words of the soldiers and spouses he interviewed. He traces their origins to the interlocking insecurities felt by senior leaders, and he assesses their impact on morale, familial solidarity, and combat readiness. He demonstrates how ostensibly unrelated policies interact at the level of the family to create anxiety, mistrust, and a sense of helplessness. He describes a culture of fear in which the principal underlying dynamic is not fear of attack by the Soviets, but fear of being found wanting with respect to some obscure regulation or requirement—and a culture of suffering. The army of alienation was led by men afraid that the personnel—soldiers and members of their families—for whom they were responsible would be deficient in readiness, cleanliness, politeness to members of the host country, obedience to traffic regulations, punctuality in returning library books, children's deportment, or any of a long list of other criteria. Anything could be grounds for career-ending sanctions.

To alleviate their own fears, superiors induced anxiety in their subordinates by blizzards of regulations, harsh punishments, and demands to take "effective, aggressive action to preclude recurrence" of deficiencies or mistakes of any kind. Spouses often participated in the soldiers' fears and, not being as well-versed in the web of prohibitions as their husbands, experienced yet greater anxiety as they sought to avoid a misstep.

With exquisite sensitivity to human social dynamics, Dr. Hawkins explains how commanders used the prospect of Soviet attack to invest the measures they took to alleviate their own professional insecurities with an urgency appropriate for the defense of Europe against nuclear holocaust. No one could challenge the sanctity of such a mission, and leaders, in many cases, unconsciously recognized that they had a blank check on their subordinates' time, energy, and spirit. Mission creep went unchallenged, demand overload was endemic, and families had to make do with almost no support from their frantically anxious husbands. Dr. Hawkins's record of how soldiers' trust in the integrity of the command structure was abused is sobering. He details these processes in two carefully studied military communities, and he provides additional evidence that the processes were widespread from six other communities studied less intensively. We infer that similar patterns could have been obtained in many other communities throughout Germany. His analysis, for example, rings true to my own experience as a unit officer in Germany during an earlier period.

John Hawkins is not a professional soldier; he is an anthropologist. One of the cardinal rules of anthropological fieldwork is to minimize the effect of the study on the cultural processes being observed. Dr. Hawkins therefore did not intervene in the lives of the soldiers and families he studied. In the conclusion, he offers limited suggestions, mostly in the form of principles, about what could have been done in the late 1980s or what might be done in the future. His exposition of patterns of fear, mistrust, and incompetence; his descriptions of regulations promulgated without regard for possible second- and third-order consequences; and his vivid presentations of the despair, depression, and alienation that resulted from lack of consideration for subordinates will be useful tools for analyzing how and why leadership can go awry.

Given an army of hope peopled by soldiers imbued with professionalism and idealism, officers and policy makers are honor bound to treat them with the trust, respect, and interest that their commitment deserves. The alternative is to turn soldiers into an army of alienation whose members are ill equipped to survive psychologically on the battlefield, much less have the judgment, compassion, and courage necessary to accomplish the subtle and complex missions of the twenty-first century.

John Hawkins is probably the one person best fitted to have carried out this investigation. *Army of Hope, Army of Alienation* is a rich resource for scholars in anthropology, social psychology, and management as well as for military leaders. Moreover, it is a pleasure to read. His concise, vividly documented account of life under the guns of the Warsaw Pact and within a military culture of fear reads more like a thriller than an academic work.

Faris R. Kirkland, Ph.D.
Bryn Mawr, Pennsylvania, October 1999
Lieutenant Colonel, Field Artillery (Retired)
Research Social Historian, Walter Reed Army Institute of Research,
Washington, D.C.

NOTES

1. Two other books, both first-person accounts, provide authentic detail about the attitudes, behavior, agendas, policies and consequences that make up life in the post–World War II Army: Christopher Bassford, *The Spit Shine Syndrome* (Westport, CT: Greenwood, 1988), and David Hackworth, *About Face* (New York: Simon & Schuster, 1989). Hawkins's book, although not a first-person account by a participating member of the Army, is a participant observer record with ethnographic and psychological analysis that the others do not provide.

2. See Cincinnatus [pseud.], *Self-Destruction* (New York: Norton, 1981); Richard A. Gabriel and Paul L. Savage, *Crisis in Command* (New York: Hill & Wang, 1978); William L. Hauser, *America's Army in Crisis* (Baltimore: Johns Hopkins University Press, 1973).

3. U.S. Department of the Army, *Study on Military Professionalism* (Carlisle Barracks, PA: U.S. Army War College, 1970).

4. Larry H. Ingraham, *The Boys in the Barracks* (Philadelphia: Institute for the Study of Human Issues, 1984).

5. James Kitfield, *Prodigal Soldiers* (New York: Simon & Schuster, 1995): 109–113.

6. Richard D. Mallonee II, *The Naked Flagpole: Battle for Bataan* (San Rafael, CA: Presidio Press, 1980): 16, 29; Jay Luvaas, ed., *Dear Miss Em: General Eichelberger's War in the Pacific, 1942–1943* (Westport, CT: Greenwood Press, 1973): 32.

7. David H. Marlowe, et al., *Unit Manning System Field Evaluation*, Technical Report No. 5 (ADA207193) (Washington, DC: Walter Reed Army Institute of Research, September 1987); Faris R. Kirkland, "Assessing COHORT," *Army* 40, no.5, (May 1990): 44–50.

8. Kitfield, *Prodigal Soldiers*, 208–14, 228, 302–3, 326.

Preface

This is a study of United States Army communities in Germany between 1986 and 1988. Much has changed in the intervening dozen years. To reflect this, I use the past tense predominantly in my text. Sometimes I use the present tense when I discuss general processes that particular events reveal, especially if I feel the conditions continue into the present or apply to all U.S. military services. I let the tense of the people who spoke to me remain as they said it.

To document both historical context and recent changes in the military community in Germany, I use the German and European editions of the *Stars and Stripes,* whose masthead in 1945 and 1946 declared itself "the Daily Newspaper of European Theater of Operations." The *Stars and Stripes* offers a wealth of detail on the life of soldiers and conditions in the American military communities in Europe from World War II to the present. Quotes from headlines leave major words capitalized.

Quotes from interviews sometimes needed editorial modifications to provide context or to make the pieces flow grammatically. Such additions are indicated [in brackets]. In all cases, the use of *italics* inside quoted material indicates the speaker's or writer's original emphasis.

I have changed the names of all persons who helped me understand their way of life. I list the pseudonyms of all those I regularly interviewed and quoted, together with their salient data, in chart form in Appendix II. I use "Mr." or "Mrs." to indicate that I interviewed a Department of Defense civilian employee with whom I had made a specific appointment.

To further ensure anonymity, I have changed the names of the two communities I studied most closely ("Richberg Kaserne" [a subcommunity of "Grossberg"

Military Community] and "Middleberg Barracks"). Likewise, I changed the names of the other communities from which I sought comparative data, including "Central Barracks," "General Barracks," "Sudberg," and "Welby General Hospital," which were all subcommunities of "Grossberg Military Community," the military community of "Newberg," and "Alpenberg," the latter a sub-community of Middleberg. In the text that follows, these pseudonyms will no longer be marked by quotes. All other community names are unchanged, as are the names of elected, appointed, or historic public figures (Secretary of Defense Frank Carlucci, General Dwight D. Eisenhower, and so forth). The names of persons quoted (or spoken about) in newspaper sources are their own, if they gave their names. "Name withheld" after a *Stars and Stripes* newspaper quotation indicates that the newspaper withheld the name at the request of the writer.

Throughout the text I use "double quotes" around words and phrases commonly used in military speech—marking them thus as native technical or cultural vocabulary. When I choose to direct attention to the analysis of a non-native word, or to be ironic or sarcastic regarding its use, or cast doubt upon it, I use 'single quotes,' unless it is a quote within a quote by a member of the military community. Finally, a word about photographs. At this time period in Germany, members of the communities were extremely security conscious. No one carried a camera or took pictures in or around military facilities. Even though I had permission, I felt—and I was stared at—as though I were a spy whenever I took photographs. I include a few of the limited selection that I have.

Acknowledgments

After a decade of work, my list of debts to people who have helped me is impossibly long and rudely incomplete. I can but touch the high points.

The Department of Military Psychiatry—now called Soldier and Family Studies—of the Walter Reed Army Institute of Research (WRAIR) funded the fieldwork on which the study is based and sponsored my linkage to the U.S. Army Europe. I conducted the fieldwork as a civilian employee of Brigham Young University under provisions of the Intergovernmental Personnel Act.

I appreciate the patience and collaboration of many colleagues at WRAIR. Among them, I give special thanks to David Marlowe, Ph.D., then chief of the Department of Military Psychiatry, who trusted me to be independent and to explore as fundamentally as possible the issues underlying the rewards and difficulties of military family life in Germany. Also at WRAIR, Joel Teitelbaum, Ph.D., provided wise guidance throughout. Lieutenant Colonel Robert Schneider, Ph.D., and Colonel Larry Ingraham, Ph.D., each read various manuscript incarnations of my thought and gave me detailed critical feedback that helped me sharpen my presentation and avoid error. Lieutenant Colonel (Retired) Faris R. Kirkland, Ph.D., a guest scholar and Intergovernmental Personnel Act fellow at WRAIR, has throughout the years been a wonderful support. He has encouraged me at every step and recently gave my manuscript an exceptionally helpful and profound critique.

In Germany, Colonel Robert Gifford, Ph.D. (now executive officer of WRAIR), commanded the United States Army Medical Research Unit Europe (USAMRU-E), the Heidelberg research station of WRAIR, and gave me much encouragement during 1987 and 1988. Subsequently, he has kindly and helpfully spent many hours going over my data and arguments in Washington, D.C. From their work posts at USAMRU-E, Lieutenant Colonel Ed Van Vranken, Ph.D., Charlene Lewis, Ph.D., and Mary Tyler, Ph.D., also assisted and critiqued, and helped me adjust to life in an army community. Evelyn Golembe, USAMRU-E administrative manager, solved the occasional problems that arose.

Captain Bruce Leeson, Ph.D., sponsored our family's arrival in the Grossberg Military Community and assisted in all aspects of liaison with the Psychiatry and Neurology Clinic of Welby General Hospital, where I was a guest research scholar. Colonel George Pierozynski, M.D., commanded the clinic and was a gracious host throughout our stay. Colonel Pierozynski, Captain Leeson, Captain Jack Dodd, M.D., and Colonel Louis Kurke, M.D., (commander of a supra-regional psychiatric ward) seemed to enjoy discussing my work with me. I probably abused their intellectual hospitality. They helped me to understand that what I was uncovering for completely ordinary soldiers and spouses chosen by random sample existed "in spades" among many of those seeking or requiring assistance in the psychiatric medical channels. The individuals and family members they had treated in the hospital psychiatric system had confronted particularly exigent versions of the stresses and strains recounted in this book, or they had substantially less effective coping skills or capacities. In either case, they had the misfortune of being overwhelmed. But most of those treated were not different in kind from those who were coping without official medical help.

Perhaps it need not be said, but the ideas expressed herein are entirely my own and do not represent the views of the Department of Defense or the Walter Reed Army Institute of Research. To their credit, no one in the military has ever tried to squelch any of my field procedures, analysis, or conclusions; my military colleagues have only encouraged me to say more clearly what I felt should be said.

Dr. Norman Schwartz, of the University of Delaware Anthropology Department, has been a consistent friend, colleague, and critic, even of these materials rather out of his area of academic emphasis. Dr. Anna Simons, of the University of California at Los Angeles Anthropology Department, gave my manuscript an excellent critique.

Drs. Mark Grandstaff, Von Call, John Clark, Stephen Houston, and David Crandall, all faculty members of Brigham Young University, gave me particularly useful critiques. Department staff secretaries over the years typed and corrected the many drafts. Colleen Bernhard, a graduate student in the English department, helped me streamline prose. Dr. Don Norton read the entire manuscript in an earlier incarnation. David Snow read the manuscript in detail and was a helpful critic. Several anonymous reviewers gave useful suggestions for revision, many of which I have been able to incorporate.

In the manuscript's final stages of preparation, Linette Sparacino served as editor to help me greatly improve it. Her skilled attention to outline, transition, and shortening, and her help in managing the details of camera-ready copy preparation aided me substantially.

Carol Lee Hawkins and our children deserve special mention because they were participant observers during the research. I came to understand much about military family life on-post and in the German villages through their experiences. Family conversations about a day's events often confirmed the concepts that were emerging in my interviews and observations. Sometimes they connected me to fresh lines of investigation or insight.

Finally, I owe the entire result to the soldiers and spouses who candidly opened their lives and shared their perceptions with me. Without their unending patience and willingness to explain—again and again—I never would have "gotten it." Or at any rate, I would not have gotten what I was able to get of it, for this is by no means a perfect or a complete book. Its shortcomings are plentiful, and I take full responsibility for them.

Introduction

Army life has always been known as a life of sacrifice, challenge, and frustration, yet one filled also with deep satisfactions. This is so for the soldiers' families as much as for the soldiers themselves. Over the years, military and civilian leaders of the U.S. Army have tried to reduce the hardships of military life by creating an array of community services designed to provide social support for soldiers and military families and help them live satisfying lives in military communities. The effort continues today.

Unfortunately, this effort has not been particularly successful, and frustration, dissatisfaction, and alienation persist among soldiers and family members in the U.S. Army communities in Germany. Yet, given the social responsibilities of national and world defense and the devastating weapons entrusted to young soldiers, it is unlikely that the American public would want such unhappiness to linger. Discontent does continue, however, because the underlying sources of alienation in the Army and among its families are highly complex, poorly understood, and therefore hardly addressed by the Army's quality-of-life programs that are intended to make soldier and family life more bearable.

In this book I seek to penetrate the logic, social structure, and daily practice of life in American military communities that lay scattered along the frontier between East and West Germany during the final years of the Cold War. These American families lived their lives fully prepared for war. Indeed, most soldiers—and therefore their families—existed on two-hour alert, obligated to be in contact with their unit at all times and able to move within two hours of surprise notification from home life and even sleep to a state of high alert, fully armed in military vehicles moving toward their assigned off-post forward defensive position. These soldiers and their families lived the bitter tensions of the Cold War at every moment.

In coming to understand the life and thought of these American soldiers and families in Germany, ordinary American citizens can learn much about their military forces and about their own society and culture. Moreover, because the Army is one of the most important and highly empowered institutions on the American scene, the deep social and cultural contradictions that interfere with efforts at improving the quality of life in the military must not remain ill-understood or neglected. Improving the Army and the life of its soldiers and families—to the benefit of both American and German society—demands otherwise. In addition, a greater understanding about how people work in and live around an institution that is at once so important and yet tasked with a mission so different from that of ordinary pursuits can stimulate social scientists and concerned citizens to think differently about culture, society, and behavior in general.

STUDYING THE AMERICAN MILITARY COMMUNITIES IN GERMANY

This analysis of American Army family and community life in Germany is based on interviews with and observations of soldiers and spouses living there between July 1986 and July 1988, the last full years of unmitigated Cold War. During that time, some 345,000 American military personnel faced the much larger Soviet forces. By some estimates, Soviet forces were 1.5 to 2 times more powerful across the entire North Atlantic Treaty Organization (NATO) front and would have been able to effect much larger disparities in an attack, through surprise concentration of mobilized forces, perhaps exceeding Western defensive forces by 20 to 1 in some weapons systems. Computer modeling of such disparities suggested NATO would lose a strictly conventional war.[1]

In this situation, many of the American soldiers and family members in Germany felt alienated. My study shows, however, that their alienation did not derive from fear of the military disparities but from anger over lost opportunity to train effectively and be more ready. Soldiers felt alienated because they frequently saw the product of their labor diverted from effective preparation for their military mission, sometimes commandeered to protect the careers of seniors, sometimes simply disappearing in mismanaged waste. Soldiers felt alienated psychologically as well, distrusting their superiors, their peers, their units, and the Army. Soldiers called such alienation "low morale," especially when describing the collective mood of a military unit. The goal, of course, was to have "high morale"—affirmative, enthusiastic attachment to the military unit, devotion to the wider military community, and possession of a sense that their efforts served appropriate and worthy goals. Conversely, "low morale,"—alienation in any of its forms—undercut unit effectiveness, savaged community cohesion, and spread infectiously, amplifying the misery of everyone. Not incidentally, persistent low morale in units, if detected, could topple the careers of those officers deemed responsible.

There is, then, a conundrum that needs to be understood. Military leaders have succeeded in instilling a high and clear sense of mission and urgency in the minds of soldiers, yet they remain plagued with dissatisfaction, "low morale," and alienation. Why? What institutional secrets blocked Army leaders from achieving the goals they had so successfully inculcated in their subordinates? More specifically, what turned the U.S. Army in Europe from an army of hope into an army of alienation? In this book, I will demonstrate that the conditions leading to alienation and persistent low morale were endemic, built into the structure and practice of the U.S. Army as it was then (and is still) constituted. There is hope, however, in saying that the conditions leading to alienation are *built* into the *structure* and *practice* of the Army, for relatively small changes in military structure and military practice can—if this argument is correct—make substantial differences in unit and military community morale.

Although much has changed on the world political scene, the lessons embedded in the case of Germany during the Cold War have yet to be learned. In July 1988, when my fieldwork ended, no one foresaw that these were the closing days of the Cold War. In November 1989, the Berlin Wall fell. In October 1990, Germany reunited. By the end of 1991, the Warsaw Pact had dissolved and the Soviet Union had ceased to exist. With the promise that Soviet troops would be removed from the former Warsaw Pact states by 1994, East-West tensions eased and U.S. Army troop strength declined from 213,000 in October 1990 to 65,000 in September 1995.[2] Force levels had changed radically, to be sure, but the *structures* and *practices* leading to alienation have remained, as have some 30,000 families still posted to Germany. These can still learn from the experience of those I studied. Moreover, many soldiers and family members stationed in the United States can also learn from the experience of forward deployment in Germany. In the aftermath of reductions in Europe, military units stationed in the United States have increasingly taken over rapid-response missions in which they must be ready to depart their home installation, combat ready, on a few hours' or days' notice. As a result, soldiers and their families serving on American soil now face conditions similar to those experienced by soldiers and families stationed in Germany during the Cold War. Learning from the struggles of their European predecessors would be wise. Finally, the intensity of Army life and family process in the clear-cut isolation of Germany lends a kind of clarity and saliency to processes that are present and similar but easily overlooked in the sometimes less dramatic circumstances of Army family life, and indeed, *all* family life, in the United States. To begin to learn from the soldiers and families living in the American military communities in late Cold War Germany, we must examine the historical path that led to today's military enclaves and explore the social conditions within which they were created.

THE ORIGIN OF THE AMERICAN MILITARY COMMUNITIES IN GERMANY

The American military communities that I studied in 1986–1988 originated forty years earlier in the ashes and aftermath of World War II. Conceived to support the soldiers assigned to govern, control, and punish Germany, these communities were soon transformed by world events that forged a Western alliance to defend against a Soviet threat.

Beginning the Occupation, 1945–1946

The May 1, 1945, headline of the *Stars and Stripes*, the official but semi-autonomous newspaper of the American military forces, bannered "Hitler Dead, Germans Claim; Seventh Army Seizes Munich." Capturing Munich was an important symbol, for it was the birthplace of the Nazi movement under Hitler. By this date, U.S. troops had liberated prisoners from the concentration camp at Dachau, pushed into Bavaria, and crossed the Elbe River. From the east, the Soviets had hoisted their banner over the Reichstag. The end was very close.[3] During the next week, American forces entered Czechoslovakia and captured significant portions of what would later become southern East Germany. On May 8, the *Stars and Stripes* declared that the war in the European theater of operations had ended.[4]

May 8 was, therefore, the first day of the American occupation. The U.S. Army's task shifted from how to destroy Germany to how to govern it, clean it up, rebuild it, suppress the ingrained Naziism suspected of its citizens, and extract reparations. The tasks were immense and were correctly perceived as such. From the senior leaders' point of view, the first task was to govern, to restore order. From the junior soldiers' point of view, the first task was to go home.[5]

Congress renewed demands for a quick return home for all but a small occupation force of about 300,000 soldiers.[6] War-weary soldiers would go home, and new draftees and career soldiers would staff the occupation. Huge armies skilled in the arts of destruction now turned "awkwardly" to the tasks of creating order.[7] The four powers announced the division of their governing responsibility, with the United States generally to the south and Berlin to be administered jointly.[8]

U.S. military personnel were prohibited from contact with German citizens, in part to protect the Americans from contamination by the stain of Naziism, and in part to punish the Germans and limit the transfer of American goods and services in the emerging black market. Rather at cross-purposes with the quickly eroding policy of nonfraternization, American military leaders wanted soldiers to behave as young ambassadors, "avoiding actions tending to discredit the U.S. in European eyes."[9] The American goal—of every soldier an American representative—was marred, however, by occasional criminal and sexual assault, grounds for seeking a measure of isolation. The sharp contrast between abundant food and food wastage among the Americans and severe food shortages among the Germans also proved embarrassing and justified further separation.[10]

Building Occupation Communities, 1946–1948

Establishing the Garrisons. In the face of hunger riots and general social collapse in Germany, and given the large numbers of American soldiers who were not always self-controlled, the Office of Military Government of the United States for Germany (OMGUS) organized a military occupational police force, known as the United States Constabulary, on May 1, 1946, to handle security in the American zone.

A huge apparatus of support units and physical facilities existed that had to be administered throughout the zone. On March 15, 1947, the First and Second Military Districts were created, each "put in control of a simplified system of military posts" covering the U.S. occupation zone. The First Military District, under the command of a major general, included seven "posts," with the Bad Tölz, Garmisch, Munich (München), Nürnberg, Würzburg, and Regensburg posts each commanded by colonels, and the Augsburg and Nürnberg posts each commanded by a brigadier general. Grafenwöhr and Bamberg were "designated as subposts of Regensburg and Nürnberg, respectively." The Second Military District was commanded by a major general who presided over the posts of Heidelberg, Darmstadt, and Wetzlar (each commanded by a colonel), and Stuttgart, commanded by a brigadier general.[11] The senior headquarters of EUCOM (European Command), at Frankfurt, and of USAFE (United States Air Force Europe), at Wiesbaden, had separate self-contained status. The two military districts in the late 1940s became the basis for the two corps areas into which military communities were divided in the 1980s, though the boundaries had shifted.

The whole system ran under a "dual hat" organization. That is, the post community commander was also the commander of the major troop unit at the post. Similarly, the military district commander was also the senior troop commander of the senior corps or army assigned to that military district. Day-to-day post or district responsibilities were handled by a deputy of the senior commander at that level. In case of mobilization for a "tactical emergency," the troop commander was to "shed the installation hat"—in other words, give command responsibility for the installation—to a deputy or other "rear echelon" commander.[12]

Thus, virtually all of the characteristics of the American military community in Germany during the late 1980s were firmly in place by mid-1947, including "dual hat" organization, a subdivision of the 7th Army into two corps-level regions, and a distribution of military communities and subcommunities covering the whole American occupation zone that provided economic, recreational, and support services for soldiers. All that remained was for the Army to assume responsibility for the presence and care of family members, for there were as yet no spouses or children in the American occupation zone. Transition to a family-sustaining community, however, would require much additional housing and logistical support.

Planning and Building Family Facilities. Within weeks of the war's end in Europe, the *Stars and Stripes* reported high-level discussions of the "desirability" of bringing "dependents and fiancées" to occupation troops on indefinite assignment of a year or longer, but suggested that conditions of unrest combined with shortages of transportation, food, and housing still precluded such arrangements. While President Harry S Truman "expressed opposition to bringing soldiers' wives and families overseas," Representative Margaret Chase Smith declared, "I don't see how we can continue our American way of living unless families can live together," suggesting that "American families could 'set an example for the natives' of occupied countries," were they sent overseas.[13]

On November 27, 1945, the *Stars and Stripes* revealed plans for 102 "specially-built communities for . . . families." In 1946, in the first description of what military family and community life might be like, the commanding general of the American sector of Berlin ordered Americans to "live in 'simple dignity' without ostentation or lavishness." "The Army is going to take prime care of the women and children coming to Europe and a once enemy country to be near their men." There were "plans [for] commissaries . . . for family use in much the same manner that shopping is done in neighborhood stores in the U.S." Families would be issued an allowance of $35 per month per spouse or child, which, given the Army's price advantages at the commissaries, would be "more than adequate for a . . . gourmet." However, spouses would need to get used to a few inconveniences, including no fresh vegetables or milk, and would have to learn to use powdered or frozen eggs. "The Army has undertaken to provide two major items: fuel to heat homes and fuel to run automobiles. Many families are bringing their cars to Germany. . . . There will be Army-operated gasoline stations, . . . beauty parlors and post exchanges." "Bring a year's supply of clothing," families were advised.[14]

Plans called for "10,000 dependents of military personnel a month" to pass through the port of Bremerhaven en route to American military communities in Berlin and in seven other key cities and their surrounding satellite installations. On Sunday, April 28, 1946, five months after the plans for communities had been announced, the first group of approximately 250 wives and 100 children arrived on a converted troopship. At first, family housing frequently came from homes "requisitioned" from Germans. Such requisitioning, however, created a major protest from the German population, with expressions of "indignation" and "horror" that "hungry Germans were being 'chased out of their homes' with no place to go."[15]

Such discontent accelerated the effort to complete construction of the planned military family housing compounds. For example, the April 28, 1946, *Stars and Stripes* described the homes that "await arriving families." A picture shows twelve long apartment buildings, parallel and close together, within the Frankfurt "compound." About two-thirds of each building was a three-floor walk-up, and one-third was a four- or five-floor walk-up. "The homes which await the Army dependents are amazingly like those they left behind," and were supplied with "central heating, telephones, gas stoves, oven, hot water heaters, and abundant [120 volt] electric connections . . . so that American-made appliances can be used." The size of home one would receive depended on one's rank. For example, "lieutenant's and captain's homes may have three bedrooms, one bath and two toilets, but maid's room, pantry, dressing room and study [available to more senior ranks] are not included." "In rubble-strewn Frankfurt, families will live in apartments and small houses within the barbed-wire enclosed USFET [United States Forces European Theater] compound." "Conveniences . . . include a post exchange with a wide variety of goods, a filling station where gasoline will be allotted on a ration ticket basis, beauty parlors, men's barber shops, yard areas between apartments, and a complete shopping center. Small cities and villages outside Frankfurt would provide homes for other Army families." Army recreational facilities will be open to the families, including "golf courses, riding stables, ski runs, and swimming pools . . . night clubs . . . tennis courts . . . baseball diamonds . . . [S]everal have stadiums . . . clubs for EM [enlisted men] and for officers . . . [movie] theaters . . . [whose] films are American and up to date," and stages for drama and opera.[16]

In addition to housing, families would require schooling and medical attention. In spite of statements that the War Department would assume no responsibility for schooling, "plans for fully accredited schools . . . representative of prevailing U.S. Standards" were announced by U.S. Army leaders in Europe. "Plans call for a civilian-staffed primary school in every military community where there are children of school ages, but high schools are planned only in a few centrally located places," setting a pattern that persisted through the 1980s. The "mostly American curriculum" also offered German language classes. "Wives and children" would go to military dispensaries and regional military hospitals at nominal charge. The regional military hospitals experienced a baby boom in 1946, with 601 births, of which 341 were to foreign wives of U.S. soldiers. A year after the first families arrived, there were "approximately thirty thousand dependents in the American occupation zones," of which 17,000 were women over eighteen, most of them wives.[17] Martha Gravois treats this period in considerable depth, concluding that American officer families lived in some degree of comfort and had at least one relationship to the German populace because they were required to have a German maid.[18]

In the context of the war's aftermath—the first anniversary of victory less than a month away—distrust, nonfraternization rules, and an isolated life inside Americanized compounds set up patterns of behavior and expectation that persisted for four decades and beyond.

Becoming Cold War Communities, 1948–1949

The Berlin blockade in 1948 crystallized perception of a new enemy and precipitated a change in the mission of U.S. forces in Germany. The task would no longer be to control Germany but to contain the Soviets. Germany, as a result, became an independent ally. Its reconstruction became paramount, the better to confront the Soviet threat. Prior to the blockade, the press had referred to powers occupying Germany in the plural. They were "the Allies," or "the Big Four" (United States, Britain, France, and Russia), "the Big Three" (United States, Britain, France), or "the Big Two" (United States and Russia). As tensions mounted, the term "Western Powers" emerged, though still decisively plural. After the blockade, the term "the West"—singular, unified—came into general use. How did this change occur? What implication did the new Western unity have for the American mission?

Immediately after the war, when the U.S. troops vacated the southern portion of the Russian occupation zone (land that became the German Democratic Republic or East Germany), Russian–American relations, as evidenced in *Stars and*

Stripes, came to be viewed cooperatively and positively. Allied agreement on problems about the joint military government in Berlin were reached in "such a spirit of harmony that responsible participants were highly optimistic regarding the prospective outcome of future meetings of the quadripartite Allied Control Council, whose job would be to divide and then coordinate the governing of the rest of occupied Germany." "Ivan is an All-right Guy, Yanks in Berlin Discover," gushed the *Stars and Stripes* headline.[19]

The extraction of war reparations gave further evidence of the favored status of Russia and the enemy/occupied status of Germany. The Potsdam Accords had arranged to dismantle and allocate to the Allies virtually the entire German industrial infrastructure, especially the heavy or complex industries potentially useful in war. On December 11, 1945, the Allied Control Council agreed on the first "industrial equipment to meet reparations" to be dismantled, of which 48 percent would go to Russia.[20]

Some leaders, however, were quite vocal in their distrust of Russia's leadership. On March 5, 1946, as a guest of President Truman, Winston Churchill delivered a lecture to the faculty of Westminster College, in Fulton, Missouri, in which he asserted that "Russia constituted a growing challenge and peril," a "threatening 'shadow' over both Europe and Asia." In this speech, Churchill coined the famous phrase that soon enough came to describe an even harsher division of Europe and the world than yet existed: "From Stettin on the Baltic to Trieste on the Adriatic, an iron curtain has descended across the continent." The speech was "received unfavorably by most members of Congress, who said they wanted no formal alliance [with Britain] because it might arouse suspicion on the part of Russia and would link the United States too closely with British foreign policy." Indeed, General Lucius Clay, as senior U.S. commander in Europe, committed the United States to a ten-year stay in Germany because that length of time would be required to monitor the prison terms of high Nazis, supervise the implementation by Germans of new laws designed to root out the Nazi influence, and punish officials of the Reich guilty of offenses less than war crimes. He did not mention Russia. From the military's point of view, we occupied Germany because of the war, not because of anxiety about Russia or its allies.[21]

A rapid succession of events eventually converted the U.S. Congress to Churchill's view. Russia's failure to remove its troops from Iran, its conflict with the United Nations Organization over the matter, and its "seizure" of Manchurian factories grabbed headlines. Adding to the tension, an unidentified spy ring in search of atomic and radar secrets successfully managed to breach British and Canadian security. Russia was accused of actively spying on U.S. divisions and their movements in Europe. Soviet sources, for their part, attacked Churchill and accused "the three powers" of undermining legitimate peoples' revolutions against fascist states and illegitimate colonialism.[22]

In this world-political environment, the OMGUS struggled to maintain the appearance that four-power cooperation was alive and well. In spite of such efforts, the relationship was in deep crisis. The United States Army, for example, had to issue a "special military scrip [paper money] for use by authorized personnel in the American Zone" because the Russians had consistently exceeded their printing allotment of the occupation marks, which were directly convertible into U.S. dollars. Russia's lack of restraint undermined the currency of all occupied Germany as well as that of the United States.[23]

Other evidences of crisis proliferated. U.S. fears were encapsulated in the accusations of Father John Cronin (and taken up later by Senator Eugene McCarthy) that the U.S. government was filled with subversive communists. Russian troop movements in Iran and their obvious interest in Iranian oil threatened to explode in regional conflict. On May 4, 1946, a series of meetings concerning Russia's insistence on further war reparations from Italy led to "the long awaited showdown between Russia and the Western Powers." The United States and Britain had poured $500 million of aid into Italy and the United Nations relief organizations had donated another $400 million. The United States and Britain flatly refused Russia's request for $300 million worth of war reparations from Italy, since to extract this amount from Italy would constitute a direct flow-through of dollars from the United States and Britain to Russia. Russian insistence that Italy transfer border lands to Yugoslavia furthered a "Stalemate [of the] Big Four." Increasing divergence between Russian and American approaches in world politics led Truman to pledge the U.S. commitment to peace in spite of disruptive "war rumors in 'certain places.'" On October 23, 1946, Truman invited support for the U.N., urged unity among the democracies, and recognized that "the Russians will try to socialize their sphere of influence, just as we are trying to democratize our sphere of influence."[24] Thus, slowly, the fractured postwar world began to coalesce in people's perceptions into two new systems-in-opposition. "Soviet"—the larger system—began to replace "Russia" in the emerging American perception of threat.

Something of this emerging new threat is indicated by the fact that the commander of U.S. forces in the European theater stated firmly that even if all U.S. goals with regard to the American sector were completely met—including full German capability of self-government and possession of a true concept of democracy—United States "[o]ccupational forces will not leave until the armies of all other countries have evacuated." Thus, control of Germany was no longer the sole expressed goal of the American presence in Germany. Between March and November 1946, the task of counterbalancing the Russian occupiers had been added to the perceived if not yet official U.S. Army mission.[25]

By November 1947, the separateness of the Big Three had consolidated somewhat into such terms as the "Western Powers," still in the plural, but conceptually more unified. On January 22, 1948, the British foreign secretary asked for "a confederation of Western Europe to balance the Soviet bloc," noting that "Russia[n] expansion may lead to war." The idea of blocs, as well as explicit notions of Western and Eastern Europe, continued to develop.[26]

On March 6, 1948, the Big Three, surmounting grave differences, agreed to federalize Germany. They spoke for the first time openly of "Western Germany," instead of separate zones, and saw Western Germany having "a major role in the European Economic Recovery Program." Germany was now seen as a valuable partner that needed to become industrially and militarily strong rather than be stripped to rural powerlessness.[27]

Berlin, always a source of tension, became a point of crisis when the Russians demanded the right to search the military trains formerly granted free passage through the Russian zone. The United States and Britain, rather than submit their military trains to search, canceled all military trains and, on April 1, 1948, began to ship military personnel and military supplies to Berlin by air. (Nonmilitary foods, fuel, and other supplies continued to enter by land transportation, unobstructed.) The Soviets then "ended their participation in the Allied *Kommandatura,* the four-power body . . . running the city of Berlin." German authorities, international press, and military leaders declared that the Western powers must not be squeezed out of Berlin. American family members were told they could choose whether to stay in Berlin or go home to the United States. None left.[28]

Shortly thereafter, a Russian fighter plane, while "buzzing" or harassing a British transport in the air corridor, presumably miscalculated, ramming the transport. Both crashed, killing the Russian pilot and the two Americans and twelve Britons aboard the British craft. The British military governor protested the "appalling incident" and ordered fighter escorts for the air re-supply. Russian officials said the British plane was out of the corridor; the British said that was untrue. The mood was captured by the British military governor, speaking to a German state parliamentary body: "War or Peace: once more the dread alternative is being whispered. Once more fear clutches the heart. . . . A war of a different kind is being waged today—it is a war of nerves."[29]

Adding to the tension of the moment, United States Secretary of Defense James Forrestal affirmed that Russians knew how to make the A-bomb, but did not yet have it for lack of industrial capacity. He "warned against public hysteria over the possibility of war," saying, more cautiously, "We are in a state of continuing tension" but affirming that "we will not tolerate the destruction of the Western civilization of Europe." General Clay expressed related thoughts: "I expect the Russian pressure to drive us out of Berlin will continue, but we are not going to be driven out."[30]

The crisis created fertile conditions for new perceptions. On April 15, the *Stars and Stripes* reported that German leaders called for an "immediate state of peace" between Germans and the "Western Occupation Powers" and pled for the "establishment of . . . [a] West German . . . federal government."[31] The notion of a friendly Federal Republic of Germany, good ally rather than an occupied monster, grew.

On the night of June 23–24, 1948, Russia converted the blockade of military transport into a total blockade by completely shutting off all rail, road, and water modes of transportation into Berlin. Without Western intervention, the city would soon starve. General Clay responded by immediately gearing up the Berlin airlift to include not just military cargo but civilian food and fuel as well. The details of the Berlin airlift are well documented and need not concern us. The airlift successfully resupplied the entire city and continued for an additional four months after the Russians had ended the blockade on May 11–12, 1949.[32] These heroic efforts saved the Berliners from starvation or subjugation. Moreover, the fact that the American military families did not evacuate from Berlin firmly established military families and family evacuation policy as a part of America's Cold War statement of intent to stay and not be bullied.[33]

The Berlin crisis and the collaborative airlift, however, effectively pushed the American, British, and French military and civilian leaders into finally accepting a new world reality. Germany would be needed as a partner; German independence and industry would be an essential element in this partnership. The term "Big Three" faded in importance. In postblockade newspaper coverage, the "Western Powers," formerly divided into a plurality, became "the West," singular, unified, with West Germany included. West Germany gained substantial independence in June 1949, with the passage of the Basic Law, essentially a new German constitution for a parliamentary democracy covering the American, British, and French zones.[34] The Federal Republic of Germany emerged so quickly as an independent state because the Berlin blockade forced a shift in the perceived threats.

Three subsequent events sealed the message of the Berlin blockade and served to propel Germany to the center of the Western alliance: the 1949 Soviet nuclear detonation, the 1949–1950 defeat of Chinese Nationalist forces and the related rise of Communist China, and the June 1950 invasion of South Korea following the withdrawal of U.S. troops in 1949. The structural similarity between divided Germany and divided Korea—now invaded—could not be missed. In response, American troop strength in Europe soon returned to the 300,000-plus level, having dropped to a low of 79,495 in 1950.[35]

The United States Army, after Germany's independence, ceased to be an occupying army and became a guest, interdependent with Britain, France, Germany, Holland, Belgium, and other nations in the North Atlantic Treaty Organization, or NATO, partners in the defense of Western Europe. Thus, by 1950 the main factors integral to understanding the social process in American military communities that I studied from 1986 to 1988 were in place: soldiers facing an imminent Soviet threat, families in isolated military communities, and West Germany as a sovereign partner in the West's defense against a Soviet threat in a cold war.

I have treated the period from the end of World War II to the end of the occupation in some detail, using the *Stars and Stripes* as a source of original detail about the structure of life in the American Army communities in Germany, the Army's relation to Germany, and the emergence of the Soviet Union as a primary threat, because these factors set the primary trajectory for the evolution of the communities for the next forty years. The intervening history I will treat in a more cursory fashion, using secondary sources, in order to move more quickly to the social and cultural analysis of my ethnographic experience of soldier and family life from 1986 to 1988. In doing so, I follow Daniel J. Nelson, who provides an excellent treatment of the social and political implications of maintaining U.S. forces in Germany in a *A History of U.S. Military Forces in Germany*, and in *Defenders or Intruders? The Dilemmas of U.S. Forces in Germany*. Nelson divides the four decades of U.S. military presence from the end of the war to the publication of his book into five periods (each a chapter): "military occupation"

(1945–1949), "semi-sovereignty" (1949–1955), "consolidation and normalcy" (1955–1967), "deterioration" (1967–1973), and a period of struggle to rebuild around the all- volunteer force (1973–1985). Having dealt with the period of occupation, I use his time periods, for they reflect watershed points in the emergence of the American Army communities.

Building a Credible Forward Defense, 1949–1955

American troop strength, as calculated by Nelson, experienced a precipitous drop, from 2.6 million at the end of World War II to 79,495 at the low point of U.S. force levels in 1950, followed by a rapid rebuilding to 350,000 by 1955.[36] The turnaround, as we have seen, was a response to communist threats evidenced in Berlin, China, and Korea. During this period, Americans enjoyed unprecedented wealth relative to the rebuilding German economy, and considerable respect. From the German point of view, the Western occupation had been for the most part dignified and constructive, and the Soviet alternative, visibly close at hand in East Germany, appeared grim indeed. Some two-thirds of the German population saw the American presence as a necessary response to external threat, and only 19 percent felt American troops should be withdrawn.[37] A 1955 Army poll showed "A clear majority of Germans said there was nothing in particular that they did not like about American soldiers. . . . Even of those who said the troops behaved badly and whose who found nothing pleasing about the soldiers' appearance or manners, majorities said that rapport between the two groups had improved."[38]

Under the 1949 Basic Law, the Federal Republic of Germany became only quasi-independent. First, the country was clearly dependent for its security on the Western powers, and especially on the strength of NATO. Second, Germany exercised a limited semi-sovereignty, for the occupation powers still retained essential veto capacity. That, however, soon would change, for it became clear that Germany would have to be rearmed and incorporated into NATO as a full partner if the NATO defense were to be credible. The treaties to end the occupation were signed in October 1954, and the Federal Republic of Germany became a member of NATO. As Nelson puts it succinctly,

> For West Germany it was a momentous occasion. The Occupation Statute was abolished, the Allied High Commission was dissolved, and the Federal Republic was accorded the rights and duties of a fully sovereign state, subject only to allied reservations concerning Berlin and the reunification of Germany. West Germany became a full member of the WEU [Western European Union], and hence an associate member of NATO. The Federal Republic agreed, in turn, to allow French, British, and American troops to remain in Germany as the first line of NATO defense in Western Europe.[39]

German rearmament not only added to the troop strength of NATO, its territory became the platform for staging the forward defense of the entire West. German participation, however, was not without a degree of contradiction. West Germany formally "gave permission" for the American presence—hence it could formally rescind the permission and perhaps thereby end its participation in NATO—but it also desperately needed the Americans and the security and stability they provided. For Germans, the relationship of formal sovereignty and yet complete security dependence on a continued U.S. presence created dilemmas of considerable complexity and even pain in the coming decades.

Consolidating the American Presence, 1955–1967

Though Nelson sees this period as "the calmest and most stable period of German-American relations," it was also a period when the U.S. Congress sometimes repeatedly cajoled Germany into paying increasing portions of the cost of U.S. personnel stationed on its soil by threatening to withdraw if Germany did not pay more. The tactic did little to improve relations between German leaders and citizens and the Americans stationed there. Nevertheless, American troop strength remained relatively steady during most of the period in question, oscillating from 240,000 to 280,000 but returning regularly to about 260,000. In 1966, however, U.S. troop levels in Germany started to fall, reaching 210,000 in 1968.[40] The reasons are complex.

Some of these reasons were economic. Germany started to emerge as an economic power, and that invited the Americans to seek their larger participation in funding the American presence. When the costs became politically prohibitive, the German government balked and Congress began to force partial withdrawals. In addition, changing technologies of warfare—especially the positioning of nuclear-armed cruise missiles during 1983–1984—brought the image of nuclear demise to the center of German political discourse. Protests called into question German reliability and made American demands for greater German funding to offset American costs all the more coercive. Finally, American adventurism in Vietnam began to drain the purse and the supply of personnel away from Germany and toward Southeast Asia. But the Vietnam War would have much more profound consequences within the American military communities and for German-American relations than the simple wrangles of who would pay for how many. At the same time that calls for cost savings suggested to Congress that there be cuts made in Germany, the Vietnam War tore the American fabric where it was weakest—along deep-seated seams of racial inequality. Those same weaknesses devastated the U.S. military communities in Germany and diminished the respect in which Americans were held.

Wallowing in Decline, 1967–1973

In the late 1960s and early 1970s, three social processes conspired to isolate the American military within Germany and overwhelm the prestigious status Americans had enjoyed until then. A series of *Washington Post* articles documented the problems. First, the Vietnam War drew the best military leadership out of Germany and left the units undermanned. The units suffered, and were described as "hollow." Moreover the political and social contradictions inherent in the way the

United States conducted the Vietnam War had demoralized soldiers throughout the U.S. Army. Racism and class hypocrisy in the choice of who went to Vietnam and who suffered most there became patently visible. Doubts over the way the war was prosecuted turned into doubts about whether it should be prosecuted. Racism became increasingly intolerable at the same time that the assassination of Martin Luther King deprived the protest movement of its wisest and most calming leadership. The processes of social dissent and racial anger raged epidemic in American society, and, exacerbated by the Vietnam War, influenced soldiers in Germany, leading to strife and violence within the military community. Violence boiled over into attacks against Germans. Unused to such levels of violence, and perhaps not yet experienced or comfortable with the diverse racial makeup of the American Army, the Germans began to turn against the Americans, increasing the isolation and frustration of both peoples. In addition, the decision to "float" the dollar added further instability. In the first six months of 1973, Americans experienced a 23 percent increase in the cost of living in German towns and villages. American soldier families were no longer the wealthy icons they once had been.[41]

In the fall of 1971, reporters from the *Washington Post* detailed the festering sores of military life in Germany. Deteriorated living conditions, isolation, violence, race hatred, and gutted leadership made Vietnam-induced instabilities all the more volatile.[42] Race hatred and race-related violence seemed to be out of control in, if not endemic to, the military communities. What Nelson or the *Washington Post* document through cold sociological reporting, Robert O'Connor makes palpable through a novel—*Buffalo Soldiers*. His work suggests that racial gangs, violent intimidation, fear, drugs, sex, theft, assaults on Germans, and a profound failure of leadership savaged the U.S. Army communities and disrupted German society as well.[43] One expects a novel to be exaggerated, but one also expects it to point out the nature of a crisis and the nature of the human reaction to it. *Buffalo Soldiers* does this masterfully well. Though not specifically devoted to Germany, Ingraham confirms the broader context of decline in the leadership of the U.S. Army during this period.[44]

For Germans, the reaction to American disorder was disgust, and Nelson documents the widespread German revulsion with and fear of American soldier behavior, for German society was quite law abiding. How much American disorder would the Germans tolerate in the interest of maintaining their external security? No one knew the answer, and no American leaders wanted to find out. Clearly, the U.S. forces in Germany would have to change and strive to regain German confidence, lest they lose their status as invited guests and thereby undermine NATO and the Western forward defense strategy. But how to do so?

Rebuilding the American Military Community, 1973–1986

The crisis within the American Army in Germany derived from the much larger processes afflicting American society generally. So the struggle to return to military competence in Europe, and regain host-nation acceptance, would be multipronged and not limited to actions taken by leaders in Europe. First, the inequalities in draft selection for a pernicious war led to the initiation of the all-volunteer force concept for staffing the U.S. Army. Wages were raised to attract volunteers. The draft ended. The conversion to an all-volunteer force by 1973 offered hope of internal change. By 1986, when I arrived in Germany, the all-volunteer force had been recruiting a substantially higher caliber of soldier for a number of years. Second, Army leaders attacked racial inequality within the Army by rigorously training the underprivileged of all races and then offering them meaningful leadership positions based on proven competence rather than racial preference. Race relations were substantially improved throughout the Army by rigorously ensuring fair treatment within the Army's processes of advancement. Moskos and Butler best trace this aspect of change in the U.S. Army.[45] Third, leaders implemented a variety of measures designed to quash the use of all drugs but alcohol. Random and frequent drug-use testing, severe penalties for dealing, and forced removal for using all led to greatly suppressed drug use and drug trafficking within the military.

Levels of violence in the American communities and attacks against Germans did decline in frequency. But a perception that American soldiers were extremely violent had crystalized in the German cultural consciousness. That perception would linger, contaminating German-American relations and adding to American social isolation. In 1986 through 1988, soldiers and spouses still met Germans who feared and resented American soldiers because of their perceived high levels of violence. Moreover, much of the restrictive policy of the 1980s was set by senior leaders who had experienced the turmoil of the late 1960s and early 1970s as junior troops and young officers. These now senior noncommissioned and commissioned officers were not about to permit drug abuse, perceptions of racial discrimination, or a laissez-faire attitude toward violence to destabilize the military community again. Their aversion to disorder in the military communities would have, as we shall soon see, a variety of unintended consequences.

Created in this historic process, the factors of German sovereignty, American military community isolation, Soviet threat, and the economics of the continuing dollar-Deutsche mark exchange-rate deterioration set the stage for my study of this overseas American Army community and its family behavior. To see how these intertwine, I now shift from the historical record to the ethnographic experience of 1986 to 1988 for my primary data.

I begin by showing the motivations of soldiers as part of an army of hope. Then I outline the basic institutions—military community, military unit, and military family—and show the impact of German society and culture them. Succeeding chapters lay out one by one the difficulties and contradictions soldiers and their families confronted as they dealt with various aspects of life in the U.S. Army in Germany during the Cold War. Collectively, the latter chapters illuminate the dynamics of discontent—the morale problem—the nature of alienation that military life persistently engenders in spite of the obvious benefits and satisfactions it provides. I conclude by reviewing the downsizing and community reorganization that took place after the fall of the Berlin Wall and assess what we have learned both about the nature of Army society and about the theories that help social scientists examine and understand the nature of society in general.

NOTES

1. NATO Information Service, *NATO and the Warsaw Pact: Force Comparisons* (Brussels: NATO Information Service, 1984): 8, 13, 19; James M. Garrett, *The Tenuous Balance: Conventional Forces in Central Europe* (Boulder, Colorado: Westview Press, 1989): 93; Joshua M. Epstein, *Conventional Force Reductions: A Dynamic Assessment* (Washington, DC: The Brookings Institution, 1990): 15–26.

2. Steve Vogel, "Training Squeezed by Budget Cuts, Environment," *Army Times*, 2 January 1994, 41.

3. "Hitler Dead, Germans Claim; Seventh Army Seizes Munich," *Stars and Stripes*, 1 May 1945, 1 and throughout. For brevity, endnote references to the *Stars and Stripes* will be abbreviated to *S&S*, date, page (with "uk" indicating page unknown).

4. "ETO [European Theater of Operations] War Ends," *S&S*, 8 May 1945, 1. A theater or theater of operations is large war zone.

5. "Berlin May Require 20 Years to Rebuild," *S&S*, 9 May 1945, 4; "What Now for the ETO Soldier?: Some Will Go to Pacific, Some Home, Others Stay," *S&S*, 9 May 1945, 3.

6. "Age Limit May Drop in 10 Days; Congress Lashes Army Strength," *S&S*, 30 August 1945, 1; "Army Faced Collapse, Ike Tells Congress," *S&S*, 17 January 1946, 1; "Idea Growing in Congress to Let Draft Stop May 15," "How GIs Are Deployed Abroad," *S&S*, 18 January 1946, 1; "Demobilization Plan Attacked in Congress; Quicker Action Urged," *S&S*, 12 September 1945, 1; "Senate Probe of Discharges Ready to Start," *S&S*, 12 November 1945, 1; "Ike Pledges Speed in Returning Men," *S&S*, 15 November 1945, 1; "Slowdown Tops Agenda in Congress," *S&S*, 15 January 1946, 1; "Army Will Keep Promise On Discharges, Ike Says; Congress Studies What Draft Can Do," *S&S*, 21 January 1946, 1.

7. Win Fanning, "Military Districts—Each Post Must Be a Stateside Town," *S&S*, 16 November 1947, 4.

8. "U.S. Army to Occupy Southwest," *S&S*, 6 June 1945, 1; "3rd and 7th Will Occupy Germany," *S&S*, 11 June 45, 1.

9. "General Wants Forces in ET [European Theater] Smartened Up," *S&S*, 12 November 1945, 3.

10. On the food supply for Germans: "Continuing of Rationing, Control of Prices Asked," *S&S*, 12 November 1945, 4; "Thousands of Europe's Children Seen Facing Death This Winter," *S&S*, 4 December 1946, 4; Glen Williams, "Europeans Are Hungry, But No One Is Starving," *S&S*, 10 February 1946, 1; "Food Rioters Loot Train, Raid Shops," *S&S*, 21 March 1946, 1; "U.S. Reduces German Food Ration," *S&S*, 30 March 1946, 1; "MG [Military Government] Launches Campaign to Avert Reich Famine," *S&S*, 4 May 1946, 4; "Germans Face Ration Cut to 500 Calories by British, U.S. Zone Slashes Bread One-Third," *S&S*, 17 May 1946, 5; "Current German Diet Termed Inadequate; 1,550 Calories Too Little for Winter, Report Says," *S&S*, 11 November 946, 4.

On the U.S. troop rations: "ET Troops Get Fresh Milk by Fall," *S&S*, 5 June 1946, uk; "One Fresh Egg Daily Included in ET Ration," *S&S*, 14 October 1946, 1; "The Eye Is on You, Joe—A German Eye; Teacher Says GIs Are Good Ambassadors But Their Waste Creates Ill-Will," *S&S*, 14 December 1945, 3.

11. Win Fanning, "Military Districts," 4.

12. Ibid., 4–6.

13. "Wives May Travel to ETO Later: WD [War Department] Promises Ban Will Be Lifted as Soon as Possible," *S&S*, 17 June 1945, 1; "Travel to ETO for GI Wives Indorsed [sic] in U.S.," *S&S* 25 June 1945, 5; "Truman Tells S & S He Will Get Troops Home as Quickly as Possible," *S&S*, 30 July 1945, 1; "That Makes it Unanimous With Everybody," *S&S*, 31 July 1945, 1.

14. Robert Marshall, "102 ET 'Villages' Are Planned for GI Families," *S&S*, 27 November 1945, 1; Cynthia Lowery, "Army Families to Live in Simple Dignity in Germany," *S&S*, 16 April 1946, 4.

15. Ron Marshall, "ET Dependents Due at Rate of 10,000 Monthly," *S&S*, 6 March 1946, 1, 8; Alan Dryfus, "First of U.S. Families Arrive Today, Official Parties at Port for Hearty Welcome," *S&S*, 28 April 1946, 1; Dorothy Gies, "Happy Reunions Mark Arrival of First Families, *S&S*, 29 April 1946, 1; "Germans Protest Seizure of Houses by U.S. Army," *S&S*, 8 June 46, 3.

16. "Modern Homes Await Arriving Families," *S&S*, 28 April 1946, 2; "Military Districts—Each Post Must Be a Stateside Town," *S&S*, 16 November 1947, 5.

17. "Accredited Schools Planned by USFET," *S&S*, 9 May 1946, 5; "Dependent Tots Attend Bad Nauheim 'School' Three Days Weekly," *S&S*, 24 October 1946, 5; Dorothy Gies, "Bobby-Sox Outpost," *S&S Weekend*, 17 November 1946, 6–7; *S&S*, 18 March 1947, uk.

18. Martha Gravois, "Military Families in Germany, 1946–1986," *Parameters: Journal of the U.S. Army War College* 16, no. 4 (Winter 1986): 62.

19. Don Whitehead, "Accord in Berlin Sets Example for All Reich," *S&S*, 15 July 1945, 3; Jack Sullivan, "Ivin is an All-Right Guy," *S&S*, 20 July 1945, 2.

20. Normal Palmer, "Allies Divide Reich Plants," *S&S*, 12 December 1945, 1.

21. "Unite to Stop Russians, Churchill Warns at Fulton," *S&S*, 6 March 1946, 1, 8; "Congress Hits Churchill Anti-Red Speech, Press Divided on Alliance of Britain, U.S.," *S&S*, 7 March 1946, 8; "10-Year Stay in Reich Likely for U.S. Army," *S&S*, 6 March 1946, 1, 8.

22. "U.S. Protests to Russia on Iran; Note on Manchuria Also Coming," *S&S*, 7 March 1946, 3; "Loss of More Important Secrets to Spy Ring Feared by Canada; Atom Scientist Admits Giving Information," *S&S*, 6 March 1946, 8; "Moscow Calls Churchill 'Warmonger'," *S&S*, 12 March 1946, 1.

23. T. Norman Palmer, "Ivin of Berlin Belies Tales of Hate-Mongers," *S&S*, 10 March 1946, 4; Robert A. Hoeger, "Army Weighs Issuance of Scrip as Soviet Marks Flood U.S. Zone," *S&S*, 13 March 1946, 1.

24. "Reds Said to Fill 2,000 U.S. Jobs," *S&S*, 13 March 1946, 3; "Iran, Turkey Warn They'll Fight . . . Russians Are Told," *S&S*, 16 March 1946, 1; "Soviets Demand Oil Before Quitting Iran," *S&S*, 19 March 1946, 1; "Italy Border Dispute Stalemates Big Four; Western Group, Russia Refuse to Alter Views," *S&S*, 5 May 1946, 1; "Truman Pledges Full U.S. Support to Peace, Asserts War Rumors Block World Recovery," *S&S*, 24 October 1946, 1.

25. Harris Peel, "ET [European Theater] Chief Says Troops Won't Leave," *S&S*, 8 November 1946, 1.

26. "Belvin Calls for Bloc to Counter Soviet," *S&S*, 13 January 1948, 1; "Marshall Backs Western Europe Bloc," *S&S*, 14 February 1948, 1.

27. "Big 3 Agree to Federalize Germany," *S&S*, 7 March 1948, 1.

28. "Russ Sift Berlin Travel—Order Trains, Cars Searched," *S&S*, 1 May 1948, 1; "Berlin 'Island' Fed by Air—U.S. Trains Halted in Russ Row," *S&S*, 2 May 1948, 1; "U.S. Berlin Wives Are in No Rush to Return Home," *S&S*, 3 April 1948, 3.

29. "Russ, UK Crash Kills 15—Red Pilot Rams Liner; 2 Yanks Die," *S&S,* 6 April 1948, 1; "Russians Blame British for Fatal Berlin Crash—London Terms Russ Story Untrue," *S&S,* 8 April 1948, 1.

30. "Forrestal Says Russ Hold A-Bomb Secret—Adds Only Lack Now Is Capacity," *S&S,* 13 April 1948, 1; "Berlin Squeeze Won't Drive U.S. Out, Clay States," *S&S,* 15 April 1948, 1.

31. "West German Rule Urged by Ehard," *S&S,* 15 April 1948, 1.

32. Henrik Bering, *Outpost Berlin: The History of the American Military Forces in Berlin, 1945–1994* (Chicago: Edition Q, 1995): 115.

33. Gravois, "Military Families," 66.

34. German Bundestag, *Questions on German History* (Bonn: German Bundestag Press, 1984): 352.

35. See Daniel Nelson, *A History of U.S. Military Forces in Germany* (Boulder, Colorado: Westview Press, 1987) and Simon Duke, *United States Military Forces and Installations in Europe* (Oxford: Oxford University Press / Stockholm International Peace Research Institute, 1989) for more complete discussions of the impact of Soviet acquisitions of nuclear weaponry and Chinese and Korean events on United States troop policy in Germany.

36. Nelson, *U.S. Military Forces,* 45.

37. Ibid., 55.

38. Nelson, *U.S. Military Forces,* 56, citing Anna J. Merritt and Richard J. Merritt, *Public Opinion in Semisovereign Germany* (Urbana: University of Illinois Press, 1980), 58.

39. Nelson, *U.S. Military Forces,* 53.

40. Ibid., 81.

41. See Nelson, *U.S. Military Forces,* 83–127, for a thorough discussion of the decline.

42. *Washington Post,* September 12–20, 1971, one or more articles per day. Nelson, *U.S. Military Forces,* 104–119, extracts the substance of the *Washington Post's* report on the U.S. Army in Germany and documents German newspaper reactions to the series.

43. Robert O'Connor, *Buffalo Soldiers* (New York: Vintage Books, 1994).

44. Larry H. Ingraham, "Fear and Loathing in the Barracks—And the Heart of Leadership," *Parameters: Journal of the U.S. Army War College* (December 1988): 75–80.

45. Charles C. Moskos and John Sibley Butler, *All That We Can Be: Black Leadership and Racial Integration the Army Way* (New York: Basic Books, 1996).

1

Army of Hope

The basic role of an infantry leader is to keep hope alive.

Brigadier General Bernard Loeffke

The American soldiers and spouses assigned to duty in Germany lived a hard life, something they often told me during our first encounter. What motivated them and justified the hardships that they took upon themselves in their moments of choice? Why did some soldiers and families stay with the Army for a career when it was often so difficult?

Soldiers and spouses experienced a range of benefits from their military life. At the crassest level, they benefited materially. Compared with what they might have expected of civilian life based on a high school diploma from an often underprivileged school in a disadvantaged urban or rural setting, enlisted soldiers in the Army had job security, good pay, housing, medical care, subsidized prices, and travel opportunities. They also found ample opportunity for personal development through in-house schooling, broad social experience, and constant change. Indeed, the Army provided a true working middle-class haven for the enlisted—many of whom came from lower class backgrounds—and a diverse managerial middle-class life for the officers, reason enough to stay in the military in a world otherwise filled with uncertainty.

Soldiers of all ranks and their spouses expressed their most profound feelings of appreciation and attachment, however, when they discussed the psychological fulfillment they derived from Army life. Black or White, Hispanic or of other origins, those attached to the Army often delighted in the task of making equality work. They found the Army and its communities to be less racist and more diverse than the circumstances of their previous lives. Many also had a thread of patriotic devotion in their Army attachment, deriving satisfaction from protecting values fundamental not only in their own country, but in the world at large. They were the army of hope for the world.

Within their work, they could build people as they crafted fighting units. They worked together and felt the sense of team precision and the smooth results of skilled cooperation. They were warriors in a largely ethical army, contributing to something that actually mattered in the greater scheme. They were not just "flipping hamburgers to make a buck." Many stayed as long as they were allowed. All sensed they were involved in an army of hope.

In the remainder of this chapter, I will share a composite of the positive aspects of Army life that soldiers and spouses of all ranks referred to as they tried to explain the motivations and meaningfulness of their often harried lives. These positive expressions are all the more interesting because the families saw me as a civilian researcher investigating how to make Army life in Germany better. The people I talked to had a natural inclination to accentuate the problems so that I could report them and invite the Army to fix them. I always asked a generic "Tell me about life here." Only once did I ask a couple to tell me what was *good* about life in the Army in Germany, after a thoughtful but unusually critical description of the lives they led. Thus, the expressions of good that follow in this chapter were insinuated into the conversation by the soldiers and spouses themselves, essentially without prompting from me. Indeed, some said explicitly they wanted to counterbalance the difficulties they had described.

Many of the couples I interviewed were quite optimistic. They expressed hope amid whatever level of cynicism, displeasure, or sometimes even anger they also felt as they tried to describe their lives and the persistent frustrations they experienced but never seemed able to rectify. I begin by exploring those satisfactions rooted in material and economic well-being.

MATERIAL BENEFITS

Economic Welfare

In one expression or another, most soldiers and spouses liked the "benefits" that military life provided: pay, provisions, and convenience. SP4 (Specialist Four) Jeff Atwood, for example, said, "The Army has good services. That is great." "We don't pay the doctors' bills. The only bill in housing is the phone bill," noted SGT (Sergeant) Adam Norton. Terry Walsh gave her list of other, less obvious benefits:

> If he is in the field and my car breaks down, I can call the post or the MPs [Military Police] and they will help me. They provide the library, and the great gym with the Nautilus room, and all of that free of charge. They have the community centers. You can borrow the sewing machines or typewriters. The Army has a real good child-care system set up. They have the travel agency . . . that will set up special discounts in recreation areas.

Soldiers and spouses also saved money in the subsidized commissaries—the military's grocery stores.

If living off-post, married soldiers received a "housing allowance" with which they paid their rent, perhaps saving a bit or perhaps spending from basic salary, depending on rents and utilities. If issued government quarters, the soldier forfeited the allowance but had no housing or utility expenses other than telephone. The on-post apartments were generally spacious, well-painted, furnished, and in good repair, much better than a young couple with a high school education might expect to afford as civilians in the United States. Sponsored families both on- and off-post also received a cost of living supplement, intended to cover some of the additional expenses of overseas life.

Repeatedly, families stressed the value of free medical care, an important part of SGT Norton's feeling that "Army life is pretty good." Barbara Norton agreed. They liked the benefits, and at the top of their list stood the fact that they had virtually no medical expenses, the birth of their child having cost "about $20 . . . as opposed to thousands if you are not in the military." In Germany, they also got "free dental" care.

Many of the enlisted soldiers joined the Army from impoverished backgrounds. Ruth Rodgers favorably compared her life now with her travails as a daughter raised in a family of sharecroppers in the South. Others described backgrounds of urban ghetto poverty and welfare assistance. They appreciated the economic and social stability the Army career offered compared with their prospects outside the Army in what they called "the civilian world," "the real world," or simply "the world." "One good thing about the Army," said SSG (Staff Sergeant) Jeremy Strong, who claimed he came "from a ghetto, a bad place," was the fact that "I ain't never been broke." To Jeremy, family housing and even the barracks were decent places to live. In a similar vein, "I don't think that we would be this well off in the U.S. without the Army," admitted SP4 Betty Atwood. "We have a new *schrank* [German for wooden wardrobe], and a new dining set. Eventually we will have a new living [room] set. I make good money, she makes good money. We are just 20 years old. We have a new car, a nice house, and secure jobs. There is no way we could have gotten that in the civilian life. We are definitely doing better than my parents at this age." For all of these people, the Army benefits offered not just income, but economic stability and the opportunity to start a family. Indeed, as we shall see shortly, Army life put them firmly on the road to a better life.

Convenience

Those who lived in government quarters liked the convenience of Army life; so much was provided so near at hand. Gretchen McCormick said, "I love it. The apartment is big and it's quiet, most of the time." CW3 (Chief Warrant Officer Three) Bill McCormick then joined in listing the conveniences: "It's close to work. School is right across the street. If you need something fixed, they come right in."

Indeed, a substantial number of military community resources were but two or three blocks away from those who lived on or next to a military installation in Germany.

Travel

Assignment to Germany provided a "rare opportunity" to see and tour Europe, to learn its history, and to experience German culture. Though many families said they did not see as much as they would have liked, they recognized, as SGT Adam Norton put it, that it would "cost a lot of money to get back over here" just to see it. After an impassioned discussion of a number of the difficulties of life in the Army in Germany, Terry Walsh pulled back, affirming, "I want to be sure to plug a few points. I'm still very thrilled to be here in Europe in spite of the little inconveniences, to see things here. . . . Every day I wake up and think, 'You're in Europe.' They haven't ruined that for me yet." Her final words intimate the problems that will concern us throughout the remainder of the book. For now, it is sufficient to see there was much good, much promise, and much hope. Most families managed to accomplish some sightseeing on their own. WO1 (Warrant Officer [initial level]) Vance Mantock noted, "Geographically, this is a nice place, wonderful for traveling. We are close to Austria, Switzerland, Luxembourg, and France." SGT Larry Bracken felt much the same about the travel opportunities: "Our friends and relatives can only dream about it."

A few imaginative company commanders managed to make some touring in Europe a part of official activities. According to SSG Nate Cobb, "In my company, the commander and the first sergeant comes up with company tours. . . . Quite a few of the single soldiers from the billets and some of the couples went to Spain. They put it on the training schedule. . . . They had a family day, with a free trip to Vilseck to see the men perform in combat training." If touring was too expensive, one could visit the local bakery, dance in the German clubs, attend the village *fests*, hike the *volksmarches* (organized weekend country hikes complete with food, first aid, and even entertainment along the route), drink in the music and the malt at a German beer hall, or find more kinds of wine, cheese, or sausage than one thought possible. The little villages had small bowling alleys, swimming pools, ice-skating rinks, castles, old churches, and 800-year-old farm buildings. Nearby cities had art galleries and museums. Throughout Germany, hundreds of hobby clubs catered to every conceivable interest. Indeed, an infinity of cultural possibilities lay within the circle of a two-dollar bus or train ride. "Basically," SGT Norton observed, Army life "lets you see the world," whereas, his wife, Barbara, pointed out, "If you stayed in the States . . . you probably wouldn't go too many places." The travel, the range of friends, and the diverse experiences constituted an environment not just financially favorable but also rich in developmental opportunities.

DEVELOPMENTAL OPPORTUNITIES

Self-Improvement and Personal Growth

The Army and its structured rules helped many acquire self-discipline and personal organization, what was often called "being squared away" or, less gracefully, "having one's shit together." A form of pride accrued to those who learned well the trait. Said one soldier on night watch,

> The Army has kind of force-fed me on keeping my stuff squared away and I can apply this to my civilian life. I have a lot of self-pride. Maybe I'll set an impression on some high school kid. He will say, "Hey, he looks good." In basic training, I said, "Hey, this is ridiculous." But I can see now where this will help me a great deal: a good outlook and esprit de corps has a lot to do with the cleanliness.

Some soldiers expected their training to lead to good jobs after they quit the military or retired. Likewise, for spouses, the frequent job changes added variety and a range of experience. "You have to enjoy the work," said Barbara Norton. "I have a two-year degree in engineering tech. . . . I can take this experience back to the States so I can get a decent job." Before he became a first sergeant, MSG (Master Sergeant) Oscar McDonald repaired tank turrets. "When I get back [to the U.S.] to retire, . . . I'm going to work on tanks in the civilian side." Indeed, the hardships of military life, the exacting training, and the "can-do attitude" that soldiers learned prepared them to succeed in almost anything they might try. As MSG McDonald put it, "Being in the military . . . if you can take it, you can succeed in anything."

The Army provided soldiers and spouses with multiple opportunities for self-development, and soldiers said they gained considerable satisfaction from seeing themselves so develop. For some, the Army gave an opportunity to "be an adult and get a first job." For others, it provided for a future education through the Army's college saving fund, or it offered a structure for getting free college credit by attending the military community's evening schools while off duty. The Army also offered all soldiers leadership training at various schools for all levels of noncommissioned officer (NCO) and commissioned officer. The military had (and still has) an extensive system of in-house training, one largely available to the "working class" enlisted and not just to the officers.[1] Every soldier could qualify and attend the in-house schools needed to advance to the next rank or to secure a more interesting job classification. SGT Juan Salinas, from Grenada, said, "I come to America and take the opportunities. The Army can't do nothing better than what it is doing." Compared with the relative closure of opportunity for America's rural and urban poor, and especially for the high school graduates of America's many ethnic and racial minorities, the Army offered exceptional and fair opportunity to learn and rise in the system. Indeed, the Army offered hope, and for some soldiers and spouses, it was the only hope they had ever had.

Soldiers and spouses likewise expressed satisfaction in the broad range of social experience and social development they acquired. Although life in the barracks is "tough," according to another single soldier standing night watch,

> It is also a time of life that will help you the rest of your life. For example: learning to deal with people. There are a whole bunch of people all in same spot, with different interests. Some keep their area clean all the time. Some relax and do not. If you're the clean-living type living with somebody else who isn't, that is the way you learn to deal with people. It helps you communicate with different people. I'm a nonsmoker. I live with a smoker in the same room. We talked. Now he cracks the window. Now we get along great; he is my best friend.

Out of such experiences came much personal growth.

Overcoming Obstacles

Soldiers and spouses consistently expressed satisfaction born of overcoming obstacles. "It is fun to be resourceful," said CPT (Captain) Peter Lawson, Richberg's chief legal officer. With the right attitude, some felt obstacles could even make a couple stronger and more resilient: "We really haven't encountered any problems that we haven't been able to overcome. If anything, it has made us closer—by hardships, by moving, by money being tight. We communicate more," said one husband on night watch. The link between obstacles, growth, pride, and success became obvious when I asked SGT Todd Jasper what it took to be successful. He chuckled a moment and launched: "You have to be dedicated. At times you are called to do things beyond the call of duty. You have to have pride in yourself and fortitude to do things without being told what to do. Opportunities are here and you have to grab them. They are not going to come to you. I personally believe the obstacles can be overcome by one's own fortitude of succeeding." Overcoming obstacles or finding in each day a new experience also were forms of change and progress.

Change and Progress

Americans for the most part like variety and change. Indeed, developmental change is one of the core American premises, the premise of "progress." Compared with a number of other societies, Americans have short time horizons, and frequent changes keep Americans from getting bored. Military family members experienced the general value of change when they moved to a new residence every one to three years. One savored a new country or a new state, and always, a new job. Of course, moving and change could be disruptive and difficult. But for some, the difficulties of a move hardly diminished the anticipated refreshment of a change. "I have always seen it as a great way to live," said MAJ (Major) Quintin Scott, the senior chaplain of the Grossberg community region, referring to the satisfactions of Army life. After being at a post for a while, he continued, "We get to feeling we ought to be moving; it's time to see a new place." Likewise, "I've had good travel in the military," said MSG McDonald. "Four tours in Germany, a year in Kansas, a year in Colorado, a year in Kentucky, a year in California, a year in Texas, and three years in Hawaii"—ten moves in twenty-one years. Barbara Norton listed the "good things" about moving often: "You meet new people. You see new areas of the country. You can get a new job before you're bored with it." Obviously, not all was good: "You have friends," Barbara noted, but "in two or three years you have to move on." Older couples even reconceptualized the forced separations of field maneuvers, emphasizing as advantage that they "get to have breaks" from the stresses of close life together.

Every change in living assignment involved changes at work. Often the job change included a change in rank and therefore a substantial change in the managerial level of one's duties. Here the changes brought development and indeed were perceived as progress. But even if the duties did not change, the supervisors and the subordinates were all different. Soldiers anticipated the inevitable change of superiors if their current boss was less than desirable. "I couldn't see myself in one job for twenty years," said SGT Adam Norton. "Here you are forced to move to a new position." One lunch hour at Richberg, I met 1LT (First Lieutenant) Hal Vinney, who was complaining about all of the changes in a soldier's life. I suggested that he apply to stay in the same location and unit for a number of years. "That would be too predictable," he retorted in disgust at my lack of understanding. "Also, there would be less chance for commands. The more you see, the more you know, the better you are. Unless I am a real screw-up, I'll be moving every eighteen months. I like that. You expect change. You know it is coming. It is the day-to-day change that irritates." Short-term change in one's daily work plans created frustration. Long-term change meant new sights, new friends, new work, new challenges, and no boredom; every change expanded the range of one's experience; changes fostered growth; change and variety begat promotion. The variety and change in the military jobs and the opportunity to explore German culture added up to a confirmation of the general values of challenge and adventure. Change enabled personal progress, a durable American value, and allowed soldiers from underprivileged backgrounds to move firmly into middle-class life.

Middle-Class Anchorage

The Army offered much more than just relative economic stability. The range of opportunities and the structure of normative stability in the Army enabled soldiers from a lower-class background to gain access to working middle-class American values. As SSG Frank Barnes put it, "You're in a controlled situation most of the time. You know where you're going to live. You have a stable wage. You know what is going on. Not knowing—that is the fear of going back to the civilian world." In spite of the many challenges in the system, the Army provided an overarching social structure that gave all young persons, no matter their background, helpful bearings and an opportunity to establish a working middle-class life in the NCO corps. The best could aspire to the managerial middle-class by qualifying for the officer corps. For both officer and enlisted, the secure achievement of middle class status represented more than mere opportunity achieved. Middle-class status and the broad range of personal development it entailed was one of several sources of profound psychological fulfillment.

PSYCHOLOGICAL FULFILLMENT

Sense of Community

Another source of psychological fulfillment came from the sense that the couples were unified within an organization and with a set of people living together and trying to help one another. They frequently expressed this idea in the often-heard term "Army family." The people in this or that installation were "like family" or were "my Army family."

Many soldiers and spouses enjoyed helping others by volunteering in community activities. They coached youth sports, gave out household goods at the "loan closet," assisted at Army Community Services, tutored children at school, and served in any of a hundred other tasks unfunded by the day-to-day military and civilian service agencies. Sometimes they helped their peers connect with Germany and its resources. Some leaders gave guided tours or put barracks-stranded soldiers on trains, encouraging them to be adventurous. Volunteering brought satisfaction because, underlying much of it, the volunteer helped develop the capacities of other human beings. For the most part, the mutual helpfulness within the community bridged racial difference, and the resulting experience of equality-in-practice added to the sense of satisfaction.

Making Equality Work

Indeed, one of the most gratifying aspects of Army life derived from the relative success the Army has had in integrating racially. The institution was by no means perfect in the human execution of the intended irrelevance of race. Yet, given the racial problems of the society from which the Army had drawn its members, soldiers and spouses have done remarkably well in the task. In Germany, units were fully integrated, with persons of all minorities demonstrating leadership, experiencing success, and achieving advancement. Housing areas were likewise integrated, with a moderate amount of interaction between racially different households. In the barracks, single soldiers still clustered into largely segregated friendship cliques. But compared with the civilian world, and compared with the Army of the 1970s in Germany, the racial atmosphere was substantially free and open. As SSG Frank Barnes, who joined the Army from his home in an American urban ghetto observed, "If I go home right now, the first thing I am expected to do is to go and hang with the brothers [other blacks]." When he did so, however, he felt intensely uncomfortable, out of place. The Army experience had transformed his behavioral and mental links to race. "To me," he went on, "that environment is so far in the past, you don't want to be a part of it. At home, I got to fight the obstacle of race. The number one reason that racism is out [unacceptable] in the Army is you can't afford to lose a friend in the military 'cause that same guy can either kill you or save your life in combat." Many similar conversations confirmed in detail the conclusions of Moskos and Butler, that Blacks, Whites, and the many other varieties of Americans for the most part took pride in their interracial, intercultural experiment and enjoyed having made the core ideals of American culture work reasonably well.[2]

Worthwhile Work

Transcending all these benefits, the nature of the work itself was the main reason soldiers found Army life in Germany satisfying. The soldiers trained, learned, assumed responsibilities, and thereby developed themselves. One competed with other units and identified with one's own unit. One acquired a sense of possession, a feeling that "this is my army." CW3 Don Brenton narrated how, at one point early in his career, he was thinking about leaving the service. "When I was a W1 [WO1, or junior warrant officer] and I wanted out [of the Army] . . . a chief warrant told me, 'I would want you in *my* army.'" When he adopted this perspective, that it was "my army," Brenton decided to stay in.

Soldiers spoke of the challenge and adventure of Army combat training and, most important, they found satisfaction in the immediate reality of the threat they faced. The work was "real work." "I like being assigned in Europe more—the mission is more real, the threat is more real," said MAJ Matthew Taylor, who regularly devoted sixteen-hour days to running the division-sized brigade operations center. Because the work was more authentic, a soldier's herculean efforts were well spent, and the sacrifices were justified because they were made in defense of one's country.

For some, this core ideal of patriotism motivated their desire to stay in the Army. MAJ Rodney Kimball, for example, said, "I get chills because of the flag." WO1 Vance Mantock's medical problems were pressing him out of the service. Yet, his wife, Fay, ruefully remarked, "What is really sad is all he wants to do is serve his country." In both instances, patriotism stood central.

The best of the leaders found enormous satisfaction helping their younger charges accomplish authentic missions and develop their lives and leadership skills. To SFC (Sergeant First Class) Arthur Baldwin, a platoon sergeant, "The best part of Army life is the . . . chance to help someone. I hate to see someone come in and fail and we put them back on the street. It is like we gave the society a problem child back." Such leadership was rooted in the competence of the leader and in the caring basic to his or her character. Out of it came the capacity of the "real leader" to bring soldiers and weapons to bear in a "real mission" where the soldiers trusted one another and their leaders. When such trust-infused relations matured, the most difficult missions could be executed in training and presumably could be accomplished in combat with minimum loss of life. The esprit had to be nurtured in training, however, and in the waiting period of garrison duty, where caring, competence, and truthfulness built basic trust. Hoping for just such moments, some soldiers felt it worthwhile to stay in the Army in spite of its aggravations. Many other soldiers, however, lost patience and departed, their hopes dashed by a series of painful experiences with leaders.

In the final analysis, a fine unit was defined by its human qualities of esprit, trust, competence, communication, and other qualities of well-honed interaction, not by its material assets. Only soldiers—through good leadership and adaptive participation—could make the needed qualities coalesce. Conversely, only soldiers—through poor leadership and maladaptive participation—could corrupt the trust and alienate themselves from the unit and from each other. The highest satisfactions of Army life came from working under, and being oneself, a "real leader." Here is how SSG Alan Evanson described his concept of "real leadership":

> You have to be able to get people to do things that they wouldn't ordinarily do in normal circumstances. You have to tell the person that he is the one . . . who will walk point on the patrol. Your decision may affect that guy's life. That is where the real leadership comes in, at the squad level. Being the squad leader is the most difficult job in the Army. When you manage people . . . you tell them and they go do it. Real leadership is more inspirational: you want to follow. . . . You *manage* paperwork and things, but you *lead* people. It requires trust—that he has the ability, and the responsibility, and that he will support you and make sacrifices for you, that he will do everything he can to support you and your mission. You believe in his ability, and he in yours. He should know, because he trained you.

When competence, caring, and open communication come together through "real leadership" and proud soldiering to create trust, the sense of identification soldiers experience is indeed a treasured and savored feeling—a burst of esprit, of high morale—contagious, something one hopes will last or something to hope for if current conditions made it evaporate.

CONCLUSION

The promise, the valued goal—the hope—was there in Germany, and understood by most. Indeed, hope, according to General Bernard Loeffke, is the essential contribution of leadership in the difficult circumstances of either war or peace.[3] But hope was hard to implement and maintain in the forward-deployed garrison communities of Cold War Germany. The rest of this book is an attempt to understand why the promise of satisfaction and trust too often seemed to break down and dash the hope of so many. The Atwood couple expressed the dilemmas well. Jeff's ideas set the stage: "A lot of people knock the Army. It is something to knock, for the civilians and for us. If you're mad, it is the Army." Betty then observed,

> The Army is very positive in a lot of ways. There are very many benefits that every soldier gets. But to be honest with you, there is too much bullshit that goes along

with it. I feel that the bullshit outweighs the positive, and that many soldiers feel that way. I feel that the Army should have been so much more positive, and that the bad should not be blown up to where everything is bad, but that is, in general, how it is.

How is it that the bad gets "blown up," out of proportion, so that the "bullshit outweighs the positive"? Somehow, for this and other soldiers and military families, the promise, the hope had become corrupted. They felt alienated. And yet they felt saddened that their hopes had dissipated. Jeff went on: "Do others have these problems?" he wondered, "or are we just bitching and crying? Should we be getting treated better? Or is it like this in the world?" Betty amplified the idea: "It's like saying, 'We are spoiled.' We do have things good. We will have a roof and food. Are we spoiled and keep asking for more? Are people in the Army spoiled? Is it handed to them on a silver platter, and now they want it on a gold platter?" MAJ Quintin Scott, the Grossberg regional chaplain, saw the problem this way: "This is a volunteer army. Most of the soldiers take a real pride in doing what they are trained to do. This is the first time in their lives they have stuck with anything. They want to leave feeling they are good citizens; the job fulfillment is important." But it does not always work out that way, for something undermines their hopes. Chaplain Scott went on: "A lot of their complaint is that the basic training—the humiliation—is supposed to be over. They then go to AIT [Advanced Individual Training] and [to a school to] learn a job. And then they get *here* to the job and find that the humiliation is *worse*." As one soldier put it succinctly, "Success is if you're happy at what you're doing. But most don't like the Army." By implication, they are not successful in the Army and the Army itself is not fully successful.

Does the Army have an interest in whether its people are happy? The evidence strongly suggests that persistent unhappiness at the family level affects unit performance and that alienated soldiers reduce combat effectiveness and undermine retention of trained personnel.[4] What soldiers call "low" or "bad" or "shitty" morale—what social scientists call "alienation"—reflects the breakdown of trust, competence, caring, and communication in military units. The idea that the good life includes the pursuit of happiness suggests that if soldiers and their spouses do not achieve a positive balance between the satisfactions and the frustrations of military life, they will leave the service—or wish they could and gripe because they cannot. Thus, the Army has an interest in raising morale, in preventing alienation, in providing satisfaction, and in understanding the systems that affect them. In the remainder of this book, I will explore those aspects of Army life in Germany that undermined the hopes and alienated the attachments of soldiers and their spouses to the Army, to the community, to the way of life they had adopted, and even to each other.

My goal is to capture and share the soldiers' and spouses' experiences and insights and through them explore the strengths and weaknesses of theory in military sociology and in anthropology. By contrast, the soldiers and spouses that

I interviewed cared not at all about theory. They saw me as a conduit to send a message to U.S. Army leaders regarding the sources of the pain they were experiencing. Hence, the dual functions of this book: an exploration in theory and an exploration in practical change. In the conclusion, I will show that both these facets—theory and practical change—are complementary. More important, I provide an interpretation of the nature of military life and military institutions that will make Army life more understandable to those who have to live it and to the civilian citizens who may be baffled by or worried about the differences they sense between themselves and those sworn to defend them. But to achieve these dual goals, one must thoroughly understand both the hopes held and the contradictions lived by soldiers and their spouses. They took their precious free time and worked with me, again and again, in the hope that if I thoroughly understood the difficulties and frustrations they faced, perhaps my experience with them might bring change to the Army in Germany, change that would benefit others. In this regard, even in their most profound expressions of alienation, they were an army of hope.

In Germany, however, soldiers and spouses often felt their work or their lives were counterproductive to their hopes. They sensed a kind of theft by coercion, an alienation of their sacrifices. My goal in the next several chapters is to detail the multiple interrelated structures and processes of this alienation, this dashing of hope. I begin with the perplexities and stresses of moving to Germany and establishing one's life in the Army community.

NOTES

1. Charles C. Moskos and John Sibley Butler, *All That We Can Be: Black Leadership and Racial Integration the Army Way* (New York: Basic Books, 1996).

2. Moskos and Butler, *All That We Can Be.*

3. Brigadier General Bernard Loeffke, "Values for Infantry Leaders," *Infantry* 76, no. 5 (1986): 12.

4. Faris R. Kirkland and Pearl Katz, "Combat Readiness and the Army Family," *Military Review* 69, no. 4 (April 1989): 63–74.

"Inside the Fence": Community, Army, and Family in Context

It's Little America: They try to make it as close to home as possible.
Elsie Kimball
Middleberg Military Community

Germany in the mid-1980s was suffused with a multinational military presence. Military aircraft frequently darted across the sky. At Germany's international airports, one noted soldiers in uniform, arriving from or departing to any of several countries. A train ride of any distance would likely pass a string of flatbed cars loaded with tanks or artillery waiting on a sidetrack or traveling in the opposite direction. On the autobahn, one encountered convoys of military trucks—loaded with troops, tanks, artillery, or sometimes even rockets—bound for training exercises or returning home. Each vehicle bore the stenciled flag of its North Atlantic Treaty Organization (NATO) country of origin, most commonly of Germany, France, Britain, or the United States. From the autobahn one also observed small, low, discrete pointers, each displaying a NATO flag and the name of a nearby military installation—directing the observant driver to the off-ramps and access routes to the many dispersed military installations. West Germany in the mid-1980s was indeed substantially impacted by NATO forces, among them the American Army communities that I now explore.

THE MILITARY COMMUNITY

Perhaps the best way to begin to understand soldier and family life in the American Army community is to form a picture of the military communities in which they reside. Here I describe Richberg Kaserne, one of the two military communities I studied intensively, a community quite representative of the many military installations throughout the American sector.

Facilities

The first-time visitor could easily miss the sign for the off-ramp to Richberg Kaserne. At the end of the ramp, a smaller sign points up a gentle hill, through a dense, verdant forest. In a clearing to the right, three-story apartment buildings smartly dressed in new brown-trim panels make up the family housing area. Pine trees, grassy areas, playground equipment, children playing, and parking lots lined with oddly oversized American cars fill the areas between buildings. To the left, wide dirt trails branch off, with signs in both German and English that identify a military training area, prohibit unauthorized entry, and post the maximum speed for tanks. At the gate-guard shack, a helmeted soldier with an M-16 at ready peers into the car and asks for military identification. Those who have it are waved on quickly. Those who do not, park to the side, enter the Military Police (MP) station, provide paperwork justifying their visit, and wait for a responsible escort from their destination. The military escort signs for the guests and returns them afterward to the MP station for clearance.

Inside the compound, tires and tank tracks chatter on cobblestones. Troops in organized squads and platoons trot in squared formations from one location to another, loudly chanting cadence. Tanks and armored personnel carriers move slowly, their high-pitched safety horns bleating incessantly. Old 1930s four-story concrete and stone buildings house various military units, community offices, and work activities. Neat signs announce the denizens of each building. On the left is a theater. On the right, a World War II Sherman tank bespeaks an armored unit. A miniature castle and a placard beside it tell of engineers housed in the barracks. Other placards identify community activities and facilities: an elementary school, a chapel, a bowling alley, and a gym.

Half a kilometer from the gate, the road loops around a rectangular parade field surrounded by command and service buildings. A community headquarters building with a library and post office lines one side, a small PX (post exchange) and a liquor store another, a battalion headquarters and barracks the third, and a burger bar with ice cream shop and bookstore the fourth. Another 200 meters of military service roads connect the equipment parks, repair buildings, and barracks at the far end of the installation. Military trucks and jeeps rattle in and out of the equipment lots; family cars come and go from the PX area. Throughout the installation, the vegetation is intensely green, the grounds absolutely litter-free, weeded and trimmed, the stone architecture gray and austere. Fifty years after the fact, if one looks closely, one can still discern the vague outlines of Nazi eagles and other emblems of war and politics that were chiseled away. Such is the first impression of Richberg, a fenced military compound that is the work site and home of 4,000 American soldiers, 2,000 spouses, and 2,500 children living on it or in the surrounding German towns and villages.

Richberg Kaserne, like most installations acquired in the aftermath of World War II, served as a German military post. These former German military installations did not match the American pattern of much larger military facilities and attached training areas, referred to as "posts" or "forts." Perhaps for this reason, none of the American facilities in Germany was officially called a fort. Any piece of military property under United States control could be called an "installation." Installations provided space and shelter for training, repair, storage, planning, residence, and all other activities Army units needed while "in garrison," as opposed to "on maneuvers" or "in the field." With the exception of training centers, recreation sites, medical facilities, and a few maintenance depots, most installations housed a combat unit and the support units that sustained it, and therefore included residential buildings for troops. In casual speech, any installation with troop residences could be called either a "barracks" or its German equivalent, a "*kaserne*," denoting the large buildings for troop lodging. Full official names typically commemorated a distinguished military person. When an American war hero or a high-ranking officer was commemorated, the installation was officially called a "barracks," as in "Sitwell Barracks." If a German name (person or town) was commemorated, the installation was called a "*kaserne*," as in Rommel Kaserne. If the area consisted exclusively of family housing, it was often called a "village"—"Alexander Hamilton Village," for example. The word "*kaserne*" was common in American military speech in Germany, properly applied to any relatively large installation, whatever its formal name.

Some installations were isolated, completely surrounded by farmlands or forest. More commonly, the American compound and housing areas stood on the edge of a German town. A few were completely engulfed by urban centers. Stout fences of barbed wire, chain link, and razor-sharp spirals of concertina defined an installation. Armed guards protected its entrances. People spoke of "being inside the fence" or of "life inside the fence." Within the fence, one found headquarters buildings for each battalion; barracks buildings containing both the command areas of each company and the lodgings of its unmarried troops; work and repair buildings; warehouses; storage areas for military equipment; offices of the community headquarters; and buildings for community activities, support services, schools, shopping, and recreation.

Single officers and single senior enlisted—soldiers used the adjective as a mass noun—lived in apartments, sometimes contiguous to the family housing areas, as at Richberg. Junior troops lived in troop barracks, invariably quite separated from the family areas and always "inside the fence."

On many Army installations in the Federal Republic, family housing stood just outside the fenced and guarded area, compact rows of three- and four-story walk-up apartment buildings called "government quarters" or "family housing." On a few installations, family housing was inside the fence. Each building had from two to four entrances, each giving access to a stairway that led to a pair of apartments on each landing. The stack of six or eight apartments connected by a common staircase and sharing a single entrance was referred to as a "stairwell." Indeed, "stairwell living" summed up both the constraints and the convenience of close residence in military family housing areas, and "stairwells" came to be an alternate term for "government quarters" in ordinary speech. Among the conveniences, basements had laundry facilities and overflow storage areas. Shopping facilities and work areas were just a few minutes' walk away. Among the constraints, one put up with close living in a judgmental community, which I will explain in detail later. In the 1980s, from a third to a half of the military families assigned to a particular military community were housed in "government quarters." The remainder of the families found apartments in the surrounding German towns and villages.

Middleberg Barracks and Richberg Kaserne, the two major sites of this study, were very similar in circumstance. In both, family housing for all enlisted and company grade officers (lieutenants and captains) lay about two minutes' walk from the installation's front gate. At Middleberg, field grade officers (majors, lieutenant colonels, and colonels) and the commanding general lived in a circle of large homes and duplexes inside the guarded compound.[1] At Richberg, field grade officers lived just outside the guarded area in three single-entrance walk-up buildings distinguished by their newness, upscale exterior finish, and slightly secluded location—across the access street from the slightly plainer housing area for married and single company grade officers, single senior NCOs (noncommissioned officers), and all enlisted families. Both Richberg Kaserne and Middleberg Barracks had small forested training areas—Richberg's adjacent to and Middleberg's inside the fenced compound. In the 1950s and 1960s, Middleberg Barracks was separated from Middleberg city's urban area by perhaps a kilometer of open area. By the late 1980s, Middleberg Barracks' family housing area was contiguous to recently built German housing and community sports facilities. The two entrances to Richberg Kaserne lay on the side of the forested training area, giving a first impression of isolation. However, the end of the government quarters area was only 200 meters from the civilian apartment buildings of Richberg city, and the back fence of the *kaserne* abutted the city's dense urban housing. Having described the physical facilities, I now explore the organizational cadre tasked to manage them.

Organization

Because not all military families could live on installation property, and because the German government, by treaty, made the U.S. Army responsible for all the American soldiers and their family members, the entire American defense sector in Germany had been divided into forty-five large, nonoverlapping administrative territories, called "military communities." Each community took responsibility for one or more installations and for the American soldier families and Department of Defense employees living in the surrounding territory. The larger installations generally housed a major combat command, with its constituent combat battalions and the support battalions and smaller service support units needed to sustain them. A few military communities housed a significant combat service support asset, such as a hospital complex.[2]

Each military community had a "community command cadre," a staff of military and civilian personnel responsible for maintaining the buildings and their contents, utilities, grounds, and roads—indeed, everything that was not mobile combat equipment. In addition, each military community provided services that supported the morale and welfare of the soldiers. This included the PX, commissary (grocery store), laundromat, recreational facilities, and other family services.

The military cadre was responsible for the safety and well-being of the families of soldiers and for families of the U.S. citizens employed by the Department of Defense who happened to reside within an Army community's boundary. Unit commanders, by contrast, had exclusive responsibility for all of the soldiers. The community cadre also handled all issues of law and regulation regarding the post. They controlled access to the facilities and dealt with all aspects of German civilian relations, business contracts, and local government concerns.

The resources available to the members of a military community flowed out of several agencies of the military support system, called directorates. The Directorate of Personnel and Community Affairs, or DPCA, administered most nonmedical social services, including drug and alcohol abuse therapy, marital counseling, and family financial management training; recreational facilities; and evening education programs. The Directorate of Engineering and Housing (DEH) managed construction contracting, repaired and maintained buildings, administered housing assignments to government quarters, and maintained apartment referral lists for those unable to be quartered in government facilities. The Directorate of Industrial Operations (DIO) maintained the motor pool, ran the commissary, supplied military clothing, and issued troop equipment other than weapons. A Civilian Personnel Office (CPO) handled recruiting for various post positions open to nonmilitary employees. The possession of essential directorates made a military community relatively independent. Some military communities, however, were subdivided into a central or core community at one installation and one or more subcommunities at satellite installations. Subcommunities were dependent on the central community to provide the essential services of one or more of the core directorates. Because the range of services offered affected both the quality of soldier life and the status of the community within the community/subcommunity hierarchy, we must detail the services typical of the various military communities.

Services

Although each community or subcommunity varied somewhat as to services available, most had family housing, a child-care facility called the Child Development Center (CDC), and an elementary school. Communities had at least a small PX and access to a large one within an hour's drive. Most military communities also had a commissary and a medical clinic staffed by military medical personnel (though Richberg, the community I described in the opening of this chapter, had neither). The PX and commissary were both extremely useful, providing soldiers and family members with familiar American products. One expected to find a bank, a post office, a barbershop, and a beauty parlor. The community provided a range of recreational opportunities: all had a post library and a "rec center" with a lounge, television, videocassette recorder, and a variety of games. Most communities and subcommunities also had a theater and a bowling alley. Other recreational facilities might include one or more well-equipped craft centers for carpentry, picture framing, photo development, or pottery making. Some communities had a "rod and gun club," and/or a self-service auto repair facility. A few communities had a pizza parlor. Some had a Burger King; the remainder had a generic burger bar serving American fast food.

In the past, each community had separate clubs for officers, NCOs, and enlisted soldiers. In the mid-1980s, the NCO club was increasingly combined with the enlisted club. Officers' clubs existed on most installations, but many were experiencing financial deficit and declining memberships. Reductions in funding had pushed some communities to collapse all the clubs into a single "community club" shared by all ranks.

Army Community Services (ACS) offered a wide range of family supports, including relocation assistance for its arriving and departing families. A "loan closet," staffed by volunteers, supplied basic living supplies until one's shipment of household goods arrived. ACS also offered formal financial counseling and the informal advice of experienced military wives. Volunteers supervised community sports leagues and other services. Indeed, the Army in Europe probably provided more recreational services to its communities than did the Army in the continental United States because there was no external English-speaking civilian community to which the soldiers and family members could turn.

Military units provided police, medical services, and finance offices to active duty members, though not all subcommunities had a resident MP (military police) unit or a medical clinic of their own. Community Command operated the Security, Plans, and Operations Division (SPO), which arranged transportation access through East Germany to Berlin, granted permission for travel in Eastern bloc countries, and debriefed travelers on their return. SPO also managed the Noncombatant Evacuation Office (NEO), which was responsible for alerting and, if necessary, evacuating military spouses and children in the event of impending or actual hostilities. NEO invited spouses of soldiers and civilian employees to attend training sessions that explained evacuation procedures. It maintained maps and rosters of off-post families for emergencies.[3]

The overwhelming majority of Army families expected their children to attend an American school. The Department of Defense Dependent Schools (DODDS) supervised curriculum and staff. Every military community and subcommunity in Germany had an elementary school. The more centrally located communities provided a regional junior high school or high school. Contracted school buses picked up and delivered elementary children across broad territories in each military community and hauled teenagers as much as two hours each way to high schools and middle schools serving several communities. Except for a few children sent to German kindergartens, Army families enrolled their children in the American military schools.

Community as Multivocal Symbol

The concept of military community took on the characteristics of physical installation, social organization, services provided, work done, and people present. When soldiers or spouses used the term "military community," they might refer to any of these distinct facets of the military community. First, soldiers or family members sometimes identified the *unit* as the community because of the central, dominating influence the military units exerted. Indeed, the military community existed only because military units needed to be supported, supplied, and staffed. The physical, social, and intellectual life of the community revolved around its military units. Second, a military community could be thought of as one of the forty-five *geographic areas* into which the American zone was divided. Third, "military community" might refer more narrowly to a *particular installation*—the fenced compound maintained in an operational state to support unit missions and to protect the military systems. Fourth, "military community" often referred to the *organization* and the *cadre of personnel* that performed the tasks necessary to maintain the post so as to support all the activities necessary for combat readiness and support of family life. Finally, the term "military community" was used to refer to the *web of friendship, cooperation,* and *idealized trust*—the *network of social relations*—between all persons connected to the military as soldiers, civilian employees, and family members of soldiers and civilian employees. Depending on context, the term "military community" was used to emphasize any or several of these facets.

In spite of the term's multiple uses, the military community existed primarily to support military units. If a major unit were withdrawn from the military community and a different kind of military unit brought in, the activities of military community personnel changed considerably. If no replacement units were assigned, the installation itself would be closed. Military communities and military families moved to the tempo set by the military units. Consequently, to fully understand the community, we must understand how Army units were organized and what their tasks were.

THE ARMY UNITS

Army installations in Germany pulsated with the energy of their military personnel, who worked feverishly to ensure that they were constantly ready to resist surprise attack by Soviet forces. Soldiers had to be physically fit. Before dawn, companies of soldiers assembled in rectangular formations to exercise and run. Equipment had to be constantly operational, so part of one's task included maintaining, cleaning, and repairing equipment. A soldier also had to be skilled in the craft of warfare. Soldiers spent much time training with their weapons and honing the organizational and physical skills of bringing all weapons to bear on a military mission in mutually supportive coordination. A military unit had to train for immediate action. Soldiers, trucks, armored carriers, tanks—everything had to be able to roll out the gate, fully prepared and armed for combat within two hours of an "alert," a surprise notification that tested how quickly the organization could rush to its designated forward defensive positions. For two hours after such an alert, the post was a frenzy of activity—a constant roar of diesel engines, an earsplitting mixture of screech and clatter, as the tracked vehicles surged through the front gate in an ordered race against time. Such readiness had to be continuous. Communications systems had to be staffed twenty-four hours a day. Guards had to be posted. Everything had to be repeatedly tested to ensure that it could respond as needed "if the balloon went up"—that is, if war began. Finally, the installation and its personnel had to "look the part," with uniforms, barracks, buildings, and equipment maintained in good order. Appearances were important because, it was thought, good appearances indicated good discipline, a factor in high readiness.

Everyone had a part to play, an assigned responsibility for which they were in charge or a unit over which they were in command. Indeed, precisely ordered rank relationships between units, soldiers, and leaders made it all possible.

Rank and Organization

The U.S. Army is a hierarchical organization, with rank the pervasive organizing principle of responsibility and control. The principle of rank is simple. A person of senior rank can order a person of junior rank to perform mission-related behavior and can expect to be obeyed. Authority, on one hand, and responsibility to obey, on the other, extend broadly, so that orders need not always be mission related. But they must always be legal. A leader expects also to be rendered the customary behaviors of military courtesy, including proper saluting and rank-sensitive forms of address, such as "sir" for addressing officers and "sergeant" for addressing NCOs. These practices—indeed ceremonies—served as symbols of readiness to obey orders and confirmed the direction from which orders should come.

All soldiers were divided into "officers" and "enlisted soldiers," or "enlisted," for short. All officers were senior in rank to all enlisted. Officers were subdivided into commissioned officers and warrant officers. Commissioned officers were further subdivided into "general officers," "field grade officers," and "company grade officers" closest to the troops. Enlisted soldiers were divided into noncommissioned officers (NCOs) and "troops," with the NCOs further subdivided into senior NCOs and junior NCOs. Every soldier had a rank, and every rank was associated with a pay grade. Rank referred to one's position in a lineal series of levels of authority in the hierarchy of decision making. Rank was recognized, for example, in direct address and was central to the organization of military life. Grade indicated the pay level associated with a rank, was used more in paperwork, and therefore was officially secondary to rank. However, both codes were common and nearly interchangeable in soldier speech, with a tendency to refer to the officers in one's own unit by rank ("the captain said" meaning "our captain said") and those more distant or less known by grade ("an O3 [pronounced Oh-3] at battalion said"). Understanding these structures of rank and pay grade helps one see the perspectives of soldiers and spouses quoted throughout this book. The linkages are summarized and further clarified in Tables 2.1 and 2.2.

Commissioned Army officers had command or staff responsibility for the operation of military units. They generally received their commission as a result of training received at the United States Military Academy (West Point), through a Reserve Officer Training Program (ROTC) completed in association with pursuit of a college bachelor's degree, or from an Officer Candidate School operated by the Army. Officers advanced through the ranks when promotion boards reviewed their record of accomplishment recorded primarily on Officer Evaluation Reports (OERs).

Warrant officers filled positions that required a high degree of specialized training, technical skill, and responsibility. The five levels of rank and experience were termed Warrant Officer (WO1), Chief Warrant Officer Two (CW2), Chief Warrant Officer Three (CW3), Chief Warrant Officer Four (CW4), and Master Warrant Officer (MW5). They did not have command authority, but their judgment was highly respected in their skill areas. The warrant officers I met in Germany served either as helicopter pilots or physician's assistants, both examples of specialized tasks.

Enlisted soldiers "did the real work" of the Army, as they were quick to say, manning the equipment and weapons and maneuvering to positions. NCOs were placed in charge of troop units, executing the orders issued by unit officers. Troops, of course, pulled the triggers and moved the supplies, doing the physical tasks. Troops and junior NCOs advanced from rank to rank based on point systems and the recommendation of company leadership. Senior NCOs advanced on the merits of their Enlisted Evaluation Reports (EERs) after these were scrutinized by promotion boards.

A division or independent brigade included all units deemed necessary for the conduct of warfare. Battalions of infantry, armor, artillery, and air defense were supported by transportation, engineer, maintenance, military police, communication, medical, postal, finance, and personnel units, giving the division an independent, organic wholeness. The division (and larger units—corps and army) was able to stand alone, fight alone, and provide itself with all necessary internal supports. It did need to receive supplies from outside—ammunition, fuel, and replacement equipment and people—and it needed orders and intelligence from higher commands. Other than that, a division or independent brigade was designed to be capable of carrying out any military mission within the capacity of its weaponry, equipment, and personnel. Each division encompassed two to five brigades; each brigade, two to five battalions; each battalion, two to five companies (or batteries for the artillery); each company, two to five platoons; each platoon, two to five squads; each squad, two or three fire teams; each fire team, two or three individuals.[4] At each level, smaller components included a heavy weapons group and one or more lightly armed components, with the heaviest weapons, such as nuclear rockets at army or corps level, descending progressively through heavy artillery,

Table 2.1
Officer Ranks in Europe, 1986–1988

Category	Rank	Abbr.	Grade	Synonyms	Typical Unit Responsibilities *
Company Grade Officers	Second Lieutenant	2LT	O1	Butter bar	Commands a platoon of some 30 to 40 soldiers
	First Lieutenant	1LT	O2		XO (executive officer—second in command) of a company or manages a staff section of a battalion HQ (headquarters)
	Captain	CPT	O3	The old man	Commands a company of 66 to 350 soldiers, or staff at battalion HQ
Field Grade Officers	Major	MAJ	O4		XO or S3 of a battalion, or staff at brigade
	Lieutenant Colonel	LTC	O5	Light colonel	Commands a battalion of 500 to 900, or XO or S3 at a brigade HQ, or staff at a division HQ
	Colonel	COL	O6	Full bird / Full bull / Full colonel	Commands a brigade of 1,500 to 3,000 soldiers, or XO or S3 at a division HQ
General Officers	Brigadier General	BG	O7	One star	Commands an independent brigade, XO at division, or staffs a corps unit
	Major General	MG	O8	Two star	Commands a division or staffs a higher unit
	Lieutenant General	LTG	O9	Three star	Commands a corps
	General	GEN	O10	Four star	Commands an army, or commander in chief of a theater

* Typical responsibilities are necessarily schematic and simplified.

Table 2.2
Enlisted Ranks in Europe, 1986–1988

Category	Rank	Abbreviation	Grade	Typical Unit Responsibilities
Troops	Private	PVT	E1	Recruit trainee
	Private	PVT	E2	Beginning soldier
	Private First Class	PFC	E3	Soldier with responsibility
	Specialist Four	SP4	E4	Skilled soldier
	Corporal	CPL	E4	Soldier with small-group leadership responsibilities
Junior NCOs	Sergeant	SGT	E5	"In charge" of enlisted in a squad (circa 10), or staff worker at battalion HQ
	Staff Sergeant	SSG	E6	"In charge" of enlisted in a section (larger than squad), or staff worker at battalion HQ
Senior NCOs	Sergeant First Class	SFC	E7	"In charge" of enlisted in a platoon (circa 40), or staff worker at battalion or higher HQ
	Master Sergeant	MSG	E8	Staff worker in a battalion or higher HQ
	First Sergeant*	1SG	E8	"In charge" of enlisted in a company (66 to 360)
	Sergeant Major	SGM	E9	Staff manager in a battalion or division HQ
	Command Sergeant Major*	CSM	E9	"In charge" of enlisted activities in a battalion, brigade, division, corps, or army

* Technically, first sergeant and command sergeant major are not ranks but positions. A first sergeant is a master sergeant with company leadership responsibility.

41

tanks, mortars, and machine guns, to rifles at the individual troop level.

Although we need not detail the structure further, it is important to remember that a war-fighting organization is extremely complicated and that the picture I have given is rather simplified. Indeed, above corps level, the multinational and multiservice organization of command and control in Europe was byzantine. Later, we will see that this complication made life difficult in the family and community domains. It is also worth pointing out that each specialty unit within a division had its own work tempo and therefore a particular ecology of relationships with other organizations and with its families. Nevertheless, all units were driven by the overarching mission of the encompassing division. In Germany, all combat units were propelled by the strategic requirement that they be able to vacate a garrison barracks in one or two hours when satellite or other intelligence data indicated something unusual was happening in the Soviet sector a few kilometers away. The expectation was that the garrison would be heavily attacked by air and saboteurs in the first moments of active war. Training for readiness held out the hope that the combat units would already be "out the gate."

"Dual Hats": The Union of Unit and Community Command

The press of such military urgency of course had its impact within the community. One way the military organization ensured its primacy was to subordinate community to military needs. It did so by having the senior troop commander wear "dual hats." In this system, the senior commander of the largest troop unit in a military community was designated the community commander. For example, where a division headquarters was located at one installation and a brigade of the division was located at another installation in the same "military community," the division commander would be the community commander of the entire military community, whereas the brigade commander at the other installation would be the latter's subcommunity commander. For day-to-day management purposes, each community was administered by a subordinate officer appointed to be the deputy community commander (DCC). If a community had subcommunities, the DCC was senior in rank and commanded the deputy subcommunity commander(s) of the subordinate installation(s). While officers decided what needed to be done, the tasks were executed by an NCO in charge of each installation, called the installation coordinator, or IC. Other NCOs staffed the various activities of the community and constituted the "community cadre." By contrast to the practice of delegating community command responsibility to a DCC, command of military units was never delegated unless the commander was absent.

Sometimes this structure put subcommunity commanders in a difficult bind. The deputy community commander reported directly to the senior troop commander of that installation, providing for the troop commander's needs and being rated by him. The subcommunity commander, by contrast, reported to and was rated by the deputy community commander but had to provide for the needs of the senior troop commander at the subcommunity installation. The latter gave a letter of input to the deputy community commander, who wrote the deputy sub-community commander's OER. Subcommunity commanders felt their careers were too easily drawn and quartered by the cross-cutting expectations of the DCC and the subcommunity's troop commander. The effect of "dual hat" organization was to ensure that the military community physical plant and personnel responded to the war-fighting and training needs of the resident tactical units. In so organizing, however, the military ethos penetrated the entire social community being served by the physical plant, and thus, penetrated also the military families that constituted part of the community.

THE MILITARY FAMILIES

At three in the morning, in a small village in southern West Germany, SGT Carla Hamilton groped for the insistent telephone. The rumored alert was confirmed. Within minutes, every soldier assigned to this U.S. Army installation was awakened and called to his or her duty station. SGT Hamilton and her husband—who also is a soldier in the U.S. Army—hastily put on their BDUs, camouflage battle dress uniforms of mottled olive and forest green. An alert might last twenty-four to forty-eight hours—sometimes more. The Hamiltons knew that if either of them were late for regular formations or special alerts more than once or twice, their careers might suffer. They quickly readied their two children. On the way to their unit, they had to deliver their children to the home of a trusted caregiver, where the children would stay until the alert was over. The Hamiltons had to remain calm for the children's sake, for crying children did not enhance the vital relationship with the caregiver the Hamiltons so desperately depended on. Later in the morning, the caregiver would wake two sleepy children, disoriented by the early morning change of beds, houses, and custodians, and make sure they got off to school and to the day-care center.

The damp cold knifed through their uniforms as the Hamiltons scraped the windshield of their car, using up more precious time. Finally in the car, they rushed first to drop off their children and then raced to work. On the way, they tried to guess which of them would be free first, and whether it would be in time to pick up the children before the day-care facility closed at 6:00 P.M. Any children not picked up by 6:15 P.M. were taken to the military police station. Their parents were charged a stiff late fee, and a notification of the offense was sent to their commander. Would a neighbor or the caregiver have to retrieve the children this evening? Or would one of the Hamiltons be free? They simply did not know, and according to them, that was the hardest part of it all—the uncertainty. The continual tension of not knowing was harder to bear than the call in the night, or the ice and cold, or even the work they would do in the long day ahead.

Although I have changed the names of the Hamiltons and all the people quoted or discussed in this book, every event was experienced by the people who talked to me, and every quote is theirs, word for word. The Hamiltons represent the 5 to 6 percent of military families in which *both* partners were serving in the military. As a result, they experienced particular stress regarding child-care arrangements, for adequate child care was essential to the maintenance of dual careers.[5] About 80 percent of military families were couples with only one spouse a soldier, usually the husband.[6] In many of those couples, the wife worked in a civilian-staffed support job on her husband's post or some other military installation. If she did not, she most likely devoted her time to caring for her family and household and often was involved in voluntary service in the community. In Germany, civilian husbands were not common, and did not show up in my random sample, though I sought out and interviewed two during fieldwork.

Soldiers who were single custodial parents (accounting for about 8 percent of married enlisted soldiers, Army-wide, in 1993[7]) faced problems similar to those of the Hamiltons. In addition to accomplishing all the tasks that a couple had to complete, a single parent with child custody had to be particularly careful to maintain child-care arrangements that could function for days, even weeks and months on end, should she or he be deployed. Even the "married unaccompanied" soldiers confronted the challenge of reconciling their military and personal lives, interacting at a distance with spouses and children who had chosen to remain "Stateside."

Germany is now and was then an overseas assignment that allowed a married soldier to take her or his family on an "accompanied tour." Almost 60 percent of the soldiers were married. If the soldier was eligible, the government "sponsored" his or her family, paying the costs of transporting the family and household goods overseas and providing a local cost of living and housing supplement in addtion to the soldier's basic entitlements. Though the policies were in frequent flux, rank determined whether a particular soldier's family would be "sponsored." During the 1986 to 1988 period, a married soldier in the rank of corporal or specialist four or above was entitled to live in "on-post" housing (if space was available) and to be fully "sponsored." Married soldiers of lower ranks who wanted to acquire immediate sponsorship for their families had to sign up for longer overseas tours, four or more years instead of the usual three.

A married soldier assigned to Germany could choose to go unaccompanied, and some did. Spouses remained in the United States for a variety of reasons, among them, to preserve a job, to tend a parent, or to accommodate a child who could not adjust to conditions overseas. Going overseas unaccompanied was considered a hardship tour for a married person, and the duty assignment (or "tour" length) was shortened from three years to eighteen months. Family members who chose to join a soldier on an unaccompanied tour were "unsponsored," paying their own costs of transportation and moving, living "on the economy," and forgoing the overseas cost-of-living adjustment to their basic housing allowances enjoyed by the sponsored family. Thus most married soldiers who elected to take the half-as-long tour of duty lived either as "married-unaccompanied" residents in unit barracks for enlisted and junior NCOs, or in separate "bachelor quarters" if they were senior NCOs or officers.[8] A few soldiers did bring their families at their own expense and lived in local German communities as unsponsored families. Whether sponsored or unsponsored, all legal dependents were entitled to receive and use USAREUR ID cards, (the acronyms standing for United States Army Europe and Identification), and thereby had access to military facilities such as the post exchange, the commissary, the health-care system, the post recreation areas, and most other services available to soldiers.

In 1985, 50 percent of all soldiers in Germany had a spouse and/or child with them in the duty area. Soldiers in Germany claimed 173,700 dependent minors, of whom 120,400, or 69 percent, were living with the soldier.[9] As the children grew into teenage years, a declining percentage accompanied the soldier parent, again for a variety of reasons. Divorce may have divided the family, with custody going to the nonsoldier. The spouse might not have wanted to move, and even if the spouse were in Germany, some teenagers probably balked at an overseas move, perhaps because they wanted to complete high school with their friends or perhaps because they felt unable or uninterested in adjusting to a foreign environment. Furthermore, by the time the oldest child in a military family was a teenager, many spouses had raised their youngest children to school age and had advanced into careers they did not want to abandon as their soldier-partner approached retirement. If the spouse stayed in the United States to preserve a job, then the children would be less likely to reside with the soldier-parent in Germany, for being a single custodial parent in a forward deployed station was extremely difficult.

The process by which Army families rotated to and returned from Germany left little reason to believe that Army families in Germany could have been substantially different in attitude or basic culture from those who remained in the States. According to a Rand report, "Army families stationed outside the continental United States (OCONUS) do not differ markedly in their structure and makeup from those stationed within the [continental] United States (CONUS)."[10] Most who served in Germany returned to the United States after a three- or four-year tour. A few extended to a total of six to eight years. As soldiers and families rotated back to the United States, their replacements came primarily from the States. In my samples, even the soldiers with German spouses regularly rotated between the two countries. This continuous turnover homogenized the military families and maintained their primary ties to the United States. A few families, for one reason or another, managed to remain in Germany a much longer time than most and became labeled as "homesteaders." For most Army families, however, geographic mobility was a fact of life.

Because the American troop presence in Germany was (and still is) a combat-oriented forward deployment, and because combat occupational specialties were exclusively male (whereas support and service support specialties admitted both sexes), there was a somewhat higher percentage of male soldiers in general and therefore of male family sponsors in Germany than in the United States. Other than the possibility of a lower percentage of female soldiers sponsoring families in Germany, no event, no interview, and no analysis of my data led me to suspect that the Army families living in Germany were at all unusual in cultural outlook or character compared with Army families generally. Army families overseas seemed to have substantially the same backgrounds as Army families in the United

States. They performed technically similar work tasks; they were moved around, promoted, and paid by the same personnel/management system; and they had access to parallel community support systems because the services were mandated by regulation. In terms of unit structure, military community services, and family structures, I found only minor differences between USAREUR and CONUS military communities. Such differences resulted from the Army trying to provide certain culturally expected community services that would otherwise have been unavailable in Germany. Indeed, the system of services and activities was so similar to what was available in the States that the American military community complex in Germany was occasionally referred to as "Little America." The Army did try to make the military community "as close to home as possible." Nevertheless, the members of these American military communities, adrift in a sea of German culture, faced a more intense mix of challenges with rather weakened support systems compared with the members of an American military community anchored in the harbor of American culture.

GERMANY: THE CONTEXT OF STRESS AMPLIFICATION

Many soldiers and spouses living in Germany believed both the soldier's life and Army family's life to be more difficult in Germany than in America. SGT Sam McGregory put it this way: "I feel it is bad to send a guy overseas, 'cause it messes them up. There is more stress overseas." Implicitly, the comparison was with assignments in the United States. Similarly, a captain's wife noted, "My husband has been a company commander twice, here and in the U.S. He has been gone more here than in the U.S. Here, it doubles up. They must help NATO and they help the infantry. The taskings come down from Heidelberg, and they still do the infantry division support." Although their references were more oblique, Meg Barnes and her husband, SSG Frank Barnes, emphasized the difficulties of life in Germany. "We came here; we hated it," said Meg. "We've learned to live with it for three years. We will manage." Frank tried to soften the message, but in fact could not: "There are good things here. But at the moment—my right hand to God!—I can't think of them. I can't think of one thing good to say of the Grossberg area." Six months later, the same couple summed it up: "Life in Germany is difficult." Or, in the words of Laura Thompson, married to a specialist, "It's a lot different than in the States. They treat you bad here." While serving as the rear detachment commander (the officer in command of the troops remaining in Richberg during a month when all its healthy soldiers were away on maneuvers), 1LT David Zark observed, "It is a lot more stressful here in Europe." MAJ Matthew Taylor said "It is tougher in Europe. Everything is harder to do here." LTC (Lieutenant Colonel) Max Newell, Richberg's deputy community commander, remarked, "Installations are less difficult to manage in the States."

These quotes highlight the *perception* that stresses are greater in Germany than in the United States and that these tensions give rise to family and personal problems thought to be greater than those they would have experienced back home.

Each of the above respondents went on to explain and give examples of the nature and causes of the stresses. We shall return to their comments throughout this book. The point is that for many, military and family life in Germany was difficult—more difficult, they believed, than in the United States. Nevertheless, major institutional systems of Army life—work, community services, and family—were fundamentally similar whether the post was in the United States or Germany. Therefore, the perception that life was more difficult in Germany must have derived from the context of being in Germany. What pressures arose simply from the fact of being in Germany? And how did those differences reverberate throughout community and family processes? Detailing the differences and the amplified impacts in community and family life in Germany is, of course, the task of this book.

The major contextual differences were first, the German cultural environment, and second, the proximity of immediate military threat. In an assignment to the United States, the surrounding nonmilitary culture was familiar and comfortable to the soldier and family members, and the source of threat lay an ocean away. In an assignment to Germany, by contrast, the surrounding nonmilitary culture was foreign and relatively unknown, and the perceived military threat was constant and very near at hand.

There were several subsidiary sources of stress. First, Americans were garrisoned in a large number of small installations scattered throughout a heavily populated German region. Military sites that were large enough to allow armored vehicles and soldiers to practice combat maneuvers or engage in "live-fire" practice were separated from the garrison areas. As a result, realistic training required soldiers to load and move weapons and equipment by truck or train to separate training areas—Grafenwöhr and Hohenfels, for example, creating extra work and frequent periods of family separation. Second, a variable exchange rate added stress. During the time of this study, the "mark rate" declined steadily from Deutsche mark (DM) 2.10 per U.S. dollar to DM 1.46, though by mid-1988, the rate had climbed back to approximately DM 1.80. Soldiers on their second or third assignment to Germany kept alive the memory of the "good old days" when a dollar bought 3.25 or 3.50 or even 3.75 marks and German goods were relatively cheap. The general decline in the dollar's value created difficulties and uncertainties, especially for junior enlisted personnel—those with the lowest pay—who earned dollars but had to pay for their rent in marks. Although the government continuously adjusted soldier allowances to compensate for exchange fluctuation, the adjustments always seemed to be late and did not diminish the psychological anguish of seeing German products become perceptibly more expensive from day to day. Third, the legal system of the Federal Republic of Germany added complexity to life at the unit, family, and community levels. German laws had to be obeyed, in addition to American laws and Army regulations. Fourth, German public opinion had to approve the presence of the NATO guest armies. Because the American government felt (and still feels) that a military presence in Germany was of the highest priority, there was intense pressure on Army leadership to prevent any behavior or incidents that might create embarrassment of any kind. This sensitivity added to the stress families felt in Germany. Finally, the fact that most soldiers and most family members lacked substantial German language ability and had quite limited knowledge of German culture and society made it more difficult for them to provision the household outside the American resupply system or to emotionally and spiritually recharge themselves by escaping the Army milieu.

Essentially, this book describes how couples functioned within the military community and with the military units. It seeks to understand the problems that soldiers and spouses experienced as a result of being in Germany and to provide an explanation, an interpretive context, for understanding their real joys and their frequent woes. In the next chapters, I explore how these aspects of German society added to the ordinary aggravations of the arrival process, intensified the stress of unit activities and leadership, increased both control and disruption of the family, isolated the military community, and thwarted soldier and family modes of relief from the pace and process of Army life.

NOTES

1. See Tables 2.1 and 2.2 for a listing of ranks, related categories, and abbreviations.

2. Combat units deliver offensive or defensive weapons systems to the battlefield, and include infantry, armor, artillery, attack aviation, and air defense units. Combat support units service, supply, or position weapons and personnel for combat, and include such units as engineers, transport, quartermaster, repair, and ordinance. Combat service support units manage the less direct services needed to take care of combat and combat-support units. These include medical, postal, finance, and units performing numerous other functions.

3. In military speech, if an organization was referred to by its full name, the appropriate article was often used, as in "The Security, Plans, and Operations Division handled . . ." but if the acronym was used as a word, the article was usually dropped, as in "NEO provided maps for . . ."

4. For historical reasons, the artillery branch uses the word "battery" for units at the company structural level; the cavalry branch uses "troop" for company, "squadron" for battalion, and "regiment" for brigade.

5. Office of the Assistant Secretary of Defense, *Population Representation in the Military Services: Fiscal Year 1994* (Washington DC: Office of the Assistant Secretary of Defense, 1995), section 3, p. 10, and section 4, p. 12.

6. Office of the Assistant Secretary of Defense, *Family Status and Initial Term of Service* (Washington, DC: Office of the Assistant Secretary of Defense, 1993), vol. 2.

7. Office of the Assistant Secretary of Defense, *Family Status*, section 4, p. 4, and section 4, p. 8.

8. Normally, one expects to find separate Bachelor Enlisted Quarters (BEQ) and Bachelor Officer Quarters (BOQ). On these small installations, senior enlisted (E7 and above) and junior officers (O3 and below) were intermixed in a single bachelor quarters building.

9. Peter A. Morrison and others, *Families in the Army: Looking Ahead.* R-3691-A (Santa Monica, CA: Arroyo Center, Rand Corporation, 1989): 33.

10. Ibid., 33.

3

"Ordered to Germany": Entry Shock and Its Lingering Impact

When you come to Germany, a lot of times soldiers . . . don't know where they are going. No prior communication with a unit. . . . Right off the bat it gives you the feeling that nobody cares. Once you get that impression, it sticks with you.

SGT Todd Jasper
Richberg Military Community

Mobility was a fact of life for Army families in the 1980s. Missions changed, units moved, whole posts opened or closed. When soldiers rose in rank, quit the Army, or retired, they opened more positions that had to be filled by moving other soldiers around. Career guidebooks, official personnel managers, and local lore all concurred that a history of many diverse assignments, each handled well, improved one's chances for promotion and retention. Soldiers and their families expected to move frequently; they thought that they would get stale if they had to keep at a single job or stay in a given location for long.

During the period of this study, married soldiers on accompanied tours—that is, tours in which spouse and family travel were authorized—usually contracted for three-year assignments to Germany. Thus, at any given time, approximately one-third of the families had been at their present residence and military job a year or less and were still unsettled. Another third expected to move within a year or less. In addition, many changed their work assignment at least once during their stay.

Any move creates difficulties. Homes and Rahe developed a scale of life-event stressors that, as a kind of stress benchmark, assigns 100 points for the death of a spouse, with fewer points for other disruptive events, whether they be positive or negative changes in one's life.[1] They further theorize that the effect of multiple stressors is additive. Thus, one can roughly calculate the impact of a move to Germany by adding up the points of the stressors encountered. A move to Germany entailed a change of residence (20 points), a change in schools (20 points), a possible change in work hours (20 points), a change of living conditions (25 points), and a change in responsibilities at work (29 points). Soldiers reported that their moves often coincided with a vacation (11 points), required a small loan (17 points), precipitated a change in social activities (19 points), involved the spouse both stopping work and beginning a new job (26 points each), and imposed a temporary marital separation (65 points). There were additional stressors in this foreign setting—such as inability to speak the local language, and cultural dislocation—that Homes and Rahe did not investigate. For soldiers and spouses, assignment to Germany precipitated a major series of stressful events.

To understand more intimately the stresses that a person assigned to Germany had to absorb, I will describe a family's path through a move and examine the problems that a soldier and military family encountered. In the Army, a move to a new post is a PCS, a Permanent Change of Station. For simplicity, I gloss over the PCS tasks in the United States—getting orders, arranging tickets, packing up and shipping one's belongings; detaching children from school, spouse from work, and soldier from military assignment; and enduring the transatlantic flight with children. I begin with the moment of arrival in Germany and examine the stresses that together precipitated a kind of entry shock.

ENTRY SHOCK

Arrival and In-Processing Complexity

Just how one entered an American Army community in Germany depended on one's rank. On touchdown, usually in Frankfurt, a first-term enlisted soldier and accompanying family, if any, was picked up at the airport by "Replacement," a personnel unit responsible for distributing junior personnel throughout the American sector. Troops and sergeants (E1 through E5) generally went to Germany without knowing where they would be stationed. At Frankfurt, they were told which unit needed their MOS (Military Occupational Specialty—a job skill classification) and rank. After a few hours or a few days in Frankfurt, they continued by local military transportation—sometimes in a vehicle sent by the receiving unit, sometimes in a private car belonging to a sponsor or friend, often in a shuttle bus—to the installation of the receiving unit. By contrast, senior NCOs and officers knew before they left the United States the specific unit and job assignment they were going to and traveled directly to the station. Moreover, the receiving unit often knew of their impending arrival.

Soldiers with families were taken to a military "transient billets" hotel if space were available. If not, accommodation was found in a hotel or small German *gasthaus* off-post. From such temporary lodgings, the soldier began the tasks of in-processing and finding a permanent residence.

Each military community's "in-processing" involved the soldier in a course of paperwork, military equipment procurement, language training, family member registration, and apartment finding, ideally done at a centralized facility. One of the first in-processing steps was to register with the Housing Office. "Housing," as it was known for short, had a "Government Quarters" section that managed on-post housing assignments and a "Housing Referral Office" (HRO) that maintained lists of those in need and offered them the apartments that German landlords made available through their office. On arrival, one first checked with "Government Quarters" to see if space was available and how long one might have to wait in "transient quarters" to get "permanent quarters" on-post. The answer depended on three factors. First, each category of rank was housed separately, so far as possible, and therefore had a separate stock and separate list of available apartments. Middleberg, for instance, had a circle of separate houses for its commanding general and field grade officers. Richberg's battalion commanders and deputy sub-community commander lived across the street and in a stairwell with a slightly fancier entrance than the rest of government housing. Company grade officers, sometimes joined by command sergeant majors, were clustered in another nearby area. Enlisted had a generally distinct housing zone, often subdivided into a section for senior NCOs and a section for midlevel and junior NCOs and the few married troops who might have been eligible for housing.

A few categories of officer and NCO had housing priority. At Middleberg, the division forward commander, the assistant division forward commander, and the division command sergeant major had specific houses designated for their positions. Division staff officers (Middleberg only) and battalion commanders, company commanders, and first sergeants at both Middleberg and Richberg were also required to be in "on-post housing" so they could be on call to solve any problems. Just who was required to be on-post varied from installation to installation, depending on command priority and housing availability.

The second factor affecting the wait for housing was predicated on the Army's perception of appropriate housing for any given family. Thus, one was listed according to the number of bedrooms required, calculated according to a formula that considered the number, ages, and sexes of one's children. Personal preferences or previous housing were not factors.

Third, the lists by rank and bedroom size were maintained in order of seniority, based on one's date of separation from his or her previous permanent (i.e., family-supporting) station. Unless one had been on "temporary duty" (TDY) attending a military training course at a location that did not allow family accompaniment, or to Korea, where families were not officially sponsored, one joined the bottom of the list. For most, the wait would likely take longer than one's thirty- to sixty-day "temporary living allowance" (TLA). Indeed, in most military communities, the government quarters waiting list for married enlisted soldiers required a twelve- to eighteen-month wait. The only choice for most soldiers of junior rank and some officers was to place one's name on the bottom of the appropriate government quarters list and walk across the hall to the HRO to be put on the bottom of the appropriate (but much shorter) list of those seeking quarters "on the economy." The person at the top of the list would be told about the next available apartment in that size category. If he or she rejected it, the next person on the list could opt for it, and so on down the list. Each hoped that something would "come up" before one's TLA ran out.

Private house hunting was possible. Perhaps someone in one's squad or platoon was leaving economy housing. If, however, the apartment being vacated had come originally from the stock of apartments that the HRO listed for the German landlords, then HRO would offer it to the person at the top of the appropriate number-of-bedrooms-required list. One could check classified advertisements in the local papers. One could even place an ad in the newspaper; this, however, was unusually resourceful behavior. To succeed, one had to discover which newspaper was suitable for placing apartment ads, find the phone number of the classified department, talk to the newspaper staff in rudimentary German, construct an ad in German, and figure out how to pay for it. Then came the calls in German through a transient billets desk clerk who spoke no German. Often one was simply cut off after trying a few words in German, the accent immediately indicating one's status as an American soldier. Some landlords, however, liked to rent to Americans because Americans would leave regularly (whereas German law made it exceedingly difficult to evict a German tenant) and because the rent was almost guaranteed, for one could force payment by contacting the soldier's unit leaders. These landlords listed their apartments in the HRO office, assured of quickly filling any vacancy.

Until the end of 1987, orders often authorized "concurrent travel," enabling spouses and children to travel to Germany with their soldier-sponsor and find initial lodging in "transient billets" (a government hotel) or in a German *gasthaus* while they sought permanent housing. During 1986 and 1987, families had a sixty-day TLA, a per diem payment intended to cover their costs while changing residence. In 1988, however, the TLA was reduced to thirty days in length, with a renewal possible but difficult to acquire. At the same time, the Army terminated the practice of concurrent family travel. The new regulations called for a married soldier to go to Germany alone, find a suitable residence, and then apply for one's family to travel to Germany. Only after finding an apartment could they initiate the paperwork that would bring their family to Germany. Spouses who came on a delayed basis, however, were at a disadvantage. From their point of view, there was virtually no orientation and no sponsor, for the sponsor had oriented the soldier and dropped away. Moreover, the spouse was made more dependent on the soldier by virtue of not having participated in the decision process that resulted in their apartment.

For thirty days, soldiers attended classes that offered information on finding housing and getting settled, gave beginning language training, and oriented soldiers to the military facilities and the local resources. Married soldiers began hunting for an apartment during this critical time. Soldiers assigned to a subcommunity of a larger military community, such as Grossberg, remained in the central community for the thirty days of orientation before being moved to the assigned subcommunity, where they would use the subcommunity's local area housing office to help them find housing "on the economy." As the married soldiers had used up their TLA allotment during the central orientation, they moved into the barracks in the subcommunity while continuing their search for an apartment so they could send for their family. At the same time, they began to work in their military jobs, part time at first if their commanders understood their need for time to find quarters for their family. Soldiers appreciated the in-processing orientations, even if they were somewhat inefficient at times. They generally liked their month of language lessons; some even desired more. Though orientation was helpful, it demanded time during a period when time was urgently needed to find housing.

Lack of Affordable Housing

Finding suitable housing "on the economy" was difficult. Germany limited urban development to preserve as much of its remaining farm and forest environment as possible, so apartments were scarce. Consequently, apartment rents were very high near the urban and military centers, often above the monthly housing and cost-of-living allowances merited by the soldier's rank. Farther away, in rural areas, rents were cheaper and housing was somewhat more available.

Given the difficulty of securing an apartment, families who came on orders authorizing concurrent travel faced a major financial disaster if their TLA ran out before they found an apartment. They would have to cover the expenses of temporary residence out of pocket or send their family back to the United States, though this seldom occurred. But the possibility was always rumored, and the stress was considerable, for the soldier was obligated to a three-year residence in Germany once the government had paid for family transportation and the shipment of their household goods, whether the family stayed or not. Even with TLA, many soldiers paid substantial sums out of pocket during their apartment-hunting period.

The TLA deadline, combined with the added daily costs, created substantial pressure for the soldier to choose an apartment quickly. Families felt forced to take what was available. Meg Barnes expressed the sense of urgency: "As long as you're less than an hour away, you have to take it [whatever HRO offered] if you're on TLA." Although TLA was reduced to thirty days and the orientation classes consumed them, some soldiers still came "concurrent travel" with their families because the Army-wide system was not fully consistent in suppressing the former practice. But in Germany, the reduction to thirty days of TLA eligibility was enforced, putting those few families in a bind. They had less access to the apartment market in their subcommunity area while being held in the central community for general orientation, yet they needed to find housing before they ran out of money.

Pressure to Return to Duty

Once the thirty days of in-processing was completed, the military units acquired the soldiers and began to put demands on their time. Most unit leaders said they tried to be sensitive to the soldier's continuing need to find family housing. As LTC Keith Bateman, a mechanized infantry battalion commander, indicated, a leader faced a constant balancing act between his responsibility to the unit and to his soldiers:

> The biggest problem we have here is off-post housing. At what point must I say to a soldier, "We have given you adequate time and adequate help to settle your family. It is now time for you to come to work eight hours a day." . . . The vast majority manage to solve housing within thirty days of in-processing. So that is kind of the cutoff that I use: the thirty days to in-process at Grossberg [i.e., at Central Barracks, the central military community], then thirty days here [at Richberg subcommunity].

In practice, the pressure to begin duty varied with the commander and the importance of the tasks to be done. For example, field maneuvers required complete crews and sometimes pulled a soldier away from apartment hunting for several weeks. As Laura Thompson, a specialist's wife, lamented, "When I got here, my husband had to go in the field. My son was sick. We could have starved. We had no transportation. Nobody cares. It's like 'duty first.'" Work pressure created a bind. If the soldier arrived accompanied and worked hard, he or she could not spend time finding an apartment, yet supplemental TLA payments were running out. If family travel were delayed and the soldier worked hard, he or she did not have opportunities to look for housing, thus delaying family arrival even further. CPL (Corporal) Richard Howard:

> I have been here seventeen months, [but] in [government] quarters four months. I stayed in the barracks . . . five months—so I could look for an apartment. You can get apartments but they may be fifty Ks [kilometers] away. I came alone, and looked for a close place. . . . [When I got here] I went straight into the field for twenty days, and we just got married. . . . [Had she come with me] I'd have to have left her in the hotel for twenty days. . . . They [unit leaders] need a body, so you are going to go. They don't care if you are new or not.

On the other hand, if the soldier did not work, but spent his or her time looking for an apartment, the soldier's performance evaluations might be affected. The conflict was endemic to the garrison situation but became acute during the all-important field exercises.

Overwhelming Start-Up Costs

In Germany, the new householder faced heavier initial costs than was usually the case in the United States. SSG Frank Barnes observed, "You gotta save a lotta money to have the deposit ready. Then you gotta take an advanced OHA [Overseas Housing Allowance loan] to get your [security] deposit." A few landlords asked for a security deposit of three months' rent. Many required two. Start-up supplies, curtains, food staples, and the excess costs of living in a hotel all had to be covered. Such costs could be met with a low-interest loan. But the income of the young low-ranking family was not substantial, and a loan created a repayment burden. On the basis of his experience as a first sergeant, MSG Oscar McDonald suggested, "These young people they are sending concurrent travel, they need

2,000 marks deposit, plus one month's rent. For a private, that's hard." In 1987,
Dr. Charlene Lewis studied the economics of soldiers arriving in Germany, reporting that prior debt, caused mostly by car ownership, was often very high in relation
to a junior enlisted person's salary. "The majority of families (42 percent) had
monthly payments between $100 and $300. Twenty one percent of respondents
had monthly payments between $300 and $400, and a rather frightening number of
respondents (26 percent) had payments in excess of $500 per month." Such debt
loads, combined with high start-up costs, were difficult to surmount.[2] SGT Jasper
described the problem eloquently:

> You have costs which are unforeseeable at the time that you move. For example,
> two months' rent in advance, utilities in advance, and the cost of the PCS move in
> itself. You already have bills prior to coming here. That ends up putting you in a
> financial burden [i.e., a bind]. At the time, all you are concerned with is getting
> into housing. Later, you find it may have put too much of a burden on your
> family. . . . You get orders to Europe, but you don't know what you are getting
> into. Personally, it was very hard. Putting me in a house, buying the things needed,
> put me in the hole. And it took me a year and a half to get out of it.

Erratic Support Systems

When families moved, they experienced added difficulties, yet often had less
support from their own networks and inadequate support from community or Army
systems. One's personal vehicle, shipped from the United States, took six weeks
to arrive, yet was urgently needed in the first month of apartment searching. The
need to comply with German and American laws and with military regulations
generated much paperwork at the start of a tour. Complex paperwork led to human
errors that later caused problems and delays for the soldiers. A sergeant I bumped
into at lunch in the mess hall complained, "I came in February, got an apartment by
April. It takes a month to get paperwork done to get your wife over here. They
lost the paperwork three times. She came in September. That was a lot of suffering for me." Families often found damaged items in their household goods'
shipment. Disconcerting in itself, the more frustrating part was the bureaucratic
paper chase required to get reimbursed for repairs or replacement of damaged
goods. Start-up pay was often incorrect or delayed, occasioning further paperwork.

All these stresses and frustrations occurred during a period when contact with
supportive relatives or friends was effectively severed by distance, time zone
differences, and the high cost of international phone rates. Mr. Trevor Foote, the
civilian social work supervisor for Grossberg Military Community, noted, "One of
the things the Army family in the USA has, but not here, is the support units:
uncles, grandparents, cousins. That is pretty major." Within the United States,
families told me, calling a mother or friend for advice was easy and relatively
inexpensive. Calling from Germany was also easy, but it was not inexpensive.
Telephoning was approximately three times more costly calling from Germany to
the United States than from the United States to Germany. The German phone bill

did not list each call, making it impossible to determine from the phone bill where one had called or at what cost. For the unwary or for the severely homesick, the result was financially disastrous. "I don't write because they don't write. And then I get kind of sad," said Anne Granville, concluding, "You have to spend a fortune on the telephone." COL (Colonel) Wayne Keele, the corps senior psychiatrist, put it succinctly: "They really do feel isolated, because they don't have the family ties. Especially the younger families."

Older "career" soldiers, in contrast with young officers or first- or second-term enlistees, developed friendships scattered in most military locations and had experienced other moves. By the third or fourth move, officers and NCOs were likely to have former friends or working acquaintances at any post in the world. MAJ Matthew Taylor observed, "If you don't have primary acquaintances, you have a whole list of secondary acquaintances." Abigail, his wife, gave an example: "We just happened to come here, and one of the battalion commanders here was his company commander in school." COL Felix Carson of Welby General Hospital felt officers would have friends virtually everywhere "after about seven years" and as a result, "now I turn down sponsors because I have friends wherever we might go." Thus, older Army couples had both experience and friends scattered around the military globe, resources with which to meet the stresses of the move. But even senior people sometimes regretted the disruption of relationships occasioned by each move.

Lack of Knowledge

Young spouses and first-term soldiers experienced additional stress because they lacked knowledge of Army procedures and facilities. Although the soldiers all went through the official in-processing orientation, few of the spouses did, even though they were eligible if space was available. During the early period, when family concurrent travel was possible, spouses probably had other family obligations, and the preponderance of soldiers in the orientations may have felt overwhelming to the spouses. With concurrent travel blocked, spouses arrived two, three, and sometimes more months later, to live in an apartment they had no voice in choosing. Moreover, spouses who arrived later missed any opportunity to participate in the in-processing orientation or share the experience of discovery. They also missed the informal learning that took place in the lobby of the military transient hotel, where those beginning and ending their tours told their tales of survival skills and of pitfalls to avoid. Yet it may have been healthy to miss out on some of the "war stories," as we shall see later. Generally, late-arriving spouses received only a half-day greeting and orientation at their destination community.

Soldiers or spouses often received misinformation. Because of the complexity of the system, civilian and military service providers and leaders did not always know the regulations or the procedures to get problems solved, for they were often new to their jobs. Sometimes the information was transmitted correctly but was so complex that the user misunderstood or received just part of the message. Regardless of the reason, misinformation frustrated a soldier or spouse and caused major loss of opportunities or resources. I will return to this complexity issue in later chapters; for now it is sufficient to recognize the deleterious impact of bureaucratic and legal complexity on new arrivals.

Cultural Disorientation

Even the older couples who knew the military system usually lacked knowledge of German society and its resources. Several cultural differences added to the stress of getting settled. For instance, an "unfurnished apartment" in Germany had no light fixtures and sometimes no light switches. Generally, German bedrooms had no closets. A kitchen often had no sink, refrigerator, oven, cabinets, or countertops, for the German expectation of long-term renting allowed each renter to provide to their personal taste. Although the Army's Quartermaster Supply lent these "amenities" along with more traditional furniture, looking at "stripped" apartments caused a bit of a shock for many American families. Finally, compared with the United States, German landlords demanded higher security deposits and larger advanced rental payments. Soldiers arriving in Germany found that cultural differences complicated the moving process and created substantial economic hardships.

Beyond the initial phase of settling-in stresses, military families experienced the longer-term buildup of culture shock: the sense of disorientation and frustration or even depression that builds when one cannot read the signals and figure out what to do because of subtle differences in fundamental premises, laws, customs, and everyday signals and body language. I discussed some of these cultural differences in Chapter 2, "Inside the Fence." In many small ways, the cultural assumptions and institutional structures of Germans affected the American Army families, especially if they were living off-post in the German towns and villages, as most had to during their first year. Linda Sims put her finger on the language aspect of cultural disorientation when she recommended, "They need to make everybody take a pre-German course before they get off the boat." "Coming to Germany is exciting," said Marla Bracken, but also "a real traumatic experience. . . . The whole new culture can be hard on a family." According to Marla, soldiers, spouses, and children suffered "virtual culture shock," which they simply "had to survive." Germany, for most, was indeed a difficult place to adjust to. The country's cultural and administrative system was quite exact. Everything had to be done the German way. Young high school graduates, with little experience outside of their home state or even their hometown, took on the major cultural challenge of a new country while still trying to adjust to a new marriage and adapt to a new and considerably intensified military job.

Simultaneous Stressors

Unfortunately, stressors did not come one at a time, but simultaneously. SP4 Betty Atwood, recently married to her specialist four husband, Jeff, responded to my probe of "Tell me about life here" with a litany of hardships:

It sucks. It is really hard. Number one, because we are in the Army. Number two, we are young and we just got married. And there is a big pressure: away from home for the first time. . . . It is a really poor duty station. I don't think that first-term soldiers should begin overseas. Because in the Army it is just hard because it is a new experience. . . . [You] have to deal with 400 different things, and it makes a lot of people quit. . . . And it just ruins the attitude of a lot of the first-termers. . . . We are both getting out.

For Betty, the simultaneous stressors included a new marriage, first time away from home, new work, first duty in the Army, and residence overseas. For SSG Gary Hatch, the jumble of stressors included a breach of promise, financial stress, foreign language, and cramped temporary accommodations:

They promise you housing, and they bring you over, and the TLA is up [runs out]. And they say you may have to send your family back. If your family come over here for more than that [TLA] time, you might be on your own. The biggest problem: it's all in German. They throw you in this hotel for two months—200 marks every night. It is a fortune, more than you make in a year. If you have a family of five kids, it's $1,700 every ten days. That is big bucks. . . . Then they got to take any old little apartment 'cause their TLA is up. That is the biggest thing: no housing. The military hotel is always full to max capacity. . . . I've seen a family [divided up] in three or four hotels. I had to move out of the Valley [the transient military hotel] just to have money to eat with.

They needed to find housing in the first thirty days, because the search became even more difficult once they moved on to the subcommunity, where they became part of a working unit, the company, which became yet another stressor: "At the company you can't find yourself that much time off to look. At the [central orientation] class they are breaking you in right. And you hear all these guys telling you where to look. At the company they are thinking about the field, not about your housing." SSG Hatch thus described a fairly full range of the stressors: concurrent travel in the face of a housing shortage and TLA deadline, the possibility of having to send one's family back to the United States, the German language deficit, excess per diem costs, forced acceptance of an apartment that was too distant or too expensive, and conflict with the unit ("the company") for time to house hunt versus time to work. The sense of desperation comes through clearly.

GOVERNMENT RESPONSES

Army leaders recognized the stresses of arriving in Germany and that people needed help. They funded several costly programs they hoped would reduce the difficulties. First, Army leaders throughout Germany made a diligent effort to centralize in-processing so that all of the agencies responsible for assisting with the tasks of arrival (and departure) were in one accessible location. This greatly reduced the inconveniences newly arrived soldiers experienced. Second, for the spouses, every community had a monthly community commander's welcome and spouse orientation meeting that introduced key community leaders, agencies, and their support services—among them Army Community Services, Child Development Center (the child-care center), Army Emergency Relief, and the bank. In Middleberg, at the end of the morning session, those attending went downtown, had lunch at a restaurant, learned to use the various forms of public transportation, and walked around town. The orientation helped greatly, though a day of instruction was not enough and in any event was sadly underattended.

Third, the Army community offered a considerable number of services to help alleviate the difficulties of a move. Each post operated a "loan closet" where various household items could be borrowed until one's household shipment arrived. Army Community Services gave solid information from experienced "old hands" who had been through the process several times. One could get child care while searching for apartments or setting up. Army Emergency Services gave financial loans for the initial period.

All these services helped, but the human element of sponsorship was even more important. Ideally, every new arrival, whether single or married, was assigned a "sponsor" to help the newly arrived get oriented and settled. The sponsor was supposed to write the family or single soldier before their departure from the United States and personally help him or her through all the tasks after arrival. In theory, it was a good program.

Unfortunately, sponsorship seldom worked well in practice. The reasons were legion. Low-ranking troops did not know their assignment until after they arrived in Frankfurt. New soldiers often arrived unannounced, and even senior-ranking sergeants sometimes did. Anyone available at the moment became a sponsor, regardless of compatibility. Work demands made it difficult to let both the new soldier and the sponsor off work at the same time to find an apartment or orient the newcomer on where to run errands. Single sponsors did not know what married couples needed. Time was short and sponsors had their own families and needs to consider. Personality conflicts between a sponsor and the new arrival sometimes interfered. Whatever the reasons, in all the places I visited, leaders told me one or another variant of "around here, sponsorship is broke." Even a moderately well-functioning case of sponsorship could easily be interpreted in a negative light, given the anxieties. This was the experience of SSG Frank Barnes on his first tour:

When I came here, everybody knew I was coming. I received a welcome letter from the unit. . . . They assigned me a sponsor. The sponsor should have given me a letter: dos and don'ts, the housing situation, little helpful notes. Instead he sent me a note, "The PX is forty-five minutes away." But it's not helpful to me because important details are left out, like where the medical facilities are set up at. I get over here, this guy says, "So you're Sergeant Barnes." He introduces me to the first sergeant, the supply sergeant, and the NBC [Nuclear, Biological, and Chemical] sergeant. Then he leaves me. . . . If it hadn't been for a guy I went to school with: he helped me out. . . . I sort of in-processed myself. He [the friend] took me to finance [forty minutes' drive away]. I had to catch the bus back. I said, "Damn!" I gave *him* a few words of wisdom!

Now on their second tour, from Meg's point of view, "When we came here we had no sponsor. We had to find out all by ourselves. If he hadn't been here before, I don't know how he would have done it."

THE PERIOD OF ADJUSTMENT

Soldiers and their families are resilient and most do adjust. But it takes time to construct a stable new universe and get comfortable within it. How long does it take? Several times I was told "six months." Such was the opinion of both COL Bert Parsons, the senior psychiatrist at Welby General Hospital, and Mr. Carl Vogel, the regional Alcohol and Drug Abuse Control Program director. Some felt it took even longer. SSG Martin Webster suggested that it took a year and a half for them to get out of the debts incurred in their move. Abigail Taylor said, "It takes a good year until you're comfortable—unpacked and set up and it feels familiar and you learn your way around the new environment and form friendships." Thus new arrivals took a minimum of six months and sometimes up to a year or more to adjust. Interestingly, this is also the length of time officers and NCOs claimed it took to learn a new job assignment and get competent in and comfortable with its tasks. By inference, between one-sixth and one-third of the married soldiers and families (on three-year assignments) and between one-third and two-thirds of the single soldiers (on eighteen month assignments) were not yet adapted or comfortable. When such a sizable portion of the community undergoes discomfort and stress simultaneously, and when all have been through it so recently, the community as a whole can easily experience alienation or, in common military language, "morale problems."

LINGERING IMPACTS: UNINTENDED CONSEQUENCES OF THE ARRIVAL PROCESS

The shock of so many initial stressors resulted in a variety of unintended and deleterious consequences both to the individual and to the system as a whole. Even among those well adapted to Germany, the lingering consequences of entry affected the individual and family well beyond the initial period, because decisions made under stress had to be lived with. For example, where soldiers chose to live during the TLA phase had a continuing impact on job well-being and family life. The initial experience guided, filtered, and defined the interpretation of subsequent experience. As the soldier quoted in the epigraph put it, "It gives you the feeling that nobody cares [and] once you get that impression, it sticks with you."

Trouble from Unsuitable Housing

Unless a family found a good, close apartment quickly, the impending loss of TLA forced them to take an apartment either too far from the post or too expensive for their monthly budget. Renting an apartment too far away led to several harmful consequences. SSG Webster, for example, lived about an hour-and-a-half drive away from post. His car had broken down, and without funds to fix it, he arose at 3:00 A.M. daily to use public transportation to be to work to "wake his section" at 6:00 A.M. He often didn't go home at the end of the duty day, overnighting in the barracks instead, because it wasn't worth the effort when he had to be back at work so early.

> Why do I live way out there? It wasn't my choice, in a way. When I got here, they put you in a hotel, they give you sixty days to find a place on the economy. When I arrived, my family and I were living with a member of the company and his wife [to not go over the TLA amounts]. I was putting ads in the German paper, looking for an apartment in the Richberg-Grossberg area in a price range I could afford. About thirty days went by, and I still hadn't found an apartment, and we were starting to get on each other's nerves.
>
> So I hired a German realtor to find me an apartment quick. The realtor found me a place in the boondocks. I asked them to put it on hold for me, because I wanted to live somewhere closer. In between all of this, I'm going to HRO and military channels. And time is starting to run out. I believe I had about eleven days left. So I took the apartment where I am now. It is a very nice apartment. [Rent is] 900 marks. Three bedrooms, a full kitchen, one-car garage. It would cost me 2,200 marks here in Richberg.
>
> I haven't moved back in [closer to the installation] because with a 2,800-marks deposit, it's not feasible for me to try to move back. [He would lose his deposit if he left before completion of the year contract.] I couldn't afford to pay the deposit on another apartment. So we adjusted our lifestyles. We have adapted very well. But that is in the course of about a year and a half.

The savings in rental payments were not as large as he thought, for there were many direct and indirect costs associated with living in a distant apartment. Some of the savings were canceled by additional fuel and maintenance costs. Moreover, without a second car, the distant spouse was isolated both socially and emotionally. As Linda Sims, a volunteer staffer in the Richberg Housing Referral Office, put it, "The further out that they [soldiers] put them [spouses] to get cheaper rents, the more lonesome they get, and the more they run up the phone bills." Moreover, the spouse on the economy without a car could not do needed family maintenance chores or find work on a different military post. Yet if a second car were purchased, the savings from having chosen a cheaper apartment dropped substantially because of added insurance costs and car payments. The long commute consumed the soldier's and spouse's most scarce commodity—time together. The soldier and spouse had to deal with added stresses and resentments if the soldier decided to spend the night in the barracks from time to time rather than return home in the evening. Finally, a distant home meant a soldier was more likely to arrive late to formations. Being late left a poor impression with superiors and could have a lasting, delayed career impact. Unintended consequences of the entry process thus reverberated within the family and could affect unit operations and the soldier's career evaluations.

Instead of moving far out, some soldiers chose a nearby apartment that was too expensive for their budget, creating lasting economic stress within the family. Whether stressed by high rent or isolated by distance, the soldier and the spouse often resented the forced conditions, disliked living on the economy, and counted the days until they rose to the top of the government quarters list. Once on the economy, however, families were required to remain there at least one year so as to not distress the pool of available German landlords through high rotation. Frequently, the end of the economy lease did not correspond with the family's arrival at the top of the government housing list. The family then felt forced to forfeit the large deposit made on the German housing to gain timely entrance to on-post quarters. I interviewed several who, long after the fact, remained bitter about this turn of events.

Stress from Marital Erosion

The stresses of moving to Germany were sufficiently great that the settling-in period put pressure on almost every marriage and tore at the fabric of some. CPT Darren Cornell, the Richberg chaplain, mused, "I have people sit down crying in my office, 'cause they are going to break apart. They have no furniture, not knowing they got to buy their own sinks. . . . The bureaucrats don't have to see how miserable the people are. They don't have to look at people day after day. They are not sensitized to what it does to people."

Some spouses did not like delayed travel status. They saw the separation as a potential threat to the marriage. For example, Julia Martinez, Korean by birth, reminisced about the difficulty and the initial costs. She elected to come with her husband, Ricardo, paying her own way, even though it would have been paid had she come later. As she put it, "If we stay apart, we don't save any money." But the real reason soon emerged. In her fractured Korean-English, "So long wife and husband apart, not good. Specially the man. They like to drink, they have a night out—divorce case. The married people, they should stay together, wherever you go." Many felt the same way: too long a separation put the marriage at risk. So a few paid the high costs of staying together. But they deemed it unfair and added, through their grumbling, to the perception of communal alienation.

Disruption of the Unit

The lingering effects of entry shock also affected the functioning and integrity of the unit. While talking about entry problems in general, Chaplain Cornell focused on housing—an entry decision—and summarized the intertwined bundle of consequences on the units: "What it does, if there is no housing: It could affect the re-up rate, or it affects the marriage. It causes chain of command problems. The soldier gets unmotivated, and that leads to a lack of readiness." In a word, the severe initial stress helped create and sustain a culture of alienation that undermined the operation of the units and the retention of trained personnel.

Difficulties at Work

As already indicated, distant housing resulted in soldiers' more frequently arriving late to work. This and other initial stresses and financial woes increased the probability of a soldier having difficulty at work and having his or her career evaluation downgraded.

Severance from the Service

For some, the difficulties were more immediate, resulting in either a forced termination or in their voluntary decision to terminate their Army career at the next opportunity. Crusty old MSG Oscar McDonald gave one example from his first sergeant experience: "Man brought his family over. Wife stayed three days. She broke; [then] his mind just went. So they decided to get him out of the Army." The Atwood couple, who resented "400 different things" thrown at them in the beginning of the assignment, decided that they would both get out of the Army. Although the Atwoods' decision was not exclusively related to entry shock, initial stressors did contribute substantially.

Early Mind-Set and the Culture of Alienation

For many, the entry difficulties left a lasting negative first impression. For both the soldier and the spouse, the first weeks after their arrival set the tone for much of the family's perception of the unit, the *kaserne*, and their life overseas. Although people heard each other's "war stories" throughout their stay, new arrivals were particularly likely to listen attentively. The lobby of the transient billets hotel figured prominently in the process, though it was by no means the only location. The exhausted new arrivals there mixed with the departing old hands, the new desperate for "how to" and "what to expect" information, the old pleased to confirm their hardened-veteran status that made them centers of attention for the day or two that they remained. Thus, the anxious were socialized by the disgruntled. As with King Leontes's suspicions of his wife in Shakespeare's *The Winter's Tale*, once the Army was suspected of unfaithfulness by virtue of the difficult arrival experience, almost any subsequent event could be interpreted as a failure to meet expectations, with the self-fulfilling negative consequences eventually spiraling out of control.

Thus, Linda Sims, the HRO volunteer and spouse of a senior NCO in Richberg, resented

the Army bullshit. Seriously, you get a runaround, trying to get a place to live. They send you command sponsored but there is not a place to live. They need to centralize. They should at least tell you to ship your car thirty days before. Then [they should] make you live within a thirty-mile radius. And then they tell you wrong. They tell you something and it's not that way. Then everybody gets bent out of shape. . . . Spouses get to hate it. It's real stressful; you can't relax.

From her position in the housing office, Sims frequently saw soldiers and spouses who experienced the cycle of frustration, misinformation, and consequent alienation of trust rooted in the entry experience.

CONCLUSION

Clearly, the arrival and settling-in process was a key transitional period for each person or family. The physical tasks consumed perhaps three months, but the emotional and cognitive tasks—learning the system, adjusting to its limits, making new friends—took up to a year. If this initial entry experience was substantially negative, soldiers and spouses tended to interpret the rest of their experience negatively. First impressions did stick, and because the arrival process was so stressful, many soldiers and spouses became especially irritable. When the service providers they dealt with seemed rude or cross, perhaps as a mechanism of self-defense in the face of caustic comments flung out by highly stressed new arrivals or those leaving, a self-perpetuating downward spiral of ill will resulted. Then, any naturally difficult or complex task was interpreted in the most negative light and became one more proof that "everything about Germany is bad." Moreover, these same negatively disposed people socialized the next generation of new arrivals, telling them "war stories" about their experience. This predisposed the new arrivals to interpret all the rest of their experiences in Germany negatively.

For example, I asked SSG Frank Barnes and his wife, Meg, now on their second tour in the country, to "tell me about life in Germany." To try to make sense of their experience to me, they immediately presented their arrival day as a metaphor for the whole experience.

"We got to the 21st Replacement [Depot, Frankfurt], exhausted. They put us on a bus to take us to Middleberg. They are no longer sending people from the unit to pick up new people. We rode for three and a half hours. The person that met us at Middleberg said: 'Hi. I'm sergeant so and so. You're not supposed to be here. You're supposed to be in Richberg'" [one and a half hours away and about one hour closer to their origin point had they gone directly].

"No problem!" Meg interjected with cheerful irony. "I'm pregnant, feet swollen, everybody wants to go home."

"They call Richberg," Frank continued, beginning to get excited. "They sent a truck—not a van, not a car! They said they didn't know that it was concurrent travel. They said, 'We got you a sponsor.' But he was unmarried, living in the barracks. He doesn't know how the system works. We've got no place to stay. They didn't call Valley [transient military hotel] before. So they go around to the gasthauses [German hotels]. They didn't take Brothers [Blacks] there. I thought this happened only in the States! Oh, shit! So we go downtown. So we check the Asia place."

"He [the driver] said, 'You better wait in the truck.' You know why they told us to stay in the truck?" Meg cut in incredulously.

Frank concluded, visibly showing contempt, "What I had the ass about was this: The Asia Hotel is the place where the guys get a quick lay. A flophouse."

Of course the Barneses were insulted and chagrined that they were accommodated at the local whorehouse. Word of such treatment gets around. The character of their first impression conditioned the interpretation of everything that happened later. Thus, a year afterward, Frank concluded, "Right hand to God, I can't think of one good thing to say about Germany." As commonly expressed, if the Army "pulls this shit on me," wasn't it all right to try to "get over on the Army"? Here soldiers used a phrase that referred to escaping or getting out from under the control of the Army, often gaining illegal recompense or exacting surreptitious retribution in the process.

The repercussions of an unpleasant arrival on individual and family morale, unit readiness, and ultimate retention were complex but no doubt costly and destructive. By contrast, if the initial entry experience were positive, then the family confronted the considerable rigors of the Army experience in Germany positively, without the morale-undermining impact of a bad first impression. For the most part, stress and financial urgency, and structures that impeded getting one's family settled hit the soldier with an initial social shock, leading to an initial alienation, an attitude that easily colored the interpretation of subsequent events throughout one's stay in "Little America."

Anthony Giddens, a sociologist, suggests that in all social systems, people, as decision-making agents, act according to the culture and the conditions in which they find themselves. Their actions respond to the system. Those actions also become part of the continuously created new environment that is "read" by others, and by themselves, in making their successive decisions. The process is recursive. In mathematics or linguistics, recursiveness refers to the fact that the mathematical result of an equation, or the words generated by a set of language rules, becomes the input for reprocessing by the same equation or rule, in the repeated application of a formula. Likewise in behavior, the new behavioral outcome is recursively read back into the system and responded to anew. Sometimes the new conditions generated by the customary strategies require the adaptive change of the strategies themselves, for the human system is much more flexible than the rule-based metaphors of mathematics or linguistic analysis. Giddens calls this evolving process of reflexively evaluative renewal and change "structuration." By this term, he suggests that the social system is continuously being built out of the actions and decisions of hundreds of participants, but always in a constrained or structured way that builds on the foundation of the prior structures.[3]

We see this process in all aspects of the military system. Thousands of individuals and hundreds of leaders acting as custodians of the various institutions make decisions to which every individual must then adapt. Part of the adaptation is to form a cognitive image of the process—an impression, an estimate of the nature of the system—so that one can have a strategy to guide one's adaptation in the next circumstance. In the attempt to build a cognitive map of a situation, first impressions thus condition subsequent observations, and negative responses are thereby recursively injected back into the cumulative "structuration" of the Army.[4] The continual reproduction of alienation and low morale was thus structured into the system in part by the nature of the entry shock and in part by the breakdown of the buffering systems. The community's birthing process, the process through which new soldiers and their spouses were inducted into the village, virtually guaranteed the reproduction of low morale. There is more to it, however, than the social reproduction of a bad attitude in the new arrivals. The expectation of negative attitudes recursively entered into leadership decision making so that the expectation of low morale was made concrete in other structures. In the next two chapters, I examine more closely the day-to-day rigors of leadership and work in a forward deployed Army unit, showing how the processes of leadership and the nature of the work had consequences in the family that led to endemic structural conflict between family members and unit personnel. These contradictions led to further alienation of many members of the community. Let us see how this was so by examining unit and leadership structures in greater detail.

NOTES

1. Thomas H. Holmes and Richard H. Rahe, "Social Readjustment Rating Scale," *Journal of Psychosomatic Research* 11 (1967): 213–218.

2. Charlene S. Lewis, "The Financial Status of 100 Families Beginning an Overseas Tour: An Initial Analysis of Data Collected on the Government Rental Housing Program" (Heidelberg, Germany: Untied States Army Medical Research Unit—Europe, HQ, 7th Medical Command, APO NY 09102-4428, 1987): 9. See also her "Families and Finances in Europe: Final Evaluation of the Government Rental Housing Program—Phase I" (U.S. Army Medical Research Unit—Europe, HQ, 7th Medical Command, APO NY 09102-4428, 1988).

3. Anthony Giddens, *Central Problems in Social Theory: Action, Structure, and Contradiction in Social Analysis* (London: Macmillan Publishers, Ltd., 1979). See especially Chapter 2, "Agency, Structure," pp. 53–73.

4. Ibid., 33.

"Danger Forward, Sir!": Readiness and the Corruption of Leadership in Military Units

Become his rater [evaluator] and you will be surprised what you can get!
1LT Curtis Smith
Middleberg Military Community

"Readiness for combat" encapsulates the deepest military goals and aspirations of most Army personnel. For such readiness to exist, soldiers at all levels need to practice their craft through training and they need to be good leaders, which is to say, makers of good decisions. Of course, to make good decisions, leaders must ever keep in mind their real mission—combat readiness—and they must have accurate information about the strengths, weaknesses, and location of their troops and equipment. As one component of helping to assess the qualities of the soldiers in their units, commanders are required periodically to rate their subordinates in Officer Evaluation Reports (OERs) and Enlisted Evaluation Reports (EERs). Unfortunately, the way the Army evaluates its leaders' performance in fact works to undermine a leader's ability to make decisions in the best interest of mission and troops by interfering with the transmission of accurate information and by altering the focus of the mission. As poor decision making undercuts morale, lowered morale in turn further corrupts decision making, a runaway feedback cycle. The result is a kind of self-inflicted organizational wounding, fratricide by the friendly fires of officer and enlisted evaluation.

The quote that introduces this chapter suggests that this rating process produces surprises. Such surprises include not only the prodigious effort that can be elicited from the individual being rated, but also the unintended direction that individual and collective leadership behavior and organizational activities may take, given how they are pushed by the performance rating system.

In particular, I want to explain two characteristics of military life that derive from this feedback. One is the tendency of the unit to be extremely driven—but often driven away from its own overt goals. The other is the tendency of its soldiers to perceive military life as erratic, arbitrary, and even irrational. The driven intensity of military activity derives from the culture of readiness and the obligation to obey orders imposed upon the garrison community and constantly reproduced within it by the imminence of external threat. I shall argue that four peculiarities of Army life proceed from the particular structure and practice of officer and enlisted career evaluation: first, the constant sense of hyperactivity, of being overly driven; second, the propensity to deviate from the core mission; third, the perception that Army leadership is erratic, arbitrary, and even irrational at times; and fourth, the frequent disruption of family and community institutions. In addition, the structure and practice of officer evaluation lead to the amplification and reproduction of such characteristics as micromanagement, self-protection, suppressed communication, the maintenance of misinformation within the system, and resistance among soldiers within the units. To understand how the organization is driven away from its goals toward behavior that oftentimes appeared surprising and even irrational to its participants, we must first understand why the organization is so intensely driven at all.

THE LOGIC OF READINESS

Five premises or general approaches to behavior seem particularly relevant to the understanding of institutionalized readiness behavior in the Army. First, success in combat—the required task of the military organization—is a demanding endeavor. An enemy will try to use speed, surprise, and maximum violence to overwhelm its opponent. To survive, the units of a defending army must respond by making extreme demands upon their personnel so that they respond with the speed, agility, and counterviolence necessary not only to meet but to overwhelm the demands made by the attackers. Thus, an army must have a demand-oriented ethic or culture. Such a culture is encoded in the expectation that soldiers must carry out legal commands or orders promptly and completely. In Germany, every soldier had to be ready to go to war, twenty-four hours a day, with just one or two hours' notice. In the face of perceived danger from Soviet forces—demands in waiting—any U.S. military post in Germany fairly throbbed with a sense of urgent and immediate threat, making constant demands on its personnel to be in a state of sharpened readiness.

Second, if attacked, an army must have an institutional culture that can accept punishing losses and still respond effectively. The members of a military organization must be prepared to maintain their morale and will to triumph in spite of heavy losses. Soldiers, whether leaders or junior troops, must be willing to take risks and to make sacrifices. In Germany, this striving, risk-taking, sacrifice-enduring culture was encoded in such phrases as "duty first," or, more colloquially, "suck it up and drive on." Nothing mattered but the mission. Adversity was simply absorbed, metabolized, disregarded.

Third, to survive the likelihood of surprise attack, an army must be able to endure and deal with ever present unpredictability. "Suck it up and drive on" encoded not only sacrifice but flexibility to change. Favorite phrases, such as "go with the flow," suggested adaptation, flexibility, and the existence of unpredictability.

Fourth, to deal with violence, risk, demands, sacrifice, and unpredictability, members of a military organization need to trust each other both horizontally (buddies) and vertically (leaders). Members of small groups, such as fire teams and squads, must cooperate and take risks for one another in order to overrun a machine gun nest, capture a pill box, disable a tank, or kill a sniper. In Germany, soldiers expressed such essential trust when they referred to each other as "family," or "like family," or "the Army family," for family symbolized primary trust and care one for another. Sharing food packages with buddies in the unit expressed this familial trust within the group. A military unit also must have vertical trust. A soldier in the attack might ask, "Will the artillery fire we called to our front be computed and delivered accurately, landing just beyond us and not on us? Do our leaders know exactly where we are? Will the aircraft know exactly where we are and fire their weapons accurately on the enemy? Will the senior leaders choose missions and procedures that will minimize death to our own?" If soldiers can answer such questions affirmatively, they trust their vertical relationships. In Germany, such vertical trust was encoded verbally in concepts of "loyalty," expressed also as willingness "to do anything for" or "to fight for" or even "to die for" one's immediate or more distant leaders. As a symbol of vertical unity, the importance of the hot meal delivered to the front or the presence of a commander at the point of danger cannot be overestimated. Lack of trust in a unit will also be expressed in language and "morale." In Germany, members of a unit experiencing failed vertical trust described their unit as "sorry," or "shitty," or "fucked up." Distrust was acted out in surliness, resistance, sabotage, or veiled disobedience. In one extreme case, a soldier who did not trust his superior talked about "fragging," or surreptitiously killing, the untrusted leader.[1]

Fifth, willingness to follow orders, sacrifice, adapt, and trust is of little consequence if the members of the organization do not know how to respond in coordinated concert when the demands come. Thus, a successful army must inculcate a culture of training, readiness, and perfection of immediate, articulated group response. The alternative is to suffer horrible losses at the moment of violent contact. Indeed, without training, the losses will come in peacetime, too, because soldiers must daily handle heavy equipment and dangerous materials. Inadequately trained soldiers injure themselves and die in accidents. Again, in Germany, the ethics of readiness and precision response were culturally encoded in the never-ending call for "training" and "preparation," and in the demand for "zero defects." The occasional rituals of close-order parade drill, which no longer have direct combat function, remain actively used symbols because they teach the general ethic of precision and teamwork.

Even the most junior troops in Germany knew that the mission of a military unit was to be prepared at all times to engage successfully in combat with the nearby Soviets and that this readiness had to be constantly sustained. Soldiers felt that their military activities should be clearly linked to maintaining their unit's mission readiness and that military activities that did not contribute to training and readiness wasted a soldier's time and thus should be held to a minimum. Soldiers usually sensed when they believed they had acquired sustainable combat capability, and they expressed their resulting "high morale" or "esprit de corps" through a variety of enthusiastic and optimistic behaviors. Morale and esprit—I use them interchangeably—were a product of combat readiness under good leadership. In a circular fashion, morale and esprit then added to combat readiness and power. Most importantly, morale and esprit derived from a soldier's perception of good leadership and trust throughout the organization.

Mission-essential task requirements must be translated into guiding beliefs (culture), an organization that can coordinate the efforts of many (social structure), and standardized working practices that get the job done (behavior). For example, the obligation to "follow orders" demonstrated a cultural orientation toward hierarchy—a prominent structural feature in all successful militaries, at least among those competing with each other in modern annihilation combat. Similarly, the need to coordinate action in a risk-laden situation makes trust essential and the group more important than the individual. Moreover, the only way to take losses and persist is to ensure that individuals are able to substitute for each other. Thus, uniformity, substitutability, and group orientation take priority over individualism. One saw a constant focus on "units," groups acting as one, even though in modern warfare, groups must be greatly dispersed to reduce losses.

Soldiers in Germany believed the military culture of demand responsiveness, indifference to pain and loss, adaptability to rapid change, trust in peers and leaders, and constant readiness through training would increase their chances of survival on the battlefield. Because warfare is an unusual activity and the battlefield such an extreme environment, the institution tasked with dealing with that environment had to develop a culture and behavioral patterns that were at variance with the basic premises of mainstream American culture and its patterns of behavior. The nature of the task and the extremity of the environment led the Army's participants to create or maintain a specialized institutional culture, by definition what the literature calls a "corporate culture," focused on group readiness for violence.

THE PARAMETERS OF READINESS

Although any army should emphasize general readiness, the conduct of military life in Germany entailed unusual conditions that dictated heightened readiness. There was, first of all, the close proximity of the Soviet threat. Second, there were special constraints arising from the Army's operation as a guest in a foreign country. These factors amplified the emphasis on readiness and increased the workload on the soldiers posted there.

Confrontation with the Soviets

Before the fall of the Berlin Wall in 1989, American soldiers in Germany saw the Warsaw Pact nations as a serious and imminent source of danger. Virtually all families lived and worked within two or three hours' drive of the border with East Germany. Quite a few soldiers worked and lived within minutes of the border and had frequent visual contact with potential antagonists. Generally, no matter the distance, there was a sense of standing "eyeball to eyeball" with the enemy forces, for any military installation in Germany was expected to be attacked within minutes of the outbreak of armed conflict. One soldier, an officer, described to me how he had been on border patrol with a cavalry unit[2] when he witnessed massed Soviet tanks moving straight toward the border fence. He radioed to higher command for instructions and was told, "If they cross the second fence, open fire." I cannot verify that such an event took place, but I can verify that such events were talked about as though they were real and that they were taken as real by listeners. The *Stars and Stripes* reported many border incidents, as well as spies and counterspies defecting across the border in both directions. An American officer, acting openly in his official capacity as an observer of military maneuvers in East Germany, was shot dead while observing.[3] The Warsaw Pact held maneuvers close to the border because NATO (North Atlantic Treaty Organization) had done so. But NATO did it because the Warsaw Pact had already done it, the cycle reproducing itself in a feud without end.[4]

The deep sense of mission urgency was conveyed by Mr. Harvey Renquist, a retired officer now serving as   director of the Community Counseling Center at Middleberg. "If we think like a battalion commander," he said,

> [then] my job is to have the soldiers ready at a moment's notice and fling them between what we are defending and the aggressor. They have got to be capable of pulling out and not even phoning that they won't be home. All of the ancillary people had better be able to operate on their own. There is this border, and there is the Army and the rest of the world. And the Army only has loyalty to its side of the border.

CPT Bill Olsen, a company commander, put it this way: "The Army comes first and it has to be. Our mission is to be able to get out of here [the installation] in two hours." Most soldiers felt the reality of the threat more in Germany than in the United States. The official view was well stated in the *Community and Deputy Community Commanders Handbook*, a manual of procedures for administering the garrison community:

> USAREUR personnel live, work, and travel in an extremely intense hostile intelligence and terrorism threat environment. There are estimated to be over 3,000 Warsaw Pact espionage agents operating in GE [Germany] alone. In addition, a wide variety of terrorist organizations conduct operations against U.S. targets throughout the USAREUR area of operations.[5]

The collapse of Eastern Europe's military standoff with NATO may make these statements sound anachronistic today, but for the period between 1986 and 1988, mission urgency forced mission priority. All else came second. With the possible exception of the Demilitarized Zone in Korea, nowhere in the world did the immediacy of threat better demonstrate the social outcomes of constant readiness than along the Warsaw Pact frontier with West Germany. The threat was felt to be real, near, and very dangerous.

Constraints on Soldiering in Germany

In addition to the stress of continuous battle readiness imposed by the nearby hostile forces, four additional features of the German environment increased the complexity of American military activities: legal system differences, demographic and environmental constraints, fear of embarrassment, and communication difficulties. MAJ Matthew Taylor, on a brigade staff, lamented, "We have the same [training] requirements as in the States, but there are so many additional tasks over here." What generated these "additional tasks"? In a word, the complexity inherent in conducting military training and community life within a foreign cultural milieu.

Multiple Legal and Regulatory Systems. In the United States, Army units and individuals on-post have to abide by federal, state, and local law, though federal law takes priority. Of course, they must also abide by Army regulations and the operating procedures of the particular post. Because these laws and regulations were generated within the cultural tradition of the soldiers and their families, they are largely understood. In addition, there were also the implicitly understood expectations of American culture. In Germany, however, the soldiers and families not only had to work and live within the framework of U.S. federal laws and Army regulations, they also had to work within the bounds of unfamiliar German law. Some of the differences between the two legal systems were resolved by the Status of Forces Agreement, or SOFA, a treaty that permitted the U.S. military to modify some German regulations. Much of German law, however, had to be complied with. In addition, the Americans needed to conform to German cultural expectation, sometimes even on-post. Thus the regulatory environment for American operations and Army families in Germany included American law, American customary practice, the Uniform Code of Military Justice (UCMJ), and U.S. Army regulations, *plus* German law, German customary culture, the Status of Forces Agreement, and USAREUR regulations adapted to Germany.

Obviously, this more complex legal and regulatory environment complicated military tasks and civilian activities for U.S. soldiers and families. CSM Henry Yates, command sergeant major of Grossberg Military Community, phrased the issue of regulatory complexity this way:

> I've been here [in Germany] eighteen of my twenty-six years [of military service]. I'm ready to go back. But by being here this length of time, there are a lot of these regs [regulations] I have known about. Then, in the planning sessions, one can remember these regulations and bring them to the surface for the others. In the community side, when you become the person with the historical insight, you are more of an asset than if you come in and [are] full of vigor and ready to conquer Grossberg. [When you are new] you want to come and do the wonderful things that you can in the States. But because of the legal ramifications, you can't do it. For

example, ice cream must be consumed on premises, so we would not [have to] pay *mehrwertsteur* [Germany's value-added sales tax, exempted on-post under SOFA]. These are simple things, but they make a big difference in planning and running. It takes someone with the experience and the regs in mind to make plans. Normally, our people [in the States] aren't restricted as much. But here you have customs, and German laws, in what they can and can't do.

Increased legal complexity also made the U.S. military mission more difficult for the units to accomplish. During combat vehicle movements, for instance, German law had to be adhered to as well as American law and Army regulations. The whole operation had to be negotiated across a language barrier. It follows that virtually every action off-post as well as many actions on-post took more time, required more coordination, were more complicated, and therefore could more easily fail or be delayed. In Germany, every action provided more opportunity for added stress and disrupted schedules.

Demographic and Environmental Constraints. In the United States, military training maneuvers usually could be accomplished on-post because many posts were huge. In Germany in the late 1980s, however, with some 63 million people packed in an area the size of an average U.S. state (Oregon was the usual example given), space was at a premium. Because Germany consisted of densely populated villages scattered over the whole countryside, "fire and maneuver" practice with military vehicles almost always required movement to special training areas, such as Grafenwöhr, at some distance from most installations, requiring an effort similar to that of a U.S. unit going to the National Training Center in the Mojave Desert in the southwestern United States. Units had to be loaded on trains or convoyed along the autobahns. Even a simple "roll-out" alert involved coordinating the movement of military vehicles through nearby German towns and villages. MAJ Taylor thus summarized, "It is tougher in Europe. . . . It is a major operation to go to Grafenwöhr" where all had to go to train with large weapons.

Fear of Embarrassment. A third factor that increased complexity and amplified the amount of work required of soldiers was the "zero defects" goal. The policy of zero defects was driven by at least two concerns. On the one hand, leaders wanted to protect the troops from injury. On the other hand, the same leaders wanted at all costs to avoid embarrassment before the German government and people. 1LT David Zark of Richberg felt that "at Fort Riley you could make a mistake, even as a company commander. It is a lot more stressful here in Europe, because there is so little time. It is a *no mistake* environment. No defects are allowed, so you get it spoon-fed to you." Of course, the Army everywhere attempts to avoid errors, but the pressure intensified in Germany because of the fear that an embarrassing mistake would create political pressure for withdrawal or reduction of the American forces.[6]

Problems in Communication. All these complications—legal complexity, physical limitations to mission accomplishment, and the pressure for zero defects in order to avoid embarrassment—were exacerbated by the rather limited German language ability of most U.S. soldiers stationed there. With tasks more complex, more numerous, and more politically delicate, the need to coordinate with the civilian sector was much higher than in the United States. But communication skills for dealing with people outside the military post were generally limited compared with the abilities of a soldier asked to coordinate an exercise with the local civil defense or police in the United States. Although many Germans spoke English rather well, others did not know or want to use English. The fact that few Americans could speak German increased the difficulty of their tasks and added to the propensity for complex activities to break down. Soldiers indeed had "many additional tasks" in Germany, tasks made even harder by language deficit.

These complications of regulatory complexity, environmental restriction, fear of embarrassment, and language deficit stressed the units. The workload and the complexities forced frequent changes and adjustments that generated still more stress. 1SG (First Sergeant) Stewart Powell reflected how he might plan out a particular training day for his company, weeks in advance.

> Then the distractors [nonmission taskings imposed from above] come in and just overfill your commitments. You're committed to one thing [your training plan] before, and then as you come closer, you're more and more [committed by imposed distractors] until by the day [of your plan], it is completely overloaded. Mission, mission, mission. All becomes hot [stressed by senior ranks], from that particular day. . . . What happened to a certain day of the week? Two weeks ago, that day wasn't too hot. But it gets hotter and hotter.

Things became "hotter and hotter" because of the multiple new requirements urged upon the unit by the chain of command. Obviously, this buildup of pressure increased the probability of error. In a word, typical units and soldiers in Germany faced more work, experienced more breakdowns in plans, and had to overcome the breakdowns diplomatically in spite of cultural barriers and language inadequacy. How did they do so? How did they practice the art of readiness in Germany?

THE PRACTICE OF READINESS IN GERMANY

The Conduct of Work

The Intensity of the Work. The heightened threat perception, the greater complexity of the work, and the increased frequency of breakdowns in the execution of plans justified increased demands on the units and thus on the soldiers. Inoperative combat equipment, for example, had to be repaired immediately so as to be usable in case of an assault. Parts should have been in stock. If they were not, repairs had to be made the moment the part arrived, regardless of the hour. If a repair part for a tank was delivered in the late afternoon, soldiers from the tank crew and the repair team did not return home until the tank was repaired and operational, no matter how late that might be. Plans had to be continuously updated, because, among other reasons, congressional funding cuts from time to time forced changes in unit plans at all levels. Tasks that ran into unforeseen difficulties had to be replanned on the fly. The resulting new tasks worked their way down the chain of command quickly, to be fitted into an already full schedule. A late request for some report or a staff demand for additional planning meant a lengthened workday. Inspections for readiness were rigorous and required extra effort because failure to perform well became permanently documented on one's evaluation report. Field training had to be scheduled, planned, prepared for, and coordinated with host nation authorities. Work life in Germany consisted of a succession of long days filled with last-minute tasks.

The Obligation to Obey Orders. Soldiers have to obey the legal orders of their superiors. In Germany, the position of superiors was almost deified. SP4 Jeff Atwood remarked, "In training, they tell you that what the NCO and the officer says is gods." His wife, Betty, also a Specialist Four, corroborated, "Like they are *God.*" Nevertheless, although the Army required obedience, its manuals also taught the soldiers to "exercise initiative." In the "fog of war," one was to use initiative to pursue the general intent of superiors as long as one's initiative did not contravene clearly given orders.

In the Army, disagreements between people of different rank ideally were settled by the lower-ranking person giving his or her best professional opinion to the higher-ranking commander. The commander then decided the issue, after having evaluated all opinions and counsel from below and the orders and intentions of senior commanders. The subordinate should, thereafter, help execute the decision with a supportive attitude (presuming the decision was legal) whether she or he thought it a wise decision or not. If the subordinate expressed his or her contrary opinion subversively, the subordinate could be called to task for insubordination or failure to execute an order. Whether triggered by a single incident or a perceived pattern, the openly resisting or obviously reluctant soldier—officer or enlisted—would eventually be disciplined.

24-Hour Availability and Two-Hour Response Time. After working a ten- or twelve-hour day, a soldier returned to the barracks or to his or her family household. Given that an attack could come at any time, however, a soldier was never really "off duty." Unless signed out officially for annual leave, the soldier had to be reachable, twenty-four hours a day, throughout his or her period of military service. When contacted, the soldier had to report for duty, arm the equipment, and "roll out the gate" within a specified time period. For Middleberg and Richberg, the required maximum response time was two hours. Other communities had even shorter response times. Few had longer.

Alerts. In the event of war, the U.S. Army installations expected to be attacked in the first minutes by air and rocket weaponry as well as by Soviet *spetznatz* teams—saboteurs placed in civilian jobs within the German economy, whose task was simply to wait in hiding for years until the order came to disrupt the Americans. The Americans had to be able to vacate the post, fully equipped for combat, before an attack. They would be alerted based on intelligence indications of an impending assault. Time was of the essence. So the soldiers had to practice and prove to superiors that they could in fact vacate the installation within the specified one or two hours allotted to them. An alert began with a call to the soldier at work or at home, often in the middle of the night. The soldier departed the household and promptly reported for duty so that the unit could be on the move before the allotted time expired. Frequent alerts tested the readiness of the military organization. As we shall see in the next chapter, alerts also tested the patience and integrity of Army families.

Symbols of Readiness. Many symbols pointedly reminded soldiers of their precarious, dangerous status on the frontier. One division's frequently repeated motto affirmed, "No mission too difficult, no sacrifice too great; duty first." In one battalion of that division, soldiers greeted officers by saluting while simultaneously shouting, "Danger forward, *Sir!*," before delivering messages. Even though soldiers on both sides of the Atlantic recognized that they were on call twenty-four hours a day, the Army combat mission imposed its reality much more forcefully in Germany than it did at Army posts in the United States.

The continuous use of the camouflage Battle Dress Uniform, or BDU, added to the atmosphere of constant war readiness. Of course, one would expect the BDU for manual work or field exercises. But even major ceremonial events were conducted in full field battle gear, with web belt, canteen, and M-16 with bayonet. At a change-of-command ceremony for Middleberg's departing commanding general, distinguished German community leaders, spouses, and guests came in Sunday best, and some in formal tuxedos and elegant black velvet evening gowns. The Germans and Americans attending the ceremony entered the building by passing under a colonnade of battle-dressed soldiers, each pair forming an overhead arch by touching the bayonet points of their M-16 rifles above the heads of the entering guests. The departing general attended, attired not in ceremonial "dress blues" but in battle-ready gear. With his combat helmet on, chin strap pulled tight, and field web-gear suspenders supporting a full complement of canteen, ammunition pouches, and grenades, the departing American commanding general stood at the podium and delivered to the German dignitaries and local community elite his speech about the need for constant readiness to defend freedom. Indeed, the American military in Germany used every opportunity to publicly symbolize its combat readiness.

Duty Rosters. Any army has recurrent maintenance tasks—among them guarding its assets, cleaning up, and staffing its safety and communication systems—that must be performed as extra duties, no matter what the primary task of the unit. The U.S. Army, in Germany as elsewhere, staffed these tasks consistent with American cultural values of fairness and equality by using an assignment device called the "duty roster." A duty roster was a posted assignment sheet that informed the group which individuals were required to perform a particular additional assignment by taking a soldier's name, on rotation, from the top of an alphabetical list of all those eligible for the duty. On completion of the duty, one's name moved to the bottom of the list and awaited another cycle. Generally, one's name went on a list if one benefited from the duty or if one's unit was responsible for providing the duty or service. Thus a residential barracks that had to maintain a person awake for safety and security would be staffed at night by choosing from the roster list of those living in that particular barracks. The community headquarters also had to staff many twenty-four-hour positions. There had to be an overnight watch, an ambulance driver and co-driver/medic, a phone operator for the installation, and a runner to take care of any needs or pass messages. The installation had to have gate guards. Because all soldiers working on the post benefited from the guarding, all were on the community-level gate-guard roster and again on the community command roster. Medics, because of their specialized skills, were on a separate roster with fewer candidates. Vehicles and munitions needed night guards. Because each battalion had its own vehicle park and armory, young soldiers and NCOs from all the companies in a particular battalion were on one or more of that battalion's duty rosters. Officers also had a set of duty rosters for senior-level positions that needed oversight. For example, each post required that a staff duty officer be available at night and through the weekends.

Each task had its own duty roster, with a differing number of eligible candidates and a differing frequency of task performance. Thus, it was possible, indeed likely, for an individual to be on several lists. The rotating lists ensured fair selection from among those eligible to do the duty. Soldiers were notified through the chain of command at daily formations that their names had moved to the top of the list, or soldiers could read the posted information on bulletin boards.

Although the duty roster was a venerable institution and appeared to be strictly fair and reasonable, the roster procedure created some problems. First, duties apportioned by units of a certain level actually fell more frequently on the members of smaller units. Thus, SP4 Jeff Atwood complained, "Delta [company] has 100 people and Alpha [company] has 500 people. Where in Delta you pull duty four or five times, in Alpha you pull it less. The problem is, the companies are of different size. Yet they are set to the same tasks." Understandably, soldiers from these smaller units did not see duty rosters as strictly fair.

Second, in the event that soldiers were unable to complete a duty when assigned, they were supposed to arrange their own substitutes. In practice, however, conflicting military duties came up suddenly. Soldiers might get sick or have other emergencies that did not permit a preplanned, self-chosen substitute. As a result, soldiers a line or two down on the roster who thought they would be free on a particular day could get a late call requiring them to report.

Finally, duty rosters were not synchronized. Because a soldier was obligated to perform his or her share of several duties, each duty having a separate roster, a given weekend might be cannibalized by the chance cycles of one's name on any of a variety of rosters. The untoward impact of the way the Army maintained its duty rosters will become more apparent in the next chapter. For now, it is sufficient to note that using the duty roster was standard practice to meet constantly recurring "housekeeping" demands.

The Exercise of Control

When the tasks of military life go awry, a leader reestablishes control by making decisions and ordering subordinates to complete tasks in limited times. Orders always carry with them the implicit threat, and sometimes even an explicit threat, that noncompliance will bring on sanctions. The main power behind military sanctions in Germany lay in the higher-ranking person's ability to threaten the lower-ranking soldier's job security, thereby putting monthly income, current medical and housing benefits, intangible job satisfactions, long-term career goals, and future retirement security at risk. MAJ Rodney Kimball, on the division staff, put it bluntly: "What drives it? Fear. You gotta live here. If you get fired, you're dead meat; you got no job. So when the general says 'shit,' everybody goes running for toilet paper."

A commander could take a variety of actions to enforce his or her will. He could give an enlisted soldier, whether troop or NCO, a written "counseling statement" that would mar the soldier's permanent record. He could give a negative (i.e., less than superlative) EER or OER. He could take a variety of punitive actions under the provisions of the Uniform Code of Military Justice (UCMJ). He could initiate the administrative discharge of an enlisted person, getting the person "chaptered out of the Army." He could relieve an officer of command or responsibility. The obligation to obey orders also gave a leader the informal ability to make a subordinate's life miserable by assigning unpleasant extra duties or by piling on so many demands that the inevitable failure to perform could be written up in any of the above formal mechanisms.

Let us look briefly at the ways for dealing with serious breach of confidence, and then examine in detail how the OER/EER mechanism was used for normal control. By definition, being "chaptered out" terminated a career. An Article 15 (formal nonjudicial punishment imposed by a commander) or other UCMJ action also terminated an officer's career, though a young NCO might survive an Article 15 if it did not involve drugs or assault. Relief of responsibility devastated an officer's career and slowed down an NCO's advancement. Such actions were supposed to be used only when serious dereliction of conduct merited their application. The OER and the EER reports, by contrast, were control procedures applied to all officers and NCOs at regular intervals, and thus deserve more thorough description.

The Officer Evaluation Report, or OER, and the Enlisted Evaluation Report, or EER, are documents that assess an officer's or an NCO's performance during a specified period of time. Performance has to be evaluated yearly or whenever triggered by a move of either the rater or the soldier to be rated. Thus, if a soldier leaves a unit, she or he has to be evaluated. Similarly, an officer about to leave a unit has to evaluate all subordinates for whom she or he is the rater. Company commanders rate the officers and NCOs within the unit. Higher unit commanders rate their subordinate unit commanders, executive officer, and senior NCO. Officers in charge of staff sections rate their subordinate officers and NCO assistants, and are in turn rated by the executive officer. Thus, all officers and NCOs are rated by their most immediate supervisory officer, known as their "rater." In each case, the rater gives numeric evaluations of officer characteristics or fills in boxes on NCO performance characteristics. NCOs are then given written "bullet" statements detailing outstanding accomplishments and strengths or specifying areas needing improvement. Officers are given a paragraph assessment of their job performance. In addition, the rating by the immediate supervisory officer is reviewed by a more senior officer, known as the "senior rater." The senior rater writes a paragraph, further assessing the rated officer, and then marks a "block," ranking the officer on a normal curve into one of nine performance levels. To gain some impression of the meaning of the block rating and overcome the effects of verbal inflation in the descriptive paragraphs, the Department of the Army then computes the percentage of persons a senior rater has placed in each "block" over his or her career, thus indicating whether a "top block" given by a particular senior rater is in fact a superior mark or a "center of mass" rating.

OERs and EERs accumulate throughout a soldier's career in a microfiche personnel file that is maintained centrally by the Department of the Army. Every few years when a soldier is eligible, a promotion board—a group of officers or NCOs senior to the rank of those being evaluated—assesses the soldier's progress and performance in military schools, reviews the soldier's diversity of assignments, scrutinizes a current photograph in uniform, weighs the evidence of physical fitness and body weight, and notes scores on soldier skills tests. Above all, the promotion board depends on the soldier's OERs or EERs, evidence of performance history and competence. As the Army needs fewer and fewer officers at each level of rank, these reports become the basis for either promoting or "passing over" an officer and eventually removing her or him from the service.

Although the rating system existed to evaluate leaders' performance, its effectiveness was compromised by a high degree of subjectivity. For example, it made a difference whether the rater wrote well or not; a rater's relative ability to choose flowery adjectives that conformed to the inflated language customary for describing even average performance could affect the outcome of a promotion board judgment made years later. MAJ Kimball described how he completed an OER: "I just said that the guy did a 'good job,' that 'he served 4,500 meals a day from North Africa to Norway.' And that is considered an adverse OER. The accepted words are 'outstanding, excellent, and superior,' in that rank order." Thus a fine performing officer could be downgraded and even removed from the Army at some time in the future because his or her rater chose less ostentatious words than another rater might have used (or the promotion board expected) for the same or less competent performance. Given the subjectivity of the simple choice of words, some officers even worried that personality differences or minor family faults might affect the tone and quality of the wording used in one's rating. Exceptional evaluation reports accelerated one's path to advancement in rank. Good reports, which in an inflated environment actually are poor performance reports, slowed one's advancement in rank. A positive but not stellar OER could have a delayed effect, for it could end an officer's career, if not at the next promotion board, then in the highly competitive environment of a promotion board eight or ten years away. MAJ Kimball again: "You don't get fired in the Army and survive. If you get fired from any job, you're finished. That is motivation!" One had to be careful, therefore, to please the rater—and the rater might be fickle or capricious.

Because one could not be certain how a given leader would respond, the ratee was forced to be "on alert" continuously to satisfy the rater, not necessarily for the sake of the mission, but to win the rater's approval or to avoid offending, disconcerting, or discomforting him or her. The pressures produced distortions. A staff sergeant on night watch duty: "In today's Army, that is how you progress. I have to determine 'How do you want me to act?' The higher you get up in the rank structure, [the more] it is 'Yes, sir, yes, sir, three bags full.' I say, 'Yes, I will,' but I'm thinking, 'What the hell am I going to do?'" In this climate, the rating system was viewed as arbitrary, dependent on the peculiarities of the rater and on his or her "whims," his or her capricious judgment. Thus, OER and EER performance reports were the key to advancement and retention, and created much anxiety among those who desired a long-term career. The reports were also central features in the undermining of leadership, driving it toward demand overload, micromanagement, and irrationality. In a word, the OER led to the corruption of the leadership it was supposed to improve.

THE CORRUPTION OF LEADERSHIP: UNINTENDED CONSEQUENCES OF PRACTICE

Demand Overload: Sources and Consequences

The condition of demand overload proceeded from the urgency of the mission, the obligation to obey, and the threat of evaluation. Soldiers understood that military readiness would require much of them. They did not complain of demands that clearly added to combat readiness. In this section I seek to clarify why demands seemed to deviate from the fundamental mission of combat readiness and why those demands so demoralized the soldiers at all levels.

We have seen that the nearness of the Soviet threat made the U.S. Army in Germany an intense, stressed organization. We have seen, too, that for an army to be able respond rapidly and appropriately to dangerous situations, it must be a demand-oriented, demand-responsive organization, its participants obligated to follow orders. So it was in the U.S. Army Europe. Many soldiers felt, however, that some of their leaders imposed a personal agenda of less legitimate demands on their subordinates and thereby took advantage of the soldier's obligation to obey. Said an enlisted soldier at a party, "A soldier signs an oath that he is going to uphold to the United States of America. Civilians sign those, too, but they have a job description. Soldiers have rights, too, but we have the little statement of 'extra duties,' which can be anything, and the oath to obey all orders from officers and NCOs." The obligation to obey made it possible for "anything" to be pushed down in the form of an order and become an "extra duty." For example, a leader could push some attribute, such as vehicle cleanliness, beyond mission functionality, transmitting additional stress to soldiers and families who were already feeling overwhelmed within a demand-rich environment.

The ease with which demands were imposed on soldiers at every level—and the soldier's inability to resist inappropriate demands because of the obligation to obey—quickly overwhelmed the soldiers in the threat-rich European theater, resulting in what I call demand overload. The demands were irksome if they did not contribute significantly to "real mission" readiness. Thus, the complaint of a company commander's wife:

"When he works fifteen hours a day, he wants something accomplished. Many, many fifteen-hour days in the office, all he does is churn paper. Every day since Thanksgiving he has gone in to the office at night because there is no telephone [ringing], and he can get done what he needs to do and not have somebody throwing something at him that he considers petty."

"Where does this 'churning' come from, this 'throwing'?" I asked.

"When he comes home frustrated and angry, it is never the soldiers," she affirmed. "It is the higher command. It comes from division."

Leaders loaded assignments on those below them, seemingly oblivious to the cumulative burden of demands. Here is how Holly Wilde, a volunteer worker at ACS, experienced the demand system in community affairs: "At ACS, there are so many powers that be that command our lives. So and so calls us up and says he is going to get in trouble if we don't do this or that. Too many chiefs and no little Indians." Indeed any officer or NCO could add to the demands made on the unit they were in charge of, often by trying to guess their commander's wishes. Thus, SSG Nate Cobb suggested, "They read their commander. The general of the brigade will say, 'This is what you need to do.' But by the time it gets to you, everybody has added to it. The battalion commander has added. Community has added. All down the chain, from the highest down to me, can add to it. I can change it, add to it. Squad leaders can add to the things that gotta be done." Demands could also be inserted by the staff officers of the many support functions needed to sustain either the combat or the community side of a military organization. In theory, only the commanders gave orders. But the staff officers were quite persuasive. According to 1LT Curtis Smith, "If you tell the division staff officers 'no,' they get hysterical. You can't tell them 'no.' If you try to tell them 'no,' they say, 'I'll have to get the general involved. He said I could have anything.' They don't think you are people. They treat you like a machine."

The load for many became staggering. Mr. Renquist, the director of the Community Counseling Center at Middleberg, spoke of his preretirement service as an officer in Germany:

> In the summer of '86, I was the acting DPCA [Director of Personnel and Community Activities] for a while. At the same time, I was the ADCO [Alcohol and Drug Control Officer] and the EDCO [Education Coordinating Officer]. We have a lot of taskings that are tangential: Suicide Prevention Council, Smoking Cessation Officer, Army Health Fitness Point of Contact for the community, Family Advocacy Case Management Team. We go to the schools if there is a sudden death in [among] the children.

The chronic state of demand overload entailed several consequences, all detrimental to the quality of a soldier's life and the Army's performance.

Time-Domain Violations. First, demand overload created time-domain violations. Time needed to meet the military demand overload had to come from somewhere. As we shall see in the next chapter, much of it came from "family time."

Career Risk. Second, demand overload exposed soldier careers to the risk of capricious judgment. Demand overload created a situation in which no matter how diligently junior leaders and individual soldiers attempted to prioritize the demands made on them, their capacity was exhausted. Something was always left undone. But anything left undone was a point of vulnerability, for the omission might have been the valued pet project of some senior in the chain of command, or it might simply have been seized upon as an excuse to pressure or punish a subordinate whose relationship with a leader had soured for other reasons. A group of soldiers on night watch at a community headquarters discussed the issues. First a private suggested, "People will actually try to chapter you out for some little thing. The Army has so many regulations." The NCO in charge of the group agreed, "And you don't know. I could be breaking regulations right now." Indeed so, interjected a corporal: "We are breaking regulations right now. I gave you money to buy the Coke. That is fraternization."

The pervasive tension of the demand-oriented culture created a perpetual state of vulnerability because a leader was inevitably forced to prioritize tasks and make decisions quickly about what to do and what to leave undone. Yet those priorities and decisions could easily be interpreted by one's rater as mistakes. Even the most careful decision of what to do first or best was risky if the senior officer evaluating a leader's performance had a different, unexpressed priority. That difference of opinion could result in a career-terminating negative OER or EER. The importance of the rater to one's career survival thus fostered a sense of crisis and of anxiety in a unit and diverted leaders from the tasks of strengthening readiness and caring for the troops to attending to the wishes of his or her rater.

Micromanagement. Throughout the U.S. Army in Germany, soldiers given a mission wanted to decide how best to accomplish it. They felt "micromanaged" if a superior specified both the task to be accomplished and the specific steps to be taken. Micromanagement, however, flourished in this system in which a subordinate's actions created a substantial career risk for a leader. Indeed, career risk inevitably rises if the organization or any of its leaders promote a "zero defects" environment and enforce that policy through OERs and EERs, as was the case in Germany. The leader cannot afford to take the risk that a subordinate will make a mistake for which the leader will be held responsible. Richberg's deputy DCC,[7] CPT Patrick Tall: "A zero defects environment creates micromanagement. It indicates a supervisor that doesn't trust his subordinates or is unwilling to accept that to be human is to err. But the NCOs would take care of it unless they had run out of options. The biggest frustration is the leaders who don't trust you. You allow people to perform, and then if they don't, you deal with it on an individual basis." Although some leaders let their subordinates grow, in part by making mistakes, others were less forgiving or more immediately demanding—because they themselves were being watched by their superiors. There was even a temptation for a superior to micromanage a subordinate who knew more about the job at hand than did the superior, a process that usually produced suboptimal performance.[8] SSG Alan Evanson defined micromanagement as "He will tell you what to do and how to do it" and laid out its dangers: "You got an officer breathing down your neck, and a colonel walks in and you're not giving the emphasis exactly right. It is a dangerous game; we are losing the leadership of the NCOs."

In Germany, micromanagement wasted leadership potential in two ways. First, a leader being micromanaged might withdraw and leave his superior to do it all—a form of passive retribution. Thus, SSG Evanson continued, "Behind a good officer, you got to have an NCO. Now the officers—they want to do micro-management. The lieutenant says, 'I want it this way.' And so I say, 'You heard the lieutenant,' while I think to myself, 'Fuck it.'" In other words, the sergeant gave up trying to improve the system and performed exactly as ordered, knowing that the procedure would cause harm. The sergeant achieved retribution through passive resistance.

The second way that micromanagement wasted leadership potential was by subverting leaders into working beneath their appointed level. As MAJ Rodney Kimball put it, "The backbone of the Army is the NCO. That is what keeps us going. And the strongest leadership is the senior NCO. . . . If we don't trust the NCOs, or if I don't trust my captain, then I do captain's work. You get the general doing squad leader work. It is the exception that the leader allows the people to work in their position." In other words, micromanagement was pervasive and it shifted the burden of responsibility for "zero defects" up the chain of command, leaving leaders at the lowest levels out of work and overloading their seniors. Thus, paradoxically, micromanagement tended to create incompetence rather than eliminate it, and undermined individual initiative, autonomy, and performance.

Crisis Management and Task Turbulence. The importance of the OER and therefore of pleasing one's rater fomented crisis management and task turbulence. Leaders at all levels experienced pressure to switch from their own view of the most important task to what they thought their rating officer thought most urgent. As a result, tasks were always changing and often were not completed. 1SG Omar Williams: "The ones that have the most frustration is the soldiers. We tell them to start on something. Then we cancel it and tell them to do another. They probably think we are a bunch of idiots here at battalion. A lot of times, every now and then, we put out changes that affect tomorrow, and they have to work at night to get it done."

Mission Distortion. Under such pressure, priorities get set according to one's best estimate of the rater's needs rather than according to one's best estimate of the mission needs, if these happen to differ. 1SG Floyd Green expressed the impact of rank, commenting that, "Who you really work for is the stars [the generals]. The stars have enough [rank] to turn the opinion." The sergeant's company commander, CPT Earl Halverson, listening in, quickly interjected, "No, I work for the guy that writes my ticket." The "ticket" is the performance report, the OER or EER, written by the officer immediately senior to the person being evaluated. Thus, decisions became rater-driven rather than mission-driven, as leaders sought to "cover their ass." As those making decisions looked "up"—junior troops invariably said "sucked up"—to leadership desires rather than looked "down" to soldier needs and mission realities, soldiers acquired the impression that "leaders don't care."

Moreover, the leaders' decisions began to look stupid. Responding to inaccurate "cover your ass" reports (a phrase so common that it acquired an acronym,

CYA), senior officers issued orders to deal with situations that to some degree did not exist. Orders increasingly became divorced from the on-the-ground mission conditions as seen by the junior troops. Hence, "They must think we are idiots here at battalion," not only because orders changed incessantly but also because orders often did not match local-level realities. This mismatch often created further last-minute, spastic changes to try to correct errors.

Soldiers commonly referred to orders or tasks that seemed unrelated to a unit's "real mission" as "bullshit tasks," "doing bullshit," or "more Army bullshit." One captain defined "Army bullshit" as "whims, wants, desires not needed to perform the mission—that is bullshit." Thus the desire to please a rater and the obligation to obey inherent in the rating system subtly inclined the military organization toward producing increased quantities of "bullshit." One battalion commander described a situation in which a commanding general's mere mention of a stray cat initiated a frantic attempt to capture and eliminate it. A staff officer told of how, at another post, the commanding general had casually pointed out the irony of having red exit signs telling people where they should go in an emergency since red usually meant stop. Laughing, the general suggested that green would seem to be the more appropriate color for emergency exit signs, because green indicated "go." The general apparently had no intention of his comment causing any change, but within days, red exit signs were replaced by green ones throughout the post. A company commander recounted an order to secure loose backpack straps with tape. He expressed his resentment at having been "jerked through a knothole" to get enough of precisely the "right tape" in time for inspection.

The desire of some officers to get a top OER was so great that they sometimes ignored their own knowledge of mission and situation to please the rating officers who filled out their OERs, to the detriment of soldiers and mission. "What drives someone to be a 'yes-man'?" I asked SGT Shane Ulman, who was leading a squad on cleanup duty. "You get a bad EER or OER and your career is over. They strive so hard to get a good report card that they will fuck anybody over. Someday the men in the Army have got to realize, 'Who are they serving? The men over? Or the men under?'" The more one valued his or her career—or sensed no other alternatives—the greater the pressure to orient up the system to deal with the whims of the superiors who provided the career-important rating, rather than down the system to attend to the needs one found among the soldiers or in the mission situation. Wherever people subverted each other to please their superiors, the system had become rank-oriented rather than mission-oriented.

Soldier Alienation. The result of such rank orientation was a deterioration of morale. Soldiers felt both trapped by the coercive aspects of the system and defrauded because their sacrifices were not directed toward soldier welfare or real mission. In Germany, even some of the best soldiers succumbed, withdrawing, pressed into the path of cautious inaction, alienated. Here are two examples, the first, a young sergeant, Sam McGregory, likely to become an excellent senior NCO:

"You have to be like water, and adapt to the flow. . . . I stay in trouble—that is my middle name—for trying to help people."

"How is it that helping soldiers equals trouble?" I inquired, puzzled.

"I've learned that if you show initiative, motivation, dedication, loyalty, it gets you in trouble because a lot of the NCOs don't have those characteristics and they are afraid to put their rank on the line for their subordinates."

"Can you give me an example?"

"I have an E2. He's been an E2 for eighteen months. He busted an appendix in French commando school [a prestigious school to which only outstanding soldiers were invited] and had a knee operation, so he couldn't work in his MOS [Military Occupational Specialty] that well. So the platoon leader and platoon sergeant got together and said he was 'lazy, good for nothing, fuck-headed.' I took over the section and tried to find out why he wasn't being promoted. I took him to the platoon sergeant, 'cause the guy said if he couldn't be promoted, he wanted to be chaptered out. I asked, 'Are you going to promote him?'

'No.'

'Why?'

'He doesn't work in his MOS.'

'Then are you going to chapter him?'

'No.'

'Why?'

''Cause he don't fuck up that bad.'

"I told them I was going to take him to the IG [inspector general]. The first sergeant doesn't care. And the IG doesn't help: 'You have to work through the chain,' they said. Well, the chain of command doesn't work for everyone in the Army. I was getting so much heat from them that a sergeant came to me and said I am a bad NCO. I said, 'Why? 'Cause I'm helping my men?'

"He says, 'Yeah.'

"I get CQ [charge of quarters, the person standing night watch in a barracks, as extra duty] for helping my men. After trying to help McK___ , I kept to myself. And the platoon leader comes in and says I 'got a bad attitude,' and 'if the first sergeant catches that, you will get details [extra duties], and CQ.'

"I take it and go with the flow. What makes it bad is it is the good soldiers that the system drives out. I look at the good soldiers, with potential. They are tired of it. They are tired of the BS. Two good first sergeants just retired. There are so many hindrances. I love the military, but not *that* much. The good soldiers, they are fading out or getting out."

So SGT McGregory, after helping, felt threatened and withdrew, "kept to himself." Withdrawal, however, resulted in a "bad attitude" label. Worse, he actively began thinking about and justifying "getting out." In a word, he was alienated.

In the second case, Denise Stewart, the deputy director of ACS at Richberg, said of her husband,

"He loved the Army before this, and he has been fortunate. He loves the soldiering, and he could put on a commercial: He is proud to be in. He is a career soldier. Right now, he is discouraged, but he is still good. He is just trying to keep his nose clean, stay out of trouble."

"What gets you in trouble?" I asked, trying to get her to be expansive.

"You just don't know here. You don't know who has it in for you. You don't know if someone will be talking up for you or talking down."

"Who?" I probed.

"Another NCO. Or the officers. Or the officers doing the NCOs' jobs. You don't [shouldn't] have to be liked to do your job. If you're a good soldier and they don't like you as a person, you don't know what they can do to you. They can take stripes, or take liberty, or take days. We are almost talking about fear here."

Such anxiety spread through the community, alienating its soldiers and derailing communication within the organization.

Corrupted Communication

Distorted Communication and Suppressed Feedback. Accurate two-way communication, as we saw at the beginning of this chapter, is essential to success in combat and to the rational operation of a complex organization such as an overseas combat-ready military community. Demands, however, flow one way: from senior ranks down to junior ranks. In Germany, it was hard to send negative communications up the system. Soldiers and family members asserted that complaining about problems got one labeled as a "crybaby," or a "sniveler," attributes of weakness in a culture that must be able to tolerate hardship. As a result, there was little return flow of information. For example, PFC (Private First Class) Nolan Farnsworth, a medic, described an instance in which his company commander was wrong on certain medical information about which the medic was expert. When I asked why he didn't give his opinion, he blurted out incredulously, "You're going to argue with your company commander? You're a PFC. You're going to get fucked in the middle of it! I keep quiet." But when soldiers "keep quiet," the Army loses the information it needs to take corrective action and improve. My interviews are replete with expressions that one got harassed for being the bearer of bad news, that "complainers get a bad reputation." Here is Denise Stewart, Richberg's ACS Deputy Director, on the subject: "They don't like troublemakers. They don't like you to have any type of gripe against the system. The moment that you bring up a grievance, if they bring it up here, at Richberg, the repercussions might hurt them. They might not take a stripe, but it can be a lot of anguish, just the pressure of being pressured. Chain of command pressure. Shit rolls downhill. That is the old saying in the military."

Complainers got labeled and then pressured at work. The labeling could work its way into an evaluation report, which of course was a permanent part of a soldier's personnel records. Thus, the potential for being labeled a complainer and then being subtly punished or marginalized was greater than the likelihood of receiving prompt or worthwhile relief from any complaint or communication lodged in official channels. As a result, many soldiers disregarded their feelings and did not complain through official channels, even when justified. SP4 Jeff Atwood: "Most of the people just want to be left alone, do their job, and keep a low profile—so they will swallow a lot of things, to not have to put up with the consequences. Most of the time nothing will be done about your complaint, and if you complain, then you're worse off than you were before. If you don't complain, at least you won't be labeled or harassed." Thus, some soldiers felt that "not rocking the boat" was a preferable strategy for achieving career progress than being vocal about perceived injustices or critiquing policies that compromised the capability of a unit. "Complaining was dangerous," they would say. SSG Evanson explained that it was even dangerous to ask questions at town meetings, which were regularly held specifically so that soldiers and spouses could ask questions of the leaders of the military community's organizations: "They don't give a shit about the soldiers, and about the families. They have town meetings because it looks good. But you got to be careful: I get reamed by my first sergeant if I ask a question, 'cause the sergeant major is going to call the first sergeant about why they didn't solve the problem. And now my first sergeant is in trouble and I get reamed for not asking the question to my first sergeant." Indeed, even posing a suggestion was felt to be fraught with difficulty and dependent on issues of rank. Betty and Jeff Atwood discussed the matter. "The reason that I think that nothing will change," said Betty, "is—whenever you go to them with a legitimate complaint, all they say is that you are a crybaby, and they don't want to hear it anymore." "If you were an E7, they would listen," Jeff suggested. "If you're an E4 and below," Betty clarified, "they hear you [out] but they don't listen." Thus, the pervasive "can-do" military attitude further suppressed essential negative feedback. As one of Middleberg's ACS employees put it, "I've seen the Army get rid of proficient officers, and keep the soft shoe and the bullshitters, who are better talkers. And when it comes time to give out a position, they give it to the polished rather than to the proficient."

False Reports. The pressures of career preservation began to distort the accuracy of reports on the status of the Army, its units, and its troops. Many leaders felt they had to emphasize "appearances" rather than substance; they had to "look good." A full colonel on staff duty at corps headquarters wondered out loud: "How do you tell the general what is wrong with his baby? It can affect your career. It is very difficult to tell the general. The system is primed for appearances." On another occasion, I commented to a group of staff officers at corps headquarters that in my view, the desire to "look good" corrupted the flow of accurate information. One of them, a lieutenant colonel about to retire, had turned in a report critical of some issue. He described how "six colonels" called him later to say, "Don't you want to change this? This will make the general look bad. If he wants two stars, he'd better not do that [look bad]." Implicitly, the officer should suppress criticism. The result, the lieutenant colonel concluded, was a philosophy and a practice of "looking good rather than being good."

In another discussion, a private on night watch described how the report of their marksmanship was distorted: "On range 211, the general came, and [i.e., together with] the NATO guys [high-ranking NATO observers]. And they said we did 80 to 90 percent. But we only had 30 or 40 percent. Let the [senior NATO] guys know when they [i.e., we] make a mistake! But they don't want to know." In short, the report was falsified to please expectations rather than to describe realities. A staff sergeant listening in confirmed, "All my guys got 'expert'" at the rifle range. He grinned and justified: "I'm the grader—it means promotion." Here the grader rewarded himself and his buddies, as well as pleased the leaders, by falsifying the qualifications of his subordinates. Soldiers disliked the falsification in the reporting, however, even though they participated in its corruption and sometimes profited from it.

Erratic Behavior in Military Units

Such misinformation leads to erratic behavior in military units. Goal-oriented systems, like thermostats, try to bring the behavior of the system into close approximation of the goal. To do so, they must have feedback on their current status. In the absence of accurate feedback, complex goal-oriented systems, such as a military unit, tend to miss their objectives and oscillate in wide swings. Alternatively, they may amplify and exaggerate a course of action because there is no negative feedback, until the extremity of the resulting behavior causes some other part of the system to collapse. CPT Halverson described the oscillations at Middleberg. The previous community commander had a fetish for posting all traffic regulations on public signs. The current community commander wanted a less cluttered look and felt community members should know the regulations and not have to be reminded. So, under the old commander, the signs went up, and under the current commander they came down. But, as CPT Halverson knew from his feel for the system, things would oscillate. Therefore, he advised,

> "Don't throw the signs away. The next guy that comes in [as commanding general] will love signs. The first guy wanted all the signs. The next guy wants them down. That is the bullshit. We got signs about every other foot. My definition of bullshit is whims, 'like to's,' wants from somebody. The only thing we need to complete the mission is traffic control. Why do we got so many signs? 'Cause the first guy said, 'I want signs.'"
>
> "Is there no suppressing it?" I wondered, expressing my surprise.
>
> "How? Stand up there and say, 'That is not smart. We don't need that sign'? The guy [senior officer] says, 'Captain when you've served twenty-eight years, then you can say that.' You're damned if you do and damned if you don't. Is a sign worth falling on your sword for? No. You let that one go, and you wait for a better one to fight for."[9]

Oscillation and exaggeration were anticipated, recognized as built into the system, so the traffic signs were saved. Moreover, Halverson implied that the wild swings were exaggerated by the suppression of feedback rooted in fear for career. Yet, adequate negative feedback is essential to dampen the oscillation of a system and enable it to remain on course, moving toward a goal. MAJ Taylor, the brigade G3 (officer in charge of operations), confirmed the concept:

> Here in Middleberg, you reinvent the wheel whenever the leader changes. A lot of the unit is affected by the change in personality. We got a new battalion commander and new ADFC [assistant division forward commander], all at the same time. That was just settling down and then we get a new brigade [division forward] commander. We have had three generals here since I've been here—three totally

different styles. Every time one changes, everything changes. Mike [another division officer] said, "Gentlemen, we are going to reinvent the Army again, for the third time in three months." Colonel [X, as ADFC] was very low key—got the job done, but did it low key. Then Colonel [Y, as the new ADFC]: very demanding. Then, just as it was settling down, we get a new division [forward] commander. That impacts on the families, simply because it impacts on the soldiers. . . . Every time anybody in the ladder changes . . . that has a ripple effect. It is the nature of the beast. And I'm not just talking the PCS changes. The higher you go, the more you tend to rotate jobs. Commanders [are in place] for only two years. A staff officer will hold a job for a year or less. Somebody is always changing.

On the beneficial side, the practice of frequently changing commanders would interrupt the potential for one commander's eccentricities to be amplified for very long by strict subordinate obedience. With frequent turnover, leadership would become the average of the rapidly imposed changes of course made by successive leaders. But for the soldier, the average was experienced as a constant, demoralizing, zigzag chase after extremes, and the perpetual turnover created all too frequent periods of incompetence as new leaders learned their jobs and then moved on just when, or even before, they had mastered their current assignment.

From the soldier's point of view, the constant changes occasioned by micromanagement, demand overload, crisis management, and task and leadership turbulence manifested the uncertainty and illogic in the system. I quote three different soldiers: first, a sergeant; second, a battalion commander; and third, a company first sergeant:

> Anonymous sergeant: One day they tell you to jump, and on another they procrastinate. Crisis management. You can plan months out, and they don't act on it.

> LTC Keith Bateman: Every leader wants to have his abilities noted. So the immature leader makes changes, makes policies perhaps which aren't necessary. And then the people that work for him become frustrated because they have added work and see no reason for it.

> 1SG Omar Williams: One of the things that makes people think this is a messed up place is the changes. All the changes are last minute. We don't even know when we are going to Graf [Grafenwöhr]. It's five or six weeks before we leave, and we don't know when we are going for sure. Supposedly 19 July, but that has been changed. And we don't have any idea when we are coming back. For a fact, it is pretty close to last minute before we ever get anything.

Thus, soldiers complained of working in a "crazy system," or a "screwy system," and referred to the "crazy shit" that goes on. They clearly saw leaders as the source of the craziness.

The Perception and Experience of Irrational Leadership

Senior leaders had to base their leadership decisions on information coming up from below, as they could not acquire it directly. We have seen, however, that much information that came from below was corrupted and inaccurate because of the pressure to look good and the desire not be known and persecuted as a complainer or bearer of bad news. Officers using such information issued orders that made them look stupid because the orders did not correspond to the soldiers' knowledge of reality. Subordinates perceived their officers to be "idiots." The trust essential to combat functionality was degraded because irrelevant, wasteful demands based on inaccurate information were complied with out of fear of adverse evaluation. The soldiers lost trust in their leaders and feared that they might use the same quality of decision making to send them into unnecessary danger in wartime. Trust, confidence, and morale within the units were undermined and, as we shall see in following chapters, individual, family, and community morale were likewise savaged.

Given the nature of the hierarchy and the fact that the pressures were easily transmitted down the hierarchy and amplified or added to at each level, it took only one inadequate leader in a chain of command to make a soldier's life fairly miserable. From a private's point of view, for instance, problem leadership could have come from his or her squad leader, platoon sergeant, or second lieutenant over the platoon, from the company's first sergeant, commander, or XO (executive officer), from the battalion's commander, battalion XO, or sergeant major, or from the brigade's or division's commander, assistant commander, or the division command sergeant major. Leadership that could have made the private uncomfortable to miserable could also have come from staff officers or staff NCOs from battalion to division. Junior troops had some ten to twelve people in their chain of command—and others in staff lines— that could significantly affect their lives. So if as many as 10 percent of leaders succumb to the corrupting pressures of the evaluation system, there exists a high probability that any given soldier will experience constant stress from poor leadership, even though intermediate leaders might be able to buffer the impact to some degree. If the number of leaders who are rank sensitive rather than mission and troop-need sensitive is closer to 20 percent, then the experience of poor leadership will be virtually certain and continuous for all.

The Creation of Resistance

A soldier had limited ability to resist orders or suggestions that he or she deemed unwise or even destructive, for resistance would eventually be recorded on an OER or an EER as inadequate performance of duty. Nevertheless, soldiers of any rank did have both formal and informal ways to try to apply countersanctions against the organization if they thought they were treated unfairly.

Using the Regulations. Rather than complain, some soldiers learned the applicable Army regulations and helped administrators or leaders use them to the soldiers' benefit. This worked best on unintentional errors of procedure rather than on errors of leadership judgment. Using the regulations, however, depended on the interpretation of the regulations and therefore depended on the goodwill of the leaders and their attitude about the regulations or the complainer. SP4 Jeff Atwood remembers sitting in the orderly room and overhearing a meeting between the company executive officer, the first sergeant, and the platoon sergeants: "They were saying, 'Anyone that falls out of the PT [physical training] run has to do remedial in the afternoons.' It was brought up that they could not do that legally, because if they pass the PT test, you don't have to do that. But they said that they would do it their way 'til there was an IG complaint [complaint made to the inspector general]." Leaders were able to selectively ignore regulations or use them as they saw fit. I chatted with the members of a leaf raking detail as they went about their work. SGT Shane Ulman, leading the detail, observed with postmodern acuity, "You can read into them [the regulations] what you want or take out what you want. I've seen people say, 'Well, we'll keep this one, throw this one out, keep this one,' etc. Whoa! It's the guy with the most stripes that counts." Several members of his squad joined in the conversation as they continued raking leaves:

> "If you play the game, you're in; if you don't play the game, you're screwed. It depends on who is in charge, what rules you have to play by. For example, the rule on hands in the pockets. Some leaders call you on it, some do not. I like doing the job in the Army, but it is the people that scare me," offered one private.
> "Yeah, 'cause it changes so much," said another private, who jumped enthusiastically into the discussion.
> SGT Ulman then emphasized the capriciousness of interpretation: "They take the rule book, and take what they want to use."
> A corporal on the work team immediately agreed, extending the notion: "The regulations are ambiguous. It depends on who is reading it."

SGT Ulman then repeated his core idea, perhaps to ensure that I did not miss it. He pointed at the patch on his sleeve denoting his rank: "The guy with the most of these railroad tracks, or stripes, is the guy that counts. The big brass, stars, sometimes let their personal preferences interfere." In a word, soldiers are subject to the interpretation of those senior to them, and this fact makes the system capricious, for "it all depends" on the peculiarities, personality, or whims of the leader, with little opportunity to register one's perspective as legitimate.

Climbing the Chain. A soldier could protest by making his or her issue known to successively higher leaders in the chain of command. Unfortunately, this action presented two difficulties. First, the problem the soldier needed to address might be the responsibility of a member of the chain of command itself, and that leader might react poorly to the protest. Second, even though most leaders listened to complaints, complaining got one labeled as a "crybaby"—someone with "an attitude."

> "I go to my commander about the problems I have with my NCO," asserted SP4 Betty Atwood. "The two other shift workers they—come time to talk—they shut up. They just bitch all day long to their peers."

"But you get labeled as a crybaby," her husband, Jeff, emphasized.

"The first time you do something to piss off one of your superiors, you're on the shit list," Betty continued, "and that is it. . . . They will not put you up for promotion. They will not speak highly of you. You're labeled as a crybaby."

Going through the chain of command could imperil one's career if the problem lay in that chain.

Seeing the IG. Soldiers who felt they could not go through the chain of command could go directly to the Inspector General (IG), an organization tasked with monitoring the Army's conformity to regulatory standards. Unfortunately, an IG complaint might not be helpful to the soldier. As Betty Atwood said, "You can go to the IG about anything if you feel you are treated unfairly. But everybody they shut up." Did the IG discourage the soldiers from making their complaints, or did the soldier become discouraged by the chain of command and choose to "shut up"? Regardless, the result was the same—a breakdown in a soldier's ability to communicate his or her concerns adequately. Soldiers felt there was little likelihood of getting satisfaction on a complaint and considerable risk of being labeled a disruptive complainer. Some soldiers complained to the community or division chaplain and trusted that the substance of the message would be passed up the chain of command with sensitivity and confidentiality. However, if a chaplain inadvertently revealed the identity of a soldier, the soldier might be negatively labeled.

Lodging a Congressional. Finally, a soldier could write his or her U.S. representative and ask for a congressional investigation. Once in a while, a complaint letter might trigger a congressional visit if the complaint dealt with a culturally or politically sensitive topic. More likely, the complaint would be sent through command channels from Congress to the immediate superior of the soldier, with each level given a short "suspense date" for the required reply. The leaders in the chain of command had to respond in detail, reviewing and evaluating the complaint. Most likely, one of the leaders may have been part of the problem. Even if not, the aggravation of having to respond to the required paperwork might lead a supervisor to retaliate against the soldier who complained.

Resisting Informally. Because open protest could be dangerous to one's career, soldiers who felt unfairly treated often tried to thwart the system informally. Given the wide latitude commanders had to interpret the Uniform Code of Military Justice, soldiers had to be extremely careful not to be too obvious in their attempts to protest by subverting or slowing down the system. The way one completed assignments, talked to peers, or even the way one walked while on duty could convey, or be taken to convey, negative feelings toward the organization. The object was to subtly communicate disgruntlement without letting one's body language get one in trouble and attract extra duties. A dissatisfied soldier did the minimum work necessary to stay out of trouble and the maximum possible to undermine the organization without getting caught. Some soldiers deliberately slowed down the work. They "shammed," putting on the false appearance of being busy whenever leaders monitored. "Getting over on the Army" referred to this "go slow" behavior and to any form of evading regulations, including minor theft. Soldiers engaged in a game of wits to gain unseen, unsuspected, and ideally unauthorized advantage for oneself or one's informal group of peers to the detriment of the Army.

Alternatively, a soldier "bad-mouthed" the Army whenever leaders were not present. Such talk fostered a verbal climate of alienation and even despair, promoting the idea that the Army "doesn't care about the soldier" and that its leaders were incompetent or self-serving. Insidiously, such negative attitudes could become generalized, believed, and self-perpetuating, thereby undermining the morale of the entire group and subverting leaders who were seeking to perform honorably and take care of their troops. Soldiers expected the worst and interpreted their experience accordingly, creating self-fulfilling prophecy through an endless feedback loop.

Beyond "shamming," a soldier could make himself or herself blatantly troublesome, calling in sick often or even going AWOL (absent without leave), though these actions invariably attracted the hostile attention of superiors. Taken to its extreme, an attitude of vengeance led soldiers to sabotage equipment or manipulate circumstances or information so as to get a leader relieved. A sergeant first class: "One first sergeant in a post I was working at was not liked by his men, and eventually they [the inspectors] found that he had left out a sensitive document. They [his subordinate soldiers] stole it and dumped it in a dumpster. He came up short and was pretty much ruined." This ability to torpedo a senior's career was an empowering form of protest within the organization. But it, too, had its dangers, for if one were caught doing it, it could result in dishonorable discharge or in a prison sentence.

To talk about "fragging" an undesired leader was perhaps the most extreme expression of anger and alienation from the Army. In the confusion of combat, "fragging," or executing a leader, was both easily done and relatively safe, attributable to enemy action. Executing an incompetent leader in peacetime, however, would have been extremely dangerous. Indeed, even to talk about fragging could precipitate a legal investigation, or have evaluation consequences, whereas to talk seriously about the option could be illegal. The desire to "frag" an officer was mentioned only once in my family interviews, perhaps because in peacetime poor leaders were intensely irksome but not worth the risk of killing because they were not likely to get their soldiers killed needlessly.

All these forms of informal resistance reduced the flow of negative information within a unit, thereby undercutting a leader's ability to respond appropriately to the psychosocial climate in the unit. Informal resistance thereby contributed to the spiraling climate of alienation within the unit and in the community and led to greater resistance.

PROFESSIONAL ETHICS AS BUFFER

Only the moral, ethical, and professional integrity of most of the officers and NCOs helped suppress such tendencies. But not entirely. The pressures to succumb and protect one's career were ever present, and even the most professional soldiers felt the blows and contradictions of the system. The common Army expression for how to handle adversity, "suck it up and drive on," was a perfect metaphor for self-sacrificing absorption and digestion of the fruits of systemic dysfunction and occasional command incompetence. One simply kept going.

One must not assume from this account that all those in the U.S. Army in Germany were distracted from their soldierly duties and commitments by the pressures of rank and whim. Some, such as MAJ Taylor, denied that the evaluation system pressured many into "improving" the information they fed up the hierarchy:

> You are morally obligated to disagree. And then if you lose the argument, then you have to follow it [the order]. I can't say, "Hey this is ridiculous, but the general said we gotta do this." You know who does that type of thing, but they don't survive. The guy that survives is the guy that stands up and fights the battles that ought to be fought, and then marches on. You can't see everything, you can't control everything, you can't comply with every regulation, so you take the risk. And you don't worry about it. If you're looking behind your back to cover your tracks, those are the guys that will get relieved.

Even so, those who denied they were personally affected acknowledged that the risk and pressure existed and affected some.

CONCLUSION

The first element that impelled the military to be highly driven was the ever present threat of Soviet attack from across the nearby frontier. That threat conferred great intensity on military activities throughout Germany. The second element was the obligation to obey orders. That, too, is a universal of military structure and culture. The third element, however, was the institutional practice of evaluation, intended to motivate soldiers in the performance of their duties by rewarding the best with rapid advancement in rank and removing the worst from time to time. The human response to the practice of evaluation included a natural personal interest in preserving a career for oneself and one's family, which depended on one's evaluation. This interest, however, sometimes stood at cross-purposes with the requirements of the real mission and the needs of the troops. The particular way that leadership evaluation was structured led to self-protective decision making that often resulted in deteriorating morale and efficiency in the units.

The capricious characteristics of leadership, the pressure to respond to rank-related rather than mission-related decisions within the Army, the micromanagement, the distortions of information, and the motivation of prodigious effort were all driven in large part by the structure and current procedures of the Officer Evaluation Report and Enlisted Evaluation Report systems. Hence my emphasis of the chapter's lead quote: "Become his rater and you will be surprised what you can get!" The sentence, however, does not refer simply to being surprised by the quantity of effort extracted from subordinates. The subordinate leader continuously stood in a position of conflict: either act with one's rating in mind and possibly subvert the integrity of the mission and the troops entrusted to one's care, or act with the mission in mind and possibly subvert the welfare of one's career and family. Decisions that resulted from that dilemma were unpredictable and therefore often surprising.

Inevitably, demand overload and the unpredictable behavior of the unit affected the family by disrupting family time and the family's ability to plan maintenance activities. Other Army practices, such as the frequency of alerts and the way duty rosters were maintained, likewise disrupted family process. To that subject I now turn.

NOTES

1. To "frag" is to use a fragmentation grenade or other military ordinance to kill, wound, or intimidate another soldier, usually a superior.

2. Cavalry units are heavily armored, highly mobile military organizations whose mission, at that time in the Federal Republic of Germany, was to delay and disrupt any initial combat penetration by Warsaw Pact forces. Under ideal circumstances, they would operate behind the enemy lines, some ten to thirty kilometers beyond the forward edge of the battle area. One heard estimates that in the event of an assault, some 80 percent of the cavalry would be lost in the first hours. With talk such as this floating around, it was not surprising that the cavalry had a reputation for being a rough, devil-may-care bunch.

3. Don Oberdorfer, "U.S. Officer Slain by Soviet Guard in East Germany," *Washington Post*, March 26, 1985, A1.

4. I do not have specific dates for these general impressions garnered over the two-year period.

5. United States Army Europe, *Community and Deputy Community Commanders Handbook*, USAREUR Pamphlet 10-20 (Heidelberg, Germany: Headquarters, USAREUR and Seventh Army, APO NY 09403, 1 August 1986): paragraph 125.

6. One reviewer wondered whether "West Germany really would have demanded reduction or withdrawal, thereby leaving themselves vulnerable?" To be sure, Germany was heavily dependent on United States and NATO presence for its security. Nevertheless, the perception of threat from the East was a matter of political debate among Germans, with the younger postwar generations much less fearful than their elders. Senior U.S. leaders seemed loath to test the patience or resolve of either the populace or its democratic leaders on this issue if a challenge could be avoided. In addition, as one retired American officer put it, "Overtaxed commanders didn't want the added hassle of dealing with irate Germans over problems that could have been avoided." And, I would add, they didn't want to deal with their own commanders who might intervene to avoid embarrassment.

7. The title, "deputy DCC," was quite redundant and completely unofficial. While CPT Tall awaited out-proessing for alcohol abuse, he was assigned to assist the DCC of Richberg, and was called the deputy DCC.

8. Faris R. Kirkland, personal communication, 1997.

9. Major General (Ret.) Aubrey Newman, *Follow Me: The Human Element in Leadership* (Novato, CA: Presidio Press, 1981): 119–121, describes parallel episodes. In one case a supply sergeant had saved several kinds of footlocker stands that could be and were, regularly, changed with the whim of each new company commander. In another case, a headquarters conference table oscillated from U-shaped to round and back as each division commander came and went.

5

"Living with the Army": Family and Work in Conflict

The hardest part to cope with is that both family and the Army are fighting for time.
Abigail Taylor
Middleberg Military Community

The married soldier lives his or her life bound by obligations in two fundamentally important institutions: the Army and the family. In the last chapter, we saw how soldiers oriented toward the Army. The soldiers' obligation to obey orders and the perceived urgency of threat allowed military leaders to impose substantial demands on the soldier, resulting in long days and erratic hours. In this chapter we will explore how the soldier orients toward the family.

The cultural concepts of the family embody obligations that enable the family members to make demands on the married soldier. David Schneider directs our attention to the "enduring, diffuse" obligations of kinship and family that make the family a demanding institution, an institution that, like the Army, may be called "greedy."[1] The soldier is placed at the intersection of two conflicting sets of demands, demands that are greedy in the sense that they are open or expandable, and therefore potentially incapable of ever being fully satisfied in the absence of great goodwill and sensitivity on the part of both the military leaders and the family members who each can exert pressure on the soldier. The long days and erratic hours imposed by the Army conflict with the trust and reliability required in the implicit cultural contract of what family means. Those living life enmeshed in both institutions can easily experience intense structural contradiction and interpersonal conflict as well as personal alienation from one institution or the other. Having seen how demand overload is built into the Army system, let us examine the cultural concepts and symbols of the family that enable its members to make demands on the soldier. With both perspectives, we will be able to see how structural contradiction between Army and family plays out.

CONCEPTS AND SYMBOLS OF FAMILY INTEGRITY

Trust and Reliability

For soldiers and their spouses, as with many Americans, the family is a multi-faceted and highly valued institution, central to their understanding of society and life. At its broadest symbolic level, a "family" consists of those who cooperate with and trust each other. It may include anyone brought into a circle of trust. But this broad definition, based on diffuse trust, continuously oscillates within a narrow structural definition that assigns specific legal responsibility for trust and coopera-tion to (ideally) two parents who raise their biological or adopted children to adulthood within a shared residence. I asked SGT Sam McGregory and his wife, Jean, to discuss what "family" meant to them. "As far as me and my wife and kids," began Sam, "it is a group of members, loved ones, relatives that all live under the same household." Jean countered, "Not necessarily. Mothers and sisters and brothers—they are part of the family, but they are not able to be with us." "Family is elite people that share common thoughts, morals, and scruples," Sam concluded. To the same question about what family meant, a woman sitting in the medical clinic at General Barracks replied, "Family means a mother, father, chil-dren. Home, a place to go. Togetherness, happiness, religion, school." She paused and thought. "Did I say 'togetherness'?" Her response encodes the essen-tial functions of the family: it must socialize children (symbolized by "school," the pure teaching organization) and convey to them the ethical propositions of the culture (as symbolized by religion). "Togetherness" connoted the general notion of solidarity and protectiveness, as well as the specific household responsibility of co-residence, a protective place to raise children. "Togetherness" likewise signi-fied the family obligation of spending time together.

Another woman said family was "the closest group of people in our society. And I hope that is the closest. . . . It doesn't always happen, but it should. My background is different: I'm from Korea. Family is all my brothers and sisters. But here, it is husband, wife, and kids. But again, people here say, 'I miss the family at home,' or 'I want to be with my family in the States.'"

A couple without children is in a development stage, and sometimes its mem-bers feel ambiguous about their family status.

> "Family for me is Terry," said CPL Hank Walsh. "When somebody asks me about my family, that is who I think they are talking about. Now, my parents, well, I don't have to worry about them and they don't have to worry about me. Now, Terry is who I worry about. If there is a little one running around, that would be my family—who I go home to, who I wake up with, who I see all the time."
>
> "I think of a house, two kids, a dog, and a station wagon," said Terry. "Family is who I don't have to put on makeup for, who I complain to when I don't want to tell anyone else. Because we don't have children, I don't think of us as a family; I think of us as a couple."

One senses here the oscillation between the narrower household trust-plus-respon-sibility definition of family and the broader kin-field-trust definition of extended family.

People also referred to an even more inclusive "Army family" or the "military family." I asked Hilda Paul, an ACS employee and wife of a first lieutenant, to explain what people meant when they used the phrase "the Army family": "There are two definitions: The military family—the mom and dad and the kids. And there are the things that people say when they get up and talk, [saying] 'Well, you are all family.' People that they are stationed with become part of the family."

We see throughout these cultural definitions an extended definition and a narrowed definition of family. The concepts of trust and shared experience domi-nated in the extended definition of family, whereas the concepts of social and economic responsibility were added to, perhaps dominating, in the narrowed household definition. It is this layered combination of trust and responsibility that most people refer to when they speak of "family." In the American model of family, trust is built—because it is repeatedly confirmed—through a history of reliable interactions: coming home to dinner on time, spending time and solving problems together, and, for the married couple, abiding (or appearing to abide) by prohibitions against extramarital sexual activity. A shared perception of the world, based on shared experiences, adds to that fund of trust.

Time Categories and Domain Separation

In the not too distant past, when America was predominantly agricultural, family members cooperated in food production and processing, thereby confirming the family's mutuality of trust, responsibility, and togetherness. As America industrialized and urbanized, however, work shifted to more distant locations owned and managed by others. Work and family came to be seen as separate obligation systems. One or more adults provided for the family by working outside the household. Americans tried to keep the two sources of obligation out of conflict by separating their lives into work and family domains. They allocated specific time for each. Today, ideally, for the middle class, work lasts from 8:00 A.M. to 5:00 P.M. and then is left behind.

These time concepts were well understood by soldiers in the Army, for the vast majority of them were thoroughly American. Thus, a sergeant's favorite phrase, resorted to when a job had dragged on past 5:00 P.M. and the soldiers needed motivation, was "You're on your own time now." Expressions such as "family time," or "your own time," or "my time," in contrast to "work time," "duty time," or "government time" were constantly heard in garrison speech, all expressing the idealized notion of time categories and domain separation.

The expectation of separated family and work domains, with time allocated to each, makes it easier to pattern behavior so as to symbolize trust and commitment to each. When separated and confined in both time and space, work and family cannot interfere with each other. With these generalized cultural concepts in mind, we can better understand the interaction between unit and family as the pressures on the unit escalated under the impact of mission urgency and mission complexity in Germany.

MILITARY ENCROACHMENT ON THE FAMILY DOMAIN

The ethic of mission urgency, the fact of mission complexity, and the open-ended demand system backed by the legal force of the UCMJ frequently consumed the "private time" of the soldiers to a degree that went beyond the requirements of combat readiness. Demands on a married soldier translated into demands and intrusions on the family as well. Coming from American culture, where a citizen's private life is jealously guarded, soldiers and spouses were sometimes offended by their lack of recourse in the face of these demands. Hilda Paul, a civilian ACS employee and wife of a first lieutenant, concluded, "My gut feeling is they worry more about the broken-down tank than the soldier that is operating it."

The American concept of separating "work time" from "family time" came into sharp conflict with the Army's need in Germany for a twenty-four-hour-a-day commitment from the soldier. The constant readiness, the alerts, the field training exercises, the repeated checking on everything possible, the practices of mission-first urgency, and the occasions when one had to recover from the natural breakdown of military complexity in Germany—all these penetrated family time and had serious consequences, even for families such as Abigail Taylor's, which had matured and adjusted to the Army. Thus, her statement in the epigraph that "The hardest part to cope with is that both the family and the Army are fighting for time." She continued, "And the Army is demanding time, and no matter how far you know in advance, it is hard to swallow." It takes time to perform military missions. Yet time is also needed to build and maintain family and marital trust and carry out the tasks of family maintenance. Systematically long or highly erratic work hours, as well as uncertain or unplannable hours, and interruptions by the military mission all sabotaged and corroded a soldier's ability to establish a sense of reliability, responsibility, and trust with his or her family. Such time-domain violations were especially hard on recently married couples struggling to define a relationship, for they had but a short history of accumulated trust to draw on. Unit and family group played tug-of-war for the loyalty of the soldiers and even the spouses, symbolized in time devoted to one or the other institution. This is the essence of Mady Segal's characterization of both military and family as "greedy" institutions.[2] The Army's constant emphasis on the immediate Soviet threat was used to justify any time demands, whether because of a legitimate mission, an instance of mismanagement, or a "stay late so we look dedicated" standing operating procedure (called an "SOP"), and was enforced by the punitive power of the UCMJ. As a result, whether married or not, both officers and enlisted soldiers in Germany had to work long hours that devoured their culturally expected "private" or "family" time.

Long Days

Extreme mission urgency and increased mission complexity gave rise to long workdays. Abigail and her husband, MAJ Matthew Taylor, on the brigade planning staff at Middleberg Barracks, described the pace of the work and its effect on the family. "Matthew is a workaholic," said Abigail. "Everybody here is!" retorted Matthew energetically. "Yes," agreed Abigail. "But twelve hour days aren't hard to deal with; that is normal existence. Fourteen hours can be dealt with. But sixteen? That is too much. Matthew, my husband, is missing out on what we are doing. It is not World War II; there is no need to abuse our people." Most soldiers and spouses shared these feelings. SSG Jane Ziegler, a squad leader serving in a headquarters and headquarters company observed,

> Lots of days we work long hours, not to include field problems. Starting from PT at 6:00 A.M., to anywhere: 8:00 at night . . . not every day . . . some days. I would say two or three times a week, we stay pretty late. It had been proposed by our OIC [Officer in Charge] that the duty hour be standard 'til 8:00 at night. But the NCO thought it would be too much stress. So it is 6:00 P.M. at night. We stay later—not every time—but just when we have to have special projects to be completed before COB [close of business].

For some, the schedule was not so difficult. SSG Jeremy Strong said he got off work daily at "4:30 or 5:00 P.M. It's just like civilian life, a 9:00 to 5:00 job, except we come in at 6:00 [A.M.] to do PT [Physical Training], shower, and then have breakfast, and then go to work at 9:00." Some commanders went to considerable effort to limit and control the length of the duty day. But even the best of the senior officers, such as battalion commander LTC Keith Bateman, admitted that stabilizing the duty day's length was difficult:

> One of my goals was an eight-hour workday. And we have come a long way to accomplishing it. And like any other organization, there are positions that must be filled that require more than the eight-hour workday. That is never going to change. The point that I make to the lieutenants' wives is, the reason that they married them is they were above average, extracurricular, go-getters always willing to put in more time. That is why they married the guy. Now they are upset that he comes home at 5:30 or 6:00 P.M. He will be coming home two hours later than everybody else in civilian life, too. That is what made him, and got him to take the commission. Getting ahead in the Army is no different than getting ahead in civilian organization: you've got to work hard and you've got to work smart.

But there is a substantial difference between civilian and military life. In civilian life one can only be passed over for promotion, or at the worst, fired, if one fails to work the hours one's employer demands. In military life, one can be sent to jail for failure to remain on duty as ordered. Thus, the military, as both Coser and Segal point out—can indeed be forcefully "greedy."[3]

Unpredictable Hours

Long work hours could be tolerated, or tolerated better at any rate, if they were predictable. At least the family members knew what to expect. Unfortunately, in Germany, mission complexity increased the probability of errors in the workplace. The time spent correcting those errors translated directly into erratic hours.

Thus, urgency and complexity at work disrupted family schedules and created unpredictable family hours at home. The concept of urgency justified duty assignments announced late, whether because of breakdowns, human mistakes, quantity of work, or just bad planning. With the threat so imminent, combat equipment had to be kept ready. Any inoperative combat equipment was "deadlined," meaning that it had to be repaired and returned to combat-ready status as soon as the necessary part arrived. Mechanics, consequently, had especially erratic schedules. SGT Adam Norton observed, "You never know exactly what time you get through." His wife, Barbara, elaborated: "He is a mechanic: he has to stay 'til it is fixed." Keeping combat vehicles operable was clearly an important goal if one always had to be ready to fight.

Smaller "distractors" also made the day unpredictable. Said SP4 Jeff Atwood, "You cannot tell someone what your day will be like. Nothing is really definite. There is not an organized schedule." SP4 Betty Atwood, developed the idea further: "Not one day will you ever be doing the job you are supposed to [i.e., trained to do]. Because you are a private, you are subject to every detail: mowing lawns, picking up, painting—everything. Not a day [goes by] in Delta [company] without a detail." Such "details" combined with one's real mission, the urgency of perceived threat, the need for training, and the insistence on constant readiness to generate a nearly overwhelming flow of demands. Soldiers at all levels tried to compensate by extra, sometimes herculean, effort. MAJ Taylor:

> In the States, the shorter windows of field duty are easier on the family. Soldiers in the U.S. are not missing the weekends, and holidays. Here [in Germany], because the training resources are critical, we are blind to holidays. Christmas and Thanksgiving are the only holidays we observe as sacrosanct. The Army tries to compensate by giving training holidays. And yet the workload is backed up, and you just work through [the training holidays].

So the Army system became blind to all but its own demands. Yet married soldiers lived their lives in a larger ecology of responsibilities, one of which was family.

Inability to Make Family Plans

These kinds of insistent, unpredictable demands immobilized the family's planning process. Because the Army "just worked through," household plans took second place. Barbara Norton lamented, "If we want to plan something for the weekend, you have to check if he has duty, first. That kills your plans." The McCormicks began by discussing their lack of time together, but settled on an even more stressful issue: the unpredictability of the Army's demands that disrupted their plans. Said Gretchen McCormick,

> He was in the field two weeks. Got home Tuesday. Comes home and the phone rings all night long about an aircraft breaking down. They got a three-day weekend coming up. But he has to work tomorrow. Yesterday they said he didn't have to work tomorrow. Today they said he has to work tomorrow. So you can't plan anything. I call him and ask when he is coming. If he says, "Yes," I fix something that can't wait. If he says, "I don't know," I fix something that can wait. If he says, "No," I fix something to feed the kids and then later feed him.

CW3 Bill McCormick amplified his wife's lead: "You can't plan: no way. Just time together is all I want. I've learned in ten years of marriage, you don't plan nothing until five minutes prior. You might think you are planning, and then 'Well, let's play it by ear.' Or my wife says, 'Well, let's go buy a car on Sunday,' and I say, 'If I don't have to work.'" The complaint was quite general. According to CPL Edgar Granville, "Seems like every time you got something planned for your family members, they gotta go to the field." "You don't know ahead. It just up and comes," his wife, Anne, fumed. "They are always going Easter or Thanksgiving. Never have no family time," Edgar concluded.

Training and testing alerts often caused unpredictable circumstances. According to SGT Adam Norton, "If you make plans to do something on the weekend, an alert comes up or you have duty, or you go in the field. Any plans to be made have to be canceled." Note the use of future tense, to signify the tentativeness of "any plans *to be* made," followed by the definite, "*have to be* canceled." One can't even plan to plan. Only Christmas Day could be counted on, and even that isn't firm until the week before, because, as Adam explained without emotion, the "duty schedule has to come first." The same theme was expressed by the Walsh family: "Nine to five—Monday through Friday—I'm saying that is how I think she wants it to be," suggested Hank. "I agree," responded Terry. "I could deal with him going away and staying away better than I could with the bouncing around that they do. Every time we plan something, he has duty. On Valentine's weekend, we had planned to go skiing. Friday afternoon, he finds he has duty Sunday." Being "bounced around" was often expressed as being "jerked around," or as someone "jerking my chain," a clear recognition of doglike submission to control by others, particularly those in the "chain of command." One heard complaints of being "jerked through a knothole," a graphic metaphor of a requirement to snap to some task in spite of an impossible set of constraints. The intrusions caused by time unpredictability irritated many marriages and fundamentally corroded others.

Resentment of Waste

Soldiers and spouses saw many of the demands as unwarranted theft of their "family time" unless the task was seen to be clearly essential to a legitimate mission. Shirley Lincoln, a former company commander, had resigned her commission to bear and raise a child. She reflected on her military husband's intense work schedule, he being a major, and declared in disgust, "I see my husband working sixteen or eighteen hours a day, six days a week—not because he is incompetent, but because that seems to be an accepted pattern of behavior here. . . . As long as my husband is having fun, I don't mind. But if it is just being there to be there, then it is on my time. And I hate that." This quote suggests that long hours were tolerable if they were used legitimately for authentic missions. If not, the hours were resented as a waste of personal time.

Field exercises generated even longer periods of time away from home. SSG Don Damon moaned, "There is a lot of stress here, especially in the combat units, due to the field problems. We just went through one that was forty-five days long. Just got back for a week and then in the field again." The wife of an enlisted soldier aggressively blurted while we waited for the military shuttlebus, "Put this in your typewriter: if we [the wives] are supposed to be the morale builder, why don't they give us time to be with our families!" Although younger couples complained at having to deal with the length of field exercises, older couples expressed little difficulty with field duty, considering it an opportunity to remind themselves how much they really depended on each other. The common concern, however, was that significant blocks of time in the field were wasted, making the time apart unnecessarily long and, sometimes, a worthless sacrifice.

Persistent long hours or wasted hours rubbed against the overarching cultural assumptions. Waste created antagonism toward the Army and anger within the family. Personal time was a gift of self-sacrifice given to the Army. If the gift was squandered or wasted, that, in their view, made soldiers and spouses justifiably angry. Thus, SFC Mike Koford reflected,

> The Army itself destroys lots of families. We go to the field sometimes thirty, forty-five days. Then you come out for a week. That is too long. It is inconsiderate. All they think of is train, train, train. Sure, training is important. But you need to consider the family. Soldiers don't need to be in the field that long. *Goddamn—that is too long*—forty-five days and thirty days! It's not good for the marriage life, or for the family, or for the kids.

Anger and Jealousy in the Family

Because unit leaders could compel performance and threaten the economic livelihood of the family by fining, reducing in rank, or dismissing a soldier, members of the community felt the family took second place to the Army. As time allocation symbolized the relative empowerment of institutions, the fact that the soldier's duty schedule had to come first blatantly subordinated family to work in a way that most Americans were not used to. In civilian jobs, regular hours enable the separation of the time domains of work and family and allow most Americans to maintain the fiction that job and family are equal priorities. Moreover, because the physical locations of work and family are usually separated, the family is not continuously reminded of its subordination, as it was in the Army in Germany. There, the irregularity of demands and the consequent intrusions on the family domain unmasked the illusion of parity between family and work. According to

Mr. Ken Anderson, Middleberg's director of personnel and community activities, "If the soldier does what he has to do, the family fades out of the picture: they go back to the States." More forcefully, Linda Sims fumed, "My husband is having a problem trying not to bring his work home. When shit starts rolling downhill, the family and the kids are at the bottom of the hill."

Given the high cultural value and moral force of family and marriage, family subordination to the Army generated much resentment. Pam Hill expressed her resentment this way: "We have planned to go to the zoo for three weekends in a row. And he has had duty each time. Last weekend I said, 'Let's go before they call you.' The other night they called him at 12:00 midnight, and he had to work to 5:30 the next night." She concluded angrily, "I'm his wife: then I was pregnant, and now we have a small baby."

As in many family systems around the world, the birth of a child underlines and legitimizes the rights of the spouse to increasingly separate his or her partner from the domination of other, wider, fields of obligation.[4] Thus, SP4 Betty Atwood complained, "I understand that guard duty is necessary. But they mess with you with your time off. Seems like whenever you have time off, they find something that has to be done on your time off." Her husband, SP4 Jeff Atwood, chimed in with an immediate example. "After twenty-four hours on duty [they were then supposed to have a day off but], I have to come in and give a PT class in the after-noon." SGT Scott Felsted recited his division's motto, "No mission too difficult, no sacrifice too great: duty first," and concluded, "That means my family can kiss my ass."

The resentment ultimately took one of several forms. Most commonly it emerged in anger and jealousy within the family. Spouses and children fought to preserve a portion of the expected internal loyalty symbolized by time together and reliability. The spouse's anger was often displaced from the Army, the real compe-tition, and directed at the service member, the pin in the hinge bringing Army and family together. Susan McDonald reflected: "He comes home from work late and just starts eating, and he has to leave. Sometimes just two or three hours at home, and yet he has to be there the whole next day. . . . We never could make some plans. . . . Weekends, most of the time, were worse—just crazy sometimes. And I know it was not his fault, but even if you know it is not his fault, you get mad, because you're angry." Gretchen McCormick dealt with her feelings regarding the Army by similarly displacing her anger from the Army to her pilot husband, a chief warrant officer: "I got one real close friend, and I let steam off [with her] and then I feel better, usually." "What causes the most steam?" I explored. She replied, "I think not seeing him as much as I want to see him. I get so mad. I usually take it out on my husband, and that is not fair; he is only doing his job."

All these factors were especially hard on young families. Jeff and Betty Atwood, married just four months, were experiencing severe marital stress. Said Jeff, "Like today: I was supposed to get off at 1500 [i.e., 3:00 P.M.] for 'Duty First Time.' At 2:15 [P.M.] I found I would have to do something that would take two to three hours." Betty added, "And the Army feels that you're a soldier twenty-four hours a day." In quick succession Jeff escalated a step further: "And the Army feels that they don't care about the family—you got to deal with that. But they don't think about the fact that you might be in trouble with your wife over coming home late." The problem was that the Army's demands made it difficult or impossible to communicate the simplest symbol of familial trust and reliability—predictable time together. The Army thereby undermined the family, but the family sometimes cannibalized itself by not directing the resulting anger outward.

Mutual resentments built up as the spouse tried to claim her (or sometimes his) cultural sense of marital rights. For example, I asked 1LT Larry McDugal, an acting company commander, and his wife, Lani, what they fought about. "Maybe money," she said. "That is a contention in everybody's life," Larry responded. Lani then offered another source of contention: "Or sex—my being pregnant." The mild tone of voice and mutual laughter indicated that these were not the most serious issues of distress. Then Larry launched resolutely, "The Army just consumes so much time. You got to get up at that hour, 5:30. You don't know when you're coming home. You gotta do your fatherly things—pay the bills. We make plans and then—boom—something happens at work, and you're not home 'til 8:00." Lani supported this line of argument energetically. "It took me a long time to figure it out. He finally had to shake me," she said as she cupped her hands as though facing and holding herself at shoulder height, shaking vigorously. "'I have no control,' he said. That causes stress at home, if you make little family plans, even to go to a movie. Yet the poor guy doesn't have any control. Yet he gets jumped on by the wife. He is the bad guy." The McDugal family had made an accommodation: they didn't fight with each other as often. Having transferred their resentment from each other back to the Army, they had decided to get out of the Army, and thereby came to peace with themselves. The McDugals illustrated a second way soldiers and family members dealt with resentment toward the Army rather than fight with each other: they directed as much resentment as possible back onto the Army. Though there were other dissatisfactions, the McDugals attributed much of their resentment toward the Army to its deleterious impact on their family.

SFC Brian Marshall felt angered by the conflict between work and family. "It is aggravating. If I'd known seven years ago the hours I put in, I think that I'd have tried to start another career in the civilian world. Being in the Army, there is not enough time with the family. If you're not dedicated to work, your job performance will suffer. If you're dedicated, you gotta work late. You're in training in the day. Then you gotta file and do paperwork [at night]." 1SG Stewart Powell showed me the conflict visually: "Here is my calendar," he said, thumping the month spread out before us. "As a father of a family I ought to have something on here for my family. This is a typical first sergeant's calendar: it is all about things for my soldiers. But I should have listed time to swim with my family." The complaint was quite frequent, here voiced by a SFC Mike Koford:

The Army says they are family oriented. And there is no way that they are, or it [Army and family] would be equal across the board. . . . They can't be family oriented with the hours that we put in. And during POMS [postoperation maintenance services—the big cleanup after a field exercise], they keep us from oh-dark-thirty [before dawn] to twenty hundred hours [2000 hours = 8:00 P.M.]. In the Army, you're not guaranteed every weekend off. There is a CQ [charge of quarters] and a runner [required on duty]. When I'm off, I want to relax. . . . I get home, and all the stress rushes out of you and you don't feel like doing anything. But I've been getting out of that; you just gotta start doing something—a game, or play catch with my kid. Before, all I wanted was to eat and go to sleep. Being in the Army and being dedicated to it—with the time [you put in]—you take away from the time that you owe your kids. When I retire, my kids will be nineteen and seventeen. All this time, I couldn't go to the PTA [Parent Teacher Association], or the basketball games, because of the long hours in the military. We have [some] jobs—finance and clerical—where they have a set program. But our schedule may say we get off at 1600, and it may be 2000 due to any change that may come down from the company commander or higher. . . . It makes it very rough to plan. I hate looking in my boy's eyes, and tell him "No, I can't watch a school play." The kids don't understand that you have to do it, not that you don't want to do it. Anybody that has people that they love wants to go watch them so they can go brag off of what they do. Kids think that you don't want to see them.

In other words, the Army's insistent consumption of all available time corrupted and destroyed the quality of family relations that soldiers sought.

Like time allocation and reliability in meeting a family schedule, sexual fidelity symbolized family trust. Conversely, infidelity—or the intimation of it in gossip—powerfully symbolized the breakdown of trust within couples and throughout a community. Two specialists, Mike Thompson and Stan Mercer, ruminated, Mike first:

"I'm a mechanic. We can be working up to 9:00 at night. Depends on your leaders." Stan gave details: "Depends on where you are at. At [he named a U.S. post], the mechanics didn't work. Here, they really work."

"It is a serious strain on the wives," Mike cut back in. "Everywhere you go you hear of the wives cheating on the husbands."

Stan implied that male soldiers also suffered. "I'm gone at night a lot. And I'm still a newlywed."

Rumors or fears of sexual immorality serve as a symbolic index of widespread breakdown of family trust. As family trust deteriorated, the quality of life for the whole family deteriorated and began to affect the soldier's morale and performance on the job. Unit leadership often responded to the resultant lowered efficiency by requiring the soldiers to stay late even more often. Family and unit began a competitive spiral of mutual deterioration, the death knell of morale in both.

FAMILY RESPONSES

Accommodation

If the soldier consistently chose to place the military first, then the spouse had essentially one of two choices: adapt or resist. Some spouses responded to their soldier's erratic work requirements by becoming highly independent in conducting family affairs, by volunteering in the community, or by working. Whether she (or occasionally he) worked or not, such spouses recognized that "military first" for the soldier meant "family first" for the spouse. The most successful of these spouses planned and executed family activities, solved family problems, or inter- acted with community service suppliers without regard to the soldier's presence or absence. A service provider who gave any version of "I can't provide the service without your military spouse's signature" was likely to get severely rebuked. Other spouses, by contrast, became extremely passive and dependent, allowing the soldier, usually a male, to dictate the flow of family decisions according to the gyrations of the unit. In either case, accommodation required that the spouse comply with the schedule of the Army and not press her (or his) legitimate time demands. As CPT Bill Olsen expressed it, "My wife is a real blessing. It took her a while to do it. She understands. If I call her up at 4:30 and say, 'Honey, I don't know when I'll be home,' she understands." Likewise, SFC James Frazier said, "I told my wife a long time ago, 'I'll get there when I get there. Don't worry about it.' They get used to it." The phrases "it took her a while to do it" and "they get used to it," however, imply that the accommodation was neither quick nor easy.

Family Violence

Although the quotes in this book suggest that contradictions between military and family life led to anger and frustration within the family, I have no direct evidence regarding any linkage with family violence. The Atwoods briefly entered a cycle of violence, physically hitting each other, in part aggravated by the tensions of Army life. Other cases of violence, if there were any, were hidden from me because they were actionable under the UCMJ. Indeed, I always told couples not to tell me about violence toward children, as I had no way to shield them from a legal and ethical requirement to protect minors.

Divorce

If the spouse did not adapt to the soldier consistently placing the military first, then endemic conflict often developed. Some families tolerated conflict, but others opted for divorce or separation. In this regard, CPL Winston Green complained, "We won't have a family if it keeps this up. Twenty percent of the families I know are getting a divorce. Most are alcoholics, now. It was not like that at the start." There was indeed considerable pressure on marriages. Though the divorce rate among Army families was said to be lower in Germany than in the United States, such statements are quite difficult to interpret because one could not in fact termi- nate an American marriage while in Germany. Separations, the spouse returning early to the States, became the de facto substitute, though not counting as divorce.

Leaving the Army

Finally, too much unit pressure on a family could result in the soldier and spouse deciding to get out of the service rather than split up. MAJ Quintin Scott, the regional chaplain, explained:

> The problem is that we are over here to do a job, to get the people trained. From that standpoint, long hours makes sense. But they [leaders] know if they are to retain the troops they [the troops] have to have a certain amount of contentment. And they [leaders] strive to accommodate that. But in light of the mission, sometimes families do suffer. It is not by design; it is circumstances. Everybody's priority has got to be the mission. That is why if the Army really had its druthers, they would have an unmarried military. But that is simply not possible. If they are going to continue to have married soldiers, they are going to have to try to keep the training schedule in the bounds. There is going to have to be sufficient breathing room to be able to have a family. If it is lost in the mission shuffle, or in the overuse of training, we are going to lose a lot of good soldiers.

Because the Army's demands easily intensified beyond reason, those who said they placed family first often spoke of their intent to get out of the Army.

CONCLUSION

The cross-cutting military and family demands on a soldier's time made the soldier a pivot of structural contradiction and threw family and unit into competition for the time that symbolized commitment and reliability. Because the family was a primary, culturally valued institution at the same time that the Army in Germany was thought to be on an essential, dangerous mission of defense, the conflict was severe and endemic. If mismanaged, as it often and easily was, this conflict resulted in structurally persistent unhappiness in both the family and the unit, a major component in the dynamics of discontent that soldiers described by saying a unit had "low morale" or "morale problems." Given ordinary leadership—leadership that attended to the pressures of the job and neglected family issues—the nature of military life easily engendered soldier and family alienation as it crashed blindly against the underlying bedrock American values of sexual need, marital unity, and family integrity. Sometimes the Army 'won,' with divorce, family passivity, and soldier alienation the result. Sometimes the Army lost, with the soldier leaving the Army to protect the family. Win or lose, Army leaders recognized the difficulties that were imposed on soldiers of all ranks and tried to provide them, their spouses, and families with a compensatory support system that I describe and analyze in the next two chapters.

NOTES

1. See Lewis A. Coser, *Greedy Institutions: Patterns of Undivided Commitment* (New York: The Free Press, 1974), for the origin of the concept, including a brief reference and recognition of an army's "greedy" nature within his definitions. See also Mady Wechsler Segal, "The Military and the Family as Greedy Institutions," *Armed Forces and Society* 13, no. 1 (1986): 9–38, a fine paper detailing the specifics of the U.S. Army's and the military family's competitive "greediness" for the time and devotion of its respective participants. David M. Schneider, *American Kinship: A Cultural Account* (Englewood Cliffs, NJ: Prentice-Hall, 1968): 61.

2. Mady Wechsler Segal, "The Military and the Family as Greedy Institutions," *Armed Forces and Society* 13, no. 1 (1986): 9–38.

3. Coser, *Greedy Institutions*; Segal, "Military and the Family."

4. J. K. Campbell, *Honour, Family, and Patronage* (New York: Oxford University Press, 1964).

6

"The Army Takes Care of Its Own": Breach of the Support for Sacrifice Contract

Take care of me. Take care of my family, especially while I'm gone. That is my Army. Here [in Germany], personal life is difficult and they say, "I'm getting out 'cause the Army doesn't take care of me."

CW3 Don Brenton
Middleberg Military Community

Soldiers and military spouses in Germany believed that the disruptions and restrictions of military life merited support or recompense for the families. The soldiers gave up liberties, exposed themselves to mortal risk, and locked themselves into erratic, family-disrupting schedules driven by "mission first" logic. Military leaders and community service employees understood and agreed, sharing an implicit contract that soldiers and their families should be provided with supporting services to help them better sustain the stressful peculiarities of military life. Vernez and Zellman, referring to the 1980s, suggest "the Army's efforts on behalf of families are based partly on a philosophy of 'partnership' or 'reciprocity.'" The authors elaborate, "The military member pledges strong commitment and a willingness to give her or his life, if necessary, to meet the army's mission; in exchange, the army assumes an obligation toward members and their families to provide those benefits and services that insure them a reasonable quality of life."[1] In short, as leaders and soldiers frequently put it, "The Army takes care of its own." I call this mutual belief in reciprocal services the support for sacrifice contract, though the phrase is not used by the soldiers.

THE SUPPORT FOR SACRIFICE CONTRACT

The idea that hard work deserves good treatment is a fact of American culture, today just as in the past and in the Army just as in American civilian life. All agreed that Army families worked hard—indeed, sacrificed—for the Army.

"There are some guys here whose wives and children went back to the States because it's too expensive," said SP4 Betty Atwood. "Or they're here [alone] for just one and a half or two years. One of the NCOs in our unit might not see his kid—just born—for another year. I don't know how they can deal with that, and the pressures from the Army."

"My job is not hard," suggested her husband, also a Specialist 4, " but the Army . . . demands more of your time than most civilian jobs. And most people have had the jobs that demand less, and they come in the Army and are used to the other. That also goes for barracks personnel that are here single. And these are the problems that they are dealing with: They are in a post that is in a city that is nowhere near like back home. They walk in there after a hard day, and being crowded into a small room with two or three people that you may not like."

"And," Betty couldn't resist adding, "you don't have any choice who you are going to live with."

The passages speak of the sacrifice of major cultural values—personal time, personal space, privacy, flexibility, personal choice, and income—all for the benefit of the Army.

Can the perceived sacrifice continue if it is exclusively one way? CPT Glen Cooper of Richberg Kaserne observed: "The lower enlisted here really gets the shaft. Anything that happens, they [leaders] say, 'Let's go to Richberg Kaserne and take all of their people and do it.'" His complaint stems from the fact that during any rise of tensions—for example, the bombing of Libya on April 15, 1986—soldiers from Richberg Kaserne were "detailed" (i.e., ordered) to provide security patrols on the other installations and housing areas twenty-four hours a day because Richberg had the only infantry unit in the region. Cooper went on, "But the barracks at Richberg Kaserne are falling apart. Yet the funding goes to fix the officers' club at Central Barracks. I don't understand the priorities—or the funding constraints." Given the sacrifices, the supports seemed misdirected. CPT Cooper was not alone in his concern. At all ranks, soldiers lamented the fact that those making the greatest sacrifice often received the least support. As SFC Mike Koford of Richberg reflected, "We are the people that go to the field thirty or forty-five days. But we don't have no commissary, [and] no gas station. This post is just forgotten. We got raggedy buildings, and no hot water for six months. If you didn't get in the shower first, you got cold water. This post is more or less run down. It should be better, for as much as we go to the field." "It should be better, for as much as we go to the field" is a clear expression of the support for sacrifice contract—one's sacrifice merited reciprocity through better, supportive treatment.

Families, too, suffered from the failure of reciprocity. Said Julia Martinez. "I don't have any complaint with his job—what he is doing in the Army. I married him because I can take care of him, and he wanted to take care of me. . . . Sometimes it is very lonely, and you're alone in the house, but that is a part of being in the Army. We both understand that. Why doesn't the Army understand how we feel, too?" Julia thus lamented the reciprocity that seemed to be missing. She and her husband understood the Army and made sacrifices for the Army's needs. They wondered why the Army didn't repay their sacrifices by providing better for their family needs. SGT Sam McGregory felt similarly: "I look at it as a two-way street: We adapt to the military, and the military needs to adapt to the military families. Not that the single people don't have a rough time. If the military expect[s] the soldiers to give 100 percent of their time, or more, then they have to take care of the soldiers and the families."

Some, like the Walshes, felt a higher salary would help compensate for their sacrifice.

> "Do the Americans in the U.S. realize that their [defense budget] cuts are going to affect the guys that are going to have to go out and face death at every hour? What is this with the Congress denying hazardous duty [pay]? The soldiers are out there facing machine guns, and they are making less than the guy that is fixing your toilet," said Terry, with a touch of bitterness.
>
> "Our concern," Hank added in detail, "is 'Are we going to have enough to pay the electric bill?' I get 850 dollars a month [basic pay] for 'on-call death.' The average American citizen gets two to three times as much as me."

Perhaps not "two or three times as much," especially if one includes housing and other allowances. Still, many in the military community felt they were underpaid, given the hours, the disruptions, and the technological and political sophistication asked of soldiers. Whether in salary or in services, virtually all of the soldiers and their families subscribed to the support for sacrifice contract, and most felt they were sacrificing more than they were being supported.

Community administrators also understood the contract. Here is how Mr. Ken Anderson, Middleberg's director of personnel and community activities, put it:

> The mentality is: You need to take care of your families, but your first responsibility is the mission. . . . If mission is first, somebody has got to suffer. It is going to be the family members. That is why these programs are important. . . . The programs ease that difficulty. That is our responsibility. . . . We have troops that spend an inordinate amount of time in the field, so we have to have things to entertain families.

The administrators knew that the families shared this contract. CPT Darren Cornell, one of Richberg's battalion chaplains, put it thus:

> The command has to be very sensitive about caring while you are in the field. If the battalion commander lets his [company] commanders know that making sure soldiers' families are cared for while they are in the field is important, it gets done. Whoever is in the rear [detachment responsible for personnel left at the installation during maneuvers] contacts the home to make sure all is OK. Is ACS calling? Are platoon sergeants and section leaders checking: "Are your men's families taken care of? Is there money at home for groceries? Is the family car available?" It's got to be a part of the commander's ethic and philosophy. . . . If you value human beings, you take care of the caring program.

The support services personnel in the military community clearly understood that the "caring program" symbolized the way leaders "valued" human beings. Long hours, irregular schedules, spouse away from home, and risk of injury—all these sacrifices on the part of soldiers and families invited reciprocal support from the community. From the point of view of the married soldier—including most officers and senior NCOs—the family system was the primary institution disrupted by the erratic and intrusive nature of the sacrificing the Army required, so family deserved reciprocal support from the Army. SP4 Joe Pile: "If they'd have taken care of the family, I could have put out 100 percent on the job. It is their responsibility to take care of the family." Implicitly, one could not "put out 100 percent" in the Army job without violating important obligations to one's family. Thus, within the Army community, unit and community compliance with the support for sacrifice contract benefited the unit because it enabled soldiers to go beyond the cultural understanding of an ordinary work effort.

Service providers as well as those served believed the supports should redress the specific hardships imposed. For example, soldiers exposed themselves to injury, disease, and death on behalf of the nation; the Army reciprocated, "taking care of its own," by providing soldiers with first-rate medical care in peace or war. Families taken overseas were deprived of access to American goods and services; the military provided a wide range of American products and services in PX (post exchange), commissary, and recreation sites. The military mission disrupted families with irregular schedules; the military community centers provided child care, convenience stores, laundries, post offices, and other services to alleviate the disruptions. Training and missions demanded intense concentration; a wide variety of recreational facilities helped soldiers and family members relax and recharge. Because of the perception that Army life in Germany entailed more difficulty and more sacrifice than in the United States, members of the community believed there was a need for greater support in Germany.

The Army took care of its own primarily so it could be more efficient, successful, and ready for combat. Conversely, if the support system broke down while demands remained high on the married soldier, the impact on the family led to alienation of both family members and soldiers. Whatever the source of the family's difficulties, community beliefs and Army regulations required the institutions to respond. According to 1SG Ray Penrod, of Middleberg, "You can't have a good unit if the families are unhappy." Indeed, Penrod continued, when a good soldier starts to not do so well, "You ask, 'What is going on?' and they say, 'Well, he has problems at home.' It usually increases the problems that he had. And that is when you have to go get outside help. But if there is a good support network, and good chain of concern, it [the support network] is hidden. But if it is not there, it becomes very apparent, through something as drastic as a suicide or infidelity." The fear of suicide was undoubtedly exaggerated, for suicide in the Army is below the national average,[2] but the expression of fear indicated the importance the first sergeant attached to family well-being and hinted at the psychological consequences of inadequacies in the support system.

KEY FAMILY SUPPORT AGENCIES AND THEIR INADEQUACIES

Although the goal of support for sacrifice was plain to everyone, the support part of the contract was not always well implemented. In the remainder of this chapter and in the next, I describe the various support systems available to the soldiers and families, focusing on the "official" services provided formally by Army-associated organizations.

I will also unravel, as far as possible, the causes of the failures in the support systems and the repercussions that failed support systems had throughout the units, the families, and in the community. In Germany, failures in the support for sacrifice contract seemed especially irritating to soldiers and families because they saw themselves constantly sacrificing to maintain combat readiness on a tense frontier, and most perceived no alternatives to the military facilities. Feelings ranged from frustration over the relatively minor irritants, such as erratic commissary and PX supplies and less than useful hours at various facilities, to absolute anger regarding difficulties in the medical and child-care system. To understand their resulting anger and sense of alienation, we must examine briefly the services offered—which soldiers came to view as earned entitlements—and the reasons why the military's offerings so often seemed to fall short of needs. I begin with a significant family issue: child-care services.

Child-Care Services

The child day-care system was an area of major concern to military families. Dual military couples with children or single-parent soldiers with custody had to file an official child-care plan indicating how their young charges would be accommodated if the soldier-parents were called on alert or sent to war. Families in which the civilian spouse worked needed daytime child-care arrangements.[3] And from time to time, all families with children needed brief, temporary, safe baby-sitting.

For a variety of cultural reasons, German society had virtually no child care system that these Americans could use. Far fewer married German women with children worked—there being a "kindergeld" payment for women who did not work—and families often included grandparents under the same roof or living nearby. So care needs were internally covered and a child-care industry hardly existed. Even if German child care were available, language barriers would have thwarted American usage. The American military community had to provide its own child-care system. The system—which also existed on posts in the United States—included a community Child Development Center (CDC) and home-based, certified, Family Child Care (FCC) providers. To these one added informal arrangements, such as occasional baby-sitting traded between families.

Even though each military community or subcommunity had a central day-care facility, called the Child Development Center, or CDC, the demand for child care far outstripped CDC capacity. Working couples who were regular users received priority service and often filled the center, leaving those who needed occasional assistance without access. "A lot of time, day care is full. Unless you use them all of the time, you might as well forget it," declared Emma Warnock.

To handle additional needs, the staff of each community's Child Development Center trained and certified others in the community, usually female spouses living in government quarters, as licensed home-care providers, called Family Child Care providers. FCC care providers charged standardized rates per child equal to those of the Child Development Center. CDC staff monitored the FCC provider sites for hygiene, safety, and child-care technique. Before an FCC provider could begin giving home child care, both the training certification and the home health and safety inspections had to be complete. Unfortunately, the supply of home-based child-care providers was constantly depleted and disrupted because roughly half of the married population that had been in place long enough to become certified rotated out each year. The result was a chronic shortage of home-care providers and a good deal of tension centering around the availability and price of the much-needed child care.

Some families tried to find more economical solutions to their child-care needs by going outside the CDC and FCC systems. One dual military family brought a widowed parent to Germany and paid her $500 per month, plus room and board, for child care and housework. This worked well, given the family rule that when either military parent walked through the door at the end of the duty day, the grandmother was released from duty. During the parents' duty day, the grandmother cooked, shopped, cared for the kids, cleaned the house, ran errands, and prepared supper. The parents were of course satisfied because they had trusted help. Some families hired English-speaking Filipino women, almost always of illegal work status, to live with them. In one case, the Filipino nanny had a master's degree in accounting and helped the kids with mathematics and other homework. Halfway through my field observations, however, the German government asked the American military to police themselves strictly regarding illegal aliens. This forced the Americans to stop using Filipino help or risk paying substantial fines and back social security taxes to the German government. One couple brought an English nanny into their home. The practice was completely legal, since the woman had work rights within the European Common Market. But her repeated use of the family phone for calls to England raised the monthly phone bill to more than $1,000, and the arrangement ended quickly.

Often, couples tried to arrange their own informal baby-sitting with trusted friends, paying them for their regular work. Post regulations, however, required that paid child care be provided by the CDC or by a licensed FCC person. Thus, personal arrangements stood in breach of post regulations. Those living in on-post housing feared that neighbors might inform post authorities of their irregular child-care arrangements, which could result in a reprimand. With an inadequate authorized child-care system and the risk of great expense or possible career damage for seeking an unauthorized form of child care, couples with younger children experienced great frustration.

Beyond the critical shortage of supply, soldiers and spouses often complained about the limited hours of operation at the day-care center. As Frank and Meg

Barnes explained, the CDC hours were not compatible with the needs of working couples. The center opened at 7:00 A.M., yet SSG Frank Barnes had to report to PT (physical fitness training) at 6:30 A.M. and his wife had to leave their quarters by 6:30 A.M. just to get to Central Barracks on time for her job. Other couples faced similar scheduling difficulties. Thus, any morning, "You can come and the kids will be sitting in the car," waiting in the predawn darkness for the CDC to open, while a parent did PT in a nearby field. To SSG Barnes, "They have banker's hours. They don't care about the soldier." Meg confirmed, "What about those spouses that come to work early to stock the PX? . . . They [Army leaders] don't care." For Frank, the result was that "nine times out of ten, I have to be late for formation."

If dropping a child off at the CDC posed problems, picking the child up could be treacherous. The CDC closed promptly at 6:00 P.M. If Frank happened to be kept late at work or was sent to the field, Meg made the pickup: "She gets off work at 5:00. Normally she gets home [one minute from the CDC] at 5:40. But if there's traffic, and she arrives after 6:00, she will not find my daughter at the day-care center." "After 6:00," Meg jumped in, "I have to pick her up at the MP station; and they charge ten dollars per fifteen minutes for late [pickup]." The MPs not only levied the fine, they were required to report late pickups to the soldier's commander. Several such reports could be construed as evidence of child neglect and might harm a soldier's career evaluation, even if the soldier's spouse had been designated to make the pickup. The difficulties were worse yet for the single-parent soldier.

Restricted freedom of choice created additional problems for the child-care user. Donna Chalmers, a spouse, explained the implications of the child-care shortage: "If we were in the States, I'd not be running myself ragged trying to find a baby-sitter. I'd have so many facets, so many outlets." Most saw military control and lack of alternate opportunities in Germany as impediments to the operation of market forces that provided greater convenience and competitive pricing in the United States. At a party in Newberg, Cindy Ashton, a former FCC child-care provider who found other employment and therefore needed child-care assistance herself, knew the difficulties from both perspectives.

> They have so many strict rules [for home care] that they don't even follow them-
> selves in the child-care facilities. . . . We were supposed to have seventy FCC
> homes, and we only have thirty. So they had parents leaving children alone. If
> you're a single parent [soldier] and you can't find someone to take care of your
> children, they will chapter you out [administrative elimination from the service].
> And yet if you use someone not certified, they get mad. [Angrily, almost shouting:]
> If I want to leave my kids with a friend, someone that I trust, that should be my
> choice. I shouldn't have to go to someone in the community and ask who I can and
> who I can't use.

The requirements, training, fees, and hours of availability existed to protect both the government and the care providers from liability and to reduce the possibility of mistreated children. Still, from the family point of view, the Army's requirements seemed to undermine family efforts to create a trusted, efficient, flexible, choice-based child-care system that had enough qualified baby-sitters to serve the families in need.

From the soldier's point of view, inadequate child care constituted a clear breach of the support for sacrifice contract. Soldier-parents were required to report to work early and had long, erratic workdays. At the junior ranks, spouses, too, had to work for economic reasons, but treaty law required them to work only on American bases, and the paucity of on-base jobs at a combat-oriented installation meant that many commuted to administrative centers at distant installations. According to the culturally understood contract, child-care services existed to facilitate and ease the demanding erratic life schedule of the military family. But the CDC's rigid policies and inappropriate hours added to family aggravation and frustration rather than providing relief. Moreover, the child-care service, though intended to help the military career, potentially put the career at risk if the erratic demands of the military or chance intervention of traffic or work demands blocked both parents—or the single parent—from a timely pickup. What was provided was insufficient and therefore "dangerous" to use for home-care providers were scarce and constantly changing yet regulatory prohibitions made the use of anything else a risk to career. Soldiers and spouses felt defrauded by the double bind.

Housing

Single soldiers often lived in poorly maintained, shabby barracks captured in World War II. By contrast, the married family apartments on-post were generally well maintained and spacious.[4] Government quarters for married personnel usually had a spacious living room that joined with a dining area, a small kitchen with the expected conveniences (refrigerator, stove, oven, dishwasher, disposal), and one to four bedrooms, depending on family size. Most had a basement or top floor storage room and access to a common laundry room and bicycle storage in the basement. Having described the family housing area and the layout of the government quarters complexes, I will simply note the shortcomings.

Despite generally favorable circumstances, married soldiers and spouses had several housing complaints. First, the married soldiers arrived and were forced by the waiting lists based on seniority to seek residence away from the post in local German housing. As officers and enlisted would occasionally point out, the lower-ranked families were the least able to afford a car and rarely had a second car for the spouse. For some, economy housing costs exceeded their overseas housing supplement. Finally, one heard complaints about rental deposits, the distance from the post, and inability to access on-post entertainment. In essence, the complaints regarding housing took the same form as complaints regarding child care: high price, inadequate supply, lack of choice, and government control. The breach of contract and associated alienation were felt because the family was "sent by the Army" to Germany and then forced by the housing shortage to live inconveniently "on the economy" during a demanding forward deployment. In Chapter 10, "Living in a Fishbowl," we will return to the nature of life in military housing to see how the housing the Army provided created risks to one's career and family, engendering a yet more corrosive form of alienation from the Army.

The Supply Systems: PX, Commissary, and Shopettes

As noted earlier, the Army provided an impressive array of stores that supplied the needs of its soldiers, family members, and civilian employees living in Germany. Occasionally, a large-population community such as Richberg had few facilities, its soldiers and families being expected to use central facilities at nearby (twenty minutes by car or shuttle bus) General Barracks or more distant Central Barracks. These latter commercial centers served several communities and subcommunities and offered a comparatively large commissary, a large PX, and a plethora of specialty shops selling such commodities as sporting goods, Oriental rugs, German souvenirs, audio and video equipment in great variety, flowers, and a number of services from fast food to haircuts.

Soldiers at Richberg complained that they had to pay more for essential food items than soldiers on other posts having access to a commissary. CPT Glen Cooper groused, "How come I go to General Barracks and get a half gallon of milk for 52 cents [at the commissary], and here in Richberg Kaserne it costs $1.29 at the PX?" The differential occurred because the military consumer supply system operated through two entirely different command channels. The commissary system focused primarily on food-type items—standard American groceries as well as a range of European "gourmet" foods. By law, the commissary subsidized food, selling at lower-than-Stateside prices. The second supply system, the Army Air Force Exchange System (AAFES), ran the PXs that provided virtually all the department-store goods: clothes, bedding, household utensils, some furnishings, tools, auto supplies, audio and camera equipment, decorations, basic German memorabilia, and so on. AAFES also operated the "shopette" convenience stores. By law, the PX had to make a profit and be priced to compete with, but not undercut, volume commercial enterprises in the United States. Thus, the military shopettes matched convenience store markups in the United States.

Some communities, including Richberg, did not have a commissary. But every installation did have at least a small AAFES combination PX/Shopette. The Richberg PX, for instance, also functioned as an AAFES convenience store by selling basic food items: milk, lunch meats, snack foods, beer, and soft drinks. However, the unsubsidized prices did not compare favorably to prices available at the commissary at General Barracks. Single soldiers without a car were at a disadvantage, and married families and single troops resented having to go so far to obtain the better prices.

Military personnel and families also felt they suffered from a lack of choice in products. They complained about the Army's "monopoly" in Germany. For American goods such as plastic-wrapped sliced bread, peanut butter, 120-volt toasters, and American clothing styles, the military supply system was the only source. Because many families tried to preserve their American lifestyle, and because food and clothing products were important symbols of cultural identity, the

Army monopoly on goods symbolizing "Americanness" could be irritating. For example, a staff sergeant that I happened to sit with at an awards ceremony observed: "There are things missing at the commissary. Last year we had a hard time getting shoe polish on this post." Indeed, one or another specific item was frequently out of stock. Transoceanic supply lines, human error, bureaucratic organization, and such imponderables as the bankruptcy of an ocean shipper helped explain the occasional shortages. Nevertheless, as one woman put it, if one's child could not live without Skippy peanut butter, or if one's best recipe for the officer's dinner called for broccoli and broccoli was not available this week, the unpredictability could be frustrating. If the missing item was imperative—in the Army, shoe polish is an essential—then the shortage could be quite distressing.

Because even the largest PX was barely the equivalent of a medium-sized Kmart or Wal-Mart in the United States, it was obviously impossible to cater to all the needs of the Army's diverse population. Some lower-ranking soldiers or their spouses felt the PX selection was a bit upscale, having mostly middle-quality, middle-priced goods, with a few high-end items for a touch of class. Jane Cooper, even with a captain's salary in the household, felt the problem: "They don't carry items there that people at Richberg can afford. They don't offer a wide enough variety in good buys, compared to [the fact that they have] lots of designer clothes. They say they are accommodating everybody, [but] I don't think that they are." Commissary and PX problems may seem like minor irritants, but one could complain at length about shortages and monopoly in the PX and commissary without fear of career retribution, for one was complaining about something the career judges had no hand in creating. Consequently, I suspect, complaints about shortages in the erratic supply system became a symbolic substitute for more substantial grievances about life and leadership in a system that did not respond well to complaints concerning more central aspects of military life.[5]

Transportation

A military shuttle-bus system connected the major installations and subcommunities within a larger community. In the case of Grossberg and its subcommunities, the buses were scheduled every two hours on weekdays from Richberg (and some other subcommunities) to Central Barracks. There one could shop in the largest central facilities, take care of most support chores, including issues of travel and pay, or catch an hourly shuttle either to the hospital or to other support services such as quartermaster supply. Buses were less frequent on Saturdays and did not operate on Sundays. Inadequate bus transportation particularly constrained the single soldiers, who often did not have cars. SSG Gary Hatch, in charge of a squad of mostly single soldiers, observed: "On Sundays they have no bus. They have to catch a cab. So last Sunday somebody took someone's car that wasn't supposed to. One of the problems is that you just can't get around." To make matters worse, funding cuts at the end of 1988 put the entire shuttle-bus system at risk. SFC Arthur Baldwin, a platoon sergeant at Richberg, expressed his fears regarding the pending cuts: "General Barracks, for the married soldier, is twenty minutes away. For the single soldier it is not available. And with the budget cuts, all the buses are gone." Recent transportation cuts had indeed confined soldiers without cars to their installations, unless they were willing to learn the German transportation system.

Recreation and Personal Maintenance

I have previously listed the wide variety of recreational facilities available on most military posts, and will not repeat them here. Soldiers and spouses had two complaints about Army recreational facilities: inconvenient hours of operation and a limited variety of activities. Hours were inconvenient because recreational facilities tended to be open during regular duty hours, when the civilian employees could staff them, rather than after work and on weekends, when soldiers and family members needed them. A variety of other services that soldiers and families needed for personal maintenance had similar problems with inconvenient hours of operation. SFC Baldwin again: "The facilities here—such as the haircut place, the bank, the [dry cleaners] pickup point—it could all be open Saturdays and closed Mondays or Tuesdays. It takes so much of our duty time. A soldier doesn't mind doing things on his own time. He doesn't want to be away from his work. If he could get up at 10:00 A.M. on Saturday and get his hair cut, he would. But it is not possible." Intended to renew, maintain, and lighten the load of soldiers and family members, the service suppliers missed the mark, and even became a burden because of inappropriate availability.[6]

Regarding the complaint of limited available activities—of "nothing to do"— almost every installation with family housing had one or more fast-food outlets (Burger King, and perhaps a pizza outlet), an ice cream bar, a theater, a bowling alley, one or more craft or hobby centers for picture framing, woodworking, pottery making, or self-service auto repair, and at least one all-ranks community club or more than one club, divided by ranks. Frequently, a shooting range and a rod and gun club completed the list. Compared with recreational facilities of many small towns in America, the military facilities were rather impressive. I propose that the real reason for the perception that there was "nothing to do" was not the lack of activities offered but the fact that the activities provided were controlled by the Army and therefore did not represent any relief from the Army's influence. I will explore this theme of the need for escape further in Chapter 11, "You Gotta Get Away."

PROBLEMS COMMON TO ALL FAMILY SUPPORT AGENCIES

Bureaucracy and Complicated Paperwork

Soldiers and spouses shared a widespread distaste for the effects of Army bureaucracy and fouled-up paperwork. Terry Walsh: "I'm not sure if the problem is poor organization, or lack of adequately trained personnel, or if the turnover is too great, or are the people just doing their time? But it is a real problem in the

Army. And you have to have paperwork for everything in the Army. If it's not done right, you screw up everything."

When pay is lost and not recovered quickly or spouses do not arrive in Europe in a timely manner, soldiers resent the suffering and are quick to inform others. Terry continued, joined by her husband, Hank:

> "The biggest problem is that the Army is totally unsympathetic," complained Terry. "They lost my husband's pay. . . . The paper[work] drags. That happens a lot. It happened with the furniture: He got here in July, found an apartment in August. In September, he got moved in here. I came in October. We still didn't get furniture until December. The reason is . . . somebody losing paperwork."
>
> "They do it when they are ready to do it, not when we need it," Hank explained.
>
> "On the pay," Terry continued, quite irritated, "we used our savings for four months. They didn't attempt to find it—not until we raised hell."
>
> Hank confirmed his wife's assertion: "You have to watch them every minute. You have to hold their hand."
>
> "Once you get in financial trouble, they don't go back and find out the source of the trouble, they just make it your fault," Terry concluded with finality. "It just eats me up that they don't take any responsibility. We still haven't got it straightened out on his new rank."

Thus, bureaucratic rigidity, underskilled or incompetent staffers, or understaffed offices undermined many services provided to families, making the Army appear to be in breach of contract, alienating its soldiers and families, and thereby undermining the loyalty essential to its success in combat.

Lack of Knowledge

A few family members, especially those new to the Army, lacked knowledge about the variety of services available. Worse, some service providers lacked knowledge about the regulations governing their services because of the substantial turnover rate of military spouse employees. Indeed, the rate of employee turnover probably exceeded 50 percent per year in the lower-level jobs because spouses often arrived well into the soldier's three-year tour, occasionally waited several months before applying for a job, sometimes returned to the States before their spouse's military tours ended, and frequently changed jobs during the tour for better pay or conditions. The soldiers and spouses needing service resented the lack of knowledge or the inadequate service provided by unskilled recent hires.

Funding Cuts

Sometimes community programs were disrupted by unpredictable shifts in funding. For example, a number of programs for the soldier and the family had taken two years to build up during 1986 and 1987. By mid-1988, the Army began cutting the staff of these family programs because of funding reductions. Kim Farley, the Army Community Services director at Richberg, quite bitter after a community leadership meeting, suggested, with rhetorical flourish, "The scapegoat for everything is 'We don't have the resources.' If they think that the mission is so essential over here, and if the families are essential, why don't they provide the resources to provide the needed assistance?" Similarly, MAJ Rodney Kimball, on the division staff at Middleberg, commented on the loss of slowly acquired family programs due to funding cuts: "This year, all the budget cuts were in the family area. As soon as that program is gone, it will be forgotten about, like the volunteer coordinator. The full understanding of the necessity of a volunteer coordinator has now been lost." From the military community member's point of view, when the Army cut the family support services more than the weapons programs, while still requiring heroic soldier efforts that disrupted the family, it stood in breach of its support for sacrifice contract.

Distrust of Community Leadership

Many military leaders and community members felt that the Army placed second rate officers and NCOs in the community cadre. They reasoned that the best soldiers stayed in their own branch doing "fast-track" jobs—jobs involving troop leadership in their unit conducive to promotion. Community cadre, by contrast, had a reputation as a "holding area" that hurt one's chances of promotion and retention. Richberg's deputy subcommunity commander, LTC Max Newell, for instance, was a "fast-track" armor officer who had injured his back jumping off a tank. The "community" assignment gave him the opportunity to do something worthwhile at a lower level of physical activity. CPT Patrick Tall served as LTC Newell's unofficial and quite temporary executive officer, and was called the "deputy DCC" in spite of the term's infelicity. Tall had been removed from his combat unit and placed "in community" while awaiting removal from the military for alcohol infractions. Other DCCs and officers in corps-level community positions readily admitted that they were off the "fast-track," in a "holding pattern," awaiting retirement. Several of the senior NCOs had been sent to community staff because they had failed to get along with their battalion or brigade officers. This was a convenient place to get them out of the way. When the units were tasked to lend someone to community, community leaders expected unit commanders to send their worst soldiers. Nevertheless, MSG Nick Morrow, who would not bend to a battalion commander's possibly unethical wishes and had therefore been "sent to community," did a first-class job. LTC Newell was an exception to the sidetracked officer practice because he truly was fast track—but temporarily injured. As a "go-getter," he did more for Richberg in three years than had been accomplished in the previous two decades. CPT Tall supervised a renovation that gave the community an excellent new post office. In spite of such positive accomplishments, the pervasive suspicion that community leadership got less than the best personnel undermined community confidence and left the impression that "family and community didn't matter" and that the Army "really didn't care for its own," thus placing the Army conceptually in breach of contract.

Some senior commanders made efforts to overcome this negative perception of the community cadre. In Middleberg, the DCC appointed was definitely a fast-track officer. The cynics, however, pointed out that he had already been slotted to attend Command and General Staff resident schooling eight months hence—barely enough time to learn the job, let alone accomplish anything—and was therefore an eyewash appointment. Upon his departure, his civilian administrative assistant served as the acting DCC for the second time during my stay. LTC Newell of Richberg commented on the belief that the community's staff was substandard, saying,

> I was handpicked. I've been trying to increase the quality of community manage-
> ment. Rather than having a person coming to me with a stigma because he was
> relieved, or inefficient, I would rather have no one. Prior to me, the adjutant and
> the deputy community commander were passed over [for promotion] and riffed
> [removed from the service by a reduction in force—RIF] because they were below
> average.

LTC Newell confirmed that putting the stigmatized or rejected personnel into the community cadre was "in vogue in Europe." The 'best' officers avoided getting "sidetracked to community" leadership because it did not count toward an officer's primary or secondary career specialization and thus hindered promotion.

CONSEQUENCES OF THE BREACH OF CONTRACT

Deterioration of Community Morale

The breaches of the support for sacrifice contract undermined far more than just the unit-soldier trust bond and the soldier-spouse trust bond. Ultimately, the frustration and anger induced by these repeated breaches isolated community members from each other, for those responsible, or deemed so because they represented an offending institution, were also members of the local community. The breaches attributed to them, combined with the fear of adverse evaluation of complainers, undermined potential circles of friendship, support, and trust. MAJ Spencer Doty, a psychiatrist, felt "unable to trust anybody here." The fact of distrust constituted the essence of community breakdown. Failure of the support for sacrifice contract corroded the ability of the soldiers and other community members to build therapeutic supports for each other. Rather, as SSG Jeremy Strong noted, they learned and then used the premise of distrust: "They make sure that the soldier gets in-processed and meets the company. But they forget the family. Let's face it, people around here are not that friendly. It is not like in the States. 'Hi! I'm your neighbor' doesn't happen around here. Here they are more or less introverts." SGT Strong thus linked what he viewed as official indifference to the family to the lack of friendliness and isolated introversion that he sensed in the community. Of course, many families did establish friendships. Social gatherings often included much spirited and therapeutic griping; indeed a friend was a person with whom one could share one's sense of alienation without fear of further repercussions. Families appreciated these trusted friends greatly, partly because of the contrast to the underlying moods of distrust that pervaded much of the community.

The family's perception of breaches in support undermined soldier and family willingness to endure the sacrifices essential to success in the face of war. Thus, according to MAJ Quintin Scott, Grossberg's regional community chaplain, soldiers even questioned their willingness to fight at all:

> Soldiers are walking around saying, "Hell, if this is the way that my country treats me, why should I fight?" I think that happy soldiers, knowing that their families are taken care of, will make for a strong fighting force. These things should not be so much at the whim of the commanders. The soldiers ought to have a right to good treatment. They ought to have a right to adequate medical care. And these things are always threatened, that they [i.e., Congress or Pentagon planners] are going to start changing. Those things should be staples. If you are going to cut budgets, cut them on the unnecessary things.

When soldiers perceived ineffective support in peacetime, they questioned the Army's ability to prudently care for the soldiers or to evacuate and protect their families in the event of war.

Furthermore, when some soldiers or spouses perceived violations of the support for sacrifice contract, they felt justified in taking retribution on the Army. 1LT David Zark hinted at such retribution when I asked him how he determined how much help to give his soldiers with their personal problems. "It depends," he said. "I have to decide: If I blow this guy off, is he going to fuck me up?" As we shall see in later chapters, the idea of revenge reciprocity was often voiced in such idioms as "getting over on the Army." The suggestion of serious impacts on morale emerged in such expressions as "it is all a joke," or "it is all a trick." In other words, the official talk of contractual obligation was felt to be manipulative: a "joke," a "trick," or a "smoke and mirrors" deception. From the soldier's point of view, soldiers actually sacrificed; leaders just talked of support to get soldiers to sacrifice while the leaders did nothing. The perception itself induced further alienation.

Personal Alienation

Implicit in these quotes about loss of community morale is a sense of personal alienation. The individual is not so directly or confidently attached to the Army as its leaders would like. In prior chapters, and again in this one, soldiers express their feeling that their efforts are in fact sacrifices that most would make voluntarily. The system, however, coerces behavior that is sometimes misdirected. That is, the leadership requires extraordinary time and effort of the soldiers but does not direct those efforts to what the soldiers see as essential mission. Sometimes the soldier's efforts are simply coerced and then wasted. Either way, the soldier's labor has been misappropriated. Family members, too, sacrifice when they lose valued time with their soldiering spouse or parent. Although the organization requires sacrifices, it also claims it "takes care of its own." When it seems not to do so, the organization appears to be in breach of contract. This adds further to personal alienation. That alienation leads to other consequences, among them, reduced retention.

Retention Undermined

When the opportunity to reenlist came, soldiers who felt alienated by their Army lives and work would decide to get out. "It impinges so much on the family," Cindy Ashton, of Newberg, said, "that you think 'I'm not going to go through with this.' Even if they don't have the money, I feel that they have got to do something [for family programs] because we have no other recourse. They brought us over here." The phrases "They brought us over here," "it impinges so much on the family," " we have no other recourse," and "they have got to do something" indicate belief in a support for sacrifice contract. With contract in breach and alienation seting in, some parents were planning to pull themselves out of the organization. Thus, SGT Rick Ashton asserted, "I don't see myself raising our daughter in the military." In short, the Army's contract violations undermined its ability to entice contract renewals. Even among the many who were not totally soured against the Army, there was nonetheless a reluctance to remain in Germany with its difficult support problems.

CONCLUSION

Army installations in Germany existed to support the combat functions of the tenant units at the post. One of the ways they supported the combat function was to help the soldiers and family members conveniently and economically solve their day-to-day support problems and provide a range of inexpensive recreational activities. Both convenient access and price subvention existed in part to compensate soldiers and families for the pain and inconvenience of Army life.

Sadly, the actual delivery of support service in Germany was often far less than adequate. Families recognized that deployments and long hours were requirements of Army life, but they still struggled to endure the sacrifices required of them. In Chapter 5, "Living with the Army," we saw that one source of great distress came not from the time sacrificed but from the perception that the sacrifices were often wasted, forcibly alienating one's labor by devoting it to no appropriate end. In this chapter we have seen how sacrifices by soldiers and families were gifts that demanded reciprocal recompense. The failure to provide the return gift of support further alienated these Army families. The community assistance agencies diligently tried to provide useful supports, but for a wide variety of reasons, including some beyond their control, the support efforts missed their mark. Soldiers and spouses often felt they should have been—and could have been—better served.

I have not yet treated one of the most important elements in the support for sacrifice contract—family health care. The matter was so important in the minds of soldiers and family members that the medical system and its shortcomings deserve separate and more extensive treatment in the next chapter.

NOTES

1. Georges Vernez and Gail L. Zellman, *Families and Mission: A Review of the Effects of Family Factors on Army Attrition, Retention, and Readiness*, N-2624-A (Santa Monica, CA: Rand Corporation, August 1987): v, 6.

2. Joseph M. Rothberg et al., "Life and Death in the US Army," *Journal of the American Medical Association* 264, no. 17 (7 November 1990): 2242–2243; Joseph M. Rothberg, Robert J. Ursano, and Harry C. Holloway, "Suicide in the United States Army," *Psychiatric Annals* 17 (August 1987): 546.

3. Under the SOFA, American spouces could only work at military installations and the only jobs available to them had 7:30 A.M.–4:30 P.M. schedules.

4. I am still puzzled by this difference. I was often told that facilities were generally less adequate in Germany than in the United States because Congress didn't want to spend money outside of their districts. That, however, does not explain the ramshackle barracks. One may presume that money followed rank, with E1 to E5 in the barracks and officers and more senior enlisted in married housing.

5. My editor, Linette Sparacino, spouse of a career Army officer and resident in Germany from July 1977 to June 1980, reacted to this supposition: "I think it was more than that. The shortages were *profoundly* irritating, as they were just one more reminder that the military controlled your life every single minute of every single day, including what was available to eat. Folks didn't grouse about the commissary because it was safe. They groused because they were frustrated that the Army couldn't even get the little things right."

6. Faris R. Kirkland, in personal communication, once asked, "What the hell was wrong with the community commanders that they tolerated all this?" I'm not sure I have a full answer. In part, the installations had to abide by German labor laws, which pushed for stable, nine to five hours, like businesses. Perhaps a senior commander decided to minimize divergences from German custom to help maintain good relations. Perhaps parallel hours helped accommodate delivery of goods, services, and repairs from German suppliers. But there were exceptions, so I am not sure that I have an answer. Linette Sparacino, in personal communication, suggested that perhaps the service facilities "were structured to be efficient for the organization and not the customers. If they were open when the rest of the Army was open, problems or issues could be referred immediately to commanders during duty hours."

Fire and maneuver exercises at Graffenwöhr: Moving to a firing point.

Fire and maneuver exercises at Graffenwöhr: The M-111 Infantry Fighting Vehicle takes a firing position.

Fire and maneuver exercises at Graffenwöhr: M-111 with rear hatch open for infantry dismount.

Fire and maneuver exercises at Graffenwöhr: Infantry in live fire training.

Barracks at Graffenwöhr.

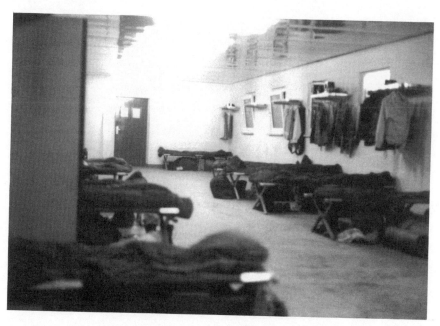

Inside the Graffenwöhr barracks: Officers' sleeping arrangements.

Graffenwöhr: Inside a mess hall.

Graffenwöhr: Enlisted troops on a break from duty.

Middleberg: Government quarters, otherwise known as stairwell housing. On military installations, even the housing stands in formation.

Middleberg: Government quarters, with barbecue area to the left.

Middleberg: Stairwells forming a quad, with parking and playground (center of quad).

On the corner of every stairwell, a plaque lists the name and rank of the ever present building coordinator. In this case, the coordinator moved recently.

Middleberg community facilities: The Officers' Club.

Middleberg community facilities: A Youth Activities Center used by early teens after school hours.

Middleberg's Child Development Center, with family housing on both sides.

Middleberg's elementary school.

The Middleberg commissary

The interior of Middleberg's commissary, a commissary of medium size, showing most of the interior. The woman at the right is looking at the display cases along the right wall.

Middleberg: A mother and two children inspecting spring blossoms.

Middleberg: A dinner honoring community volunteers. Note the original murals dating from World War II.

Middleberg: A reception marking the departure of a deputy community commander.

Richberg: Families were invited to come to the units and climb aboard their equipment.

An after-hours get-together. These senior sergeants were from different units and said they preferred to socialize that way.

7

"The System Is Totally Screwed to Hell": Space-Available Health Care for the Military Family

The biggest problem that we have had is the medical. With our little boy, he has had chronic throat and ear infection. And they didn't want to do the surgeries here. They don't have the facilities. They are understaffed—tremendously. So we have to have fevers [from infections] every three or four weeks.

Jane Cooper
Richberg Military Community

Soldiers and spouses alike viewed health care for the family as one of the most important returns in the support for sacrifice contract, a core symbol of the military's commitment to the life and health of those who exposed themselves to danger and death for their country. I will therefore devote considerable attention to this key symbol of Army commitment, more than I gave to the other support systems that were both less culturally significant and less complicated.

In America during the late 1980s, military families could use military medical facilities for free if they desired, but only if there was "space available." Alternatively, family members made a small co-payment when they went to a civilian physician who participated in CHAMPUS (Civilian Health and Medical Program of the Uniformed Services), the military's medical insurance. In Germany, by contrast, family members were required to use military medical facilities unless they had been authorized to go outside the system.

The medical system available to families in Germany consisted of large regional hospitals and local community medical clinics. Soldiers used these same facilities. If a community medical clinic was not available on an installation, an ill family member had to go to the nearest military community with a community clinic or to the general hospital. Ill soldiers were given basic first aid at their battalion troop medical clinic. Those diagnosed as needing more than basic treatment were transported to a nearby community clinic or the general hospital. Middleberg had a community clinic, and the trip to the nearest military hospital, Welby General, took an hour and a half. Richberg had no community clinic. Family members had to drive about twenty minutes to the clinic at General Barracks or about one hour to Welby General Hospital.

The community medical clinic was often a fairly modern building built to the needs of the medical practice. An entry and waiting area, accessible to the administrative counters, provided initial access. Once one processed the paperwork, one waited in the entry foyer until called to an examination room. A clinic had one or more doctors, a nursing staff, and a pharmacist to dispense the required prescriptions, all without cost. The clinic generally had basic equipment for outpatient minor surgery, an X-ray machine, and other instruments appropriate for first-level care. If the emerging examination and diagnosis suggested unusual lab work or the need for specialist attention, the patient was referred to a specialty clinic at the general hospital serving the region.

Welby General Hospital was one such facility, the general hospital service center for all of the communities named (by pseudonyms) in this study. Welby General occupied a set of buildings erected during World War II that had been reconditioned to meet the needs of a hospital. The main building housed all of the operating rooms, recovery areas, and wards that one might see in a regional hospital serving any large rural area in America. The hospital served the soldiers and family members and the Department of Defense employees and their families from the scattered military communities of a large region.

The hospital provided an extensive emergency room, open twenty-four hours a day. Various specialty clinics, open Monday through Friday, gave second-level diagnosis and treatment to the soldiers and family members referred by the local community clinics. The referred patient was responsible for making the connecting appointment. The specialty clinics included Child and Adolescent Psychiatric Service, Exceptional Family Member Service, a community health nurse, and separate clinics for dental care; dermatology; eye, ear, nose and throat; internal medicine; psychiatry and neurology; obstetrics and gynecology; occupational therapy; orthopedics; pediatrics; physical therapy; and optometry and ophthalmology. Additional departments provided radiology, preventive medicine, labs, and a large pharmacy. Each clinic, service, or department had its administrative group responsible for making patient appointments.

SHORTCOMINGS IN THE MEDICAL SYSTEM

Although residents in these communities appreciated the military medical system, especially because it was free, one often heard expressions of general anger or resentment regarding its use. "We got a fucked-up system," said SSG Alan Evanson when I inquired about the medical system. SSG Frank Barnes, watching me type everything else he had said, paused when I invited his opinion of the hospital and asked, "You gonna print profanity?"

When people were in more contemplative moods, two types of expressions emerged. First, some felt that the doctors themselves were good, but that the systems, procedures of access, and quality of physical facilities were the problem. Meg Barnes, for instance: "The doctors aren't bad. It is the system. It is what you have to do to get to a doctor. It is the government's fault that we don't have enough doctors." CPL Craig Hansen, whose family had sought frequent medical attention, felt the medical system "is pretty much of a joke." Rebecca, his wife, explained why:

> They have better doctors now than they used to. Before, the doctors were not the ones that I would go to if I had a choice. The new commander of the dispensary is great. I'd take him home with me if I could. But the way it is run leaves much to be desired. You get put on hold for ten or fifteen minutes. And then it gets disconnected, more times than I care to think of. It is pretty busy. It is hard to get an appointment.

The patients and medical staff mentioned the poor condition of the physical facilities in their list of complaints. Meg Barnes had recently delivered her baby, observing, "Welby General [Hospital] is the most run-down shabby shack. I mean, it doesn't look sterile. They are painting at one end while you are having a baby at the other. But the nurses and doctors were very friendly." CW3 Kevin Robbins, Richberg's battalion physician's assistant, held similar views: "Welby General? That place is the pits: the poorest excuse for a hospital that I have ever seen. But the people that go there know that they get good care."

On the other hand, others felt that the medical personnel themselves were inadequate. For some, like Yvette and Richard Howard, the medical staff were too protected from competition. Thus, Yvette Howard expressed her uncertainty: "I don't really feel secure with the doctors here. I don't think that they really know what they are doing." Her husband, Richard, drove home his thought on a reason why: "The doctors over here got a guaranteed income. They don't really care." Richard went on to describe an incident in which one of his buddies had broken his leg. He experienced delays and perceived incompetence in the first aid and ambulance procedures. Richard then concluded, "The only thing good in the medical field is the dentist. Then they took out this guy's wrong tooth. If I'm sick, I got no choice. But avoid them if you can." CPL Hansen likewise worried about lack of competition: "If you are a doctor in the States, you get paid according to the patient load. Here, they don't have to be as good, because it doesn't make a difference." Some soldiers and families felt apprehensive about military medical care but admitted they had "been lucky" when they used it. Even the lucky ones expressed several concerns, including understaffing, difficult access, fear of potential harm, and inadequate facilities.

Understaffing

Soldiers and family members saw understaffing as a key source of their difficulties when using the military medical system. The Army staffed its units with medical personnel according to the recommendations of a standardized Table of Distribution and Allowances, or TDA. The tables specified the numbers of doctors, nurses, staff, types of hospitals, and equipment needed for an army to handle the medical needs of its soldiers in combat. Every unit of a certain type had a package of standard authorized medical personnel, supplies, and equipment. Large units, such as a corps or an army, had hospitals—both mobile and stationary—and a staff of physicians appropriate for combat medical care. Battalions had an aid station, with a physician, a physician's assistant, and medics trained in the elements of combat first aid. The whole tended to be mobile and oriented to the kinds of wounds and diseases associated with combat. Combat medical personnel, such as battalion physicians and physician's assistants, were loaned to the community clinics and general hospitals while in garrison but were withdrawn when the units went on maneuvers.

In Germany, the combat-designed medical staff and facilities were asked to provide for the medical needs of spouses and children as well as soldiers. Although this assignment gave much useful training and skill maintenance in noncombat medicine, it also resulted in the medical system being immediately understaffed, given the added population to be served. A few civilian doctors were contracted and brought to the general hospitals and community clinics to help with the load, but not sufficient for the tripling in the size of the populations to be served. Though similarly tasked with caring for family member dental needs, the dental system did not have any supplementary staff at all. Thus, the clinic commander in General Barracks felt, "Medical problems result from understaffing, underfunding, underplanning." Likewise, LTC Nevin Davis, head of dental services in the region, briefed the commanding general of Grossberg Military Community: "As you all know, dental is staffed strictly on [the basis of the] active duty population. Some senior [troop] commanders have elected to concentrate on active duty. Some commanders ask us to do family members, too." Regarding medical care for family members, CPT Glen Cooper, a Richberg dentist, noted:

> I don't see anything that can be done. Doctors are staffed by [i.e., according to the number of] the active duty personnel. Dependents are to be [served] "space available." Unless the entire Department of Army changes its policy, there will never be any improvement. Dependents don't matter at all as I understand it. One of the advantages [of being] here [in Germany] is that the Army is trying to take care of the family. But as far as staffing, it is for military only.

Even with the extra medical staff in the main medical clinics, users felt the system was inadequate to handle the additional family population.

A contradiction in messages—between "dependents not mattering" and "the Army is trying to take care of the family"—constantly festered. Families were openly told they were served "space available," after the soldiers were cared for. CPT Cooper:

> Colonel S___ [the previous deputy subcommunity commander] did a survey on Richberg. The number-one problem people said is medical. But then we were told that we can't do anything about medical, because they are not here to treat the dependents. . . . Dependents are to be space available. . . . If that is the way, I think

it is stupid. They either get more doctors, or they don't bring dependents to Germany.

This policy of space-available care made families second-class appendages and contradicted the notion that "the Army takes care of its own." Meg Barnes: "I was sick last week with the flu. I went in there [the clinic] at 7:30. . . . I sat from 7:30 to 10:00. She [a woman on the administrative staff] says to me, 'We won't be able to get to you 'til 11:30.' 'Why?' I asked. 'Active duty comes first. And any emergency.' But if you don't come in at 7:30, you won't get the 11:30 appointment." Space-available treatment increased the family member's frustration by offering second-class access to a first-priority cultural value—good health care.

Even with the addition of civilian contract doctors, the combined military and civilian population needing services tended to outstrip the facilities and providers available. As SGT Larry Bracken noted, "The clinic has been understaffed for the past two and a half years." I did not attempt to measure carefully the degree of understaffing, though doctors, dentists, nurses, hospital administrators, and patients complained of it. One can fathom something of the problem by looking at well-woman care in the General Barracks Community Clinic. General Barracks clinic, the largest outside Welby General Hospital, dedicated two afternoons a week for well-woman appointments—primarily for Pap smears for early detection of cervical cancer. Two afternoons a week was felt to be a generous allocation, given all of the other demands on physician time. The clinic's capacity for ten appointments an afternoon, or twenty a week, meant approximately 1,000 appointments a year. But there were at least 3,000 service women and female spouses in the area served by this clinic who should have been having this test once a year. LTC Manny Clifford, the clinic's commander, confirmed the shortfall:

> The people that have problems are well-woman appointments. And the ones that require one particular doctor. They come over here from Stateside and expect to go to OB-GYN [obstetrics-gynecology] or ortho [orthodontics]. But here [in Germany], they have to come here [the installation clinic]. Another problem is if they want a special [i.e., specific] doctor. I will do my darndest for them, but they have to wait. Many times they won't accept that.

Regarding other issues of understaffing, COL Lee Goodwin, the Welby General Hospital commander, alerted the corps-level community commander to the recurrent understaffing problem: "We are going to have significant shortages this summer in orthopedics, obstetrics, and psychiatry. There will be no mandatory treatment that will go astray, but little elective. All required, necessary care will be done. This is not new; we go through this every summer." Understaffing, however, forced doctors and staff throughout the system to work long hours just to take care of "all required necessary care."

More evidence of understaffing came from the difficulties Welby General Hospital had in providing outreach programs of preventive medicine education and other therapy support services to the surrounding military community clinics. A social work technician (and master sergeant) at Welby General explained that the central clinics should have had outreach programs that delivered preventive education and mobile screening units to the outlying clinics. But, he concluded, "Welby General is so understaffed they can't deal with their own problems, let alone take problems from the satellite communities." Psychological and social work caseworkers reported informally that their time was totally consumed by investigating child abuse allegations and providing abuse therapy. As a result, they had little time for preventive measures such as early marriage counseling. Therefore, chaplains had to do much of the marital counseling.

Distressing Appointment Procedures

Making an appointment at one of the clinics gave yet another perspective on the results of understaffing. Although each clinic, whether in a hospital or at an outlying *kaserne*, established its own procedures, they tended to follow a common approach. Clinics opened their appointment books on one particular day each week or every other week to fill the next week or two weeks and replace any cancellations in the current week. If they allowed appointments more than two weeks away, administrators felt that patients would fill the appointments into the indefinite future. Moreover, experience had shown that appointments made more than two weeks in advance were missed too often because of changing military and family schedules, thereby wasting scarce medical assets.

To avoid constant phone disruption of the clinic staff's daily work, appointments were taken only on one specified day each week, beginning at a specific hour. Some clinics chose the opening hour of the morning. Others selected an afternoon hour that enabled the clinic to finish with morning sick call for soldiers and family members before taking on the rush of appointment calls. Thus, everyone who needed an appointment was forced to call at the same time, once a week, overloading the two phone lines into Richberg and Middleberg from the German phone net. Weekly, this four-hour surge of calls for medical appointments tied up all of the phone lines between the post and the German phone system, blocking post leaders and employees from using the phones for military calls to off-post locations. The General Barracks medical clinic commander, LTC Clifford explained, "I open at 1:00 P.M. [for calls for appointments]. That way I am past sick call. . . . It ties up the phones from civilian access [i.e., off-post] for the whole day." Formerly they had made appointments by requiring a person to call in on a different day for each kind of appointment, one week before the day devoted to that purpose. But "When we opened up one day at a time—two days a week for Paps; one day, Wednesday, for well-baby; Thursday for well-woman, etc.—they were going, 'Aghghhhhhh!'" The present system of opening for all types of appointments on the first and third Wednesday afternoons of every month was better, he explained, because a woman could make all the appointments she or her family needed for the week at the same time and would not have to spend a half day redialing for each kind of appointment.

Some clinics dealt with the phone problem by giving those who walked in first priority in securing an appointment. Here is how CPT Andy Finley, Middleberg Barracks dental clinic commander, justified his appointment policy at a public town meeting:

We have changed the appointment policy, working to better the community. Once a week, a week of appointments will be opened for two weeks out. I believe that the folks who have the gumption to get up and come in should have priority. Or you can call in Tuesday afternoon by phone to get an appointment, if slots are left. The priority is soldiers: they must be fit to fight. Second is family members. Third is retirees. Fourth is civilians. We have 2,200 soldiers and 4,000 family members. Soldiers have priority. We will take two-thirds soldiers and one-third family members. We have two dentists now, and a third one promised for another month from now.[1]

Three days earlier, at another meeting explaining the procedures, CPT Finley detailed how troops had to "miss work" on the appointment-scheduling day and then "miss work on the day the dental work was done." If any "follow-up" was needed, they had to miss work twice more. The process was frustratingly inefficient. Giving priority to walk-ins, moreover, gave enormous advantage to those living or working on-post. Spouses without a car living off-post could not arrange an appointment and complained bitterly of the unfairness. The policy exacerbated the difference—and the tensions—between high ranks tending to live on-post and low ranks and new arrivals tending to live off-post, and resulted in much lost work time, as soldiers left work to make appointments for spouses and children.

Family members had more frustrated views of the appointment system. SGT Ian Warnock observed that his wife, Emma, "has been trying three months to get an appointment." Emma detailed the situation:

There are only two times a month that you can call to make one. You have to call on the first and third Wednesday, for all of the nonemergency appointments. Then you finally get through and they put you on hold for fifteen minutes. I dialed continuously for an hour and ten minutes. Then I was on hold for ten or fifteen minutes. I needed a well-baby appointment. I asked for it and they said, "fifteen months checkup is not needed." Then I asked for myself. They said they were filled, and they said I would have to call again. Mine was for a well-woman yearly physical. They said, "We're all filled up," and that I would have to wait and call the first Wednesday of next month.

Ian repeated for emphasis: "She has been trying every day that you can call, for three months." Again, the problem is not the quality of the medical care but lack of access to it. As I have indicated, once people got past the appointment-keeping system, many were satisfied with the care they got.

The appointment system was actually a rationing mechanism for an overloaded and understaffed military medical system where no perceived alternatives existed.

People had to compete for the available slots. Families suffered and soldiers lost work time. CPT Bill Olsen, a company commander in Middleberg: "The appointment system is the sorriest thing that I have ever seen. I have to excuse a soldier at 6:30 [A.M., to go make an appointment]. The receptionist comes in at 7:30 [A.M.] The soldiers miss PT. They can schedule the week that is two weeks away, but not any further away. God bless K___ [his wife]! On appointment day you just about have to give her Valium at night." MAJ Rodney Kimball complained of the "Catch-22" effect of the medical appointment system:

> We have now gone to the centralized appointment system. But a lot of people are saving money on phones [by not having one], and can't drop by. All the clinics have different ways to make appointments. Some places you have to show up in person. Some places it's Tuesdays. At our medical clinic, Monday is the only day to call. But you can't get through [on the phone], and you're not allowed to go in person.

Marla Bracken represented parents expressing concern for her children: "It's sad that your child has something wrong, and they will give you an appointment two or three weeks out. They don't have enough personnel. Our community is growing, but our dispensary is not." The problem was perhaps worse at the regional medical center. In Jane Cooper's view, at Welby General Hospital, "any given clinic is a four-week or a three-month wait—to see OB-GYN (obstetrics-gynecology) or eye, ear, nose, and throat."

Given the inability to make clinic appointments easily, soldiers often took their spouses or children to the regional emergency clinic at Welby General Hospital, a two-hour drive from some communities. All knew that the emergency room required no appointment and eventually would see everyone. According to CW3 Robbins, the physician's assistant at Richberg's Troop Medical Clinic, "The system works—not very well—but it works. They get treated. . . . The mother with a routine appointment tries to call in, but the phones are jammed, so she shows up at Emergency. And then they jam Emergency, and it takes hours to be seen there." He didn't blame them for going to the emergency room. "You should try to call for an appointment," he admonished me, mimicking what the call would be like: "'Today is Wednesday. You need to call Tuesday,' they tell you. So you call Tuesday: 'Sorry, all the appointments are gone. Call in two weeks.' Just try to get an appointment! And the larger clinics can't take walk-ins or it would be total chaos." As a result, the Welby General emergency room facilities were constantly overwhelmed. The emergency room personnel had to triage the patients, and those needing minor care routinely waited hours. Most were willing to wait, though, because they felt close to care in case what bought them there developed into an authentic emergency.

Discourtesy and the Climate of Belligerence

Soldiers and spouses consistently complained of a lack of courtesy in the medical system. "We're not being treated bad," said SGT Larry Bracken, "but knowing they are not going to lose their job, it's not, 'Good morning, may I help you?' but someone leaning over the counter saying, 'Yeah?'" Terry Walsh put the same problem in different, mixed images: "It is a jungle. I walk into a clinic to make an appointment and I feel like a piece of paper." Then she made a telling contrast with her civilian medical experience: "I worked in a county hospital; we saw mostly indigents and we still treated them like human beings." By implication, soldiers and family members in Germany were not treated like humans. Repeatedly, complaints focused on the desk staff rather than on the doctors or the nurses delivering the actual treatment. Marla Bracken: "I didn't mind sitting and waiting. But their attitude was, 'She thinks she is going to see a doctor!'" Her intonation conveyed her sense of their skepticism, bordering on mockery. By contrast, "The doctor was apologetic. No problems with the nurse, but the reception people made matters worse."

Why did the clinic desk staffs so often draw this reaction? In essence, understaffing directly contributed to the lack of courtesy. To some degree, the staff at the check-in counter was required to impose a rationing function through the appointment system. Desk staffers had to become inured to the distresses of the clients, learning to ignore them. The clients strove to overcome the rationing by becoming increasingly demanding and openly venting their frustrations. Each fended off the demands of the other in an escalation of discourtesy. The problem of escalating discourtesy described here extended well beyond the medical system to include all military systems that were inadequately staffed to meet the needs of the community population.

Meg Barnes described how she attempted to use the medical system politely and patiently, but experienced a continuing "runaround" because of changing doctors and delays in getting appointments. To get what she felt she urgently needed—an appointment in the allergy clinic—she eventually had to give up being nice and became belligerent: "Finally I said, 'Forget it!' I said, 'Excuse me!' and I explained the symptoms. I cried! I played stupid! And I had to play stupid. That was the only way to get to Welby General." When she got to Welby General, she began the explanations again, and had to resort yet again to making demands: "The appointment was for 2:00 P.M. I didn't get to see the doctor 'til 5:00. By then, everything was closed. I had to go back the next day. 'Fine,' I said. 'Tomorrow I'm coming back, and you're *going* to do the tests!'" Meg's husband, SSG Frank Barnes, added, "She went three times by herself. Then I took work time off and went with her. They tried to send us away again. I said, 'I'm not leaving 'til my wife is seen.'" A system that doesn't respond until its clients "raise hell" trains its clients to raise hell.

Occasionally soldiers would "pull rank" rather than use belligerence to meet their needs. The Coopers, for instance:

"I was having blackouts" explained Jane Cooper. "I was calling every week for an appointment. My husband [Glen, the post dentist] said, 'This is getting dangerous,' so we went to the emergency room. This went on from October to the end of August."

"Why did it take so long?" I enquired.

"Because nobody would treat her, because she needed a specialist," Glen explained. "So you see a clinic doctor for a referral. But if they mark it 'routine,' they will take three to four months to get her an appointment with the specialist."

"But this was dangerous!" Jane jumped in emphatically. "But because I was only a dependent, and because it wasn't life threatening, they didn't assign an immediate appointment."

Glen then explained how he went to a physician's assistant for the battalion, and got him to intervene to make an appointment, thereby using his friendship with the physician's assistant to get around the system. Jane recalled how "the receptionists got mad at us because we had the physician's assistant do it for us." But Glen was simply pragmatic: "That system works better than if the patients call themselves." More blatantly, Cindy Ashton of Newberg Military Community also pulled rank:

I need treatment for an ongoing problem. I was at a crisis level, but went to the hospital. They said, "You're not dying; go see your [community clinic] doctor." Clinic said, "[an appointment is available in] six weeks." The doctor said, "Call Emergency." Emergency said, "It's not an emergency." So my husband went to the colonel and said, "We've tried everything we can." The colonel called the doctor. We had an appointment the next morning.

Some spouses brought their military partner to the clinic, partly to provide familial support, but also to make a more belligerent scene if necessary, as did the Barneses above. Spouses managed to be pushy without any assistance: "I'm supposed to be seen every week," said Meg Barnes, "but it [the appointment] comes two weeks later [than when it is made]. They only open the books once a week. You are supposed to call in at ten o'clock. On Tuesday, I had to get mad and use profanity. And then they just happen to pull an appointment." Unfortunately, the staff of any service-providing agency that faced such repeated belligerence necessarily developed further resistence and assumed an even more uncaring or withdrawn attitude, inviting yet more aggressiveness in the clients. Thus, a feedback loop developed that progressively amplified community frustration, tension, and discourtesy. One created an increasingly strident scene, because "the squeaky wheel gets greased." Few felt proud of having to behave that way, and the process created unhappiness, discontent, and low morale. This behavioral escalation was by no means limited to the medical clinic system. In any agency, the same pattern of receptionist-as-triage-agent fostered throughout the Army population both the unpleasant belligerence pattern and forced the service providers to protect themselves by withdrawing behind defensive walls of resistant procedure or attitude.

Lack of Choice

Some people resented what they felt was a lack of choice in the Army medical system in Germany. COL Carson, the senior administrator of Welby General Hospital, noted, "For in-patient treatment, you are almost locked into going into the military hospital." Kathy Brenton reflected, "In the civilian world, you have a choice. If you don't like a doctor, you go to another. In the military normally you don't have a choice. My daughter is two years old, and she has seen seven pediatricians. And she is healthy! Only one was actually a pediatrician. There are two doctors serving thousands of people here. They just can't do it." Kathy's child could not be seen by the same physician because she lacked choice and the system lacked resources.

Most soldier-families felt they had to use military medical facilities. To use nonmilitary facilities, one had to get authorization from the administrators of CHAMPUS, the military's family medical insurance program. CHAMPUS regulations contributed to the perception of no alternatives. As a supplemental medical insurance program, CHAMPUS covered 80 percent of the allowable cost of civilian medical treatment if military medical facilities were unable to handle the medical needs of civilian dependents of soldiers. To use CHAMPUS in Germany, one first had to acquire a "statement of nonavailability," which declared that the service was not available in a reasonable time period. If an installation did not have a clinic, then one had to travel to the nearest clinic or the general hospital to do the necessary paperwork. Some parents complained that referrals were not easily given, even when the required clinic could not see a patient for an inordinate amount of time.

CHAMPUS covered emergencies in full, regardless of who delivered the services. But an insurance representative or a military physician had to confirm subsequently that the situation had been an authentic emergency. To be safe, one had to call Welby General to get preauthorization establishing that the symptoms one experienced qualified as an emergency. But once again, military families felt it was difficult to get a timely decision under the pressures of a possible emergency. If a family member decided to go to a German hospital without preauthorization and the precipitating event was declared later by the American military medical personnel not to have been an authentic emergency, the family was required to pay the full cost of the service. Because this could be financially devastating, the only safe alternative was to go directly to the Welby General Hospital emergency room.

Family members felt trapped, locked into a single source of medical help. Kathy Brenton observed: "In the States you've got more places you can go to get medical and dental. Here you've got one ball game." Meg Barnes, full-term pregnant and living an hour from Welby General, expressed her anxiety: "If I go into labor, I cannot just go to the German hospital. I have to call Welby General and they have to decide." Exasperated at her condition and the risks implicit in the distance to Welby General, she blurted out, "I might not make it to the corner!" The requirement to use military medical facilities rode roughshod over the American cultural value of freedom of choice and the time required to get clearance to use German facilities for a suspected emergency added to the medical risk.

Language Difficulties

One way the military attempted to provide additional medical services for the families was to hire additional contract doctors, civilian employees of the Department of Defense. Some of the contracted doctors spoke English as a second language, making communication difficult. The difficulties so exasperated SSG Frank Barnes that he blurted, "The system is totally screwed to hell! I gotta get a nurse to translate the damn doctor. Want to talk to a doctor? You can't! On a scale of one to ten, Welby General is negative zero." Given how concerned people were about their health, they resented any difficulties communicating with health-care providers.

Bureaucracy

Quite apart from simply getting an appointment, negotiating the bureaucracy and dealing with paperwork requirements became a daunting task for a family. "I have a little boy that has been in and out of the hospital since he was two and a half," said CPT Cooper. "The amount of bureaucracy that you have to do is ridiculous. The amount of paperwork to get a second opinion—it is just about out of the question." Bureaucracy even incapacitated the bureaucrats. The NCOIC [noncommissioned officer in charge] of one clinic described the senior therapist in command of another clinic thus: "He's wore out. The bureaucracy just wore him out."

The bureaucracy also created health risks. In Kathy Brenton's case,

I had a kidney stone, so I needed surgery. I had to go to the German hospital, as there was no urologist at Welby General. My surgeon needs me to go to get laser surgery. But CHAMPUS doesn't list the newest techniques, so I'm going to have to go and get my side sliced up because CHAMPUS doesn't pay for modern stuff. If CHAMPUS won't approve it, I'm going to have to wait until the stone is big enough and makes me sick enough to get it out. Just one of the other stupid little stresses that you have to . . .

"Endure," or "put up with," I suppose she would have said had she finished her sentence. Thus, bureaucracy not only created a frustration, in Germany it endangered one's health.

Lost Test Results

Loss of test results repeatedly caused delays and frustration. The paperwork simply did not get back to the local clinic. With soldiers and employees continually circulating and with a central hospital doing lab work for medical clinics scattered over a catchment area of some two hours' drive in radius, accurate record keeping was a difficult problem. The Brentons recounted their experience. "I have a little medical problem that has been going on since 1985," said Kathy calmly. Her husband, Don, with obvious irritation, cut in to give more detail: "She took the tests, I don't know how many times. They lost the samples, they lost the results, they lost the biopsies." "We're dealing with two different clinics—the Middleberg clinic, and the Welby General clinic. And both the twain shall not meet. I have to wait six to eight weeks to get the results back," said Kathy with a hint of resignation, "and then make an appointment for two months later." Of course, whenever results were lost, one began again the frustrating task of making an appointment.

Breaches of Confidentiality

I will discuss breaches of confidentiality again in Chapter 10, "Living in a Fishbowl," where I focus on information flows within the tightly knit and judgmental military community. Suffice it to say here that the Army needed physically, socially, and psychologically healthy individuals to be ready for combat. Because medical information could affect military abilities, certain kinds of medical information flowed to commanders so that they could ensure combat readiness. Within a small community with many people on required oversight committees, key people could decode even veiled references to medical issues, and medical information could accidentally become widely known in the community. Such information created a risk to the soldier's career, however, and the risk in some cases led to suppressed use of medical services. Thus, soldiers and family members sometimes avoided using available medical facilities if their use might result in unfavorable judgment in the community. Virtually everyone felt betrayed by the contradiction that facilities that were intended to help one physically and mentally might actually hurt one's career and family. Thus, the potential for breach of confidentiality was felt also to be a breach of the support for sacrifice contract, especially because breaches of medical confidentiality could have substantially harmful long-term consequences.

HARMFUL CONSEQUENCES

Delaying, Deferring, and Avoiding Medical Help

Inadequate staff levels, impossible appointment procedures, belligerent attitudes, communication failures, repeated tests, and violations of confidentiality, whether required or inadvertent—all of these shortcomings resulted in soldiers or spouses delaying, deferring, or avoiding medical treatment. Such delays created serious health risks. Terry Walsh, a former critical care nurse, offered testimony from experience:

In an understaffed system, nonemergencies get delayed. Some of the delays create emotional stress only. Other delays potentially allow a dangerous medical condition to critically develop. Women with high blood sugar [potential diabetes] might wait six months to get it seen. And that six months can make the difference between using pills and having insulin shots. A young woman waits three months to get a breast biopsy. That can mean the difference between nothing—a lumpectomy—versus a radical mastectomy with chemotherapy. The same for the soldier—a forty-year-old has a high risk of colon cancer. If they wait three months or six months, that can be [i.e., create] a major problem.

Delays in treatment increased family stress as well as heightened risks. CW3 Don Brenton recounted Kathy's experience with military medicine:

> She can't get one of those appointments. If I was in the States, this would be handled immediately. But here it can't. I can't blame her [for being upset and not wanting to remain in Germany]. She has been trying at least every month to get help. She finally got an appointment for three months off. She called again to see the result and found they had lost the tests. She got another appointment for three months off. They lost it again. It took one year. Three times they lost the stuff. She says, "To heck with it. I'll deal with it another day."

"To heck with it [until] another day," only *sounded* voluntary. In fact, it constituted accommodation or resignation to a forced delay. Unfortunately, after a forced delay, any negative medical outcome will be blamed on the military, whether deserved or not.

Indeed, "military medicine horror stories" and tales of one's medical frustrations circulated widely in the community, undermining morale and contradicting the notion that "the Army takes care of its own." For example, LTC Max Newell told how his wife had needed an operation. Delays in the military medical system aggravated the problem until she almost lost her life. The officer shook with anger as he recounted the treatment of his wife and contrasted this with his own sacrifice for the military.

Even the medical personnel distrusted the system. MAJ Spencer Doty, one of Welby General's psychiatrists, said, "In matters pertaining to my family's welfare, I have felt really threatened here and unable to trust anybody here. If my family were to get sick, I would send them back to the States. This is a combat-oriented place and is not able to deal with family problems." Because the military medical system symbolized to all soldiers the Army's commitment to the well-being and physical survival of its population, families bitterly resented their inability to get prompt military medical service. In telling the tales of their experiences, they undermined trust and engendered fear regarding the medical services, and sought retribution for their mistreatment.

Such fears led some soldiers and spouses either to avoid medical services or to keep their families away from the military community system and its services. Gwen Cobb, for example, felt that "the doctors in the Army can't get a job outside.

I feel like a guinea pig sometime, like they experiment on you." Her husband, SSG Nate Cobb, emphatically asserted, "I will not let her go near the military doctor. I ain't got no faith in the medical system." So Gwen will be kept away or elect to stay away from Army medical care as much as possible, out of distrust of the system. SSG Frank Barnes also will try to stay away: "I would never go to the hospital again. I was treated pretty well in Hawkeye General [a military hospital in the United States]. But here—no damn way I'm going to a military hospital. I know I'm going to die if I go to Welby General." Jane Cooper felt the same even though her husband was a dentist in the medical system: "The emergency room is a joke. If it came to life-or-death urgent, I would take my family to the German facility and pay for the service. You can go any given day or time." When community members avoided medical services because they feared the services or the social consequences of having used them, the whole community suffered a sense of loss.

Reduced Personnel Stability

The difficulties incurred led some to seek assignments in the United States when they might otherwise have remained in Germany. CW3 Brenton said it best: "I love it here. I want to stay. The kids think that is OK. But my wife hates it. She has female problems, and [here] she can't get the care she needs. . . . So I'm not going to stay."

Helps That Hurt: Betrayal and Alienation

By far the most vexing breakdown in the support for sacrifice contract occurred when support service personnel, especially medical personnel, created unexpected harm even as they delivered the expected help. The cases above have already touched on this issue.

Soldiers and spouses bitterly resented being delivered benefits that paradoxically had the potential to be prejudicial, detrimental, or dangerous to self, family, or career. For example, a young first-term soldier suffering mildly from arrival shock sought help in getting used to the new country and job climate by attending the widely advertised group therapy sessions at the military hospital's psychiatric clinic. He later regretted the decision, lamenting bitterly, "It did help me, but it blew my security clearance for the rest of my life." No one had told him that "secret" clearance required "stable" individuals and that getting help from anyone for anything made one appear unstable.

Such betrayal was by no means limited to psychiatric medical services. The Atwoods, who sought professional marital therapy, are unlikely to seek any further help from unit leaders or military social work marriage counselors because they believe their seeking counseling lowered their esteem in the eyes of their immediate leaders and probably affected their career evaluations negatively as well. Soldiers and spouses told stories of similar damage arising from lack of confidenti-

·ality in family counseling, alcohol and drug abuse therapy, or the chaplains' counseling services. As detailed in Chapter 5, "Living with the Army," even the relatively inconsequential services—such as the library, traffic control, and housing management—were thought risky because, as we have seen, when traffic errors were made or library fines had to be levied, the Army retrieved its fines or gave reminders by sending them through the unit commander. The procedure generated fear that even minor offenses might have a career-damaging impact. When combined with the sense of medical betrayal, the result was profound alienation.

CONCLUSION

Given the value people placed on their health and the health risks they incurred to be combat ready, military medical care was perceived by all to be an essential component of the support for sacrifice contract. The shortcomings in the care provided made the soldiers and spouses feel deceived and alienated. Medical and counseling services were believed to be potential booby traps, innocuous at first sight but laden with danger to the unwary. The perception of unwarranted danger itself undermined the delivery of the services, scaring away some who needed help. The potential for betrayal, or the direct experience of it, generated much anger and cynicism, multiplying the intensity of soldier and family alienation well beyond that covered by simple breach of contract. Potential for betrayal made the Army a hidden enemy double agent rather than an open and well-meaning, if sometimes unreliable or inept, assistant.

To a considerable degree the medical care and social support services offered within the support for sacrifice contract ameliorated symptoms only. That is, medical care for families compensated for lack of access to local medical facilities overseas; commissaries provided American-style foods unavailable overseas; recreation relieved stress created by intense Army activity. But none of the supports dealt in fundamental ways with the structural sources of the malaise in the military community. To further unravel that malaise, that alienation, I proceed with a closer examination of the pressures placed on the military family in the overseas context.

NOTE

1. Such figures offer another measure of understaffing. The American Dental Association does not provide a recommended dentist-to-patient ratio. However, over the United States as a whole, there are 138,499 dentists serving a population of 270,299,000. (American Dental Association, *Distribution of Dentists in the United States by Region and State*, Table 1.) This suggests a ratio of 1,952 patients per dentist. The figures in this quote indicate a ratio of 3,100 patients per dentist, a 59 percent higher patient load than exists per dentist in the United States.

8

"If You Can't Control Your Family": Law and Informal Military Control of the Family

Even though your wife doesn't raise her hand and swear in, she is in the Army, too. Your family is in the Army.

SGT Rick Ashton
Newberg Military Community

Military families reported they felt more controlled in Germany than in the United States. I suggest that the perception is well-grounded and derived from four factors. First, the commanders felt a need for increased control, given their belief in increased threat. Second, military treaties with Germany required additional family control. Third, and most important, leaders wanted at all cost to "avoid embarrassments" that would compromise the goodwill of the German electorate. These three factors account for the Army's increased interest in controlling the family in Germany. The fourth factor—the American military family's tenuous legal status in a foreign land—helps us understand how and why leaders often tried to influence the family indirectly, through their powers of formal and informal control of the soldier.

The mechanisms for exercising control over the soldiers were considerable, backed by the legal force of the Uniform Code of Military Justice (UCMJ). Legal controls over spouses and children, by contrast, were minimal, for American law generally did not apply within German territory, and German officials generally did not want to intervene in what they considered to be American issues. Consequently, military leaders tried to influence family behavior with the formal but limited instruments of regulatory access. Alternatively, they had to exert informal, indirect pressure on the family by manipulating the soldier through the latter's obligation to obey. Backed by the UCMJ, the obligation to obey orders gave the leader the capacity to make a subordinate's life hellish, or even to end his or her career, if the soldier's family did not conform to a leader's expectations. Although most families did behave well by almost anyone's standard, mere availability of this informal, indirect, coercive approach cost family and community morale heavily. Indeed, the practices threatened careers, fostered ultracautious behavior, induced dependency, eroded spouse identity, resulted in a kind of withdrawal from the community, and in general, undermined the sense of personal and familial integrity of family members in Germany.

CAUSES OF INCREASED ARMY CONTROL OF FAMILIES

General Control

In Chapter 4, "Danger Forward, Sir!" we saw that control is a key premise of military culture, essential to the successful management of forces in combat. As SGT Todd Jasper put it, "In the military, they want to have control of you." In Germany, moreover, we saw that the premise of control was intensified by the perception of a very close and dangerous Soviet threat. This interest in control spilled into the family domain, manifest in the belief that "a soldier is responsible for his family" and in the common rhetorical question, "If a soldier can't control his family, how can he control the troops?" Control of the family, then, became a symbol for good leadership. Conversely, the out-of-control family could not be tolerated comfortably. Why did this need for control spill over into the family domain?

Obviously, the Army needed to control its soldiers while on duty. Not so obviously, such control extended into the off-duty personal life of the soldiers—especially officers and NCOs. Because the development and practice of leadership qualities were vital to military activity at all levels, especially in the ambassadorial atmosphere in Germany, a leader's personal life came under close scrutiny. LTC Keith Bateman:

> The hardest part of being a commander is trying to influence the actions over which you have no control. In the civilian world, your boss doesn't care if you get DWI [Driving While Intoxicated] or beat up the wife, as long as you fulfill the work time. [But] we are in the business of developing leaders: you will either fulfill the requirements of becoming a leader or you will get out. A leader must be trusted completely. And if a person has [pause], if a *leader* has a weakness, even in his personal life, that deviates from accepted standards of our [American] society, he or she will not be trusted. The family that gives us their sons to come in the unit assumes the leaders to be role models, and failure to live up to that will be a failure as a leader.

That the personal life of an officer or NCO ought to be exemplary was an inarguable premise. Military leaders were expected to deal with the personal problems of their soldiers because a soldier's irresponsible or out-of-control personal life, it was feared, might diminish goodwill in the host country or otherwise compromise mission readiness. Personal problems thus came under Army purview and could adversely affect a soldier's career.

So, as 1LT Russ Masterson, a battalion S1 (officer responsible for personnel administration), put it, when German citizens had a problem regarding a soldier or the soldier's family members, such as not receiving rent payments on time, "they immediately go to the individual's commander." Indeed, the senior command invited Germans with complaints to contact company commanders regarding any issue of displeasure. "We have written the individual, and then the [company] commander, with no response," 1LT Masterson recited from experienced memory. "Could you [the battalion commander] help us in this matter so important to German-American relations?" As he spoke, the phone rang, and 1LT Masterson took the call. I overheard him say, "The situation is this: She has money to last to Friday, for food. The rent was due on the 15th [this was the 18th] but no one has come by to collect. His [the soldier's] pay goes to the unit. So we need to catch him before he spends it all in Grafenwöhr. If needed we will take her to ACS." After finishing the call, 1LT Masterson returned to our interview and explained that he had just dealt with what we were discussing. A soldier had gone on a monthlong field exercise without making arrangements for his wife to access his paycheck. She had no way to buy food or pay rent. Food could be obtained by an emergency trip to ACS. Rent was another matter; it created an embarrassing situation with the German landlord. As the lieutenant rehearsed the circumstances to me, a sergeant came in and handed him the translation of a letter just received from this soldier's landlord, calling for the family's immediate eviction. The letter cited overdue rent, general noisiness, and other disturbances as reasons for the eviction—another small offense in the cumulative German-American dialogue. "How often does this happen?" I queried Masterson. "It's routine. Not a day passes that we don't have some crisis. Our function back here is to handle crises."

Accountability Required by Treaty

German leaders of course desired to maintain sovereignty over the country's borders and control its economy, adding to the requirement that the U.S. Army control the families brought to the country. Sovereignty implied control over such matters as permanent residence, illegal aliens, work permits, enforcement of contracts, obedience to laws, and payment of taxes, to include customs, income, and value-added (sales) taxes (VAT). Residents abided the obligations of their status. In the instance of soldiers, however, Germany, the United States, and the other NATO partners had negotiated a Status of Forces Agreement (SOFA), a treaty that allocated responsibility for the soldiers assigned to a given NATO partner's territory. Within the SOFA treaty, the German government agreed to admit soldiers and their dependents outside normal visa channels, on an American "SOFA stamp" supplied by the Army. Treaties granted the military the right to maintain post exchanges, commissaries, and other islands of untaxed economic activity within Germany to support military and family needs.

The German government held the U.S. Army accountable for everything brought into the country in support of military activities, including military families. Army leaders therefore sought to control military families and the economic and social enclave communities in which they lived, limiting access to them to

American soldiers, Department of Defense civilian support staff, and diplomats; to their dependents; and to the soldiers and dependents of other NATO countries. The U.S. Army monitored family members and soldiers so that they did not work in the German economy or make illegal transfers of duty-free goods to German citizens. In short, the Army acquired a treaty obligation to control family members because they were "sponsored" dependents in a foreign nation.

The Army-controlled personal life of a married soldier in Germany thus included his or her family. "You [the soldier] are the sponsor," said 1LT Larry McDugal while serving as company commander. "You're responsible for their [your family's] behavior in the Federal Republic." The chief of social work services for the large community of Grossberg, LTC Clyde Simmons, confirmed the principle:

> The sponsor is responsible for his or her family members. In the States, if your wife got picked up for drunk driving your boss may or may not know about it, but it wouldn't have an effect on your job. But in Grossberg, that is a reflection on the Army. . . . The soldier is always responsible for dependents. If a person is alleged to have abused [his or her] spouse or children, that can't be handled outside the chain of command. The Army is interested and somebody will have to answer for this.

At the highest level, the Army was the sponsor of all the Army families brought to Germany, held liable by treaty. Military leaders took a serious interest in managing this family responsibility. This of course applied pressure on the soldier and on the family. According to LTC Simmons, soldiers Stateside experienced many of the same pressures, but to a diminished degree, because the Army held the married soldier responsible for family member behavior only while they were physically on-post. In Germany, however, because of the treaty requirements and increased political sensitivity to embarrassment, there was no "off-post."

Fear of Embarrassment

In working through the issues of general control and treaty obligation, I have already alluded to the military leader's fear of embarrassment, the desire to avoid any behavior that might diminish the German citizenry's support for the American military presence in their country. Without question, the stationing of U.S. troops in Germany required a continuing invitation from the Federal Republic and depended, ultimately, on the goodwill of the German electorate. Thus, as guests, it was imperative that the soldiers and family members brought to Germany avoid offending the government of Germany or its citizens. One cannot stress the concept too much, for fear of embarrassment was a central consideration in military decision making and in military control of the family. Indeed, avoiding embarrassment became an obsession with some leaders, who sought to prevent compromising incidents by exercising ever tighter control.

MAJ Eric Buckley, a Judge Advocate General Corps lawyer[1] who headed Middleberg's committee that evaluated family misbehavior, asserted, "You have an obligation as a soldier not to cause embarrassment to the command." Irregular family behavior drew a sharp reaction if it created an "embarrassment to the command," said 1SG Gerald Hickman. He continued, "If a[n American military] kid gets picked up for dope, it hits the papers twice [as big as] any German kid's [problem would have]. Basically [when] that happens, they are going to pack them up and send them home. Embarrassment to the command with Germany is the biggest thing." So Army leaders made every effort to avoid even the appearance of problems. "They [Army leaders] bend over quadruple backwards to not offend any Germans," said 1LT McDugal. Any behavior by either soldiers or family members that might attract unfavorable attention drew close scrutiny from commanders and thereby endangered the career of the soldier in question. Thus, emphasized MAJ Buckley, "The command will not tolerate embarrassment. Diplomatically we cannot afford embarrassment." The increased Army control of the family in Germany flowed not only from a heightened sense of threat and imposed treaty obligations, but also and more importantly from the Army's urgent need to avoid embarrassing itself vis-à-vis the Federal Republic of Germany and its people.

MECHANISMS OF FAMILY CONTROL

Military commanders found themselves comprehensively responsible for the families of their soldiers and sought to exercise control over them through the use of law, Army regulations, and informal, indirect coercion through the soldier.

Law

Curiously, the highly complex combination of American and German laws and U.S. Army regulations that so constrained a soldier's work had something of the opposite effect on the family. To a degree, the military family was beyond the law in Germany. In American culture, law is the primary mechanism of official control. Soldiers are controlled through the UCMJ. The UCMJ, however, had no jurisdiction whatsoever over civilians and therefore had no application to military spouses and children in Germany. Dependents were completely exempt from the military legal system. Because the American legal system had little practical jurisdiction in Germany, neither were family members effectively covered by American law, the normal means for their official control. German law, however, did apply to American soldiers and to their spouses and children, both on and off American military property. According to the Status of Forces Agreement, "The authorities of the receiving State shall have jurisdiction over the members of a force or civilian component and their dependents with respect to offenses committed within the territory of the receiving State and punishable by the law of that State."[2] The *Community and Deputy Community Commanders Handbook,* which

governed community management, reiterated the principle: "GE [German] authorities are responsible for maintaining public order and security in GE, including
U.S. installations. U.S. installations are not extraterritorial; they are GE territory.
The U.S. is obligated to provide access so that GE authorities can safeguard GE
interests. . . . GE police do not, however, have an unrestricted right of access."[3]

The German government, however, often ceded its interest in the American
soldier to UCMJ for disposition in military channels. In part, this was related to
the SOFA agreements, which granted to the sending state (in this case the United
States) the right to handle its own internal military affairs:

> The military authorities of the sending State shall have the primary right to exercise
> jurisdiction over a member of a force or of a civilian component in relation to
> > (i) offence solely against the property or security of that State, or offence
> > solely against the person or property of another member of the force or
> > civilian component of that State or of a dependent;
> > (ii) offence arising out of any act or omission done in the performance of
> > official duty.[4]

In other words, the Germans wanted the Americans to handle their own internal
affairs. Although German law likewise applied to military family members,
Germany granted "primary" authority over dependent persons to the sending state
if offenses were "against the person or property" of that state. American military
authorities noted that the Germans cared little about American dependent behavior
unless it created a problem with Germans citizens or involved child abuse. As one
deputy community commander put it, "SOFA gives jurisdiction over dependents
to the Germans. They pass it on to us." The Germans preferred that the Americans handle their own dependent family problems. German legal disinterest,
however, left military spouses and children in a vague state of "lawlessness," for
there were no applicable American laws, nor did military leaders have judicial
authority over the attached civilians. Yet the military had an intense interest in
assuring appropriate family behavior so as to avoid embarrassment.

In the absence of a well-defined body of law and juridical mechanisms for
dealing with dependents, the military had two options to exercise control over
family member behavior. The first was formal and quite legal: Army regulations
gave its leaders the power to deny misbehaving persons access to military services.
The second mode of control was informal and not always legal: a leader could
pressure a soldier, add to his or her workload, or threaten the soldier's career
because of a family member's behavior.

Army Regulations

In the absence of law, leaders sought to control families by applying relevant
Army regulations. Without question, the Army exercised a clear right to control
its installations and services and to withdraw a dependent's privilege of access
when justified. Housing and all other post services except medical attention were

"privileges" under the governance of Army regulation. The *Community and Deputy Community Commanders Handbook* described how to deal with misconduct by family members:

> MISCONDUCT BY CIVILIAN EMPLOYEES OR FAMILY MEMBERS
> a. Purpose. Community commanders may take a variety of administrative actions in response to misconduct by civilians eligible to receive individual logistic support. The local host nation has jurisdiction for criminal prosecution of U.S. civilians in Europe, except when U.S. Federal statutory authority extends criminal jurisdiction to Europe.
> b. Community Commander Responsibilities. The community commander will:
>> (1) Designate an officer as civilian misconduct action authority (CMAA) for investigating and determining the proper administrative action to be taken in response to incidents of civilian misconduct. Actions may include counseling, suspension of privileges, community service, early return of family members, and request for host nation prosecution.[5]

I will examine each in turn.

Counseling. At the first level of intervention in family issues, the deputy community commander could request that a family member who had misbehaved come in to receive counseling—advice regarding how to behave, why it was important, and what might happen if he or she did not change. The DCC could recommend that the family member receive evaluation and, where appropriate, help or treatment from any of the community's available social service providers. Attendance at such a counseling session or at any recommended follow-up services was voluntary, for the DCC could not impose any punishment except suspension of services. Recommendation for counseling was, by far, the mildest exercise of authority to regain control.

Suspension of Privileges. The DCC could also recommend that one or more of the offender's privileges on-post be revoked. There was a general agreement that the privileges suspended should be those abused in the infraction. Thus, if one bounced a check, the privilege of using checks in the military facilities would be suspended, forcing the offender to conduct all transactions in cash. Similarly, at a community town hall meeting, BG (Brigadier General) Nathan Watkins, Middleberg community commander (and commanding general), described the consequences of student misbehavior on the school bus: "If there is a problem, the school bus will go to the nearest military police [station] and the child will be taken off. The parent will be reprimanded. Second offense and the kid will be off [the bus] for the year. No appeal. The school bus is a privilege that I can withdraw if conduct indicates a problem." The reprimanded parent is, of course, the soldier-parent, who is responsible for her or his child's behavior.

In flagrant cases of misbehavior, all privileges could be withdrawn. One could be denied entrance to the post generally, thereby limiting access to duty-free food, postal services, schools, and post recreation, including English language movies and videos. One could be removed from government housing. One's Army-issue

European driver's license could be withdrawn. Only medical services were inviolate.

Community Service. As an addition or alternative to counseling (and less harsh than suspension of privileges), the deputy community commander was authorized to try to correct behavioral problems by recommending compensatory community service hours for children or spouses. As explained by LTC Douglas Call, deputy community commander of Sudberg, the service hours he imposed always required that the military parent agree and be present with the child in the performance of the service. In point of fact, service hours could not actually be imposed on family members. If family members refused, however, the DCC could recommend that the soldier-parent give service hours, or he could proceed to the suspension of privileges that I have already noted.

Early Return. In cases of severe misconduct, the community commander withdrew military sponsorship. The misbehaving person immediately became an illegal alien, because most military family members came to Germany with the SOFA stamp in their passport as their only visa. Thus, withdrawal of sponsorship triggered a forced deportation. Speaking of his stint as a first sergeant, MSG Oscar McDonald put it bluntly: "I cut the orders and send them back. If they don't want to go, the MPs or the [German] police escort them to the plane. If they don't have a valid visa, off they go." Thus, the military family existed in Germany at the pleasure of the American military authorities.

Conversations with community members were replete with recognition of their conditionally "privileged" status. CPT Darren Cornell, Richberg's community chaplain, agreed that "having one's family in Germany is a privilege." At one of the regular welcoming and orientation meetings for newly arrived spouses at Middleberg, the military leaders of the community gave their greeting and departed, leaving the civilian heads of various community agencies to describe the services available and to give survival advice. With the military personnel gone, Middleberg's director of Army Family Services, Mrs. Tanya Griggs, cautioned, "There is always the fear here that if your child does this or that, you're going to be sent back to the States. They hold that high over your head here." Because gossip and complaint ran rampant, everyone had heard of someone who had been returned. The threat implicit in this knowledge sustained military control and demanded family conformity. It also irritated many community members. As CSM Barry Cutler, of Richberg Military Community declared, "The power I have is to keep them out of the post, or to send them out of the country, because I don't have UCMJ authority over civilians or dependents. The power I have is to cut privileges or kick them out. That can aggravate."

In reality, expulsion from the country was a rather infrequent last recourse. MAJ Quintin Scott, as regional chaplain, said,

> It is only in the unusual situation where the Army will put pressure for return of dependents. . . . If a spouse becomes a serious embarrassment, the Army has the right to return the person. The person brought the family as a guest at government

expense, and if they don't live up to the obligations, the Army feels it has a right to cut short the stay. Those kinds of problems are brought on [the family by] themselves.

Though well aware of their guest status, military families sometimes perceived the possibility of early return as a form of extralegal coercion that could be used at the whim or caprice of someone in command. The resulting sense of uncertainty induced a feeling that one had to be extremely careful not to create any embarrassment or attract the negative attention of any leader in the soldier-spouse's chain of command.

Host Nation Prosecution. The final resort of the community commander was to request host nation prosecution, but such prosecution was used so seldom that I found no anxiety in the community about being turned over to German authorities. American officials much preferred to send their problems home to the States rather than expose the problems publicly through host nation prosecution.

Pressure on the Soldier

These regulatory approaches to influencing the behavior of family members—although direct, authorized by regulation, and completely legal—were usually considered the last resort for dealing with family problems. Before taking direct official action, Army leaders usually tried an indirect, often informal approach, one that attempted to elicit acceptable family behavior by applying pressure on the soldier-spouse.

Increased Workload. For example, a commander or NCO could apply informal pressures on a family by increasing or altering the married soldier's workload. Such duties were easy to impose, and it would have been hard to prove that they were based illegally on a spouse's offenses. Although soldiers considered these informal pressures preferable to formal actions that would mar their careers, such informal measures still had a drastic effect on the soldiers, their marriages, and on community morale. For instance, if a deputy community commander found a family member unwilling to submit to counseling, the DCC could ask the soldier's commander to order the soldier to attend counseling or remedial therapy. Likewise, if a unit commander felt there were too many family problems, he or she could order the soldier, but not the spouse, to attend an appropriate remedial course. Some soldiers, for example, reported having had to attend a driver-training refresher course as a result of tickets issued to their spouse.[6]

Hostile Environment. In the ordinary conduct of work, a careless or incompetent leader could be aggressive, intimidating, or verbally abusive toward a subordinate. A leader could socially isolate a soldier he did not like, sending the soldier to a remote site or to accomplish an impossible task. A leader could manipulate the flow of information so as to exclude a subordinate from receiving essential instructions. In these and many other ways a leader could create a hostile environment and make a subordinate's work life utterly miserable. Likewise, if a boss decided he did not like you because your family offended him or her, you were in trouble, for you could neither avoid the onslaught of duties nor show disrespect. Thus, family member acceptance of, and therefore family member conformity to, conservative expectations became a matter of pressing soldier concern, for family behavioral or social incompatibility could become a covert threat to one's career, especially among officers.

Career Threat. In a harsher form of control, leaders overtly threatened the career status of a soldier in one of two ways. Command might bar an enlisted soldier from reenlistment on the basis of an accumulated perception, backed by documentation, that reenlistment was not in the best interest of the military. Of course, during my time in the field, people and positions rotated. The second Richberg ACS director I knew, Christina Ivie, suggested, "If I cause too much [of a] problem, I can damage my husband. They can say, 'Do not extend him; he has a problem wife.' There is no way to deal with that; you are your husband's responsibility." Indeed, there was no way to deal with that. And that, precisely, was the source of considerable anxiety, frustration, irritation, and anger but also of effective control.

Officers were permanently commissioned and did not have to reenlist at regular intervals. Nevertheless, all officers were evaluated with an Officer Evaluation Report (OER), and all NCOs except corporals were evaluated with the Enlisted Evaluation Report (EER). In Chapter 4, "Danger Forward, Sir!," we saw that evaluation reports substantially affected an officer's or NCO's career, and that just one less-than-stellar report, even if it contained positive but not strong adjectives throughout, could trip up an officer at a future promotion board and force his or her eventual departure from the service. Because of the subjective nature of such evaluations, soldiers were dependent on their leader's personal opinion of them. If too many family problems came to a leader's attention, the leader's opinion of the soldier might sour. Of course, family issues would never be mentioned outright on the OER or EER, for it was illegal to do so. Soldiers or family members could not prove this possibility, but proof was irrelevant. Soldiers and their families needed merely to fear that a family member's behavior *might* affect an OER or EER and thereby undermine the soldier's career. 1SG Grant Kezerian explained, "There is people that will say, 'Your wife is messing up, and this is what you're going to get on your EER.' Then he will go home and say, 'You're messing up my EER—because I can't control my spouse.'" Thus the Army penetrated family life in yet another corrosive way. When I asked a battalion commander, LTC Keith Bateman, to comment on people's belief that spousal behavior indeed affected the OER, he replied, "I personally have a dilemma: If a wife is very supportive, I may mention [on an OER] that he and his wife have been supportive. But will I say something negative [if the spouse were not supportive]? No. But is there the inference? Yes."

The danger to career came not only from the spouse but also from children. 1SG Gerald Hickman said, "If I had a problem, and command had to send my kid home, that would reflect on my military career. That would reflect because I can't control my family. How can I control ninety soldiers if I can't control one teen-ager at home?" The flaw in this line of reasoning is quickly apparent to anyone who has tried to raise a teenager. Whereas a commander has the UCMJ and the weight of the entire Army system to help him or her control childish or illegal behavior among soldiers, a parent has nothing equivalent for enforcing rules and regulations in the home. Nevertheless, there existed a pervasive assumption that one's ability to control soldiers was manifest in one's control of family.

In sum, Army leaders had quite firm control of the soldier, but, from their point of view, rather inadequate control of the family. After a frank discussion in a community command meeting where participants tried to solve a community problem, Richberg's community command sergeant major, CSM Cutler, blurted in exasperation, "The bottom line is who controls the soldiers, and has influence on the family," for these were the two components of the community that he had to deal with to arrive at a solution. With this statement, however, he highlighted the uncertain nature of the Army's "influence on the family" compared with its solid "control of the soldier." Though the Army was exposed to potential risk from family behavior, it indeed had uncertain control. Given that German interest in the family was "passed on to" the Americans, that the UCMJ and American law did not apply to the family, and that cutting privileges and access were an "irrita-tion," one can understand the movement to informal modes of control exercised through giving punitive work assignments, making the work environment unpleas-ant, and/or threatening the career of the soldier. Yet these informal modes of control had highly negative consequences on morale.

CONSEQUENCES OF INDIRECT CONTROL OF THE FAMILY

Impacts on the Units

Loss of Work Time. The intense connection between the unit and the family domain, which in American culture should be rather separate and private, caused leaders and soldiers to lose valuable work time, distracted by family-control issues. I asked several company commanders and first sergeants how much time they spent on family matters, and how they felt about the task. 1LT McDugal, an acting company commander, spent "a good chunk of time on family matters—not quite half my time." Other company commanders said they spent five or ten hours a week dealing with family issues. Company first sergeants varied similarly as to time spent on family issues.

Company commanders and their leadership cadres were expected to handle a great range of issues regarding the family. Traffic tickets, notices of overdue library books, bank problems, German landlord grievances—all crossed the commander's desk. For the enlisted soldiers, the papers then passed through the first sergeant to the platoon sergeant to be handed out in daily formations. 1LT Masterson described the typical procedure by which a community agency might approach someone who needed to return something or pay a fine: "A letter was given first to the individual, then to the individual" again if needed, both distributed during formations or passed to an officer by the unit commander. "Then [a letter] to the company commander, then to the battalion commander, then to the community commander. This is not at all unusual: collection letters work the same way. They go right up the echelons of command, much to our dismay. We spend an inordinate amount of time on this." 1LT McDugal felt the explicit contrast with the job situation in civilian American life:

> "If I was [manager] at Burger King, and someone just came in to me and said, 'Your stir-fry cook is delinquent in his TV payments,' I'd just laugh at him, tell him to 'take him to court.' We end up spending an inordinate amount of time on this type of thing."
> "Why not ignore it?" I asked, trying to fathom what was driving the behavior.
> "We have a whole reg [regulation] that tells us how to deal with indebtedness. It distracts in a major way from the time a commander can deal with his good troops. It keeps us out of the field. I have spent just endless hours as a commander dealing with this, and that detracts from the mission."

Most leaders wanted to help soldiers with personal and family adjustment, but they did not enjoy their job as a collection agency, nor did it contribute to unit morale. The regional chaplain, MAJ Quintin Scott, observed, "A lot of company commanders are uneasy, as they have not had training to deal with family matters. They say, 'I'm just overwhelmed with all this baby-sitting stuff that I am doing'—paying rent, etc." Besides consuming time, resolving family matters sometimes impinged on a leader's personal morale.

Loss of Useful Information. Although the loss of a commander's time and morale was detrimental to a unit, another loss was just as serious—the loss of corrective information that could greatly assist in running the unit. When leaders controlled family members by threatening the family's primary career, families suppressed information that might endanger their career. For example, at an initial orientation meeting for families, the wives spoke openly about their concerns only after the military leaders had departed. "The general is not here. The wives want to be able to ask or complain without their husbands being gigged," said Deena Lind, Middleberg's ACS director and wife of a senior NCO. As we saw in Chapter 4, "Danger Forward, Sir!," a complex system like an Army unit needs such "complaining"—in other words, negative feedback—to adjust and improve. But in Germany, soldiers and spouses worried that even asking questions might be dangerous to the shared military career. Christina Ivie, as Richberg ACS director, realized the risks to family spouses and tried to be an advocate for them: "I continue to fight for them, 'cause they can't speak up. They will get in trouble." Spouses repressed complaints, leaving leaders ignorant of where they deviated from their goals. As we saw, distortions compounded until they created a serious problem that could be corrected only through a major change of the system—a wild oscillation. The system then lurched erratically and soldiers complained of being "jerked around." Much of this could have been avoided had Army leaders at all levels not penalized their soldiers and family members for bringing up problems earlier.

Impacts on the Soldiers

Career Jeopardy. The most obvious impact on the soldier was that his or her career could be put in jeopardy by what would be considered a private nonvocational matter in general American culture. Company commanders were called on to transmit to the families in the unit everything from traffic tickets to library fines. Ordinarily, the commander was simply a message conduit, but he or she could become a collection agent for debts or an arbitrator if a matter dragged on too long. 1LT Larry McDugal, an acting company commander at Newberg Barracks, and his wife, Lani, explored the issues. "Your commander gives you the traffic ticket," explained Larry. "If the commander wants to push it, he can counsel you all day, every day. Library books, bill collectors, housing, MP tickets, it all goes to the commander." "And the commander can send wives home if they have too many family problems," Lani added, focusing on a spouse's interest. Larry then brought the two interests together: "My commander gives me my wife's traffic tickets." Here an officer advanced his wife's traffic tickets as an example of what could add up to "too many family problems."

Later, the McDugals returned to this theme, not in the context of violations, but to explore the widespread social pressure on the spouse to conform to the commander's expectations. "In the Army," Lani observed, "you're expected to go to the coffees on-post, and to volunteer. It reflects [on your husband's career evaluation] even if they say it doesn't." "It all depends on the commander," Larry downplayed. Lani raised the stakes with an example: "This guy's wife worked 100 miles away, and she wanted to finish school. They married in the middle of the [school] year. The commander told her she had no business staying down there. She should be up here with him. She said, 'I'm a grown woman.' But now it has caused problems for him." Larry no longer held back. "He [the commander] told the guy that if he couldn't control his wife, how could he control his soldiers?"

The perception that someone lacked control depended very much on the peculiarities of those in charge and might be triggered by quite ordinary behavior. The Walshes gave two examples of such whimsy. "One of the wives wrote a letter to the *Stars and Stripes*," said Terry, emphasizing that "the husband got read up and down for that." Hank confirmed, "Over here the sponsor is responsible for every one of the family's actions. If Terry kicked the general, I'd probably go to Mannheim [military prison] 'cause I'm responsible for every one of her actions." A few months later, they reflected on an experience from their own lives, adding their impressions of career and family impact:

"The Army is very persuasive. I got a ticket in October." Terry explained: "There is a [traffic] light out [i.e., nonfunctional]. They got my picture.[7] So he gets a letter to his unit. The sergeant gives it to him."

"You like to run lights!" Hank teased.

"He didn't get in a lot of trouble for that."

"I didn't get in *any* trouble," Hank emphasized.

"For other men, that can get you in trouble," Terry affirmed. "He can get skunky kinds of details. I know of two women in his unit that were told that if they did not calm themselves down they would be sent home. There are thirty-four in the platoon. Half are married. So 10 percent are threatened to be sent home."

"The husband was told to control his wife. I think you see it more in the officers than in the enlisted," Hank elaborated. "A wife's attitude—that can reflect on their next promotion."

As I closed this interview, Terry commented on how easily a wife could "torpedo" her husband's career by deliberately messing up, though she could think of no examples. When I asked COL Wayne Keele, the regional psychiatrist, about spouses deliberately undermining soldiers, he said he knew of several cases and recounted to me an instance in which, out of spite, a wife falsely accused her husband of child abuse during a divorce custody battle. The husband, a major, lost his security clearance. That forced a change of duty and ended his ride on the fast track toward promotion. Even though the psychiatrist testified that there was no evidence of abuse and that there was ample evidence that the spouse had invented the charges, the family process had planted doubts regarding the officer's ability to control others, and that was sufficient to blight his career.

Enlistees could be similarly affected by family issues and even brought to a crisis of choice—forced to choose between Army or marriage. SSG (Staff Sergeant) Jeremy Strong related that his "wife started screwing up, big time," having set their apartment on fire while he was on maneuvers.

I bumped into the general, by chance, and the general asks, "Hey son, you look like you got a problem: tell me about it." "No, I can't." He sent his aide to me. He tells me just to tell the truth. So I did. Then the general gets real mad and comes down on the battalion commander and the company commander for not taking enough initiative with this matter. So then the battalion and company commander are mad at me. So they say, "We are gonna get this guy." So they bar me from [re]enlistment, for failure to control my wife. How can I do that? I wasn't even there when it happened. They bar me from reenlistment for something from family matters: "Failure to be responsible for spouse's behavior." I can't be responsible for a human being that you see I can't control. Now I've got a divorce, and she is gone to the States. But the bar is not lifted. I have a new company commander, and the platoon sergeant and the first sergeant and the company commander say, "Lift the bar." But the battalion commander says "no." But the problem that caused the bar is solved. If they keep the bar, I want to know why. Next week I go for second review. If that is negative, I'm history, that is it.

Thus, potential for the family to undermine the soldier's career—the family's career—loomed over all, eroding morale as well as work performance.

Separation from Military Service. Finally, we must remind ourselves of what we saw in the chapter on family and work in conflict: the pressures and tensions between family and work can bring a soldier to sever his or her link with the Army to preserve relations with the other moral values and responsibilities of spouse and family.

Impacts on Spouses

Dependency. By making the soldier responsible for all services issued, spouses of either sex were pushed into dependency. Although the word "depend-ent" had been officially banned from the politically correct military vocabulary, it was commonly used in daily speech. The official form of reference was "family member," also common in daily unofficial speech, used to refer to any member of the family except the soldier. But to an adult who could not sign for any family support resources—such as furniture or school bus rides for the kids—but had to have the soldier present to sign; to an adult who had to use the social security number of her (or his) spouse; to an adult who received her (or his) traffic tickets through the spouse's commander, the official suppression of the word "dependent" was a transparent and at times galling evasion of reality. In fact, spouses were absolutely dependent on their soldier, almost to the negation of their own identity. Yet there was nothing spouses could do or say for fear of damaging the soldier's career opportunities and the family's future financial security. Meanwhile, lacking adequate official ways to influence spouses and family members directly except by severing their access to post facilities, the Army had no choice but to operate indirectly through the legally bound and treaty-relevant soldier.

The fact that the vast majority of sponsored adult military family members (dependents) were female turned this whole situation into a sensitive gender issue. Indeed, many wives of American soldiers in Germany felt they were being treated like children. Pam Hill, whose husband had recently been promoted to sergeant, lamented,

> It makes me feel like I have to ask his permission for anything. It makes me feel like I am a child. I feel dependent being at the house, going to the bathroom, almost. One day, he was at Sudberg [post], doodling around. I asked if I could go to Grossberg and buy groceries. He said, "No, I'll go with you to buy groceries." He goes and buys groceries. . . . Sometimes I feel that whenever we go shopping, he meets me at the cash register and says, "I'll write the check." He makes me feel that things that I could be doing, he has to do for me. When we lived in the States, I could go by myself and shop. But here, he is with me wherever we go.

Deprived of the ability to take care of family responsibilities, the civilian spouse was left with no way to feel like a mutual contributor to the family system. This put tension on the marriage, exacerbated the civilian spouse's sense of dependdency, and placed even more of an overload on the solder. CW3 Don Brenton and his wife, Kathy, the post's volunteer services coordinator at ACS, elaborated on the phenomenon:

> "It is hard to get things done here as a family," Kathy stated energetically. "For example, my husband is a pilot, gone a lot. Therefore I do the household chores. And I don't think they give credit to the spouse. For instance, registering the car: I would run into brick walls, like, 'Have your husband sign this.' And I say, 'No, I take care of household items. I run the family.' For instance: getting the kids in school, ID cards, signing for furniture, bank accounts—Oh, that is a story! Everything I mentioned said, 'Have your husband sign this when he gets home.'"
>
> "In the States," Don explained, "the spouse is allowed to do all of this. Here in USAREUR, the dependent wife or dependent husband is just that, and is not allowed to perform these functions. That is really frustrating to them."

To the extent that the soldier had to be present to sign for everything and to make all decisions regarding family services, the unit lost valuable soldier labor time, family members became burdensome appendages, and the spouse sank to the status of a perpetual minor. Indeed, the spouse became a hindrance, or an obstacle, even though she (or occasionally he) would rather be a major support system, relieving rather than creating burdens for the soldier. The result was highly contradictory, according to CPL Hank Walsh and his wife, Terry. "From my point of view," said Terry, "being a wife, it really controls a lot of your life. Like the missed dental appointment—he can get in trouble over it." "What else can get you in trouble?" I asked. Her husband jumped into the conversation:

> Our checks. In general, if a spouse has a habit of writing rubber checks, the sponsor gets in trouble for it. If she misuses her ration card, I get in trouble for it. If she gets too many tickets, I get in trouble for it. It is not like your wife is a responsible adult. It is like your wife is a child and I am the only adult. Yes, she is my spouse and my wife and a dependent. But they take it farther than that—like I have to hold her hand for everything she does. In ways the Army or the commander is very sympathetic. But still, the Army is very contradictory: they want you to be there on duty all the time, but they want you to be sure she doesn't miss her appointments.

Terry's remarks about the sense of childlike dependency forced upon her were particularly poignant because she was an experienced, licensed critical care nurse and college graduate.

An insidious duplicity, a "Catch-22," evolved from the Army's tendency to create spouse dependency. On the one hand, the military community system fostered—even demanded—a spouse's dependency. Yet a too dependent spouse could sabotage the family career. As COL Felix Carson, director of operations at Welby General Hospital, put it,

It used to be, "You gotta be just a good soldier." Now, if you're married, "You gotta be a good soldier, a good husband and a good wife." I'm not sure that is all bad. The Army says, "If we can keep your family healthy, you're going to be a more effective soldier." But if she is very dependent on him, she will ruin him. The Army is set up for independent women. But we have some dependent women, and we have some dependent men, too.

On the one hand, the Army was "set up" to require "independent women"—women who could manage families during their spouse's long, erratic absences and who did not require the Army's attention. On the other hand, the Army demanded that only the sponsor—the soldier—sign for the tasks and services that a family needed to survive. Yet those essential signatures could not be provided after duty hours. Consequently, spouses were placed in a no-win situation. They could not take care of their family's needs alone, but neither were they to place any family demands on their soldier-spouse that might evoke the negative attention of his or her command. If they did, they would "ruin" them. Thus, spouse dependency was structurally built in, yet it undermined the soldier's career and the unit's efficiency. Such contradictions lay at the root of much resentment and many of the morale problems in both the unit and community.

Lost Identity. Some female spouses sensed they had lost part of their identity and reported feeling uncomfortable or even angry as a result. Shirley Lincoln, a former company commander—bright, reflective, and married to another company commander (later promoted)—resigned her commission to have a baby. "The minute I had my baby and got out of the Army, I was treated as mindless. Before, I was bright. Now I'm just somebody's mom and somebody's wife—good for volunteering." Nancy Newell, wife of Richberg's deputy community commander, had "spent the past twenty years as a model officer's wife, volunteering." She recently completed a graduate degree and began working:

I was threatened three months ago [by the community commander's wife] that I had to stop all of this [graduate study for a degree in school counseling] or it would adversely affect my husband's career. You lose your identity being married to a military man. I'm doing it [the degree] for me. I'm not Colonel Newell's wife. [As his wife] you go to the social functions and play the role of being phony, playing the role of being Mrs. Colonel Newell. I've turned my life around. He has earned what he has, and I've earned what I have. Being a colonel's wife feels good at first, but it wears off.

Terry Walsh, the critical care/intensive care nurse married to Hank, a bright but much less educated corporal, described her Army status as a "nonperson." "They are always very respectful, but at the same time they are thinking, 'You are a child.' . . . I can't get a ration card; he has to get it for me. I can't get a checking account; he has to open it for me." "Whatever she has to do," interjected Hank, "I have to take the first step, get the ball rolling." Terry then concluded: "It is kind of like you're a nonperson. Yeah, they wanted my name, but they wanted his name, his social security number, his unit. I'm a person in my own right. If I want to study, what does his social security number have to do with my education? I'm known as Private Walsh's wife, not as Terry Walsh.[8] That offends me."

Thus even the dignity of a personal name had been stripped away, leaving the social security number as the only mark of uniqueness. Yet in Germany, spouses could not even use their own social security number. "In the States," said Terry Walsh, "they don't ask me for my husband's social security number. That is a *big* issue, is the control." Sally Damon complained, "All you hear is, 'What is your husband's last four [social security digits]?' I'm Sally! I have one, too! It is terrible. Everything is under him." The idea that having a unique number is essential to express one's personal identity may seem like an ironic joke, a postmodern revenge on the citizens of a culture that they think exemplifies progress. But having one's own number was a serious symbol to the inhabitants of this culture, and the Army's approach to sponsorship offended many cultural sensitivities.

Disrupted Careers. In American culture, careers and work help define one's identity. Yet the military's treaty-defined guest status blocked American spouses from access to the German job market, for by treaty, military spouses could work only on military installations. The job opportunities, however, were limited. Even though a congressionally mandated program required military posts to hire spouses in many service and support jobs, women perceived career development to be difficult, and they attributed the difficulty to the Army. Moreover, frequent moves, good for the soldier's career, blocked a spouse's chances to advance in a career. Terry Walsh, formerly a critical care nurse and now a waitress in the post hamburger joint said, "I love Germany. I am very happy. I can cope with the fishbowl [lack of privacy, the subject of Chapter 10]. I cannot stand that the Army is ruining my career. I cannot stand that. And I'm not happy that my husband is in the field so much." Notice the intensities: the career loss created extreme distress—a feeling she "cannot stand," whereas her husband's frequent periods away from home triggered a milder "I'm not happy."

Impacts Throughout the Family

Militarized Family Interaction. Among some families the style of communication thought appropriate or effective in the military setting invaded the home and became the style of communication inside the family. For the nonsoldiers of the military family, this could be quite distressing. As Gwen Cobb put it, "I'm not an active service member. I'm just a dependent. The husband jumps on you like he thinks he's got a soldier in front of him. [When I complain] he says, 'Girl, the Army makes me that way.'"

Vitiated Family Discipline. To a degree, the Army's interest in controlling the family undermined parental authority within the family. For example, Ruth Rodgers, of Patriot Village, was trying to deal with her teenage daughter, whom she had caught stealing from home:

If you whip your kids, no matter the reason, every time you spank one of your kids—and if my neighbor hears me spank a kid—that is abuse, and they can take my kid. You have no control here. You can't raise your kids right because if your kid stole something, it is going to go to the unit. But if you whip your kid, it is going to go to the unit. You're in the middle of a situation that you can't raise your kids, and if you do, you're in trouble, and if you don't, you're in trouble. You pop your kids in the commissary, or in the clinic—they may be going to break their neck, and you want to chastise them—but you do it, the MPs are going to come. And after the MPs come, the [German] *polizei* come, and your ass is going to go downtown.

She went on to explain the consequences to child raising. "You can't do so much because the law won't allow you to do so much. I tell my teenager, 'If you don't like it, leave. I will not live with a thief, or a disrespectful kid, or a liar.' But if you tell them to get out, they're going to send you to jail." Many community members felt such contradictions undermined family integrity. The contradictions also strained the fabric of community by forcing parental conformity to "safe" behaviors.

Impacts in the Community

Coerced Conservative Behavior. Sally Damon, of Richberg, suggested just how tightly soldier, family, and community intertwined and how this resulted in danger to the family and produced caution in their behavior.

"We had a friend of ours . . . [who] got into a fistfight with another woman, and her husband got in trouble for it—not the wife, *he* [the soldier] did."

"Do you think this affects families and the way husbands treat wives or wives husbands?" I asked.

"Yes, because if two wives have a conflict about something that may not even concern the men—but if you tell your husband, he is going to say, 'Hey, this could possibly ruin my career,' instead of saying, 'Hey, you guys go and fight it out.' . . . If I went and complained to somebody, some officer or whatever, and I just told him off, he isn't going to do anything to me. He is going to get in touch with my husband. And then my husband is going to say, 'Don't you do that, 'cause I'm going down the drain.' . . . If one day I decide to get drunk and act like a fool, and if I walk outside, and some sergeant major or sergeant major's wife is going to see that and say I'm not a very good mother, because I get drunk and whatever it may be—I shouldn't have to deal with that. *I shouldn't have to deal with that.* I'm not in the Army. He [the sergeant major] doesn't mean anything to me. I shouldn't have to meet his idea of Army behavior. In that sense you're kind of walking on eggshells."

"Walking on eggshells" within the community aptly described the feelings of many soldiers and family members. The metaphor suggested the delicacy, the fragility, and the restraint required. Relationships were chilled throughout the community.

Such uncertainty, in the context of arbitrary penalties for deviation from unpredictable and changing leader expectations, fostered excessive caution and conservatism. In societies the world over, people abide by their community's cultural rules to preserve their individual and familial reputations. This is not unique to the Army. What makes the Army family's experience unusual is the uncertainty as to which behaviors are "taboo" and which are not, because the required behaviors can change from commander to commander and sometimes even from day to day, never to be known beforehand. For example, I asked Frances Orton, the head clerk of military police records, if a spouse's minor action, such as getting traffic tickets, might affect the soldier's career. "They say it doesn't. But—" she paused. "You never know what they are going to do. They can remember different things. It may not *necessarily* have any bearing. It goes back to the saying that the sponsor is supposed to have control over his dependents." For those who desired a long military career, however, this uncertainty bred cautious conservatism because the boundaries were not known. As a result, Cynthia Watkins, the Middleberg division commander's wife, observed, "There doesn't seem to be a lot of room in the system for the maverick. She [the maverick] is not destructive, but she just doesn't do what her husband's commander or senior officer thinks is just right." Uncertain how a leader will react, every member of the military family was forced to live in a state of constant vigilance and adopt the most conservative, cautious, decorous behavior possible, so as to not offend anyone who might then report to a commander or create gossip that could be passed on to a commander. Thus, uncertainty regarding commanders resulted in self-imposed but excessively restricted control. The process thoroughly chilled innovation and variety. The pressure was felt by all, especially the spouses of soldiers at the most senior levels. Cynthia Watkins, having described the problems of the "maverick" wife, reflected on her dilemmas:

> Sometimes I feel that I cop out—that the most important thing [I could do] is to serve as a role model for behavior change. There are two things wrong with this: If you're sensitive to criticism, it is hard to take the risk. Some are less sensitive to criticism. But it would be very hard to have people not be supportive of me. Or the other: If you care about your husband—you're not even career conscious—but if you *care* about *him* as a *person*, and if in any way your actions shape or form or affect the progression of his career, that is a terrible risk. Captains [i.e., captains' wives] are in the same [situation]. They may not even want the senior wives' type of life, but if she loves him, she doesn't want to hurt his career. You have to be careful just in case you happen to run into the wrong person. You really don't know who you might run into. There are some men [officers] that don't look at the wife [in making Officer Evaluation Report judgments] and there are others who may. And you don't know.

Note how closely the spouses are identified with their soldier-mate's rank: wives of captains are referred to as "captains." More important, wives who choose not to be conservative walk in the line of fire. Thus, fear-related conservatism led to a continuous social reproduction of caution and therefore to the evolution of protective traditions. Traditional understandings enabled family members to envision one way they could live with minimal career risk. Because traditions are inculcated Army-wide, both by the force of rank and by the rapid circulation of personnel, such understandings partially suppressed the whiplash dangers of the peculiar expectations that could be imposed by local commanders and their spouses as they rotated through their assignments.

Psychological Withdrawal from Community. Regarding the social pressures to conform and the possibilities of withdrawal, LTC Bateman reflected, "There is such a thing as positive pressure, which makes the soldier member better—I don't want to use the word *control*—better *supervise* his dependents and keep them out of trouble. That is positive. But if it becomes so much [pressure] that they withdraw . . ." Unfortunately, something interrupted and Lieutenant Colonel Bateman did not continue this line of thought. Yet it is clear that the behavioral balance was thought delicate. With too little pressure, families might not conform, but with too much pressure, the members of the community might begin to withdraw. Indeed, as we shall explore in Chapter 10, "Living in a Fishbowl," withdrawal was a major problem in the American military communities in Germany.

Given the career risks and uncertainties, as well as their fears of sexual infidelity, some soldiers tried to keep their spouses and young children hidden, out of contact with the unit and military community services generally. According to Cynthia Watkins, "One of the biggest problems is men not taking the communications home. Men are afraid that the wife will get involved with someone else. He doesn't want her to embarrass him. He doesn't want her to be a part of the community."

Though I have divided this discussion of consequences by focusing on units, soldiers, spouses, and families, in succession, one must remember that in fact the impacts are all interactive; what affects the soldier affects the spouse, family, and unit; what affects the unit ripples through soldier, spouse, and family relationships; what affects any part of the family reverberates within the unit and the community—negative leading to further negative and positive leading to more positive throughout the system.

And there are, indeed, positive aspects to the close connection between family life and unit activities. Spouses often performed tasks that helped their unit. They frequently passed timely information to leaders, and thereby helped eliminate problems quickly. LTC Bateman fully appreciated the contribution: "My wife and other officers' wives say, 'Why don't you go look into this? Something is wrong.' Or 'something is right'! I wouldn't want it any different." But overall, negative consequences, suppressed communication, and lowered morale seemed to predominate.

CONCLUSION

In Chapter 5, "Living with the Army," I showed how mission urgency and mission complexity generated time-domain violations. Private or "family" time was often invaded and disrupted by the Army. In this chapter, I have shown how the U.S. military's awkward legal structure in Germany combined with the desire to avoid embarrassment led to attempts to control the family by applying pressure on the soldier through extra work, rebukes, and by threatening his or her career. The pressures on the family were considerable. As a result, the Army family in Europe was bound more intensely and more closely to the Army than the Army family Stateside. Clearly, as a result, careers have been torpedoed, units have been disrupted, much time has been lost, and information flows distorted. Perhaps more important—and certainly more personal—spouses and families have been forced toward more conservative behavior. Spouses have been made more dependent and have to some degree lost identity, spouses' careers have been disrupted, and some families have felt a need to withdraw from the community into safe, isolated refuge. The results were not salutary for the morale or well-being of groups at any level, whether soldier, family, unit, or community. In Germany, indeed, a soldier's spouse and children were—de facto—"in the Army." Not only was the family "in the Army," we shall see next that family members felt isolated in a foreign country, and that this isolation had further negative repercussions on morale in the military community.

NOTES

1. Judge Advocate General Corps (JAG Corps): All military attorneys are officers that belong to a separated branch of the Army, the JAG Corps. As a result, lawyers are only evaluated by their military peers in the legal profession, thereby insulating the Army's legal system from possible external influence.

2. North Atlantic Treaty Organization, "North Atlantic Treaty, Status of Forces Agreement," Article VII.1.b, in *United States Treaties and Other International Agreements*, vol. 4, pt. 2, 1978. (TIAS 2846, pages 1792–1829.)

3. United States Army Europe, *Community and Deputy Community Commanders Handbook*, USAREUR Pamphlet 10-20 (Heidelberg, Germany: Headquarters, USAREUR and Seventh Army, APO NY 09403, 1 August 1986): paragraph 66a.

4. NATO, NATO-SOFA, Article VII.3.a, *U.S. Treaties*, 1978–1979.

5. United States Army Europe, *Community and Deputy Community Commanders Handbook*, USAREUR Pamphlet 10-20 (Heidelberg, Germany: Headquarters, USAREUR and Seventh Army, APO NY 09403, 1 August 1986): paragraph 88. (Case as in original.)

6. Such measures were not unique to Germany. Because such punishments were driven by the Army's UCMJ and the regulatory control that it had just over the soldier, spouses were similarly punished—through the soldier—in the United States.

7. Germans use electronically triggered traffic-control cameras extensively and send photographic proof of traffic infractions through command channels.

8. Since Terry Walsh's husband was a corporal, and not a private, she may be recalling a particularly galling memory or she may be symbolically emphasizing the plight of those at the bottom of the status order.

9

"Little America": Islands of Isolation in Germany

You feel isolated because of the culture.

SP4 Betty Atwood
Middleberg Military Community

Married soldiers and their families often limited their interaction with the surrounding German society, thereby isolating themselves both physically and socially within the American military community. Several factors contributed to this isolation. First, the low value of the dollar relative to the German mark, along with the subsidized on-post dollar economy, discouraged Americans from venturing into the German economic system. Less obvious but quite as important, widespread lack of knowledge about German language, culture, and society, and fear of committing politically embarrassing errors also isolated these Americans. Finally, the two social systems were structured differently. Following "American hours" or American vacation patterns led one to be out of sync with German people following German patterns. It was difficult for an individual to maintain simultaneous connection in both systems. Together, these economic and cultural factors left the Army family in Germany imprisoned to a considerable degree within islands of American military culture. Among the single soldiers, those who remained most isolated were labeled "barracks rats," an apt metaphor for their quasi-reclusive yet socially packlike existence. The term was occasionally applied to married soldiers or their spouses who similarly focused their existence almost exclusively on the military installation and its people, making relatively little contact with German society and culture, living their lives in a transplanted "Little America."

THE SOURCES OF AMERICAN ISOLATION

Economic Enclaves

Many Americans felt that most things German were quite expensive and becoming more so. The poor performance of the dollar relative to the mark was the culprit. In early August 1986, when I arrived, the carefully watched "mark rate" was 2.10 marks to the dollar. The rate declined steadily throughout the next year and a half, briefly edging below 1.50 marks to the dollar before returning to the 1.80 level during the second quarter of 1988.

The Army tried to compensate by regularly adjusting the soldiers' cost of living allowance (COLA) and housing supplement. In addition, the bank on each *kaserne* offered a favorable exchange rate, generally four pfennigs (DM 0.04) better than the rate available in German banks. The hefty sales tax of 14 percent on items purchased in German stores was also a bit of a shock, even though it was added into each item's marked price and therefore was 'invisible' to the consumer. With a bit of time and bureaucratic effort, members of the military community could get a refund of the 14 percent sales tax on their larger purchases within the German economy. The process was as follows: One first determined the price at a German store, returned to post to fill out the documents requesting the tax remission, picked up the approved documents the next day, took the paperwork back to the vendor for the sale, and returned the documents with the vendor's annotations to the post. Some vendors refused to do the necessary paperwork. Some military customers would not or could not make the extra trip. In mimicking the tax-refund procedures available to tourists upon leaving the country, the tax-remission procedure available to the military community, combined with the identity check at the gate, made the guarded fence between the military installation and German society rather like a national border, the edge of an enclave economy within Germany.

In spite of the COLA and the preferable exchange rate, the slow decline of the dollar's value left many nervous about their future ability to meet the costs of living "on the economy." Miscellaneous daily purchases on the economy were completely unprotected against price and exchange rate fluctuations. Furthermore, the rate-adjusted housing allowance often did not cover the full cost of a German apartment and utilities, exposing the family to mark-rate losses on the difference. By contrast, on-post housing was completely paid for, with utilities except telephone included, and therefore safe. The cost excess created by the early rush to find an apartment—any apartment—now pushed the families to relocate on-post as soon as they were eligible after their required one year "on the economy." The problem was most acute for the junior enlisted personnel. In Pam Hill's view, "It always confused me why they would let the lower enlisted, who don't have a lot of money, go off-post, and the people that have the money— the officers—they get the housing. I understand that is the privileges of being in the Army a long time. *But!*" She emphasized her objection but did not continue. Finally, fear and uncertainty regarding the high costs of travel in Germany left some, especially the junior enlisted, unsure of their ability to travel or to shop within the German or European area unless they went in packaged-price military tour groups.

At the same time that the mark rate inhibited "off-post" spending, the Army provided a subsidized, culturally comfortable American dollar economy on-post that encouraged one to turn inward. As we saw in Chapter 6, "The Army Takes Care of Its Own," the military community provided banking services, PX and commissary shopping opportunities, as well as a plethora of smaller specialty shops. A U.S. post office, a gas station with rationed fuel at one-third the cost of that available on the economy, convenient laundromats, American-style recreational facilities, and the fact that the 14 percent German value added-tax was not levied against any on-base purchases all favored economic insulation from Germany. To limit its tax losses, however, Germany required the Americans to admit only NATO military personnel, support staff, diplomats, and their families to these facilities. The complex of economic factors—the unfavorable exchange rate, the ease with which one could remain entirely in the dollar economy, and the German desire to limit tax losses—and the added need for military security, virtually ensured the military community's separation from the German economy and society. The American soldiers and their family members lived their lives largely within the on-post enclave societies, separated since the end of World War II in fact and in symbol by barbed-wire-topped fences and gate guards who admitted only American soldiers, their families, and other NATO personnel.

Linguistic Barriers

Poor German language skills further separated the Americans from their hosts. In response to my question about what was "toughest" on the American families, SFC Kenneth Parry, the noncommissioned officer assigned to assist Middleberg's ACS, promptly replied,

> The decline of the dollar. The second toughest is being unable to speak the language. You may receive a letter in the mail and have no one who knows what it means. Here at ACS we try to maintain a list of translators, but usually we don't have someone who can. It is hard to even know what they are asking. When I lived on the economy, the owner would list information on the bulletin, and we had no way of knowing what or when [something was going on] or [whether] to leave a key to the neighbor to be able to do the repair. So you missed out on a lot of those things.

Inability to use the prevailing language made one's stay on the economy more stressful and added to the uncertainty and isolation of the military life. Children, too, were isolated and made dependent by their lack of information and orientation. According to Kathy Brenton, "The Army gives Head Start Level One [i.e., beginning German classes] to every active-duty soldier, but not to the family. Make it so the whole family goes to the language classes! My kids are afraid to take the [German public] bus because they don't know the language."

Although some personnel made a determined effort to learn the language, most got along with a minimum capability sufficient to order food or to point and shop. 1SG Oscar McDonald had lived in Germany fourteen years out of his twenty-one-year career and had married a German. I inquired about his language ability: "None. After my second tour, they act like they can't understand me. In every area, every town got a different dialect. I said, 'To heck with it.'" 1LT Irving Quilter had a more positive attitude toward learning the language: "In twenty years I'm going to spend eleven years here in Germany. Not knowing German breeds a certain insecurity; the barracks people often refuse to get out. I'm going to learn the lingo." Jane Cooper's feelings paralleled the lieutenant's: "Things are different here," she said. "There is a language barrier. I know people who won't shop on the economy because they are afraid they won't know how to pay for this. But there are enough Germans on the economy who speak English!" SSG Nate Cobb, of Richberg, reflected, "Another reason families put Germany down: because they can't understand the signs and they will not try to learn the language. . . . And on weekends, they go to Central Barracks or to General Barracks to the PX or the shopping center. It is packed with Americans. The American soldier goes to the PX like he doesn't want to see anything else."

Julia Martinez, born in Korea, had met and married Platoon Sergeant Ricardo Martinez while he was on duty in Korea. In her slightly fractured grammar, she observed,

> "Husbands work so long, and come home. After taking a shower, they falling asleep. [She laughed.] Weekends, they want to stay home. Wives: I say 60 percent they stay home. But here small community. . . . Husbands come home, and the wives don't get out. So they get tired of Germany, and they don't want to stay more than three years. They only go commissary, exchanges, and the dispensary. Hardly see other places."
>
> Ricardo confirmed, "A friend of ours, B__, [she's been] three years here and not more than ten times in downtown. Just this month we have been downtown maybe four times—walking, driving or something. I like to go for exercise and for the window shopping."
>
> "Not only B__, but I have several friends like that," Julia continued.
>
> "B__ said she's afraid," Ricardo developed with his parallel example, "and 'I don't speak no German so I don't go down there.'"
>
> "Even if you don't speak German, it is lots of fun," said Julia gamely.

Although it helped to know basic German, these two got by on their adventuresome personalities. Others were not so daring. At a gathering of junior enlisted couples in a village twenty minutes from Middleberg Barracks, SP4 Mike Thompson evaluated his experience: "It is a big difference, [living] overseas. You can't understand anybody, and you can't get a damn TV station when you want to relax. There is nothing else to do here." Chris Mercer, from an apartment downstairs, agreed: "I came from a small town, and there was nothing else to do. But this is even worse. It's an experience! It's been my dream to visit Europe, and now I live in it and I don't like it." Unable to speak German, these soldiers and spouses represented the many who felt themselves pressed into the exclusively American military society.

Cultural Isolation

Americans were much more likely to admit their lack of language ability than to recognize their lack of cultural knowledge about German ways of thought. When the American families reflected on German "culture," they tended to focus on the restrictive "don't" rules they knew: "Do not flush the toilet or take a shower after 10:00 P.M." "Do not mow the lawn on Sunday," etc. Many were aware of the things you "can't do" in Germany, but they had little understanding of the German reasons for these rules. This caused Jean McGregory a good deal of irritation and frustration as a result:

> We can't walk past 10:00 [P.M.], can't take a bath after 10:00 [P.M.]. It's not our home; we are just borrowing a part of it. We can't even let our clock run at night 'cause it goes "ding." My kids can't play in the backyard: their Big Wheel makes too much noise. Yet the German kids do [play outside], but my kids are limited to stay in the house. You sign a contract that you will abide by their rules. Sometimes I get angry, 'cause I hate to restrict my children from what is American. On the weekend, we take them to Central Barracks, where they can run wild.

"Life is a gamble," her husband, Sam, interjected. "You win some and you lose some." His demeanor and tone left the distinct impression that this experience had been a hard one.

The irritations Jean McGregory experienced arose from important German cultural premises that differed from the root values of many Americans. Although it is not my intention to provide a thorough analysis of German premises and practice, a few examples will help us understand the predicament of those young American high school graduates coming from a culture that emphasizes freedom and flexibility. Germans valued quiet and privacy. Sunday maintenance work on the house or automobile was generally discouraged by informal social pressures. If informal pressure didn't work, there was a legal solution, such as a DM 1,000 fine for mowing the lawn on Sunday, the noise being an offense. Weekdays and Saturdays had enforced quiet times with equally severe penalties for infractions. Indignant neighbors came to tell me that our visiting niece could not play the piano between noon and 3:00 P.M. Piano practice—even her concert-quality Bach pieces—violated the quiet ordinances, and the complainer threatened to call the local authorities. Noise after 10:00 P.M. and before 7:00 A.M. was equally *verboten*. In multiunit housing, noise regulations prohibited flushing toilets and taking showers after 10:00 P.M. Germany was definitely quiet: one seldom heard the sounds of music or partying from outside a home, apartment, or passing car. In this very densely populated country that sustained premises of order and privacy, such measures—to Americans, draconian measures—had to be taken to prevent intrusion on others.

Order, precision, and tidiness were pervasive in Germany. Unlike many American vehicles, German-owned cars simply did not drip oil. German parking lots had no oil blotches from dripping engines. At a German repair shop, any oil leak was repaired, no matter the cost, because of at least four fundamental cultural premises that were encoded in law. First, things that leaked were *nicht in ordnung*— not in order, not precise, not exact—and precision and exactness were core German cultural principles. Second, oil dripping on pavement surfaces created dangerously slick conditions when the frequent mists wetted the winding country roads and the no-speed-limit autobahns. Third, oil on pavement turned into a petrochemical runoff that offended the environmentally protective spirit of this small but crowded country's inhabitants. Fourth, oil on pavement was dirty, whereas cleanliness was a deep-set cultural goal of these people. These four powerful, basic premises led to the illegality of oil drips. As a result, Americans had to repair what to them were insignificant, inoffensive oil drips. They experienced more hassle at the mechanic's shop, where the boss might not speak English. If the Americans did not repair the leaks, they might be reported to the German police by neighbors. One's German neighbors might further marginalize Americans whose dripping cars confirmed the German stereotype that Americans were careless and filthy.

American military families found many German rules unfathomable. These Americans got in trouble because they did not understand how the American and German premise systems differed. They felt uncertain of how to behave as a result. In conditions of uncertainty and lack of knowledge, fear or anxiety grew. Pam Hill, just out of high school, expressed her fears about living on the economy among the Germans she knew so little about and with whom she could not communicate: "I think that I'd be scared half to death if I had German families to the side and above me." She felt very fortunate to be living in the basement apartment of a home already rented by other Americans. SGT Sam McGregory, after remarking that he and his wife, Jean, enjoyed the privacy of living on the economy, indicated that they intended to move into on-post quarters as soon as possible. I asked Sam why they were moving.

> The mark rate is killing me. Living here costs $200 a month above my allowance. And I don't like being told when I can take a bath. . . . I abide with the "no loud music." But as far as taking a bath, I can't agree. It is a lot of things I don't agree with. Germans must face the fact that Americans have a different culture. And we have to adapt to them, but them to us a bit, too. If you are not outrageous, there shouldn't be no complaints.

For some, these cultural differences led to a sense of disconnection and isolation that became more and more intolerable as time passed. At the root of this intolerance was the fact that Americans seldom recognized the importance of the premises of cleanliness, order, and precision that guided German behavior. Americans tended to be irritated by the behavioral restraints rather than attempt to understand them. This lack of basic understanding contributed to incidents that bothered Germans, embarrassed the U.S. Army, and brought discredit to soldier careers.

Systemic Disjunctions

Several systemic differences in transportation, store hours, vacations, and school procedures contributed to the isolation of American military families. Public buses and trains efficiently connected most of Germany. However, it helped to speak or read a bit of German, and even more so, to have a sponsor show one how to use the system. If bus, train, or bicycle were unacceptable or inaccessible, one had to have a car. German driving styles were quite precise—at speeds that were utterly unforgiving—because the culture of precision led to extensive driver training among its citizens. The SOFA treaty, however, enabled soldiers and spouses with a current license from any American state to drive in Germany after completing an afternoon conversion course. The soldiers had to drive as part of their job, and licenses were required. But some spouses feared to drive in these new conditions, stranding themselves in their apartments and increasing their dependence on their military spouses.

Differing hours of operation for businesses and government also suppressed American interaction with the surrounding German society. In America, where freedom of choice, access, and convenience constitute cultural values, shopping was available around the clock. In Germany, commerce was structured to comply with the German cultural emphasis on recreation and family time. Virtually all businesses closed at 6:00 P.M. on weekdays and at 2:00 P.M. on Wednesdays and Saturdays, though all remained open late one weekday a month. Many also closed for a few hours each afternoon. They did not open at all on Sundays. These restricted hours of operation were inconvenient for military families, given their erratic schedules, and left them with little alternative except to shop on-post. Finally, German and American holidays did not mesh, occasionally frustrating those trying to operate in both systems.

American families living in Germany found that differences in the school systems also contributed to isolation. Germans considered schools to be strictly academic in purpose, with no custodial role. Rather than being in school from early morning to midafternoon, as is the custom in America, German students left school between noon and 1:00 P.M. each day. They developed extracurricular skills at village clubs during the afternoon. If, during school hours, a teacher became sick, children were simply sent home on the assumption that a parent would be there to supervise them. These differences did not mesh with the American lifestyle and made German schools difficult for Americans to use. Furthermore, the six months to a year of struggle before children obtained language skills discouraged American families from using German schools. With but one exception that I heard of, Americans attended the Department of Defense Dependent School system on-post to avoid these difficulties and also to be sure that their children would   make a smooth transition into American schools when they returned to the United States. Finally, Germans coordinated work and school vacation schedules so that parents and children could share their six weeks of time off. Americans did not, and by following the American holiday calendar, they further increased the difficulty of using German schools and other institutions.

SOCIAL SEPARATIONS

National pride, racial discrimination, and educational deficiency led to further social separation. Both Americans and Germans felt a kind of national pride, a feeling that theirs was the best way, that contributed subtly to the continuation of relatively separate systems. Americans of color—especially Blacks—found lingering, diffuse notions of German racial purity to be offensive; they were occasionally denied entry to some German clubs or beer halls.

The majority of Army personnel were enlisted persons whose highest degree was a high school diploma. With few exceptions, their lives and their school experiences had not prepared them for international living in a multilingual Europe. Terry Walsh felt it odd that "A lot of people won't give their kids milk if they can't buy it in the commissary." I asked why that was.

> They are scared. It is foreign. Most of them are from small towns, from middle- or lower-class backgrounds. A lot are not even high school graduates, and they haven't been exposed. They don't speak the language, and it is all foreign to them. Change causes anxiety. And anxiety causes fear. They aren't prepared to deal with the differences of living in Middleberg versus small-town USA, where you knew everybody all your life.

The American secondary school educational system simply did not prepare its students for international experiences.

For MAJ Rodney Kimball, so many points of system difference added up to interaction being impossible.

> If we were on the economy, there are so many variables, especially the dollar-mark value. The car breaking down. The resourcing is harder. On-post, you don't face those frustrations. The linguistic aspect affects being able to be resourceful. Systems that are easily tapped in the U.S. are insurmountable here because of linguistic isolation. The cultural differences are really enormous. The holidays are different. The husband has a day off, but it is wrong for the Germans. Husbands have one day off. If he has to work Saturday, there is no shopping on Sunday, and so on. Sunday becomes not a day where you go see the German community, but a day to drive to Central Barracks for shoes. If you have a child in kindergarten, the German stores [open] at 8:30, [the] bank at 9:00, and the kids are home at 11:00 [A.M.]. [That] leaves you an hour to do things.

He then explained that the on-post bank used to follow the normal hours of its German employees and shut down for the noon hour, thus making it impossible for soldiers to gain access to the German monetary system without leaving work. He then returned to the difficulties of interacting with the German community:

> The holiday times are different. We have a German-American Wives Club. To get dates to mesh is literally impossible. Between the post schedule and the German schedule, we can't get together as much as both communities would like to. Germans have the main meal at lunch; Americans at 5:00 [P.M.]. Coffee for Germans [is] at 3:00. But American children are out of school at 2:30—no time to do it. We are American forces stationed in Europe: they [American military leaders] want us to remain Americans. On the one hand [we are told], "Be involved in the German community." On the other, they will pull you back for every goddamned holiday.

In short, a multiplicity of differences made it difficult for the Americans to participate in both systems. Job demands forced these people to focus on the American system, producing isolated islands, ghettos of Americans.

THE CONSEQUENCES OF ISOLATION

Culture Shock and Turning Inward

By itself, each system difference was probably tolerable. Taken together, however, the effect could be overwhelming, leading to culture shock and protective withdrawal, a turning inward within the American community. Hank and Terry Walsh were among the best-adapted people I met, but the compound effects of cultural differences still affected them.

> "In a lot of ways it's hard over here," said Terry. "I've found the Germans a lot different in lifestyles [than what] we as Americans grew up with. Going to a store and not being able to ask for the simplest assistance, that is a shock."
>
> "The Army to an extent tries to help with the language courses. Basic German is taught," Hank offered in consolation.
>
> "Just the whole way they live," Terry continued, even though she was learning more German and seemed better adapted to Germany than Hank. "They walk a lot, use public transportation. The kids walk around a lot and take the public bus to school."
>
> "America has a school bus; the German system catches the public bus," Hank detailed.
>
> "The shop hours are different. You can go grocery shopping in California at any time," Terry compared. "Here everything shuts down. On Sundays—I'm not sure it is religious—it is a family day, a quiet day. People walk. They don't walk in the States; they don't spend as much time together. In Germany, the only people who smile are the kids. It is much quieter in a big department store; there is not the sound of voices like in the States. Here, they go to the grocery store every day. I didn't want to do that, every day."

Even though Terry showed an unusually sophisticated sense of behavioral aware-ness and cultural nuance, was among the best adapted to German culture that I met, and appreciated the family-friendly aspects of German practices, she did not want to adopt the German ways. Out of culture shock or due to simple complexi-ties or economic restraint, Americans tended to interact little with the German society and instead oriented themselves more toward the American military community system.

Hating Germany

Such isolation fostered among soldiers and their families a pervasive negative attitude toward Germany. As the isolation festered, soldiers or family members said they "hate it" in Germany or in the Army. According to SSG Nate Cobb, "A lot of them will just sit at home all day long, seven days a week, and then say 'Germany ain't worth ___.'" He grunted the last syllable, perhaps avoiding the usual word—"shit"—that fits this speech pattern. "They sit there, not go nowhere, not do nothing. They'll say: 'I don't have nothing for Germany.' I'll say, 'Wait a minute. Have you seen any of it? Got involved?' 'No,' [they say]. *That* is the reason they hate Germany." As the burden of anger and frustration toward life in Germany accumulated, one may presume it found expression from time to time in the behavior of the soldiers and spouses, thereby adding to the problems of main-taining good relations with the host country. The potential for angry outburst invited a self-imposed "time-out" of isolation in the American military ghetto.

Alienation

If the anger and frustration of isolation were not directed outward, they some-times were turned inward in ways that cannibalized the family. "You been around," 1SG Evan Roper rebuked me mildly for asking about conditions that to him were so obvious:

> You get a lot of frustrated wives if you're isolated. In the States, everybody speaks English. You can go around the street and see Suzie. You can walk down the street and see Mom and Dad. Here, it's an entirely different situation. A lot of times it is not the man's problem, it is the wives' problems. Some of the wives, they can't come out of the apartment unless the husband comes home. That is not healthy, sir. Sooner or later, something is gonna give. Might involve child abuse. Or somebody might get killed. Or she might kill herself.

In fact, what "gives" is not mounting violence but mounting frustration and alienation.

Boredom, Domestic Isolation, and Giving Up

One expression of such alienation is a retreat to isolation. 1SG Roper: "Back in the States they stuck together. . . . And all of a sudden, *here*, he don't come home regular. He's in the field or stops for a beer. The husbands take them to the commissary or the PX. Will you believe you got people that been here four years and haven't seen nothing in Germany? Some of the wives can't drive. Husband don't have time for them. . . . Far as she can go is walk around the corner." When SGT John Hill moved into the basement apartment of the house that my family and I occupied on the economy, I had the opportunity to observe this type of situation firsthand. Pam Hill arrived three months later. She was afraid to get a driver's license. We watched her for months as she stayed home with one and then two young children, never venturing out, except to post with her husband. She confided, "You can put this down: my most exciting part of the day is waiting for John to bring home the mail." At an Officers and Civilian Wives Club meeting in Central Barracks, Victoria Zeller made almost the same remark: "The highlight of the day is when my husband comes home and brings the mail. I write letters like, you know, fifteen a week."

Unfortunately, isolation was not unique to spouses living on the economy. Mr. Walter Stanley, serving as Middleberg Barrack's acting DCC, reflected on the isolation: "I've met the type of people that their whole life is centered on Middleberg Barracks, because they are afraid to go downtown. They would spend their whole life in a little rut between the housing area and the post. It was really strange. My wife meets that all the time, especially among the wives." These were the proverbial "barracks rats," single and married people who seldom left the protective custody of the military enclave.

Soldiers and family members underscored their isolation when they described themselves as being stationed on "Planet Mid." Terry Walsh explained the expression: "'Planet Mid' includes Middleberg Barracks and Planet Mid. It is isolated. The United States is stationed on Planet Mid." SGT Edgar Granville used the term spontaneously and then defined it for me. "Planet Mid means a lonely planet with nothing to do." In other words, being stationed in Germany was like being sent to an alien planet, Mid, on which the Americans had established an isolated space colony, Middleberg Barracks, from which some hardly ventured unless fully equipped during required military training expeditions.[1]

One might think that the isolation of living in a little German village at some distance from the military installation would draw its American families together, but it didn't. In fact, I encountered only one instance on the economy in which several soldiers and their families did much socializing. They were from the same company and had let their buddies know of nearby apartments as they came vacant. Most people were like SFC Kenneth Parry, who did not even know the other Americans living in his same building, even though his job at ACS connected him to family and community issues.

In the face of so many differences and outright difficulties, some people just gave up trying to make a connection to Germany. Deena Lind, Middleberg's ACS director, explained what happened when she offered classes on German culture: "I offered a 'Germany Can Be Fun' free class, and—max—eight came. I've met many that said, 'I'm going to be miserable, and darn it, don't try to change it on me.' I'm afraid Americans as a whole are embarrassed, and think, 'If I don't try, no one knows I can't do it.'" In giving up, people refused to explore, savor, enjoy, appreciate, or even admit the possibility of good experiences in Germany. In so doing, they added to their isolation and risked increased frustration, anger, and the possibility that they would turn that anger corrosively inward on themselves, their families, or the military community. Whether such inwardly turned anger led to increased violence, spouse or child abuse, or suicide, I do not know, though some members of the community felt it was likely. What is certain is that such feelings amplified the conditions for worsening morale, the native term for both personal and social alienation.

BREAKING OUT OF ISOLATION

If physical, social, economic, linguistic, and cultural isolation from the German surroundings fostered a negative experience, we may profitably examine the results experienced by those who deliberately overcame the obstacles and established some form of social connection to Germany. It is my general impression that those soldiers and family members who did so were able to adapt to or absorb the stresses of military life much better than those who did not. Even though the soldiers and spouses still had to deal with the difficulties of too much work or personality conflict within their chain of command, they had an outlet, a buffer, a mode of escape. They did not feel so trapped.

Prior experience helped some to connect better. Couples on a second tour to Germany felt their second tour was much easier than their first. Said Marla Bracken: "We kind of knew what to expect. But our first tour was a struggle. We were newlyweds, and it is a virtual cultural shock. E2 pay. . . . We've gone through a lot of hard times over here but we finally got it going. Seen a lot of Europe this time. First time, we had to survive." In prior chapters we heard her sergeant husband say, "It's neat to be here," and Marla called "coming to Germany . . . exciting." Prior experience took the sharp edge off the arrival process. Because a second tour years later meant higher rank, more money, increased knowledge of the American military system, and, perhaps, a greater sense of the German culture, it added up to an easier experience for many. Those who in some way connected with Germany or its people often came to enjoy their stay overseas.

Some language ability freed the people who had it, alleviating their need for Germans to use English, and lessening their frustration when Germans did not. "I've completed two courses [of German]," said Terry Walsh. "I can communicate with just about anybody I want, but I'm not exactly fluent." Though "stuck" on the economy, Terry was loving the experience. Those who tried to learn German seemed to enjoy living in Germany. Julia Martinez and her husband, Ricardo, a platoon sergeant, both thoroughly enjoying their stay in Germany, were learning

German. "I like to get to know people over here," Julia gave as her reason for learning German. "They are very nice, if you treat them nice. I was in a very lovely house, with nice people [in a community of] about 16,000."[2] "There were four or five American families," said Ricardo. "The neighborhood is excellent; we had no problems." "I have no complaints in Germany," Julia concluded. Even after moving to Middleberg government quarters, this family benefited from a positive attitude toward their residence in Germany, in part because of their effort to learn some of the language and thereby reduce their own isolation.

A little bit of cultural knowledge—not so much about rules but about the principles that underlie the differences in German daily life—helped people feel less isolated and frustrated. Often, those making an effort to learn the language, like Terry Walsh, had the more sensitive and appreciative insights into the logic of German life.

Some kind of social connection to a German—a friendship with an elderly couple or a landlord, a German boyfriend or girlfriend, a German drinking partner—helped overcome isolation. Even relationships that were completely transitory, based on a chance encounter, served this purpose. "The thing that changed me," said Jean McGregory, "was so many stopped when my car skidded off the road and they tried to help." Jean, now feeling positive toward Germany, had been "changed" by the mishap, and her husband, with other casual associations, had "no complaints." Two families mentioned a warm relation with a German landlord or grandmotherly landlady who rented them their apartment. Pam Hill, who hated her first year, came to love Germany when she was virtually adopted by a German next-door neighbor who showed her how to shop and negotiate the German system. Before this connection, Pam had been singularly miserable.

A few families deliberately engineered social encounters. The Kimballs, on their second tour, chose to aggressively move into a number of German activities, in spite of language inadequacy and on-post residence. Rodney, an avid fly fisherman, joined the local German fly-fishing club. The children took riding lessons at a German stable and joined a German ice-skating club. Though there were many strains and demands within their military life, these outside activities added balance, provided escape from the pressures, and initiated the process of learning to speak German. A military medical doctor had inquired through his contacts about enrolling his children in the German high schools and was told I was the only person in the Grossberg Military community (about 20,000 families) known to have done it. He followed suit and later claimed it was a great experience.

Of course, it helps if one has a confident, exploring personality, as exemplified by the Martinez couple, and perhaps some exposure to languages and cultures in high school or college. But for some, the connection to Germany did not require a personal relationship at all. It was enough simply to drive away from base and enjoy some aspect of Germany or Europe: skiing, *volksmarching*, hiking, shopping, or sightseeing.

CONCLUSION

American soldiers and their families tended to turn inward and cling together. On the one hand, they were pushed together by the forces of a weak dollar, linguistic and cultural inadequacy, and the fear of making mistakes. On the other hand, they were pulled together by the attractive power of unit activities, installation services, economic subsidies, English language, American symbols, and a community of shared experience. The result was an isolated, densely interconnected American military community, ofttimes angered by their forced imprisonment in an alien environment. As we shall see next, their isolation and dense interconnection greatly amplified the negative effects of military career judgment and hierarchical control within the community.

NOTES

1. The psycholinguistic effect was much better in the original usage, where the abbreviation of the German city name left a harsh, alien-sounding planet name. Unfortunately, my choice of pseudonyms did not capture the guttural effect of actual soldier usage trying to abbreviate a long German city name.

2. Julia's Korean background strongly influenced the grammar of her English. In these sentences, I have taken the liberty of moving two words to more grammatical locations.

10

"Living in a Fishbowl": Surveillance and Social Control in the Military Community

You understand that the Army family is in a fishbowl. If someone does something, it will be reported to me. Another family will "drop a dime" on the offending family.

LTC Douglas Call, DCC
Sudberg Military Subcommunity

Married soldiers and their spouses often said their military community life in Germany felt like "living in a fishbowl" of constant surveillance and intense judgment. Several factors helped create fertile conditions for both. Economic pressures and cultural inabilities had pushed these Americans into isolated, compact communities with few outside interactions, and residential closeness and interlocking relationships subjected all aspects of their lives to pervasive scrutiny. Commanders were under pressure to control family behavior to avoid embarrassing the American military presence in Germany. Finally, the military system's pyramidal rank structure, with its built-in attrition, made a negative evaluation report dangerous to a soldier's, and especially an officer's, career. Family behavior subtly became one of the factors on which married soldiers were evaluated. In this chapter, I will show how the small-town characteristics of the community made the systems of intended and unintended surveillance and judgment all the more alienating.

Certain characteristics of life in Germany amplified and fostered the scrutiny and judgment structurally inherent in military life. For example, in Germany, all telephone calls—local, regional, or long distance—accrued message units based on time and distance that increased one's phone bill rapidly. Communication through the German postal service was likewise relatively expensive. Therefore, many communications, even if personal, were passed to soldiers and spouses by routing messages through the company commanders and down the chain of command, to be handed to officers in meetings or announced to enlisted soldiers in outdoor formations. Similarly, as the "chain of concern" was used to pass information, relatively personal data became widely known. The problem was paralleled in the community counseling systems, which too often and too easily breached therapeutic confidentiality. Finally, by living in densely concentrated housing areas where coworkers by day became neighbors at night, family problems known in the neighborhood became known also in the critically judgmental work area.

The constant scrutiny and intense judgment led to distrust in the units, career damage to soldiers, and systematic withdrawal of soldiers and families from community activities to evade scrutiny. Within the community, a gossipy climate eroded community attachments, fostered caution, and undermined trust and friendship. This contributed to a feeling that things never were what they were represented to be and that safety lay in maintaining a facade. Life in the constantly scrutinized, intensely judgmental community contributed greatly to soldiers and spouses both disliking their stay in Germany and hating the Army. Many felt alienated in the extreme by the processes of judgment and the nature of military social control.

JUDGMENT AND SOCIAL CONTROL

Any army has substantial need for social control, for an army must have the capacity to move soldiers where they are needed, whatever the reason, and expect that they are there obeying orders. The U.S. Army in Germany had this same need, amplified by the desire to avoid political embarrassment and by the perceived nearness and urgency of the Soviet threat. Such control required judgment—constant evaluation of situation and personnel—and good judgment required accurate information.

The need for accurate information led to pervasive reporting, to help assess unit coordination, command, control, and readiness. There were reports on the numbers of soldiers on duty, their health, and their availability for deployment. There were reports on their skill levels in their job (MOS—military occupational specialty) assignment, on their basic combat skills, and on their marksmanship. There were reports that inventoried equipment and its readiness for combat, reports on ammunition supplies, reports on communication systems, and reports on modes of transportation. There were key reports that assessed soldier and officer performance, the EER and the OER. Not only did leaders gather data and report on soldiers and military equipment, they also reported on family and community issues. There were reports that determined whether families had adequate arrangements for child care. There were reports and rosters that mapped where families lived and ensured that they had passports, shots, and emergency kits ready so that they could grab one bag and begin evacuation within minutes of notification. These and other reports established that the Army in Germany was ready, that the installations were secure, that spies and moles might be less effective, that officers and NCOs would be promoted or eliminated from the service, and that families were ready for alerts, deployments, or general evacuation from Europe. All these reports and many more were required by Army regulations and could not be evaded without severe career consequences. In a word, the Army had an ingrained ethic of reporting on everything.

This ethic spilled over into the community, both in official community functions and activities, and in informal community life. The fusion of domains led to the informal social community and its families being penetrated by the consequences of Army activities and the styles of Army thought processes, what some social scientists would call Army ethos, and others, Army corporate culture. Thus, community members participated in the ubiquitous logic of surveillance, reporting, and judgment. They did so through constant watchfulness, as well as judgmental talk, gossip, and rumor. Some community members deliberately passed their personal knowledge or their accumulations of gossip and rumor into military channels. A few did so for personal competitive advantage, some did it purely to maintain community standards, and yet others did it quite unconsciously.

Since most adult community members were either soldiers or married to one, "pillow talk" quickly passed informal information and judgments of the family and community domains into the military domain, where it could become part of official reports or exist as background knowledge of leaders. Once in the minds of leaders, it could not help but be used as a subtle factor in the way some NCOs or officers allocated work assignments or in the way some commanders wrote up the career evaluations of others. The combination of the need for control, the ethic of reporting, networks of information, openness to surveillance, and requirement to judge and prune ranks allowed leaders to control both soldiers and their families by threatening the married soldier's career. Out of this risk and consequent fear flowed a number of behaviors that had adverse consequences on the unit, individual, family, and community, which we will explore in the remainder of this chapter. Because judgment and control were dependent on adequate information, I must first describe the processes of information flow in the military community.

SURVEILLANCE AND INFORMATION FLOW

In Chapter 9, "Little America," we saw that one source of community isolation and narrowed social interaction stemmed from the American soldier's and family members' general inability to access the culture, society, and physical environment of Germany. Cut off from outside contacts, the soldier's work community and social community collapsed into one. In Chapter 8, "If You Can't Control Your Family," we saw that another source of community closure and intense judgment flowed from the leaders' use of extra work assignments or career evaluation threats to control family member behavior by pressuring the soldier. Because a broad spectrum of activities were appropriate to the "good order and discipline" of a combat-ready unit in Germany, much of a soldier's life and much of the lives of his or her family members came under the scrutiny of the Army.

Terry Walsh expressed ably the interaction of language isolation, community closure, surveillance, gossip, judgment, and career risk: "Because you don't know the language—you draw together. It's just like the small town—everybody going on about what is going on. But if Hank's boss gets wind of . . . some problem, like a missed dental appointment, he can get into trouble over it. From my point of view, being a[n Army] wife, it really controls a lot of your life." The working unit's close embrace of the family—a fusion of domains—brought trouble. The trouble began with the intermixing of information flows in work, housing, and community areas.

In the Work/Unit Areas

Throughout the work areas, information moved down the hierarchy with ease and speed, and up the hierarchy if required. Some of the information gleaned and transmitted up the chain of command was official and required: such as reports from the Noncombatant Evacuation Office on the evacuation readiness of family members and child-care plans verifying arrangements for dependent care during mobilizations. Much information passed down the chain of command for convenience. German postage, for example, was expensive, so the command saved money by sending a wide variety of messages through the chain of command to the enlisted formations, and from there to the families. Some information passed through the chain because of the coercive value of the route. From the trivial overdue library notices to the substantial overdue rent complaints that I have already detailed in other chapters, people used the chain to get results in family and community matters that were only tangentially related to the unit's mission.

In the process of relying on the chain of command to pass information, a variety of persons became aware of family-related data that many would have preferred to remain private. As I was exiting the field, I gave a courtesy briefing to the women of Middleberg's ACS. I reviewed the fact that mail was passed out to the soldiers by their platoon sergeants, as were traffic tickets, library fines, and administrative and personal messages of all kinds. "So does your gynecologist's appointment results," blurted one woman amid gales of laughter. "My husband's company commander gave me my gynecologist's report and said, 'Everything was OK.'" All agreed when someone summarized, "So the whole company knows about your life." Thus, not only one's peers in the squad, but all members of a platoon or even a company became privy to what someone might have considered a private matter.

Workmates—fellow soldiers—also chatted throughout the day and shared information not just about work, but about events in the housing area or about personal behavior. Once such information was released, its interpretation could not be controlled. Among the junior enlisted, much of the information stayed safe, because junior troops were often rather alienated from NCOs and officers. But peers got promoted into the chain of command, and some were not fully trustworthy or were simply unthinking or careless in what they said and to whom.

Whether such information became hurtful depended on interpretation. Because the disposition of the NCOs, officers, and neighbors could not easily be known, and because various persons in the chain of command changed frequently, it was unwise to disclose family or personal information to members of the community. The fact that so much private information flowed so casually through the chain of command felt to many like a violation of trust and a subversion of the expected separation of family and work domains. Moreover, the housing areas were not just physically close to the work area; they were also close in communication paths, for the information about one's family and neighbors easily flowed from the residential to the work areas.

In the Housing/Family Areas

Surveillance and information flow extended deep into the housing areas and family life, especially in government quarters. The existence of building coordinators, the presence of work supervisors and one's commander scattered among one's neighbors, the existence of a chain of concern that laced families to units, and the fact of dense housing and the necessary interactions it entailed all contributed to the ease of surveillance and the flow of information into the military domain.

Living with Building Coordinators. Within government quarters, each building had a building coordinator tasked with the responsibility of seeing that the grounds were safe and well maintained and that the occupants of the building abided by the various housing regulations. The task was assigned to the highest ranking person in each building so that the building coordinator could use military rank to ensure that his or her instructions were obeyed. Each building had duty rosters for the chores that needed attention: cleaning the stairs and laundry rooms, snow removal, lawn mowing, picking up litter, and so on. Some stairwells pooled funds and hired a German cleaning woman for some chores; other stairwells used the roster method. The coordinator had to enforce the obligations if they were left unattended. The building coordinator was also responsible for resolving complaints about the behavior of the building's residents. If the coordinator was unable to obtain satisfactory compliance, he or she referred the matter either to the military police or to the offender's unit commander. Thus, surveillance, information flow, rank, and coercion entered the government quarters' residential areas.

Living with Commanders. In most military communities in Germany, on-post housing consisted of densely spaced apartments with "thin walls" that easily transmitted the sounds of family life. Though the housing area was somewhat segregated into clusters based on rank, the ranked areas were close to one another. The enlisted soldier's NCO supervisors lived nearby, and the officers were but a street or two away. Moreover, segregation by rank was never perfect. People got promoted yet stayed in the same apartment. By regulation, a junior troop with a large family had to have a certain size of apartment that perhaps existed only in an NCO area at the time an assignment had to be made. Other exceptions occurred because the economic requirement to keep apartments filled preempted the abstract goal of separating the ranks.

Every neighbor was also a workmate within the same general chain of command, sometimes in the same company, often in the same battalion, always in the same brigade. Thus, Kathy Brenton remarked, "When Cindy [her friend and spouse of another warrant officer living in the same stairwell] found out the commanding officer would move in next door, we were worried sick in the stairwell." The close linkage of work, residence, and command enmeshed the information networks and created yet another source of social exposure. CW3 Kevin Robbins, the physician's assistant in Richberg: "We'd never move to a stairwell. This is the only place where that many Army families would live together. You would think it would work as a support, but it tends to make people feel more isolated than ever. There is no privacy. The walls are thin." Because family and work overlapped not only physically but also socially and judgmentally, offenses in the housing area were easily and frequently carried to one's commander through official channels or informal gossip. By implication, the closer the housing was to the installation and the more the housing was occupied by persons from closely related units in a single installation's chain of command, the more problem there was with citizen surveillance and hair-trigger reporting to units.

To investigate the impact of this close attachment of work and residence, I visited Richberg families living in Patriot Village, a military housing community forty-five minutes' drive from Richberg. Unlike the residents of Richberg's nearby housing area, who all worked in the same brigade chain of command, Patriot Village neighbors worked at different installations in many different chains of command that joined only at the highest USAREUR level. SSG Victor Rodgers, who worked on Richberg but lived in Patriot Village, agreed that although major fights or misdemeanors at Patriot Village would be reported to one's company commander at Richberg, smaller disputes or gossipy matters that would have been reported had they occurred in Richberg generally did not "get back." The reason, he said, is because "Richberg is a cubbyhole. All you got to do in Richberg [housing] is holler, and they will be right there. If you start arguing, somebody is going to call the MPs. Even if the MPs came because your kid has been ringing the buzzer too much, they are going to verify that the kid is yours, and that will go to the unit." I asked SSG Gary Hatch, also living at Patriot Village and working on Richberg, if he had any concern about gossip getting back to his unit.

> That is one of the things that don't happen here [Patriot Village]. I'm the only one from my company in the building. But at Richberg, whatever you do might go back to work. Sometimes you just want to open up to someone, and here you can. At Richberg, everybody is afraid to talk, because everybody gets into your business. They got the BOQ [bachelor officers quarters] and the BEQ [bachelor enlisted quarters] right in the [same area as the family] housing. Everybody in one little group. The first sergeant is over there. The platoon leader is over there. Richberg is so small you feel like you're still at work. . . . At Patriot Village, it is so far away, the talk doesn't go back. I talk to someone here and they say, "Where is Richberg?"

That does not make Patriot Village problem free, let alone gossip free. As Ruth Rodgers suggested, "Is this Patriot Village or is it Peyton Place? Patriot Village itself is everybody tending everybody else's business." Still, all Patriot Village families who worked at Richberg agreed that the distance from their work installation and the diversity of branches in the chain of command provided considerable freedom by separating work and private life.

Not everyone complained of close living at Richberg, possibly because of differences in personality. Barbara Norton, living in Richberg's attached government quarters, observed, "We haven't had too much of a problem with privacy [in quarters]. . . . Here the stairwell has been pretty good." SGT Adam Norton felt similarly. "We don't have any problem with privacy. We get more than our share." Nevertheless, for many, the comfort and convenience of the American on-post housing and the ability to use English with neighbors was counterbalanced by the tension of being in such intimate proximity with work supervisors and potentially career-damaging scrutiny.

Living with the Chain of Concern. Standing beside the official chain of command, the informal "chain of concern" linked the spouses of those in command and formed another potential route for the widespread flow of personal information. Functioning as a sort of shadow organization, spouses of senior-ranking leaders kept in touch with spouses of subordinates in an effort to support and serve their soldiers' unit and its families. Major and Mrs. Taylor discussed the definition of "chain of concern." The phrase had come up spontaneously, and I then asked for a definition. "The chain of concern is the informal chain that in general parallels the chain of command," said Matthew. "Usually," said Abigail, "it goes up to the company commander's wife. If there is a big problem, she might call the battalion commander's wife, or the rear detachment [commander, the officer in charge at the home station when the major unit is away]. But it doesn't go up forever. If it is that bad, we call the chaplain, or the provost marshal [chief of military police]." 1LT Hal Vinney, an unmarried officer, defined the chain of concern as the "wives' chain of command—especially at officer level. I know it is there. The battalion commander said it is there. I think in Europe it is different than in America, because that is all there is: here on-post, the officers' wives, together." These two parallel structures, one of command and the other of concern but with commandlike attributes, created a ladderlike configuration of two vertical chains connected at each level by a marital rung.

Through the chain of concern, "senior rank" spouses helped "junior rank" spouses solve family problems and stay informed, especially while the soldier-husbands were on extended training or deployment. Used incautiously, however, the chain of concern could also be a route for inappropriately distributing too widely information about personal problems or for routing information about personal or family difficulties to a judgmental commander.

Influence in the chain of concern accrued from several sources. First, the higher the rank of the husband, the greater the influence of the wife. Second, wives of senior officers and NCOs usually had a great deal of experience and knowledge, a genuine resource to the less experienced families. Third, wives gained moral authority because others appreciated the service they rendered to the unit and its families.

One of the unpleasant possibilities of the close connection between chain of command and chain of concern occurred when the spouse of a senior leader used her husband's rank to intimidate or coerce spouses of junior-ranking soldiers by implying some threat to their soldier's career through the rating process. Elsie Kimball:

> There are women who have been devoting their whole life to the military community. One of the top ranking wives here, she has found a position as nurse. And she

had waited almost seven months to find it. . . . But the general's wife said in front of the other wives, "A colonel's wife does not have time to work; she has others to think of." You have to understand that the general is the colonel's senior rater.

Thus, one wife's influence over another wife was explicitly based on the first wife's husband rating the second wife's husband on the OER. That is what made her a "top-ranking wife." People believed that spouses influenced command evaluations or work distributions through "pillow talk," and this is what gave commandlike qualities to relationships in the chain of concern. Kathy Brenton remarked, "A general's wife or a colonel's wife wears the rank [saying], 'I'll expect to see you at all the coffees. Do you know who I am?' Officers' wives' structure—they pull their rank. NCOs' wives are more informal." The negative power of the chain of concern derived from fear for career. Cynthia Watkins, from her experience and current position as the wife of Middleberg's community commander and the troop commander of Middleberg's and Richberg's units, observed,

> I had another friend whose husband did not come out on the brigade command list [of promotions]. There are those who say it is because she works wherever she goes. A senior wife said to her, "It is because you work and don't support your husband." She [the working woman] is not tactless: she bends over backwards to help in the community in the time she has. It is almost as if a capable, competent woman is threatening to some of the senior wives who have chosen to do things another way.

In a word, people believed the chain of concern could have a large impact on a soldier's career, and especially on an officer's career, if a senior spouse transmitted her impression of a junior spouse to her husband, who either rated or gave input to the rating of the junior spouse's soldier-husband. Thus, family and residential life put careers at risk because of the dense interconnections of residential and military chains of social interaction.

In the Logistical Support/Community Areas

The military community's enclave nature added to the fertile conditions for open surveillance and fostered the rapid and widespread flow of information, gossip, and rumor. At the official level, the DCC and the members of the community cadre were tasked to monitor the behavior of the members of the military community, and they did so both through official reports and informally. Community leaders distributed official information through newsletters, and through both the chain of command and the chain of concern. Other community agencies could access the chain of concern or relevant portions of it as needed.

Every community engaged in the practice of holding regular town meetings. At a town meeting, the DCC and his (or, theoretically, her) assistants stood before the assembled members of the military and answered their questions or took their complaints. Spouses attended voluntarily. Soldiers often were assembled in formations and marched to the meetings so that (it was said) local or visiting leaders would not be displeased by evidence of disinterest.

Members of the community interacted, observed one another, and exchanged information in the many places and activities of community life and logistical support. Outside the housing area, they saw one another repeatedly when shopping for food or supplies, for they necessarily went to the same shoppette, and the nearest commissary or PX. They met at the on-post activities and at craft clubs, if they used them. Officers interacted in the officers' club, and NCOs did the same in the NCO club. Junior troops met each other in the rec center, at the burger bar, and at the NCO club, or the enlisted club if there was one. Catholics met with other Catholics for mass and the after-mass coffee in the community chapel; Protestants met nondenominationally with other Protestants at a different hour. The smallest religious congregations held separate meetings on- or off-post, one of the few modes of differentiation from the almost unitary military community.

The various ranked clubs were especially important for informal communication. Among officers, widespread understandings that one should not "jump," "go around," or "go outside the chain of command" at work made the apparent social informality of the officers' club especially attractive. There one could, when needed, socialize with people higher in one's chain of command, passing information and cultivating one's reputation informally, or absorbing casually a leader's approach to military life and mission. One could deliberately engineer a chance encounter with people who might be essential to the success of a current project, but who could not easily be consulted in the normal hierarchy of work. The NCO clubs had a much more noisy, playful, beer-sloshing, jukebox-throbbing casual atmosphere. After work, NCOs could "kick back and relax." But not too much, for they were being observed. Misbehavior—such as failure to "hold one's liquor"—in the clubs could come to haunt the careless. As the pressures to cut costs took their effect, communities moved toward disbanding their ranked clubs, collapsing them instead into a "community club" or an "all-ranks" club. The ever present surveillance and the premise of obedience, however, tended to make the enlisted uncomfortable in the presence of officers and the officers uncomfortable in the presence of enlisted, and undermined the possibility of relaxation in the all-ranks clubs.

In a word, the military community's island ecology focused people's interactions within a few logistical and support points—the bank, barbershop, beauty parlor, liquor store, bowling alley—facilitating scrutiny, surveillance, and the formation of judgment, gossip, and rumor. Although rumor was by definition not officially controlled, attempting to avoid being its object was in fact quite controlling. One had to act so that the pervasive ethic of monitoring and surveillance did not generate damaging impressions that might affect one's OER or EER. The pressures of constant surveillance and judgment changed one's behavior, and these changes had a variety of unintended consequences.

THE UNINTENDED CONSEQUENCES OF SURVEILLANCE AND SOCIAL CONTROL

Neither leaders and their soldiers, as members of the Army, nor soldiers and their spouses, as members of the community, were completely happy with the way of life that had grown up in the military community. Attitudes—culture and morale—and actual behaviors in the units, the families, and in the community were often less than desirable. Here I hope to show the structure and logic of why this was so.

People usually adapt their behavior so as to reduce their pain or risk as much as possible and to promote their well-being as they conceive it. In the highly judgmental community, where any information might have been interpreted negatively, many soldiers and spouses grew to distrust their neighbors, felt cynical about the community, and even despised the Army because they felt they encountered both hypocrisy and treachery in return for what they felt was their own authentic self-sacrifice. They reacted by withholding negative information. That process distorted the information base on which good leadership depended, and the poor decisions resulting from bad information and fear in the system then confirmed the soldiers' or the spouses' belief that leaders were incompetent or that they did not care about the junior soldiers.

The fact that commanders, who wrote OERs and EERs, and NCO leaders, who made work assignments for all but the officers, lived within the highly interconnected community had repercussions for the ecology of the whole community. In the face of pervasive scrutiny and judgment, many families reduced contact with the unit and withdrew from all but a few trusted, carefully proven friends. Ideally, one said nothing about self or family that indicated weakness. Those who moved into the self-protective mode did not communicate unit shortcomings to its leaders but used the unattributable indirection of gossip and rumor or simply let things deteriorate. This strategy made good sense, given the "zero defects" ethic that pervaded the Army and its communities and the tendency to "shoot the messenger" who brought bad news.

Creating a "Zero Defects" Ethic Within the Community

The Army's "zero defects" ethic, combined with the individual's interest in protecting family and career, tended to produce several unintended logical transformations and behavioral consequences. The logic seemed to develop something like this: One important premise for the Army professional was "Don't make mistakes." Given the hazards of combat and the dangers of working with large machinery and explosive materials in peacetime training, people's lives depended on careful, accurate work and reporting. Unfortunately, the overall complications of military activities made it impossible not to make mistakes. Given (1) that you were not supposed to make mistakes, (2) that it was impossible not to, and (3) that you would be judged and removed if you were known to have made mistakes, the resolution seemed to be the ethic of "Don't admit mistakes." A second premise was (and still is) that armies need to be strong. Military strength is substantially rooted in people, in soldiers. So soldiers must be strong, not weak. Now, weakness is of course rather vague and subjective. So in Germany, whatever others *might* think weakness to be or to look like, one tried not to show it. One put on a facade of bravado and confidence at all times, even when one was uncertain of the conditions or the appropriate course of action. Third, professional soldiers accept the premise that they must be able to substitute for one another. When one individual dies in combat, the next in rank takes over until there is an opportunity to officially reorganize and reconstitute the unit. If mutual substitutability is essential, the logical spin-off is "Don't be different." At first blush, it would appear that "Don't be different" is contradictory to the idea that some are going to be judged as more competent than others. But in fact, the expectation of excellence in personnel was a variant of "zero defects." In Germany, those who approximated the standard of "zero defects" by maintaining the appearance of errorless total dedication to mission were substantially alike. Those who did not were different and defective, and were likely eventually to be cut from the service. These premises were thoroughly woven into the fabric of the military's organization and daily procedures in Germany, more so, perhaps, than in the United States because of the nearness of the threat and the desire to avoid political embarrassment. The premises became ingrained in the minds of both officer and enlisted personnel.

In Chapter 4, "Danger Forward, Sir!," we saw how these premises undermined leadership and induced the appearance of irrationality in unit behavior and leadership. What is important in this chapter is that the military logic of the fusion of domains to concentrate power led to the application of the Army's premises throughout the family and community spheres. For community members—which meant family members—the premise transformations and behavioral responses were essentially the same as for the soldiers. Family members, also, needed to avoid the appearance of error, to not show weakness, and to suppress difference within the community. Let us explore how these premises were worked out in the practical life of community members.

Avoiding the Appearance of Error, Weakness, or Difference

Withdrawal. One tactic to avoid revealing weakness was to withdraw from contact with the Army and its social community. Reducing activity and interaction between the Army and one's family members helped avoid making errors or reduced the possibility of their discovery. Being "barracks rats," shielding or even hiding one's spouse from contact with unit members, limiting one's friends, or isolating one's family were all conscious or unconscious tactics that made sense, given the larger premise of avoiding the appearance of error, weakness, or difference.

Community life for the wife of an enlisted soldier entailed less social pressure than among officers' spouses. But the expected interaction with the unit could still have potentially detrimental consequences. CPL Hank Walsh and his wife, Terry, described an incident in which Hank was unjustly punished. "The bull that goes on between the ranks," she fumed. "I wouldn't put up with it, being a civilian." Hank interjected, "I stood there and took the punishment. If I'd complained, I'd have gotten in big-time trouble in the section." Terry's response was to seek distance: "I try to stay away from his bosses. You get into that small town-y thing. I don't want to get involved in that." Over the two years I knew her, Terry continued to maintain as much distance as possible between herself and the Army community. Caught between the considerable value of Hank's military career and the unpredictability of how her behavior might affect it, Terry felt it safer to isolate herself, to reduce contact. Other spouses also minimized contact rather than risk trouble for their families. Sometimes the soldier-husbands deliberately isolated their wives, even against their will.

A few soldiers and spouses tried to avoid risks to themselves even as they attempted to police the community through their gossip and reporting. They did so by making anonymous phone calls to another's home or to an official agency. As Lani McDugal noted, these calls often began with some variation of, "I'm not going to tell you who I am because I don't want this going back to my husband's unit." Similarly, Jane Cooper justified her preference for anonymity and expressed her frustration with agencies that required the name of the person making a report when she said, "You do not know if there is going to be retaliation on you or your child if you report [someone or something]. *That* [risk of retaliation] certainly needs to be fixed. Most definitely!"

Wives of high-ranking officers carried the same burden of isolation as their spouses. They had to avoid any contact with others that could have a negative effect on their husband's career. Moreover, their words and wishes were taken as seriously as if they had held their husband's rank. Cynthia Watkins, as the wife of Middleberg's commanding general, knew from experience:

> Wives go to the "charm course" [when they are] on brigade [promotion] list. You are warned: "Suddenly your words take on a meaning. You have to be very thoughtful and careful. People are very quick to try to remedy anything you do not like." You can't just talk as a normal person anymore, especially in a community this size. Everybody knows everything that their general and his wife know and believe.

Thus, among spouses of higher-ranking soldiers there was a deep sense of isolation. Unable to create the distance from the Army that spouses of enlisted soldiers were able to retreat into, officers' wives felt stranded behind what Mrs. Watkins called "a veil of tears." Later, she returned to the subject using another metaphor:

> When a husband is about to enter a [brigade-level] command, he has to go [to a pre-command course], and the wife is invited. What they say to a wife is, "There is a role for a wife to play, if you choose to play it." But the other message is, "There is a role for you to play." I feel there are oceans of tears cried behind closed doors over this sort of thing: that wives can't come out and say, "Some people just aren't cut out for the role." It is expecting too much, that every woman is to conform. There is a terrible uniformity of the expectation.

Cynthia went on to express how intense, even pathological, the situation became for some women and where she felt the breakdown occurred:

> I feel as if the pressures that I recognize are not unusual. But we don't talk about them easily. Once in a while you can click with another senior wife, and [feel sure] that she will not talk about it with anyone, not even her husband. If I have a problem, I am wary about who I can talk with. And we have some senior wives that have no other place to turn. I've seen a bit of alcoholism over this. We talk about letting people be individuals. But if you get a square peg, it had better be pounded into the round hole. It is not the senior leadership [that causes this]. [Secretary of Defense Frank] Carlucci has come out and said, "Men's careers will not be determined by wives." The problem is that it doesn't filter down to the real life on the individual base. There are so many that still have a view of the "Army wife," and they make it hard on each other. And the individual that tries to fill her own needs, she is criticized a lot. This causes tremendous stress.

I asked Cynthia Watkins how she felt families were handling the stress, what choices they had, and how they were responding. Cynthia was genuinely and compassionately disconcerted, for she saw no solutions coming from the Army. She felt that the spouse who did not fit into the role as Army wife had the following "options," which she listed thus:

> - Live miserably in a state of anxiety and discontent for months or years on end.
> - Try to leave the military. Or at least get out [retire] at twenty instead of thirty [years of service].
> - The spouse having the biggest problem could leave the marriage.
> - Numb the discontent with alcohol or some other way of coping.

"Part of the distress is the complexity of it," she concluded. It would appear that the last three choices are forms of withdrawal. The first may also be a form of withdrawal if it means that one must simply live with the discontent without expressing one's feelings for fear that doing so might affect the military career on which the family depends. None of these choices seemed desirable for the family, for the community, or for the Army. Obviously, spouses living in a "veil of tears" and "isolation" were not fully functional, either in their families or in their communities. Withdrawal and isolation sought to address key dangers inherent in the structure of surveillance and judgment in the community. Nevertheless, withdrawal amplified the sense of alienation people felt in living within the community.

Lost Sense of Community. Withdrawal to preserve privacy led to individual family isolation. Each family's individual isolation, when generalized, had a detrimental effect on the entire community, detracting from overall interaction and sense of camaraderie or fellowship. Pam Hill described the hurdles she had to overcome to get to a meeting for wives of enlisted soldiers, and her disappointment at finding no one else there: "I told him [her husband], 'You must have a girlfriend, 'cause you don't introduce me to anybody.' I don't know anybody." "Don't they have a wives' meeting?" I inquired, suspecting they did. "They have a wives' meeting once a month," Pam replied, "and John says, 'Oh, you don't want to go.

They just gossip.' I usually find the notes [announcements] in his pocket too late. One day I found about it and went when he had duty, and nobody else showed up." In a similar vein, 1SG Gerald Hickman felt, "The biggest problem I've found is getting the families together. They are reluctant to come to family things. There is more of a family unit there [in the United States] than you have here." Paradoxically, SFC Kenneth Parry, assigned to assist the Middleberg ACS and, therefore, a person who ought to have known who lived where because he worked on family issues, most thoroughly exemplified this absence of community. He knew that eight or nine military families lived in his high-rise off-post German apartment building. I asked him if he knew any of them personally. "No," he replied, and added that he didn't even know on which floor any of them lived. He knew American soldiers lived in the building only because he had seen the distinctive military license plates in the parking garage and had bumped into some in the apartment elevator.

Even those living in government quarters sometimes did not know the names of the other families using their common stairwell. Kathy Brenton, the ACS volunteer coordinator for Middleberg, socially adept and not at all shy, said, "I can tell you who lives across the hall. And the building coordinator. But others in the stairwell? They leave us alone and we leave them alone." SSG Frank Barnes observed, "People are unsociable, and they complain, and they are nosy. Families aren't as close as in the States. In the States, if I say we are going to have a barbecue, they will probably chip in. Here, we had a barbecue, and the others came out, but they all had separate grills." To Frank, the failure to "chip in" and the use of "separate grills" symbolized social distance. In summary, soldiers kept their families isolated to avoid any negative repercussions to their evaluations, families isolated themselves to prevent gossip and career status loss, and many cultivated a culture of privacy in which people chose to keep their distance from the too intrusive Army.

Fear of Asking for Help. The dense networks of scrutiny and judgment also influenced soldiers (and family members, as we will see shortly) to forgo therapy to avoid adverse impact on their careers. Even Welby General Hospital's chief operations manager, COL Felix Carson, felt the pressure: "If I go in and tell my boss that I'm under stress, I may ruin my job, my career. It goes back to the man that can destroy him: If you've got three soldiers that are superb, and only one slot, and one that is top-notch, but had to go to P&N [Psychiatry and Neurology Clinic at any military hospital] for stress management, the commander might not promote him because he had to go to P&N." Mr. Harvey Renquist, as head of the counseling and treatment center for alcohol or drug abuse at Middleberg, likewise perceived a reluctance among soldiers to use his clinic's services. "Because we are getting the 10 percent who are in trouble, we have a reputation that if you go to us, your career is washed up." He went on, "People view this place as trouble, and they are reluctant to refer people, because they think that they are going to ruin their careers." After giving a detailed example, he concluded bluntly, "The commanders don't trust us."

A conversation one Sunday morning plainly demonstrated the fear military personnel have of seeking therapy. After attending mass in Richberg, I joined the group gathered in the basement for coffee. CPT Francisco Soto, the chaplain-priest who had conducted the service, approached me, exchanged greetings, took me aside, and began to speak of his concern for one of his parishioners. He spoke of a certain major who was "dealing with so much stress" the chaplain feared he might "have a breakdown." CPT Soto felt the problem was beyond his pastoral abilities, but the major refused to go to the hospital's psychiatric clinic for fear of ruining his career. The chaplain wondered if I might be able to offer the major some off-the-record counseling, because I was a "doctor" attached to the Department of Psychiatry and Neurology but not a part of the military reporting system and therefore not a threat. I declined, of course, explaining that I was an anthropologist, not a therapist.

Other officers and spouses confided in me that they or their friends had sought care from private psychiatrists at their own cost, off-post, to avoid any report of the therapy to their units, for the use of military psychological counseling or psychiatric therapy would be reported to commanders. There seemed to be no such alternative in Germany due to language and cultural barriers. Sadly, avoiding therapy early in a troubled situation often led to more intractable crises later. Thus, the system of close scrutiny within the community and intense judgment by its citizens and leaders hurt soldiers and spouses either by directly affecting evaluations or by tempting the soldier and/or spouse to delay therapy until his or her problems grew to affect either their job or their marriage.

Spouses often shared the tactic of therapy avoidance. Problems within the family were hidden through denial and made resistant to therapy because mental health, social work, and substance-abuse therapy services were feared, all in the interest of protecting a family's primary economic support. Kathy Brenton, Middleberg's ACS volunteer coordinator, said, "If one of your family goes to a therapy clinic, it is on your record. It's 'Catch-22'. You go to the commander for help. But if you do, you get slapped on the wrist and don't get a promotion. If it didn't affect the record, more people would go for help."

My impression was that therapeutic services for children were quite freely sought after. Exceptional Family Member services, for instance, provided much that was needed for challenged children. If a child were having problems that drew unfavorable attention to the family, using one of the available therapies could actually help avoid forced early return to the United States. With spouses of soldiers, however, I saw therapy being avoided in order to minimize gossip and loss of social reputation. Like the soldiers, family members also found the German community's mental health resources impossible to access because of an inability to speak the language and lack of cultural knowledge.

Tolerating Injustice. Some family members felt they had to "put up with" more problems from the Army than they thought they should have had to. They "take it" or "have to deal with it" for the sake of the career. Ruth Rodgers: "You don't want to get in trouble. You put up with a lot 'cause everything that you do reflects back on your husband." Her husband, Victor, a staff sergeant, confirmed the view. "That is the system," he said, "and if it is bad enough, they will send them home." "But the worst is it reflects back on your husband," Ruth said, expressing the ever present fear.

Some thought increased injustice might have been tolerated *within* the family's relations with each other, likewise to avoid endangering the career. One day I asked MAJ Quintin Scott, the Grossberg regional chaplain, whether families who tried to get therapeutic help for their problems created repercussions for the soldier's job. He pithily observed:

> When you call for help, be prepared for the command to know. That is what women [i.e., spouses] don't want. A case I know: The MPs got called; he got lectured. Now his career is really on the line. She is caught in a bind. If she presses the thing, they might get a divorce. He can lose his career and she her security. There are women putting up with more abuse than before because the Army says, "This soldier is unable to control his domestic situation; how then can he control his battle situation? If he loses his cool and beats his wife, he must not have any leadership ability, as he can't control his emotion."

By making the soldier's career prospects dependent on "good" family behavior and by putting the commander in charge of defining adequate "goodness," family behavior became a matter of career risk. As a result, some families actually got less help or put up with more misbehavior within the family than they would have, had getting help been less risky.

Being Cautious and Conservative. At one level, to be different is to be deviant. To be deviant is to be weak or in error, both prohibited conditions if one is to succeed in the military. One avoids deviance by being conservative, cautious to a fault. One relies on tradition. But there is much more to military conservatism than that.

When people do not know how complex systems work, they may be reluctant to make changes out of fear that the consequences of a change, which they cannot predict, might be negative. Cynthia Watkins faced this dilemma because she, as the wife of Middleberg's community commander, was in a position to effect change easily, even inadvertently. Members of the community were so solicitous that they would try to provide not just what she asked for but what they felt she might have or should have wanted.

> Another part I don't want to miss: risks to the husband's career. Then there is this angle: you come to realize how your role is. It really can be meaningful. It can be meaningful to have the senior wife present at the change of command, to see the senior wife taking an active part in the community. There are some who say that if the senior wife doesn't take part in the fabric of the community then the whole community is going to fall apart. There are some who believe that. And there is the unknown: what if that is true? If the senior wife is not actively involved, what if it does affect the whole subculture? *There* is another terrible risk to have to take.

Uncertainty regarding consequences became an incentive to reproduce the traditions that had seemed to work. Indeed, the mix of intense judgment and perceived risk in an important endeavor led many to make the most conservative decisions possible, to not tamper with the system. The military community, like the peasant community in many parts of the world, became tradition-oriented, its citizens slow to change their behavior because overweening judgment inhibited the will to risk change until after a situation became desperately untenable.[1] Then, as we saw in Chapter 4, "Danger Forward, Sir!," the system lurched in a radical reorientation.

Creating a Facade. Some members of the military community felt compelled to present a facade, to pretend outwardly that "everything is OK." Below the surface, however, for many, there existed a great deal of distrust and cynicism. Outward appearance and inner reality of feelings began to differ sharply, all in the interest of avoiding the appearance of error or weakness. At ACS in Middleberg, Holly Wilde, who was volunteering and seeking a job, chatted with Hilda Paul, the ACS jobs assistance officer:

> "We are trying to get the job done. . . . But you keep running into walls— dishonesty, and not knowing what is going on."
>
> "Bingo!" Hilda jumped in excitedly. "Running into walls! If I know some- body is being dishonest, it is fine. But I don't want to believe somebody and then be led on."
>
> "You are supposed to give your all and supposed to pretend you like it," Holly added, qualifying her feelings.
>
> "We are supposed to pull together," Hilda confirmed, paralleling Holly's structure of normative obligation and inappropriate contradiction, " but we are not included in the picture."

When many people believe community life is built upon facades of those "pretend- ing," the essence of community disappears. Relationships are not what they are said to be. Nothing is what it is said to be. Life becomes surreal. For Gretchen McCormick, the disparity between the truth and the pretense of their social situa- tion had driven her to the point of bitterness.

> "I don't go to the coffees, or the OCWC [Officers and Civilian Wives' Club] functions. I don't go. I don't like it," she said.
>
> "Why not?" I probed for her rationale.
>
> " 'Cause they are a bunch of snobs. Not all of them; most of them. I don't like going to a place where you can't be yourself, where they talk funny. They try to be so nice to you, and when they see you on the street, they don't say hello. I'm not saying all are like that. But I want to go where I am comfortable. I'm not two- faced."
>
> "Two-faced?"
>
> "You act like you try to be somebody that you're not. . . . They don't do nothing right there. But they start talking, and it comes back all blown out of proportion."

Living the facade indeed helped avoid the appearance of weakness or error. Living the facade also came to define the nature of the most valuable friend: a person with whom one did not have to maintain a facade because they could be trusted to reveal nothing into the public system. But having to live the facade in much of one's life and believing others did likewise led to a pervasive sense of what I call artificiality.

Recognizing the Pervasive Existence of Artificiality

In creating a facade, soldiers and spouses avoided the appearance of error or weakness, thereby protecting themselves. In doing so, however, they also created the feeling that things were not what they seemed to be and that a person could not be him- or herself, but had always to be performing in a way that felt like pretending. In Germany, this artificiality served only to create even greater isolation— alienation, if you will.

Resenting Social and Volunteer Events. Especially in Europe, where few nonmilitary activities seemed accessible, a great deal of community activity for single soldiers, married soldiers, and family members depended on volunteers. Youth and adult sports teams, for instance, needed coaches. The thrift store needed staff. The German-American Club needed a president. Schools needed parental helpers. The list was long. Enormous good came to the community because of the hours donated by its members. Besides the obvious good of ameliorating the problem of understaffing, volunteerism helped morale throughout the community and provided an escape from the social tensions that existed in a person's unit-based workday world.

Nevertheless, the intense connection between private life and career introduced a sense of coercion into social events and volunteer efforts. Leaders sponsored social events at every level of the military organization—company, battalion, and brigade—and intended these events to draw the units together and foster community spirit. For the most part, they accomplished this purpose. For some people, however, the sense of having to attend social events to please a boss or to get a better evaluation undermined any feeling of true willingness or spontaneity. Thus, when I asked 1LT Larry McDugal and his wife, Lani, what bothered them most about Army life, Lani replied, "I think the social things we have to put up with, though it's not as bad now as before." "It changes with the commander's wife," Larry explained, "if she is 'white glove'," meaning, if she happens to uphold formal tradition. Lani cut in to elaborate. "In the Army, you're expected to go to the coffees on post and to volunteer. It reflects on your evaluation, even if they say it doesn't," she asserted, showing increased irritation. In an emotionless, resigned tone, Larry concluded, "It all depends on the commander," much like one would assert that the fate of a picnic depends on the weather. In the past, social risk was managed by ceremony—"white gloves" and teas or coffees—in which the dangers of close social interaction were absorbed by the structures of traditional procedure. All one had to do was attend key social functions and act according to convention while limiting conversation to safe subjects. In Lani and Larry we again find the ever present undercurrent of anxiety and uncertainty about playing to one's leader's peculiarities for the sake of one's career. Unfortunately, when people feel coerced into doing something, the opportunity to do it because they want to is automatically undercut.

Another woman described an incident in which a friend did not attend the Officer and Civilian Wives' Club meeting one month and within a half hour of its conclusion received "five phone calls" from others inquiring, "Where were you?" Of course, this kind of interest could represent an honest and healthy concern from others. Unfortunately, because of the pervasive distrust of others in the military community, a more sinister interpretation of the callers' motives was almost guaranteed. Thus, Kathy Brenton described how her husband, a chief warrant officer, "had to do extra duty because I didn't go to the social functions. He had to mow lawns, and odd things."

Many felt that the implied job coercion had a chilling impact on social events. Here three officers and warrant officers' wives from different units each described the "climate" at their respective unit coffees as they sat chatting in one of their living rooms. Only one of the three appeared emotionally satisfied by the coffees.

> "Everybody was not talking to each other because it was a mandatory party. The business portion of our coffees are not fun," said the first.

> "Even soldiers come to the MI [Military Intelligence Battalion] coffees. No rank involved: spouses and soldiers," contrasted the second, Kathy Brenton.

> "I was going to go to a coffee because I was told that the enlisted were invited," offered the third. "But then I learned that only the NCO wives were invited. Well, I'd rather not have anything to do with it if the junior soldiers' wives are excluded."

> "And our coffee group has gotten so depressed," continued the first woman. "Down to five persons, and two are brownnosers that want to impress the commander. We need to have less business and more social."

> "Does the social information from these coffees ever cause problems for those that attend?" I asked, trying to draw out the issues of confidentiality and risk in the community.

> "At our coffees, it doesn't get back," said the second woman. "What goes on at the coffee I don't brief Don on."

> The first woman could not miss the contrast: "At my unit, R__ [the commander's wife] would run right to J__ [the company commander], and it would get back. I really have the feeling that that is more the norm than the other way around." The third nodded in agreement.

Thus, two of the three women expressed fear that social conversation "gets back" to their unit commanders in hurtful ways, yet they felt it mandatory to attend such gatherings. Of course, their fears of things "getting back" were well-founded, because the "chain of concern" literally was married to the "chain of command."

The sense of job-related coercion extended beyond social gatherings. Officers and sometimes even enlisted soldiers said they were required to use the on-post clubs and other physical facilities and services. A former company commander groused, "They open a club and then they push you into using it to keep it going. So you have to go. When we first got here, we were told, 'You will support your officers' club.' They had terrible food, and horrible service. They closed it for two years, and they still wanted us to pay the dues when it was closed!" Thus, community facilities and social events intended to benefit the community became symbols of oppression to soldiers or spouses caught in the climate of coercion.

Coercion also tainted the positive values of volunteer service among members of the military community. Pressure applied through either the chain of concern or the chain of command turned what ordinarily would have been an act of goodwill into a required evil. For example, one day I asked Gretchen McCormick where the community and the family experienced stress with each other, and she replied, "I was approached by the women's groups [and asked to volunteer]. And they said, 'You reflect [on] your husband's career. It is for your husband's best interest.'" Likewise, Elsie Kimball acknowledged that many people derived a great deal of personal pleasure from volunteering, but she felt that the sense of coercion left her anxiety ridden and perhaps even angry over the volunteering she had done. "There are some wives who have had self-satisfaction in volunteerism. But a lot of times I've felt more like it's coercion for me: for the good of the family and for the good of his career—I'll do it. I've never stood up and said 'no' and see if it does hurt his career. Been frightened of doing that. My God—we don't have a house, and nothing's in the bank!" Thus, Mrs. Kimball perceived a significant uncertainty and risk and that not only her husband's career, but her family's entire future might rest on her "volunteering." This sense of forced volunteerism thwarted the development of community morale and diminished the therapeutic value inherent in true volunteering.

Some wives sensed a decided change of climate under way within the Army, perhaps related to recent court cases that made it explicitly illegal for spouse matters to affect promotion. Nikole Yardley, a battalion commander's wife, explored the shifts in culture: "Only until very recently was volunteering not coerced to a degree. And it still is, but less. I'm an exception. I'm a battalion commander's wife that went to work." She went on to say that she has had two entirely different decades of life as an officer's wife. Of the first decade, the 1970s, she said, "I wouldn't think of missing a coffee." Of the second, in the 1980s, she stated "I worked, and wondered if I could have really thought like that" in the first half of the family's military career. Nevertheless, the structure of potential coercion remained in place. Even with the apparently Army-wide change of climate, "it all depends on the commander." That contingency influenced many people to volunteer whether they wanted to or not, believing it would be safer and productive for the family's Army career.

Fostering Gossip. The perception that things were not what they were said to be added credibility to any rumor and fueled its transmission. If outward appearances and official statements were not reality, then perhaps gossip and rumor got closer to the truth. In the controlled, artificial information system of Germany, rumor was the countercultural newspaper. As CPL Hank Walsh said, "Somebody starts a rumor, and it goes like wildfire."

Given the pervasive sense of facade and unreality, gossip could be effectively used in the competition between families. "Drugs, thievery, and sex is alive and well," said Terry Walsh, "and they do use the information on each other."

Gretchen McCormick felt likewise: "They hear the smallest thing and make a mountain of it. Gossip: they say, 'It will go before my husband's command.'"

Gossip, however, also served a positive purpose in the military community. Informally, the tales educated community members, especially newcomers. Gossip implicitly laid out the rules, the unseen pitfalls, and the strategies necessary for survival. Gossip, like rumor, thrived when key information was otherwise unavailable or corrupted by the belief that the visible or the official might be facade.[2]

Trusting Few and Avoiding Friendships. Gossip and the threat of gossip coming to a commander's attention made conversational openness in casual friendships risky and undermined trust within the community. Yet trust and friendship were essential to mutual social support and, according to theory, trust was also essential to cohesion in combat. Ruth Rodgers and her husband, SSG Victor Rodgers, reflected on their experience living in Patriot Village and working at Richberg. During one part of the conversation, Ruth and Victor, both Blacks, alternated, confirming and simultaneously escalating each other's revelations in a close verbal tango. "How many friends do you have that you trust?" I had asked. Ruth started:

> "Not many."
> "Here? One or two. That I trust? Two or three."
> "We don't do a lot of socializing."
> "In the company, zero. I don't trust nobody in my unit. Only one, a Spec Four. He is White."
> "He is one of our adopted children in the unit."
> "I tell him something and it is just between me and him. And it doesn't get about to the next and the next and cause a big stink in the unit."
> "They are all trying to stab each other in the back."
> "When you get so many years in the service, the harder [it is] to trust someone. They might want to back-stab you. A lot of times, you just do your job, really."

In other words, job took priority over friendship, and friendship posed a risk to job. A friend you trust was someone who conveyed no information to others, ensuring that nothing got back to the unit through the densely intertwined and judgmental networks. But the uncertainty with regard to friends—and the potentially hurtful consequences—favored isolation. Soldiers and spouses pulled inward. Marla Bracken explained, "We have no friends like [those we had] back in the States. . . . We don't trust anyone here. We only have each other, really." With so much community judgment, life was best lived as privately as possible. As Cynthia Watkins put it, "Women are not talking to each other because they are afraid that they will go and talk to each other." The higher the rank, the more the isolation from friendship. Abigail Taylor felt keenly the impact of rank (her husband was a major), wondering aloud what she would do if she were "a brigade commander's wife. Who do you call and say, 'Do you know I've had a bad day?' or 'Do you know what my husband said?' . . . You do have to be careful. Twice last week the battalion commander's wife was taken literally. It wasn't important, but just—" She didn't finish the sentence.

The fusion of domains caused the soldier-husband's authority to be transmitted to the spouse, so the higher the soldier's rank, the more good or damage a spouse could do in the community. At all ranks, the possibilities of harm to self, to others, and to community tended to narrow the circle of friendship and trust to but a few persons. CPL Richard Howard and his wife, Yvette, developed my inquiry regarding friendship:

> "Some don't socialize at all. Just depends on who you know. Most women just keep to themselves. Or they have their little groups. They just talk to each other," Yvette began.
>
> "They gossip about each other," Richard added.
>
> "Ladies over here aren't as helpful as they should be," Yvette continued. "Over in a foreign country, you'd think that they ought to help, but they don't."
>
> "If a lady gets a friend, it will be somebody!" Richard's tone indicated the value, yet scarcity, of friends.
>
> "Other than that, you don't look for friends. People talk too much to make friends," Yvette said thoughtfully. "Officer wives, they stick together. We don't talk to each other. Enlisted wives get the shitty jobs, like their husbands. Officers' wives, they get the better jobs. And the gossip! They just make big things out of nothing. Somebody's wife is talking to somebody: [so they conclude] 'They just have to be messing around.' It's like there is a rumor for everybody. I hear things about my friend that I know aren't true."
>
> "That means you can't trust anybody!" I blurted, feeling empathy.
>
> "You can't," Yvette concluded, expressing the result: "We just keep to ourselves."

This enlisted couple was typical. Junior enlisted and the lower ranks of NCO usually found their friends within the company. Once they learned who to trust—those who shared their view of the hardships and frustrations of Army life without passing on such sharing, and those who helped in time of need—they claimed them as friends. Senior NCOs often liked to choose friends of equal rank but from outside the company; it was safer. Friendships between officer couples wove together the units and organizations they led, uniting the whole community. Yet all maintained family privacy as best they could, because the possibility of judgment was ever present. Cynthia Watkins linked the difficulty of establishing friendship to the risk of career judgment:

> "There are individuals who are so easy to talk to. And you don't always know who they are. And you live together such a short time [because of turnover]. It would take a long time to discover who those people are that you would open up with."
>
> "How do you discover who they are? What characteristics do they have?" I inquired.
>
> "Something they said—that they are on the same wavelength. Those are the friends that I make, that keep opening up that they are feeling the same."

"You mentioned [earlier in the conversation] that they 'not talk about it, even with their husbands,'" I probed to get her to elaborate on her concepts.

"It is their husband's opinion that you are afraid of, for your husband's sake. Let's say I chose the wrong person [to open up to], and given what pillow talk is, and the husband thinks that the wife has a certain role, and that started to make a difference in my husband's career. And they may be the parts that are critical."

Here again, the uncertainty of "it all depends on the commander" rings through: "They may be the parts that are critical" in future evaluations, the difference between what would have been a "superb" rating, and one that is only "highly professional." That could turn a career to a different path, ending it at lieutenant colonel instead of colonel or general. For younger officers, it could end the military career prematurely and dash hopes of securing a military retirement.

Of course, the risks of judgment were not the only reasons these people sensed difficulty forming friendships. In the first place, American men generally have friendships that tend to be functional, operating while there is a common task. Achieving "togetherness" in an individualistic society is a well-recorded perennial problem that Americans have faced for nearly two centuries, if not longer.[3] But the fact that career judgment was so intensely bound into the social community increased these Americans' problems of finding friends and achieving community, unless they were at the lowest enlisted ranks with nothing to lose. Then, collaboration in resistance—by meeting occasionally to "bitch" about the Army—created community.

Another systemic factor that worked against friendship was the rate of turnover in the community. During the research period, three years was a normal tour for families. The only people to share a complete three-year tour were those few who arrived at the same time. A third of the available population of married families would be gone within the year and another third had just arrived. So friendship, as we have seen in several quotes already, was constantly being cut off by the moving or had not yet had sufficient time to form.

There were other pressures against close friendship. CPL Hank Walsh said he rebuffed friendships as a way to resist the trauma of potential combat loss: "I've learned myself to not get very close to anybody. In a unit, you don't want to develop a very deep friendship. [That way,] if in combat he gets killed, you will feel bad, but it won't affect your job performance." One must stay combat capable no matter the effort, for the alternative might cost one his or her life. This mix of factors—fear of loss, rapid turnover, a culture of individualism and temporary friendships, risks to career through information leaks—decidedly militated against forming friendships easily while in Germany.

The major events that facilitated friendship were the shared experiences of hardship. Given the difficulties, when friendship was achieved, it tended to be cherished and special. That friendship was a notable event seems to be the meaning conveyed by CPL Howard when he said, "If a lady gets a friend, it will be somebody!" The conditional "if" indicated the task was chancy, but the tone of voice connoted an enthusiastic appreciation of the specialness of friendship once it was found. Larry and Marla Bracken likewise demonstrated the intense character of such friendships:

> "We are content: I have one friend, and his wife joined him," said Larry.
> "They are our best friends," Marla resonated.
> "What do you mean by 'friend'?" I intervened.
> "We have shared with these people," Larry began. "We share our hopes for the future, and that is a pretty close relationship. We are going to move to their hometown [when we retire], for various reasons."
> "Out of the six years in the military, this is the first time we have found a family that has been a support," Marla added. "When the guys go to the field, I can call up and have a girlfriend [come over], to spend the night here—or there." Marla looked at her husband. "You'd probably say the same: he has been a close companion. When the guys go to the field, I work through the week, so I can handle the weekdays. But the weekends are so long, it is nice to have a friend that I can call and speak 'adult' to. It has made a lot of weekends livable."

In a word, trusted friendships were highly valued but scarce because they were undermined by the pervasive risks of career judgment in the densely interconnected situation of fused social domains. The accumulation of unintended negative consequences not only created feelings of distrust, but fostered also a vague sense of having been violated.

Feeling Violated

Resenting Breached Confidentiality. Breached confidentiality led one to feel violated because, especially in medical and therapeutic support, the breach constituted a clear contract violation. Sometimes confidentiality broke down in community support or mental health services, contributing to a distrust of those agencies. Before citing examples of broken confidentiality, I must emphasize that there was enormous goodwill among the providers of social work, psychiatric, and all other support services, including ACS. Community agencies, by law or regulation, tried to preserve confidentiality. CPT Wade Anthony, a Richberg company commander, explained, "If a soldier goes to Family Advocacy on his own, him or his wife, it is kept confidential. The command is not informed of that, normally. But if you command-refer a soldier to an agency, you are more likely to hear of the progress or nonprogress." In theory, self-referral to any of the counseling systems was not reported to the unit. In practice, however, a soldier might be deliberately reported if he were thought to be a security risk.

In spite of best efforts, confidentiality was sometimes broken accidentally on a small post. A neighbor, workmate, or friend might have seen someone go into a counseling center and interpret that negatively. The gossip that "so-and-so must be having problems" because he or she was seen in the alcohol treatment clinic might return to the work supervisors or evaluators. Even when confidentiality was in theory preserved by not using names of the self-referred parties, the counseling systems had to make reports to senior unit leaders. For example, the battalion chaplain, as minister, counseled people with regard to many matters, including marital problems, stress adaptation, or alcohol abuse. By regulation, the chaplain was required to brief the battalion commander regularly on general morale and problems in the command. The briefings took place, however, in larger staff meetings. Chaplains tried to keep marital information generic and confidential. But the task was difficult. As MAJ Rodney Kimball put it,

> Going to the chaplain can be a dangerous situation. You have to know the chaplain's personality before you can confide in him. There is a patient-client relationship. But he is caught between a rock and a hard place. He must brief the battalion commander in staff meeting. Ten to one, whoever is there can figure out who it [the briefing] is about. In the environment we live in, it doesn't take long to figure who the people are. There is no privacy. So you have to be very careful.

Thus, even an attempt to get help could be career damaging.

The Atwoods, both specialists four, described the difficulties they encountered while attempting to get marital counseling after one of their arguments had escalated into physical violence. They both recognized that their initial problem was due to their own personalities and immaturity, compounded by the pressures of a dual-military couple life. They had discussed the possibility of going to counseling; the husband, Jeff, indicated, "She had brought up that she was going to see counseling, but not when." Betty spoke up: "We didn't want to go to the chaplain, because he married us. But we wanted a professional counselor, hoping that she could help us with our problems." So Betty asked her "chief," her work supervisor, for advice.

> He turned me in the right direction of counseling. But he also went to [Jeff's] chain of command and got him in trouble for something that—number one—I don't feel should have gotten him in any trouble, I was told, because we came to them. We were not referred to them or brought in to them by the MPs. We came in on our own. And with Jeff's chain of command, it went from the commander all the way down to the NCO. And it was not necessary to go past the commander, because Jeff was willing. He didn't have to be forced to go to counseling.
>
> It happened all in one day. My chief told his chain. Then the whole chain knew. He [Jeff] got a counseling statement. I was told that no action would be taken—and then *this*. So he comes home totally angry with me because I went crying [to my boss], and to get him in trouble. Even if I wouldn't have gone to the chief, the counselor told me straight up she had to do a report on spouse abuse. Just 'cause I came for help on a situation where he hit me and I hit him. I went in confidence, and then this: 200 million people know.

One wonders if this young couple or any of their friends will ever again make the same "mistake" of attempting to get "help."

In addition to the various therapy services, other agencies, such as the military police, had a problem with confidentiality in the small-town setting created by such concentrated social networks. Kathy Brenton, as coordinator of volunteer services at Middleberg's ACS, responded to a question about confidentiality with a somewhat indignant account of an apprehension by the MPs: "The MPs had blabbed the story before the ink was even dry [on the police blotter]. One of the MPs told her friend, who told my baby-sitter, who told me. Yes, the families have legitimate reason to be unhappy."

The Family Action Case Management Team (FACMT), a committee composed of relevant leaders from a community's social, medical, psychological, and legal offices, was another potential source of information leakage. Every military community was required by regulation to have such a committee to handle "problem family" situations in which either regular therapeutic support services had failed or the behavior appeared threatening to the welfare of a spouse, a child, the efficiency of the military activities, or German-American relations. Every complaint, regardless of its merit, seemed to require investigation, as the following two case proceedings (among many that I sat in on) demonstrate. In front of a committee of some ten leaders from various agencies in the Middleberg community, the team leader, MAJ Eric Buckley, a Judge Advocate General officer, initiated the monthly review of each pending case by calling the family's surname and giving the relevant details: "This case involves two boys, nine and six years old. They were asking the neighbors for food. Said that they only got peanut butter at home." The committee began discussion. The social worker assigned to investigate recommended that the case be dropped as "unfounded." His investigation revealed the kids were well-fed, but the neighbors interpreted the desire for food as "neglect" and made the report. The social worker explained further, perhaps for my benefit, perhaps to share experience with others who might have to interpret future reports of neglect, or perhaps to confirm the intense degree of suspicion and lack of privacy that military families endured: "When people say that the neighbors [children] are begging, the stairwell may be having problems between the parents. A kid comes and asks for a cookie and the neighbor yells 'child neglect.' If you live in the stairwell, you had better not get on the bad side of your neighbors. If you're on the economy, well, it is not such a problem." MAJ Buckley proceeded to the next case, again stating the family's surname and grade: "The victim is the child of an E-3. Scratch on the face of the child. Parent says child fell on a cassette. The doctor says the cut is consistent with the description, and the child is bonding well with the parent. Recommend that the case be found unfounded."

When the cases were legitimate, the FACMT group recommended a course of action to the community commander, for his or her approval. Serious or repeated misbehavior would result in a recommendation that the family be returned to the States. Other recommendations could span the possibilities described in Chapter 8, "If You Can't Control Your Family." Although it seems intrinsically good that families were helped by professionals and that the community commander's actions were often based on their recommendations, there nevertheless were potential problems. Given the various professionals present in the FACMT group, family information about "founded" or "unfounded" incidents could easily escape and flow to the company or battalion leaders through informal channels. As Mr. Renquist, the director of the community counseling center, put it, "It is real here, that things bleed back to the command." I believe that the choice of the word "bleed" was unconscious but significant. It conveyed the fear of many military families that even a simple life event or a common but minor mistake could wound their career.

Resenting Loss of Privacy. Many people felt they lacked privacy, that everything they did was under scrutiny, under observation, especially if they lived in on-post housing. The "fishbowl" metaphor came up repeatedly in interviews with families from different communities. MAJ Scott, the Grossberg supervisor of community chaplains, compared a tour in the States with his experience in Germany: "We were in paradise in Colorado; I never felt restricted. Here, I feel I'm in a fishbowl sometimes. But also in the German village, everybody knows your life. You [have to] create your own privacy in the stairwell, in crowded conditions." As Terry Walsh put it, "Everybody is in everybody's back pocket. It's a fishbowl. Everybody knows everybody's business." To this, her husband, Hank, interjected, "It's a giant soap opera. If anything weird is happening, the unit knows." "I don't know any of the men in my husband's unit, but I know all about them, and they know all about me," Terry clarified. LTC Douglas Call, Sudberg's deputy community commander, elaborated on the impact of closed information loops, using the same metaphor:

> The military family lives in a fishbowl. They meet each other everywhere—[in] school, Scouts, walking to the PX. Everything is open to the scrutiny and the judgmental aspect. And all are quick to judge. This compounds the social adjustments, because there are so many other things that come into it. The other issue is that of command involvement with a family's misconduct. This brings with it an instant scrutiny that may have severe career impact.

People not only disliked being observed "in a fishbowl," they even wearied of being observers. I conversed with SFC Alex Tanner while he accompanied his wife and child in the medical clinic in Middleberg:

> "I don't care for the community at all. This community is too small. Where you work at, you see people you know. You can't be anonymous at all here. You can't get away."
> "In the Army in the USA, you can't be anonymous," I challenged.
> "Yeah, you could: at the gas station, at the grocery store."
> "Wouldn't you rather know the people?" I pushed to find the edges of the concept.
> "Not everybody, everywhere, knowing everything. I don't want to know their personal stories. It is not healthy for people to be—" He didn't finish the sentence, but resolutely started again. "I don't want to know their dirty laundry. You tend not to like them if you know that. I don't want to know so much."

People wanted—needed—greater privacy. To get it, however, they in fact needed a sharper separation of military life and community life domains.

Lost privacy was closely related to breached confidentiality, though there seemed to be less of a sense of breached professional expectation. Oprah Brimley, the ACS financial counselor at Richberg and wife of a senior NCO, described her sense of lost privacy: "It is a lot different here. Bouncing a check here is—" She shifted her approach. "Here we are all in one place and they know where you work. Here it seems more concentrated. Here everybody in the world knows that you wrote a bad check, and it [your military ID card] is overstamped." Indeed, anyone who misused their checking account had their military ID card stamped in large block print—"cash only"—so all could see they had lost their checking privileges. Since one was required to show the ID card at virtually every point of interaction with the military—to come through the front gate, to shop, to use any services, including a cash payment at the post office—a great deal of confidentiality and privacy were lost. All such information was sinister in that it might draw the commander's attention to aspects of the soldier's life not related to the mission. As COL Wayne Keele, chief of psychiatry for U.S. forces in Germany, put it, "Only if the commander hears your name too often is he going to get rid of you." But how often is "too often"? No one could ever be sure because "it all depends on the commander."

Losing Parental Control. Families sensed they lost parental control because the "fishbowl" scrutiny of military life made all citizens potential critics of each other's style of raising children. Chapter 8, "If You Can't Control Your Family," described a mother who complained of being unable to raise her children as she felt proper because virtually any physical discipline was likely to be interpreted by someone else as abuse. Traditional patterns of child discipline—a swat on the rear in public—could get parents in trouble. Yet, young Army parents often had no training in other forms of discipline. Some were tempted to abandon child control measures entirely, but the uncontrolled child also endangered the family's career. The "Catch-22" contradiction produced emotions ranging from angst to anger. The point here is not so much that family control seemed vitiated, but that the loss of family control was a form of social violation directly attributable to the Army.

Reacting to Cultural Contradiction and Dissonance. The felt sense of coercion rubbed raw against the cultural expectation of freedom of choice and left a significant feeling of contradiction, of cognitive dissonance. Soldiers and spouses seemed to feel violated by the sense of entrapment in a web of inescapable contradictions. Thus, spouses felt they needed to exercise extreme caution in interacting with others, yet they felt pressured to get involved in the community to enhance their husband's career. Parents felt they needed discipline to control children, yet discipline could be viewed as abuse. Soldiers should report the status of their unit's combat readiness, yet the reports could harm their career. These contradictions and others led to a kind of pervasive corruption throughout the system.

The End Result: Corruption of Unit, Mission, Family, and Community

Demand Overload and Distraction From the Mission. In Chapter 8, "If You Can't Control Your Family," leaders estimated they were spending up to half of their time attending to family matters. In all probability this was an exaggeration. But it no doubt expressed the frustration of officers and senior sergeants for whom dealing with family issues was a distraction from the military mission on which they wished to focus. The processes of family surveillance and the assumption of responsibility for the family had generated a burden on leaders that was counterproductive to the organization's mission. Again, we find a "Catch-22" logic. Military leaders wanted to improve mission efficiency by attending to family needs in the community. But in the process of doing so, they degraded mission efficiency with not only the increased work burden placed on leaders, but also with the psychological burden of asking them to deal with counseling issues for which they were untrained.

Distrust, Fear, and Loathing in the Units. The potential for any information to be misinterpreted or used against soldiers' careers led to a number of distortions in the flow of information that had severe consequences in the unit and in the community.

Sharing gripes demonstrated trust at the same time that it built trust. Said CPL Ron Hammond, "We love getting together with our neighbors—from the unit—and talk about some of the bad things that are happening." But such information did not easily move vertically if the group had proved trustworthy. Out of fear that the bearer of bad news or the complainer might be punished, many soldiers withheld information that company commanders and senior military leaders needed to run the organization well. 1SG Roper, of Middleberg, explained. "They try to hide stuff [problems]. By the time we find out about it, it is out of proportion." Soldiers explained their reluctance by stating that "complainers are looked down on."

Not all felt suppressed. Terry Walsh expressed her determination to go to the unit leaders when something was wrong. Her husband said he was willing to just try to "roll with the punches" that might result. Her reply to his statement was firm: "I will say what I think." Perhaps she felt protected by her ability to function as a critical care nurse were they pressed out of the Army. She admitted, however, that as far as she could tell, "the majority say what they think the leaders want to hear," thereby passing corrupt information up the system.

To the degree that people said what they thought their leaders wanted to hear instead of sharing accurately their views of reality, the Army lost its ability to take its own pulse, to assess its own health. It lost its ability to determine where it was in relation to its goals. Leaders, of course, took action based on the information they received. If their information did not match the soldiers' view of reality, leadership decisions, though well-intentioned, appeared arbitrary, irrational, or even self-serving to those they commanded. Obviously, leaders who were supplied with inaccurate information could not make appropriate decisions. Instead, they were being set up to respond to fictitious situations. Thus the disparity between what the soldier experienced and what the leader was told continued to widen inadvertently, confirming to the soldiers and families that the system was "crazy" and "fucked up." Soldiers who perceived their leaders to be irrational and arbitrary while handling community affairs and training in peacetime said they were less likely to serve faithfully under the same leaders when their lives were at risk in combat. Unit morale was savaged in the process.

Families in the U.S. Army communities in Germany during the period of this study lived in a social climate of pain. Many, like Elsie Kimball, experienced the system as potentially ruinous to their lives: "We have so many circumstances that ruin our lives, you can't trust the system. And you can be as flexible as you want, but it hurts." She did not speak in possibilities, using words like "might" or "could," but rather in the declarative voice—that they "have . . . circumstances that ruin our lives." The circumstances of Army life in Germany drove many to consider leaving the Army. Kathy Brenton, the ACS volunteer coordinator at Middleberg, described her struggle to reassure several discouraged wives. "I tell the wives, 'Just chill out, calm down, 'til you get to the next post.' These wives are so upset at what is going on. Their husbands are pilots. This is their first assignment, and they are wanting to get out of the Army." To be sure, most families managed to make it through their tour of duty in Germany, though some paid a price in the form of withdrawal, alcohol abuse, or divorce. Virtually all families experienced anguish as they worked through the intrusions of mission complexity, mission urgency, family control, cultural isolation, and community judgment. The Army paid a parallel price in the form of diminished morale and effectiveness within its units and in the loss of personnel who had originally intended to make the Army their profession. Interestingly, all of these processes of morale corruption have been documented at least since the 1970s, especially in Larry Ingraham's *The Boys in the Barracks*.[4]

INFORMATION FLOW AND THE VALUE OF SEPARATING WORK AND FAMILY DOMAINS

In spite of the many unsatisfying and unintended negative consequences, the flow of information through the dense communication networks had positive effects in units when handled carefully and confidentially. On the positive side, having such intimate and often immediate sources of information enabled unit leaders to be more completely informed about their soldiers and dependents, for whom leaders were responsible. Consequently, leaders were better able to assist their subordinates when some aspect of military life became a problem. To do so, however, they had to handle information with discretion. 1SG Roper related how he and his wife participated as a team in the leadership of his unit:

> I get home and put on civilian clothes and they [the junior enlisted personnel] feel more comfortable. That is where the commanders' wives, or the first sergeants' wives get involved. They sit down and talk over a cup of tea. They are more likely to open up to my wife than to me. My wife has a bachelor's degree in counseling. She worked as a social worker in Fort Benning. She goes and sits with them, and they have a coffee in their apartment. They feel comfortable around her. She tries to solve the problem herself. Try and get the thing solved. Why, she may learn a thousand things. But if she tells me, I never let the soldier know. Because the wife will think, if she tells my wife, and it gets to me, then it will get to the husband. My wife may talk to me, but until the guy comes to me, I just tell my wife what she ought to tell the wives to tell the men to come in. If I tell everybody [how or what

I know], she [the soldier's wife] is going to pass the word around that the company commander and everybody knows. He [the soldier] is going to be embarrassed; he is going to jump on her. Every Sunday, on the weekend, I come in to check my office, in civilian clothes. I just sit here from 9:00 to 10:00 [A.M.] on Sunday. They may tell me, "The platoon sergeant told me 'xyz.'" No problem. I'll take care of it. But I never tell the platoon sergeant who told me. I act like it is just by observation.

This couple sensitively handled the flow of information between spouses in the chain of concern and soldiers in the chain of command without letting the process undermine trust in people's messages or trust in unit leadership.

CONCLUSION

The implications of the quote that launched this chapter sum up the impact surveillance and judgment can have on a community. With so many close interconnections, "the Army family is in a fishbowl," so exposed to view and to judgment that other families "report" on "the offending family" by "dropping a dime on them" (referring to the old price of an anonymous pay-phone call). This prospect led to a great deal of distrust and isolation between families. Indeed, the process created and continuously reproduced a community of fear and alienation. Surveillance, control, and threat led to fear, rejection, resistance, and alienation. Increased alienation and resistance led to the application of more control and the need for increased surveillance and judgment. The feedback loop easily spiraled out of control in a downward decline of morale and was managed successfully only by the most exceptional leaders.

Chapter 8, "If You Can't Control Your Family," showed that not only was the married soldier "in the Army," so also were all the members of his or her family. In this chapter I have shown that the entire community was suffused with pervasive military scrutiny and judgment, judgment that directly affected every family's career security. The fear of scrutiny and judgment induced withdrawal from the community and forced its members to reproduce safe, conservative, standardized, cautious, "traditional" forms of expected public behavior. One is reminded of Michel Foucault's assertion that the expectation of pervasive surveillance and punishment anchors systems of discipline and institutionalizes a self-motivated bodily discipline.[5]

The intense community judgment amplified greatly the sense that the family was in the Army. The fact that most Americans could not easily enter the surrounding German community further narrowed the already dense channels of communication within the American military community. Work, family, and community became tightly fused, conjoined by a single judgment system—the military chain of command. Everywhere one looked, there seemed to be no escape from the fused domains. At work, soldiers were confronted with family issues; in the family, soldier's work took priority over family needs. Likewise, the community existed to serve military needs and therefore was run by the leaders of the largest resident combat units.

This fusion of domains caused a great deal of discomfort to the families who attempted to live in these Army communities, for three significant reasons. First, families feared harming, or even losing, the family's most important asset—the soldier's career. Second, the military injected itself into every aspect of the family's life, subverting the family's normal functions and violating its members' cultural expectations of a familial domain of privacy and autonomy. And finally, the intense fusion of career, family, and community contradicted basic beliefs and values in the American cultural system. Before we can examine this last proposition, however, we must explore how the fusion of career, family, and community created an intense desire for escape.

NOTES

1. George Foster, "Peasant Society and the Image of the Limited Good," *American Anthropologist* 67 (1965): 293–315.

2. See Charlotte Wolf, *Garrison Community: A Study of an Overseas American Military Colony* (Westport, CT: Greenwood Publishing, 1969) on gossip and rumor in a U.S. military community in Turkey.

3. The difficulties come up clearly throughout Alexis de Tocqueville's *Democracy in America*, ed. J. P. Mayer, trans. George Lawrence (Garden City, NY: Anchor Books, Doubleday & Company, 1969). They reappear in Herve Varenne's *Americans Together: Structured Diversity in a Midwestern Town* (New York: Teachers College Press, 1977), another Frenchman's analysis of American life. Finally, Robert Bellah et. al. treat the topic in *Habits of the Heart: Individualism and Commitment in American Life* (New York: Harper & Row, 1985).

4. Larry Ingraham, *The Boys in the Barracks: Observations on American Military Life* (Philadelphia: Institute for the Study of Human Issues, 1984); "Fear and Loathing in the Baracks—And the Heart of Leadership" *Parameters: Journal of the U.S. Army War College* (December 1988): 75–80.

5. Michel Foucault, *Discipline and Punish: The Birth of the Prison* (New York: Pantheon Books, 1977): 170–185, 195–228.

11

"You Gotta Get Away": From Taking a Break to Making an Escape

You need to take a break from here or you will scramble your brains.
Platoon Sergeant Zeke Peterson
Middleberg Military Community

In previous chapters, soldiers and spouses expressed perplexity, confusion, apathy, frustration, demoralization, and even anger—all indications of alienation from their community and cultural circumstances. Reacting to the thorough surveillance and multifaceted judgment of their lives in these military compounds, almost all felt they needed to escape, to "get away" and "take a break" from the intensity of their lives. There were, of course, multiple avenues of escape. Recreation, family association, friendships, relaxation in one's housing area, or a broad diversity of activities within German society could all provide the needed separation of domains. For a variety of reasons, however, these modes of legitimate escape were either partially or substantially blocked by the structures of military life. Some soldiers and some spouses turned either to complete severance—getting out of the Army—or to self-destructive or hidden modes of escape, among them, divorce, alcohol abuse, misbehaving so as to be forced out of the Army, or resisting and undermining the Army with varying degrees of subtlety.

The desire to escape came from deeper wellsprings than the simple effort to escape surveillance and judgment by work leaders and neighbors. More fundamentally, it was a human response to the contradiction between the realities of their lives and their long-held cultural ideals. The closed structure of overlapping domains in military life violated the premises of freedom, openness, and separated domains embraced within the general American culture. The requirement that soldiers and spouses live both systems simultaneously threatened to "scramble your brains" unless you could "take a break."

THE NEED TO "TAKE A BREAK"

Soldiers worked hard in Germany, driven by the urgency of the mission, the complexity of the social environment, and pressure from the chain of command. Earlier, I quoted Abigail Taylor, who was complaining that the fourteen- to sixteen-hour days normally put in by her husband, a major, had increased to sixteen- to eighteen-hour days. She noted that he "had never disliked his job before," but now "he comes home *tired*. There is no time to let go of the job. For your own mental health, you need to let go. If you don't get a change and have time to do something else, you wear down." Although such rest was recognized as necessary, what I am addressing in this chapter is not a need for physical rest or recreational diversion, though much deserved by many, but a need for mental and social distance from the Army environment.

Both soldiers and military family members often expressed the sentiment that one must get away from the Army, not so much to get away from the work, but to get away from the character of the situation. As CW3 Bill McCormick suggested, "If you stay right here in Middleberg Barracks, you're going to hate it. There are guys that work for me, we go and drag them out of the barracks to go skating, or to Middleberg. You got to get out." His wife, Gretchen, agreed, saying, "You gotta get out! I know I have to get out." SSG Victor Rodgers expressed the same opinion in discussing his quarters at Patriot Village some forty-five minutes away from his work installation: "When you leave Richberg Kaserne you want to try to get as far away as you can from there." Barbra Norton and her husband, Adam, a sergeant, discussed their approaching leave: "I'm going to enjoy this thirty-days' break," said Barbara. "Are you enjoying life at this point in your lives?" I queried. "Yeah, overall it's not bad," said Adam, jumping into the conversation. Barbara continued, "I'm pretty satisfied. Sometimes it does get rough, but as long as I can take a break, it's OK." Although a break meant different things to different people, these and other expressions suggest that a good break or a "real" break—whether short or long—involved finding a form of separation from the Army, a separation of domains, so that one could live life for a while without the Army intruding or demanding thought or action.

THE DIFFICULTY OF TAKING A "REAL BREAK"

The soldier's goal was to get away from work control, to place oneself where the Army could not intrude. Married soldiers sought refuge in family, friends, the housing area, and the installation community or beyond by immersing oneself in German society and its environment.

Whereas a male soldier might find refuge in his quarters, his wife likely wanted relief from the intensity of child care and family duties, from social difficulties in the housing area, and from the Army's tendency to intrude on the family by tasking the soldier. This difference in perspective was the source of occasional argument between some spouses.

To attain a degree of separation, the soldier either had to be informally "off duty," or to be formally "on leave." In a sense, soldiers were never off duty because they had a commitment twenty-four hours a day to be on call, able to return to their posts, arm their equipment, and leave the installation in battle formation within two hours of an alert. Evenings and weekends could be interrupted by the demands of the duty rosters, or by an unexpected call to deal with whatever came up. The only way to avoid such obligations, and preserve a weekend for certain, was to formally go "on leave." A soldier on leave had no obligation and was in fact using vacation time. But even this mechanism was potentially uncertain, for going on leave depended on one's commander granting permission. Permission could be denied based on the current workloads, the upcoming training schedule, or other considerations.[1] Whether informally off duty or formally on leave, the soldier and spouse could seek respite nearby in the family and housing area, farther away in the facilities of the military community, or at a greater physical and psychological distance within the German society.

Seeking Respite in the Family and Living Area

Ideally, the family domain and the residential housing areas offered an escape, but in fact, refuge in either was subverted.

Family. In a discussion concerning the advantages of having a family, 1LT Calvin Park pointed to the difficulty of the single junior troop: "The problem with being single is that you can't really escape from the atmosphere." The contrast with the married soldier was implicit, but potent: the family provided escape. Park went on to say that single soldiers were constantly tasked to do things, more than the married soldiers, because the single soldier lived in the company's barracks housing area, which was upstairs from the company command work area. A company officer or NCO with a late-breaking task simply went upstairs and issued an order to press into service whatever number of soldiers were needed to complete the task. The single soldier lacked the social buffer of a family refuge. Thus, SGT Todd Jasper, on night watch, upon hearing I was doing a family study, suggested:

> The single soldier doesn't have no outlet. They just sit around bored. That leads to the problems of drinking. There's no recreation. I think that the married soldier has a whole big advantage, for support. Because you are in the company area, there are big ears around. You might get in big trouble complaining too much. If you are married, you can deprogram yourself from the military and be civilian. But the single soldiers are in the company work area and are in the Army all of the time. . . . In the barracks you are in an intense area all of the time.

Thus, the single soldier had a greater problem separating domains because she or he lived even closer to work than those married.

SFC Darwin Farr, a platoon sergeant, was explicit about the family as a buffer and escape: "Family helps the married soldier get away from the pressures of the job. The single soldier can't get away. They are in the billets, and it is twenty-four hours a day: someone's banging on the door to 'go clean up.' Married soldiers—they get a release of all that." The release came from having private space and a relationship with family members that served as a primary buffer from the difficulties of work. SSG Frank Barnes felt similarly. "I don't care how bad the unit is—I can handle anything as long as I can have some time in the evening, when they say 'dismissed.'" SSG Mary Donahue, serving as a squad leader, reflected on the benefits of a listening spouse: "It's having someone to talk to that helps, if the spouses are willing to listen. There are things you can say to your spouse that you can't really say to anyone else . . . 'cause you trust them. . . . For example, there might be something that your NCOIC [noncommissioned officer in charge] done to you today. You can't really tell him what you think, but you can tell your spouse, and it lets it all out, and it helps the stress a lot."

Though the family ideally served as a refuge, previous chapters have shown that the Army penetrated and disrupted the family. The twenty-four hour a day call status, job intensity, long hours on duty, mission urgency, and job unpredictability all undermined the refuge of the family and immobilized the family's planning processes. American political sensitivity to embarrassment in Germany led the military to try to control families through a climate of threat to the soldier's career. Community social closure, close observation, family judgment, and gossip further undermined a family's sense of privacy and its modes of escape. The family was inadvertently turned into a continuous risk and a burden rather than a place of refuge.

Housing. Interestingly, although most of my respondents agreed that living in government quarters was enormously convenient, cheap, and comfortable, and they liked being surrounded by American symbols and the English language, living in the government quarters next to the post where one worked offered little in the way of escape from Army influence. 1SG Enrique Gomez: "I feel uncomfortable living in the housing area. I finish here and go to the housing area and solve problems there. . . . I feel cheated because . . . I have to tell them to go cut the grass. But here [at work], that is my job. Then I get to the housing area and for me it keeps going. I have less time for myself." The result was a sense of breached domains and a feeling of alienation, of having been "cheated." Of what was the soldier "cheated"? The answer—the cultural right to family autonomy. The dense overlapping of judgmental social relationships abridged the separation of work and family, generating the need for mental and social escape, but at the same time, it prevented its easy accomplishment, thereby inducing alienation.

An extreme example of relationship concentration was exemplified in some COHORT (Cohesion, Operational Readiness, Training) units, especially if their leaders were not sensitive to the need for escape. Once a COHORT unit was formed, its personnel stayed together for a three-year period. Individual transfers were held to a minimum. COHORT units moved to Europe together. In some cases the unit's families lived in contiguous blocks of housing, by design. CO-HORT units were particularly unified and that unity, it was felt, had important functions in combat. Yet COHORT represented the maximal fusion of domains. Thus, according to 1LT Ivan Owens, "In the COHORT battalion rotation, it was stressful. We were so inundated with the military. We were so responsible for everybody's happiness. We were around each other too much. In the stairwell, there was no privacy. You are in such a close range of interaction that it is very hard." Close residence with potentially judgmental coworkers, in a situation where families, too, were being judged and having an effect on the career, presented too great a fusion of domains.

In contrast with housing areas attached to and serving a single installation, the government housing areas that served a number of installations—often called "villages"—seemed to allow more of a sense of escape or removal because one's neighbors were not from one's unit or even one's installation. Patriot Village exemplified this condition, and SSG Gary Hatch, a resident, explained: "When they get off work, they say, 'It is nice to be far as possible from work.' Puts their mind at ease. At Richberg [housing], if they call you, you gotta go in. But here, you feel that once you left work, you feel that you left work. [Living] at Richberg . . . you feel that you are still at work." Nevertheless, for some, Patriot Village was still "all military," and therefore only a partially satisfying refuge. Indeed, SGT Sam McGregory and his wife, Jean, who lived in a German village, thought of Patriot Village as the epitome of military overconcentration. "One of the benefits on the economy is peace and quiet," Jean mused. "You are away from all of the military and all their crazies," her husband confirmed. "Crazies?" I probed. Sam then clarified:

If you go up to Patriot Village, where all the military housing is, and there is nothing but military there . . . you are going to have . . . people sitting around asking you, "Why'd you do this?" and, "Who goes in? Who comes out?" You always got that few that likes to keep a mess going. I don't like them to keep tabs on me. Out here [on the economy], I can drive home and nobody is watching. It's a peaceful environment.

In short, Army housing that was attached to the work site, filled with soldier-families from the same work installation, and linked in a single chain of command, offered no escape from surveillance, tasking, or judgment. Army quarters in a separated housing area, filled with soldier families from diverse installations in distinct chains of command, was better but not perfect. Residence "on the economy" offered the greatest escape.

Seeking Refuge in the Larger Military Community

Recreation. Recognizing the value of a break, the Army provided a wide variety of recreational facilities on many installations. A movie theater or two, a bowling alley, a game-room recreation center, a library, a woodworking shop and a fast-food facility were nearly universal. A rod and gun club provided a casual bar and restaurant atmosphere for all ranks. An officers' club and an NCO club allowed the ranks to have private areas. Craft centers had project rooms that enabled soldiers or spouses to make their own pottery or frame their art. A few installations had a golf course. Many had a self-help auto repair bay where those inclined could do their own repairs. The Army also provided a range of shopping, especially at the central supply points, of which Grossberg Military Community was one. Beyond the local military community, the U.S. armed forces in Europe made several major recreational facilities available to soldiers of all services. The Lake Chiemsee facility offered a large lakeside hotel, excellent camping facilities, and a fine restaurant. One could rent a variety of boats and water sports equipment for a nominal fee. At Berchtesgaden and Garmisch, military hotels, restaurants, and a military ski lift supported remarkable year-round mountain recreation.

On-post recreational facilities were important symbols that the Army cared for its soldiers and families. But they did not fully satisfy the need for a break because they fell within the orbit of military control, and the on-post ones were patronized by one's bosses and work associates from the same community. Speaking of the local community club, SSG Hatch observed, "Most of the troops won't go up there because there may be officers, and it is like working: you're surrounded by high leaders. They [the enlisted] need a club for themselves." As acting company commander, 1LT Larry McDugal put it, "Over here you're kind of limited. You can't break away. You're sealed in. They try to provide it as a service and yet—" Lani, his wife, interrupted and finished his sentence, "—the community controls it." In this instance, "the community" meant the military community command cadre. In short, the escape potential of on-post recreation was considerably subverted by its own militariness and by the likely presence of military peers or superiors from the work area.

By contrast, the regional recreational facilities, such as those at Lake Chiemsee, Berchtesgaden, and Garmisch, were visited by soldiers and families from all over Europe. In such locations, soldiers were sufficiently distant from the scrutiny, judgment, control, and social closure of one's work installation that they offered much better escape.

Employment. Some spouses escaped through employment. This strategy not only offered the spouse diversion from the travails of household life and nearby neighbors, it also provided essential funds for young families living in a very expensive economy. The Army recognized the economic needs of its families and, by law, provided spouses with a first option on many of the jobs available in the military communities in Germany.

Money, however, was only one of the incentives in work. 1LT Owens commented on the escape value of a spouse's employment, challenging the view that employment was sought primarily to meet economic needs: "I think that sometimes the military misses the point on spouse employment. When the spouse is employed, her life is not just military. The spouse gets out of the military unit loop. When all of your support is in the unit, it is not as healthy."

But there were impediments to escape through employment. First, fewer jobs were available in the military communities than were needed or than would have been available in the States, where one could have chosen from civilian jobs as well. Second, spouses in military community jobs worked with soldiers and under officers to provide services to other soldiers or Army families. Thus, while employment helped, it did not allow complete escape because the employment involved interaction with soldiers and subordination to military bosses.

Volunteerism. Volunteer work in the community provided another extremely productive form of escape because it involved the use of one's freedom of choice. One did something one was not required to do. Unfortunately, some of the escape value of volunteering was undercut by a feeling that the chain of concern coerced a spouse's efforts and the chain of command expected officers and NCOs to be committed to such service. Having addressed this issue extensively in Chapter 10, "Living in a Fishbowl," I will not say more here.

Friendships. Friends also afforded relief from the pressures of work. The quotes on friendship in the previous chapter indicate that people appreciated having a few trusted friends and that these friends furnished mutual support and informal therapy. In that chapter, we also saw that families experienced difficulties in finding trustworthy friends because gossip and information leakage to the community could so easily have an adverse effect on a career. To a lesser degree, some people pulled back from friendships because they knew they would lose them through rotations. These factors undermined the escape value of friendship.

Finding Relief in the German Community

Living on the economy was the most thorough form of residential escape from the pervasive influence of the Army, though off-post living created significant cultural challenges. Mr. Steve Bramwell, Middleberg's Department of Defense civilian social worker, lived on the economy. He suggested, "American culture ends at the gate. I like it better out there." SFC Alex Tanner, who also lived on the economy and worked at Richberg, commented, "We like our privacy. And we have a very nice house. You give that up for quarters. Before we came here [i.e., at their previous station in the United States], we bought a house in a civilian community. No [military] neighbors. We are used to having our privacy in our own area. We turned down quarters in October." Thus, some families definitely preferred life in the German villages precisely because off-post residence allowed them to get away from the omnipresence of the Army tasking, away from the watchful evaluation in on-post housing, and away from the cultural contradictions we have seen and that I will explore further in the next chapter. Clearly, for some, all of the additional costs and cultural stresses of living on the economy were worth the escape acquired.

A few even savored the adventure in a new culture. One could use the German community's many luxurious community sports facilities to swim, skate, or bowl. One could tour the historic and architectural sites, visit the museums, or hike the myriad public trails through farms, forests, or mountains. One could escape into the amazing variety of German hobby clubs and engage in everything from sail-planing to flower gardening, from chess to horseback riding.

Escape into the richness of German society and culture, however, was not easy. In Chapter 9, "Little America," I laid out a battery of factors—high costs and mark-rate uncertainty, language deficit, lack of cultural knowledge, risk of embarrassment, and a variety of structural separations—that inhibited access to the German environment and society. From the perspective of this chapter, these same factors blocked or impeded escape to the German society.

Moreover, newly arriving young couples often did not appreciate, until too late, the escape value of their initial requirement to live on the economy. Forced to rent on the economy by the long waiting lists for government housing, and isolated by language deficit and lack of money early in their careers, many couples hated their early months on the economy. They looked forward to a more convenient and more American life in government quarters, where English was spoken all around. Accordingly, they immediately signed the lists and waited for—longed for—government housing that would become available some twelve to eighteen months later. Considering the need for escape, one might wonder about the soldiers and their families who lived away from post and yet were not happy. Apparently, they did not see their situation as a choice for escape because it was not made of their own volition. They were required to live on the economy, so that requirement made their condition another imposition of Army control rather than a restful escape.

When these families finally moved into on-post housing, however, they quickly discovered that the more closed nature of the on-post housing society—including the Army's presence in organizing cleanup and maintenance, and the too watchful eyes of neighbors—made the experience far less desirable than they had hoped. They eventually came to resent the entire assignment, both "on the economy" and then "in quarters." They literally counted down the days until their return to the United States. Indeed, it was not at all uncommon to hear a most ordinary greeting of "How are you doing?" answered with some variation of "I've got 189 [or whatever their particular number of] days to do" or "I'm doing my time." Metaphorically, such answers signaled that the speakers felt imprisoned.

Double Messages Regarding Taking a Break

Although leaders wanted soldiers to take a break and experience Germany, they sent contradictory signals to soldiers and families regarding their access to Germany. On the one hand, many commanders, as well as friends, urged soldiers to do what the *Stars and Stripes* suggested—"get out" and enjoy Germany. On the other hand, at least five beliefs held by senior leaders—and communicated in various ways to subordinates—tended to discourage soldiers and family members from making vigorous contact with Germans. First, there was the constant and powerful message not to create an embarrassment with the host country. Second, because funds flowed to where they were most used, senior community commanders wanted soldiers of all ranks to use or "support" the on-post facilities to retain funding for existing personnel and services and qualify for future funds and projects. Thus, every service provider on post had a sign-in sheet that proved use and justified continued funding. No leader—let alone a community commander—wanted to be responsible for an implosion of community services through lack of use. So all residents were encouraged—and some even felt coerced—to use the on-post facilities, from the officers' club to the barbershop. Third, because heavy use of central facilities symbolized community esprit-de-corps, commanders encouraged use of on-post facilities to demonstrate their success at building community morale. It was hard not to feel some obligation being imposed. Fourth, there were subtle fears that those who learned to use the German resources and language might be "going native" and losing allegiance to American ways. They might even compromise military security, for their friends from Germany or other nations might be spies. Thus, the very act of learning how to communicate with outsiders could get one portrayed as subtly un-American. Finally, those who learned German language and culture placed in an unfavorable light other, more senior officers who could not manage the language. Although this statement in some ways contradicts the prior point, the fact remains that the bosses were supposed to be the best, the brightest, and the point of contact with officialdom in Germany. None of the senior brigade or division/troop community commanders I met, however, could function in German beyond getting a meal. Consciously or unconsciously, the variety of pressures led some to protect their careers by "facing the flag," saluting, and cutting themselves off from contact with Germany.

MAKING AN ESCAPE: FORMS OF DESTRUCTIVE BREAK

Given that the socially acceptable modes of escape were partially blocked, some soldiers and family members created their own alternatives, with varying degrees of social acceptability or personal cost. One way to end the contradictions between Army life and the American culture was to end one's service in the Army. An officer resigned her or his commission. An enlisted person simply did not reenlist when his or her current obligation ended. Getting out of the Army these ways was perfectly proper, but the Army lost a great deal each time, having made a huge investment in training its personnel.

Alternatively, one could misbehave in order to force one's removal from the service. CSM Barry Cutler described how a fine but dissatisfied soldier came to him and asked how he could get out of the Army as quickly as possible with minimum damage to his reputation. The sergeant major showed him the regulations, and the soldier obtained a discharge by overeating. Once he weighed more than the Army's fitness regulation allowed, he was processed out of the Army. In another case, a Richberg soldier with fewer than thirty days of service remaining in his enlistment contract assaulted another soldier, the driver of a five-ton Army truck. Knocking him unconscious with a helmet and pulling him out of the cab, the assailant commandeered the truck and rammed the installation's side gate. Although I never met or interviewed the subsequently imprisoned soldier, the episode had all the exterior signs of a desire to escape run amok.

One could reduce the conflicts between family and career if spouse and children agreed (or were forced) to return to the United States. For some, this was a simple economic necessity. For others, it was a move to reduce conflict and thereby maintain the marriage or the children's welfare. Having paid the costs of a family transfer, however, the government policy did not shorten the sponsor's remaining obligation in Germany. For some couples, the decision to return part of the family to the States was a marital separation preparatory to a divorce. Presumably there was something about the relationship that they "could not stand" any longer, even if it was simply the presence of the Army fused into the relationship. Here again, contradictions between unit and family were being resolved, though the parties to the separation perhaps did not conceive it in those terms. Nevertheless, the widely held cultural concept of individual and private family domains collided with the Army's premises and practices that tended to gobble up other domains in the pursuit of unity and control.

Alcohol served as a popular way to deal with contradiction and stress in the military milieu. According to SGT Larry Bracken, "A lot of people take Stress-Tab Jim Beam. They are not a bunch of lushes, but for a large number, that is their main source of entertainment." SP4 Jeff Atwood shared this opinion: "There's a lot of people in the service with alcohol and drug problems. It is mostly the people that stay in the barracks. Maybe they don't go out, and they don't have much money." Drugs seemed to be a relatively small problem in the Army in Germany, though continued vigilance by random testing was required. Alcohol, however, had long been a socially acceptable drug. Though policy changes in the late 1980s had been putting increased emphasis on reducing alcohol use, alcohol continued to provide a traditional and widely used form of escape, and the "Class VI store," the liquor store on each installation, was always busy.

If one could not physically or socially escape the Army's control, if one could not avoid "getting fucked by the Green Machine," one could at least escape symbolically and to one's personal satisfaction through subtle and secretive acts that subverted or got even with the system. The soldiers called it "getting over on the Army." The metaphor showed superiority by getting "on top" of something, perhaps with reference to, say, winning in wrestling. Though no soldier made this connection for me, it may have been a sexual reference to the missionary position, so that "getting over on the Army" symbolically constituted "fucking the Army," taking revenge without its consent or knowledge. As explained to me by many soldiers, the Army extracted so much sacrifice and was so slow to reciprocate that soldiers often felt they had to take whatever action they could to balance the accounts. By slowing down their work or by absenting themselves during an unsupervised errand and taking extra time to get back, soldiers reclaimed some of the hours they felt had been commandeered. Sometimes they performed personal chores while on duty, especially while on unsupervised work details. Occasionally, soldiers stole articles of government property. But in most cases, "getting over" simply meant taking their "own sweet time" without getting caught. Thus, "getting over" was a mild form of escape.

Finally, in Chapters 5, 8, and 10, I showed how the dense and judgmental social networks in the nearly closed military community resulted in self-protective social withdrawal or socially imposed isolation. For some, withdrawal may have been a form of culture shock, an inadvertent reaction to a difficult system. But for others, social separation and withdrawal was a form of intentional escape.

THE INABILITY TO "TAKE A BREAK" AND
THE BREAKDOWN OF MORALE

SGT Ian Warnock and his wife, Emma, reflected on the need for a break, the difficulty of getting away:

> "Are you happy on the economy?" I began.
>
> "Yes," replied Ian.
>
> "How come?" I scrambled to draw something worthwhile out of an inherently weak yes/no question.
>
> "Because I am away from work—away from soldiers."
>
> Emma jumped in with her perspective: "Sometimes it is hard because you are so far away from the American type things. But I prefer living away from all the soldiers."
>
> "How come?" I invited elaboration.
>
> "We were raised in the country. I'm not a city person," Emma offered.
>
> Ian added the more military reasons: "A lot of my reason is I get so fed up with stuff at work that I don't like being around it. It is my way of getting away from it all."
>
> "Why do you need to get away?"
>
> "I think if I didn't, I'd probably go crazy," Ian suggested.
>
> "Why? What do you mean?" I pushed for the cultural logic.
>
> "The long days. The dog and pony show. For the Germans, you have to put on a show for them—[like] stay in the field, or work twelve and fourteen hours a day. When I get home, I just want to get away from it all," concluded Ian definitively.

Ian went on to detail the lack of sense in keeping equipment ultraclean—a matter of external show—but inadequately repaired and therefore not ready for the "real" mission of combat. I asked again for the meaning of "dog and pony show."

> "Keeping everybody in the same uniform, for example—wet-weather gear, overshoes. Your feet sweat so much that they get wetter than if you had not worn them. [Wet feet cause incapacitating trench foot, or foot rot, and all soldiers are trained to avoid the condition.] But in our unit, you wear them if anybody wears them. Like the wet-weather jacket: if the battalion commander is wearing it, everybody is wearing it, whether you need it or not. To me, half the stuff is stupid. It doesn't make any sense."
>
> "Does that bother your wife?" I asked.
>
> "Not her as much as me. That is one reason I like living off-post—to keep her away from it all."
>
> "So what makes the on-post quarters unpleasant?" I asked, again probing for the logic.
>
> "You are still right there on-post. Your commander has the right to come in and inspect your quarters."
>
> "He has the right, but does he do it?" I asked, knowing that it is not done unless there is probable cause sufficient to justify a search warrant.
>
> "No, it's never been done. But it is the thought of it. The military has too much control as it is over you."

This conversation reflects some of the basic tensions between work and culture that existed among members of the U.S. Army community stationed in Germany. The spouse missed the convenience and the symbolic affirmation that came from being around "American-type things." The soldier preferred to get away and explained his desire for escape in terms of long hours, craziness, lack of privacy, working to "appear good," and overwhelming control. "Real mission," soldier safety, and the soldier's ability to return home on time had been sacrificed. As a result, the work life began to seem "stupid." It had no point. Army life became an irrational complex of contradictions that would drive you "crazy." As a result, "you gotta get away." Hence the meaning of this chapter's epigraph: "scrambled brains" are indeed an apt symbol for a life constructed out of intense, close, overlapping social relations when such a condition violates fundamental cultural assumptions. To avoid that scrambling, one does need a break.

Up to now I have suggested a kind of linear causation—social relations that were too dense and judgmental created a need for escape that was blocked by military control of the families and community isolation. But there were additional intricate feedback loops. For example, complexity of the system induced leaders to keep soldiers for longer hours, which then intruded on the family domain and increased the tensions between Army and family. Soldiers consequently resisted. Thus, leaders' efforts to solve a problem at one point in the system actually amplified tensions throughout the rest of the system in a ripple of unintended consequences, a runaway feedback loop that exacerbated rather than resolved issues.

The pervasive stresses rooted in these contradictions added to the level of aggression within the community—and the increased aggression multiplied the stresses. As Ruth Rodgers explained, "In the States, it is more or less secluded. Here, people are stuck and don't even want to be here." Ominously, her next words indicated that verbal aggression resulted from the frustrations arising from being stuck, and that forgiveness or tolerance seemed to be reduced: "Things are said that normally wouldn't be said. If you come tomorrow to say you're sorry [for something you said the day before]—*wrong answer*." Much later in the interview, I empathized with the Rodgers family, saying, "It is a hard life in the Army." "Yeah," said Victor, "with all the regulations it is." Ruth was more explicit:

> You gotta deal with more than the normal circumstances. Then you start rebelling, and you start speaking out, and that is when people start to dislike each other. The other day, one woman looked at me and I thought, "Why in the hell did she look at me like that, like I got shit on me." And body language speaks a lot. They don't need to say nothing. When they do say something, it is when the body language won't do it any more. And then they may say, "You black so and so" or "you asshole." And that is when you may slap the shit out of somebody.

If these members of the community are to be believed—and they should be, because their perceptions drove their behavior—the inability to escape from the contradictions and the pressures supercharged the community with anger, resentment, and verbal aggression that spilled over into misinterpretation and threatened aggression based on race.

Throughout this book, we have seen many examples of this morale deterioration. In Chapter 9, "Little America," SSG Nate Cobb referred to spouses who "just sit at home all day long, seven days a week and then say Germany ain't worth —," and suggested that the reason "they hate Germany" is because they "go nowhere," "do nothing," and neither "see" nor "get involved" with the country. In short, they did not escape. Again, concerning morale, Denise Stewart, the deputy director of ACS at Richberg: "They think life is the pits here. Their husband is being treated like the pits. Ten to one, the woman is in the house with two kids, not moving out at all."

One afternoon, as I was walking through the government quarters housing area of Richberg to an interview appointment, I met a German photographer who specialized in taking family photos in the client's home. He spoke excellent English, and his clients were now exclusively American military. He, too, was walking to an appointment. He thought I was a fellow salesman, perhaps his competition, because I was carrying my computer in a briefcase somewhat similar to his camera case. He asked me what I was doing, and I told him I was studying how the American military family adapted to life in Germany. Without any further information from me, he said, "There are two types: those that love it, and those that hate it. The ones that hate it, you ask, 'Have you been to Heidelberg? or to Munich?' 'No.' 'Well where have you been?' 'To the PX and the commissary on Sunday.' Those that love it go to Munich and Heidelberg and get out of the house." In a word, those who loved it in Germany had learned to escape. CPT Peter Lawson, one of the Judge Advocate General officers that I interviewed, put it this way: "There can be a sense of isolation here, but there are ways to cope with it: Break out of your shell. Enjoy Germany as much as you can [even] with limited language ability."

CONCLUSION

The inability to take a simple but real break and the consequent urge to make an escape imposed substantial hidden costs on the military institution. Not only did the process undermine the integrity and morale of the members of the military institution, it also undermined the fabric of the family and the social community. Sometimes the forms of escape brought havoc to the family or put the individual soldier's career or health at risk. What caused the behavior to unfold this way?

When an institution such as the Army affects so much of life and is so closed into a dense and isolated social network, as it was in Germany, it takes on characteristics that Goffman labeled a "total institution." According to Goffman, a total institution is an "encompassing" organization in which the social relations and the physical places of residence, work, and hierarchy of social control are essentially identical, so that all aspects of one's activities are shared and subject to manipulative scrutiny by a "staff." One becomes an "inmate."[2] Put in my terms, the domains of work, family and residence, local community, and social judgment are fused.

For Americans, the Army's fusion of domains produced conflict within the individual because the fused structures of the total institution violated the premises of freedom, autonomy, and separation of domains embedded in the overlying American culture. I will return to these disparities in detail in the next chapter. For now, it is sufficient to say that when the premises and structures of fused domains and suppressed autonomy considered essential to the military enterprise are also used to orient nonmilitary domains such as community and family, the need for respite, relief, or escape will become critical.

In essence, the general American cultural premises provided the underlying basis for judging moral rationality in the U.S. Army communities in Germany. Military premises and practices were exempted because of the belief that the American premises could not accomplish the assigned tasks in the combat environment. The participants expected, however, that the specialized premises and practices appropriate in a combat organization would be applied only to the peacetime military domain of training for readiness. When military personnel of any level applied the combat-specialized premises and practices outside of the training domain of "real mission," such as to family and community, soldiers and spouses felt alienated. The extension of Army premises and practices beyond their culturally authorized domain caused the contradictory Army institutional system to appear irrational or crazy when judged in American cultural terms. This magnified the stress and guaranteed alienation.

Germany intensified soldier isolation. Soldiers and spouses clearly sensed a depressing inability to "get away" from the Army community and be rejuvenated. The "barracks rat" single soldier who rarely left post, the young spouse who seldom left the on-the-economy apartment, the married soldier who came home but infrequently took her or his spouse out, and the family that sought all its entertainment on-post were frequent manifestations of the fact that many soldiers perceived no or few safe avenues to escape the Army's influence in Germany. Finally, the excessive use of alcohol and the problems of aggression or perceived aggression within the U.S. Army community in Germany might have been triggered, in part, by inability to find forms of appropriate escape, removal, and respite via activities that were uncontaminated by military control. Put differently, with little access to the surrounding culture and society of Germany, all one had was the Army and the Army community, with no way to escape from the overlapping social domains of the total institution. The contrast between the relatively closed, highly scrutinized, intensely judgmental military community characterized by fused domains and the wider American culture of dispersed, separated domains and open choice, if maintained through time, would indeed "scramble your brains."

Fusion of domains was by no means the only cultural contradiction that soldiers and spouses faced in Army life. Indeed, to fully understand the perplexities and frustrations of military life for the American citizens that lived it, we will explore in the next chapter the many aspects of general American culture and military corporate culture that stood in contrast and contradiction.

NOTES

1. Linette Sparacino, in personal communication, describes a case she knew occurred in Germany just prior to my fieldwork, in which an officer was expected to formally sign out for his thirty days of "use or lose" annual leave, but to come to work full time for the thirty days, in civilian clothes, if he expected to get a decent OER subsequently. His commanding officer was not going to allow him to go on leave, nor was he going to explain in writing, as regulations required him to do, why this officer was losing thirty days' leave.

2. Erving Goffman, *Asylums: Essays on the Social Situation of Mental Patients and Other Inmates* (Garden City, NY: Anchor Books, 1961): 4, 6–7.

12

Army of Alienation

The whole American system is premised on the individual's rights. But we are probably closest to a socialist system.

MAJ Tim Waters, DCC
Alpenberg Military Subcommunity

From time to time throughout this book, and particularly in the previous chapter, I have asserted that aspects of ordinary American life and aspects of Army life are substantially in opposition. Dispersion of power versus concentration of power and separation of domains versus fusion of domains are but two of several such oppositions. It is time now to collect these juxtapositions and deal with them in a focused way in order to highlight their variety, pervasiveness, and importance. To be more precise in dealing with such oppositions, I first define the concept of a cultural premise, for the contrasts in behavior between American and military life arise largely from the fact that people implement opposite master premises in their behavior, judging an outcome to be good or bad depending on whether, on balance, it enhances or degrades the symbolic representation of the premises. Second, I lay out five key premises of American culture—atomization, pursuit of comfort, freedom of choice, equality, and readiness for discussion and compromise—and the corresponding premises of the military institution—unity, endurance, obedience, hierarchy, and readiness for violence. These are, of course, highly contrastive sets of concepts, if not fully inverse.

Premises are abstract and that abstractness entails two consequences. First, premises do not exist except in the minds of the society's members and are seen only implicitly as they are brought to life in the behavior of individuals. Thus, we infer premises as we watch the patterned practices people use to define their society, connect individuals, or otherwise orient their behavior. Second, the most basic premises have a variety of permutations—contextually specific synonyms, if you will. This is most easily shown in what may well be the master premise of American culture: atomization as a preference over unity. Thus, atomization shows up as favoring the individual over the group when it comes to defining society (individual rights) or the smaller group over the larger group (states' rights). Atomization appears as separation of institutions and domains of life rather than fusion of institutions and domains when it comes to organizing society. Thus, in the case of how to handle power, the atomization premise orients its American adherents to disperse power by locating specific kinds of responsibility in separated institutions rather than concentrating and unifying power in single institutions.

In the context of how or to what degree to connect individuals, atomization suggests primary responsibility for self rather than primary responsibility for others first. One can carry out such an analysis with other premises, though the richest and most productive synonyms cluster around the idea of atomization, perhaps indicating, as the anthropologist Gary Witherspoon suggests, that atomization is the master American premise.[1] For example, freedom of choice versus obedience plays out as freedom of choice and the open society versus control, at the level of defining society; as independence versus subordination, in the task of connecting individuals; and as individual privacy and security versus group security, at the level of orienting more specific behaviors. The synonyms in our vocabulary for the main premises are almost as vast as the many situations in which we must decide what to do.

In the remainder of this chapter, after presenting the major premises of American culture and their inversions in military institutions, I discuss a few of the many permutations of these premise contrasts under the somewhat arbitrary headings of defining society, connecting individuals, and a final catchall, orienting behavior. The headings, however, are not important. What is important is that the reader confirm to herself or himself whether the notion of general cultural premises and specific institutional premises help one to insightfully analyze broad patterns of behavior in complex society. If this is so, then we come more clearly to understand the Army as a corporate culture and discover that the soldier's alienation arises out of the difference between the two cultures and the many possibilities for breach of expectation—breach of contract—entailed in the interaction of an individual operating in two cultures. In this case, one culture—American—is thought of as basic, natural, and human nature, and the other culture—the Army's—is thought of as subordinate, contingent, defined, limited, and yet ever so important to the survival of the first. The disparity between the two systems explains the intensity of the contradictions and depth of the alienation that many soldiers and family members experience as they try to live within both the American-cultured institutions of family and community and the Army-cultured institutions of combat units located, as the soldiers so graphically put it, "on the tip of the spear" in Germany. To conclude, I will develop a theory to explain these differences and why they must exist—despite the stress they place on soldiers and family members.

AMERICAN PREMISES AND WARRIOR PREMISES IN CONTRAST

The Concept of Premises

In every society there exists a set of accepted premises or core principles that serve as the foundation for the society's value system. These premises pervade the community members' thoughts, influence their perceptions, condition the ways people approach problems, and produce a style of action that results in patterns of coherent, intelligible behavior among a people. Basic principles are so deeply ingrained in the minds of members of a society that for some, they defy ready articulation, yet they orient the lives and decisions of its members. Premises are the silent cultural assumptions that guide an individual in evaluating and deciding what is appropriate behavior, regardless of specific circumstances. To the degree that premises are widely shared and well inculcated, they guide solutions to ever changing problems within a people.[2]

American Premises

At least five premises stand at the core of our American cultural existence: atomization, pursuit of comfort, freedom of choice, equality, and readiness for discussion and compromise. These premises have evolved and been handed down to us as social facts that, Durkheim showed quite clearly, are imposed on us by their rootedness in the thoughts, actions, and demands of others.[3]

Atomization, perhaps the fundamental premise, is the notion that things exist as discrete entities and that the components of an entity are more fundamental than the whole.[4] We take this notion and apply it as a general guide in our lives. Thus, we emphasize the component individual rather than the overarching groups in our legal and political system, and we watch carefully to preserve states' rights. Having emphasized the individual, we reward siblings with separate bedrooms rather than emphasize the unity of the family by constructing a one-room round hogan, Navajo style, wherein all are in view of each other. We have students do individual projects rather than group tasks, and we grade the individual. We hire individuals rather than groups or families. There are exceptions, of course, but many of the exceptions result when specific institutions are exempted from abiding by one or more of the general premises by virtue of a social understanding that their use would not allow the institution's participants to attain the chartered purposes of the institution.

Comfort is the cover term for the second American premise, that the world is a physical world to be dominated and made comfortable. "Subdue" the earth, whose contents shall serve humankind "for meat" says an early biblical expression of this premise. We make air-conditioned cocoons of our buildings and vehicles not for survival, but for comfort. We create massive industries of leisure, pleasure, and physical comfort justified by the "self"-evident truth of the premise.

Freedom glosses the third premise, the idea that we have the right to make choices according to the dictates of our own logic (which in American culture is generally self-interest). We praise freedom of choice and enshrine it in the dozens of brands of almost any kind of consumer product, a multiplicity we prefer to be offered even though the products are often not fundamentally different and likely cost more to ensure differentiation through advertising and packaging.

Equality encapsulates the fourth premise, the conception that all citizens have similar natural endowments, that none is naturally better than another. When Americans employ this premise to guide governmental decisions, the result suggests equal and adequate access of all individuals to the benefits and protections of government. When applied to people, it suggests no natural betters, no royalty, and it calls into question the legitimacy of longstanding social practices that limit people because of some supposed physical attribute, be it race, gender, sexual orientation, or physical impediment.

I must discuss the premise of equality in somewhat greater detail, because the evident and deep-seated inequalities in the institutions of American life and in the beliefs of many individuals call into question the legitimacy of the claim that equality is a basic premise of American culture. First, institutions can deviate from the broadly applied core premises to satisfy what are perceived to be functional requirements. Thus, economic institutions have typically allowed hierarchy (in contrast to equality) to achieve organizational focus, leadership, and ownership. I will return to this point momentarily. Second, most members of the minorities that have traditionally been discriminated against subscribe to the core principles of American culture unless they have been so alienated by the difference between American premise and practice that they have withdrawn into isolation, resistance, or reverse racism or sexism.

The real challenge to the notion of equality as basic premise comes from the continuing reproduction of white racism as an ideology in the minds of some—perhaps many. How can Whites be said to embrace an ideology of equality if some of them believe (now or in the past) that other races are inferior and ought to be kept separate?

The reasons are multiple, and I must grossly simplify in the interest of brevity, for a history and theory of inequality deserves a book rather than a few lines. The first simplification is to treat, for a moment, just two of the most obvious inequalities: race and gender discrimination. In the case of race, once the power disparities of colonialism and the profit needs of Southern agro-capitalism had locked onto slaving, the obvious disparity with the premise of equality needed a powerful justification. Religious justification through the elaboration of supposedly divinely created racial differences enabled the elites to avoid thinking about the premise disparities. Indeed, the inculcation of ideas of natural and even divinely created biological difference made practices based on race the result of natural difference. They therefore conformed to the premise that natural reality is ultimate reality, or to the premise that God's will supercedes all. Once the concept was in place and became self-perpetuating, those who subscribed saw slavery, a deviation from equality, as natural. Those who did not subscribe saw it as abhorrent. In the process of our history, equality eventually drove out the secondary mythological elaborations of economic convenience, and we have spent much of our history as a nation trying to deal with the unanticipated and residual consequences of lingering but not ideal inequalities that institutionalized practice had built into the structure of our society.

Gendered inequalities have followed a different, but somewhat analogous path. To put it in a sentence, gender difference in the family workplace enabled reproduction, child care, and cooperative participation in agro-production and food processing. The functions were so important that the institutions of the family stood outside the purview of equality. With the technological transformations of both biological reproduction and food production, equality increasingly has come to the fore as the primary operational premise. Gender-based inequalities have been slowly eliminated, first by law, and eventually in the thought of an increasing number of people. A great deal more could be said, but this is not the place. I rest with the notion that the root idea of equality has been the trumpet whose sound has slowly battered down the institutional walls of many inequalities-in-practice.

Finally, I offer the fifth premise—readiness for discussion and compromise. This premise ties to an Enlightenment tradition of logic and to the emergence of a variety of institutions that structure democratic participation and representation. Again, this book is not the place for a general discourse on government. It is sufficient here to say that the modern democracies facilitate a broad range of discussion and communication and frequently use compromise to arrive at practices made into law or custom.

Warrior Premises

Every set of premises must, of course, work for its adherents, at a minimum by keeping them alive. Ordinarily, a given environment has sufficient variety that it can sustain more than one approach to life. As the environment gets more extreme, the modes of adaptive behavior that could sustain life with a given technology become more limited. The range of driving or organizing assumptions likewise become more restricted.

Combat is surely one of the most extreme environments of all. In the environment of combat violence and its attendant chaos, certain forms of behavior and organization are highly rewarded while other forms of behavior are heavily punished. Yet the behavioral response to violence cannot be fixed in precise rules of what to do because the weapons of war change, and so do the opponents' tactics. Military commanders, historians, and philosophers have long sought to describe the changing nature of the combat environment, ascertain which premises lead to best results when inculcated in leaders and followers at all levels, and determine how to reduce the tendency of national or ethnic presumptions to transform military practice or override the military premises that guide decision making best adapted to success in the combat environment. Regardless of period or national or cultural background—from China's Sun Tzu to the creators of American Air-Land Battle doctrine—the guiding principles or premises of those who have been successful in combat have been remarkably consistent and similar.

The premises of leadership and soldierly behavior in the U.S. Army are thought to be derived from these same principles of success in the uncompromising environment of combat, insofar as combat is able to be understood, and insofar as our understanding of the combat environment has not been clouded over and idealized by the deep presuppositions of our national culture and by the practices learned and expected in an American context. Though there are others, I should like to examine more closely five premises of American military philosophy—unity, endurance, obedience, hierarchy, and readiness for violence—because they stand in contrast with the key American premises above.

Unity glosses the first military premise, the idea that organizations that are more unified survive better than organizations that are less unified. The logic probably works something like this, though no one I interviewed stated this directly: In combat, powerful things survive. Power comes from the application of violence where it is needed to break down opposing violent forces. Such focused application takes coordination. Coordination requires unity.[5]

The second premise, endurance, derives from the concept that the field of combat is a hard, dangerous world. To survive in combat, one must be able to endure hardship stoically. The all-night march, the heavy loads, the inclement weather, the mud and grit, the injuries, the need to proceed regardless of pain, the dangers of capturing an objective, the loss of friends, the risk to self—all must be endured. One must "suck it up and march on" as the common Army expression puts it.

Obedience encodes the third premise, the idea that one must obey orders. Of course the orders must be lawful, but in most cases lawfulness is not at issue. Orders must be trusted and obeyed if soldiers are to coordinate their actions so as to take a military objective against violent opposition.

Fourth, the Army emphasizes hierarchy. The obligation to obey depends on the rank of the person issuing the order. Indeed, the most prominent marking on the uniform is rank, the only marking one must invariably search for and respond to, emphasizing the inequality that dominates the military system. Thus, hierarchy and uniformity coexist by designating all persons of the same rank as uniform, substitutable, and equal.

Finally, soldiers must stand in readiness for violence. To not be ready for violence is to prepare for failure, to accept or even invite unnecessary losses, for even the appearance of readiness intimidates potential attackers. In peace, one stands ready to interact violently when ordered or attacked; the soldier exists to intimidate and to be ready to destroy.

Premises in Contrast

The two sets of premises stand in sharp contrast. American atomization differs from military unity; pursuit of comfort contrasts with stoic endurance; freedom of choice opposes the presumption of obedience; equality stands against hierarchy; and, finally, readiness for democratic discussion and compromise differs from readiness for violence. One cannot survive in combat if operating strictly on the core American premises.

Thus, the distinctive military assumptions condition the practices of life in the Army just as the more generally held values affect patterns of behavior in the larger American society. The military premises guide and condition behavior in the Army, creating behavioral patterns of considerable similarity throughout the institution. In a word, the principles of combat guide the creation and continual reproduction of a specific but always changing Army corporate culture. The premise differences go a long way toward helping us understand the contrasts between Army life and life in American society generally. Moreover, at the local level—at a particular post or installation, or at a company, battalion, or division headquarters—the principles combine with specific local conditions and are interpreted (or ignored) by a particular leader whose personality and vision create a local variant of the larger corporate culture. Moreover, in peacetime, soldiers must operate in both military and civilian domains of American society, alternating as needed between the military premises that are appropriate to an organization that must train to counter violence with violence, and the civilian premises that are ideally applicable throughout the society in a fundamentally nonviolent, law-abiding environment. Soldiers, as citizens, must struggle to reconcile the incongruities between the Army's special premises and consequent practices on the one hand, and the general American premises and practices on the other. There is complexity and variability at the same time that there is recognizable similarity to the issues a soldier faces in any Army setting. Indeed, every soldier, officer or enlisted, must deal with the two cultures and handle the complexities of leadership, followership, and agency that flow from the differences.

CONTEXTUAL PERMUTATIONS OF THE PREMISES

The five basic premises—whether American or military—have multiple transformations that depend on the context in which they are used. Thus, when talking about power, atomization requires dispersion of power, whereas unity requires its concentration. In talking about the entities that compose an organization, atomization pushes one to look at the individual as the ultimate unit of society, whereas the principle of unity redirects one's attention toward the group as a whole or toward subgroups larger than the individual.

I will lay out a number of such permutations under three somewhat arbitrary and even overlapping headings that represent facets of the social process: (1) the tasks of defining society generally, (2) the issue of connecting individuals, and (3) requirements for orienting behavior. We must remember, however, that both the order and the emphasis of this division are matters of analytical convenience. In fact, each premise simultaneously helps create the nature of the society or the institution to which it applies, influences the ways individuals connect to each other, and helps orient specific behaviors.

DEFINING SOCIETY WITH PREMISES

I begin with permutations of the basic premises that substantially influence the way Americans build their larger society versus the premises that help soldiers build their Army institution and its various components. The permutations in this section are essentially variations—extended synonyms—of the atomization premise in American society and the unity premise in military society.

Individualism and Diversity versus Group Orientation and Uniformity

In Chapter 4, "Danger Forward Sir!," I showed how the unique task and environment of combat leads to distinctive military premises, setting up a corporate culture that contrasts in some aspects with American culture and with the American people's social experience. The mayhem of combat requires that people be interchangeable parts, relatively alike, relatively uniform, and mutually substitutable so that the group can overcome losses by rapidly replacing the dead or wounded with the able. Moreover, to succeed in combat, the group must be more important than the individual; the individual must take risks for the group and its goals. By contrast, Americans generally place a high value on the individual. Many of our political institutions protect the individual and safeguard his or her rights more than they protect interests of the state or the society as a whole. The rights of groups of kin are nonexistent, and the rights of families are not easily made explicit. By contrast, the rights of the individual, as citizen, are clear and codified in law. Behaviorally, individuals seek (within styles) to be unique and distinctive, and we Americans celebrate diversity, especially at the individual level. In these ways the superordinate American culture of individualism and diversity is at odds with the necessary military institutional culture of group orientation and uniformity. Individualism and diversity are clearly transformations, permutations, variations of the American premise of atomization. Group orientation and uniformity, likewise, are more specific manifestations of the military premise of unity.

Separation of Domains versus Fusion of Domains

Americans separate institutions, generally by giving each institution a single task—police, county health office, National Guard, board of education, welfare department, and so on—and by staffing different institutions with different personnel. These practices atomize the social organization and prevent the unification of power. From the checks and balances of our national government through the premise of free enterprise, which is to say, enterprise unimpeded by governmental regulation, Americans exhibit a definite preference for separate organizations, each with a single purpose.

The intense American belief that church and state should be separated represents another manifestation of atomization. Likewise, Americans expect the domains of politics and economics to be reasonably separated. To be sure, government should regulate economics, especially in the interests of safety and through the atomization—we call it "break up"—of unified monopolies. But economics should not buy politics, at least not too blatantly. Finally, the domains of family and individual are separated from community by concepts of rights, including a right to privacy, and from work and economics by concepts and practices of time allocation—the ideas of "family time" and "work time" that I have previously discussed.

By contrast, in the Army, people tend to fuse domains. In doing so, they incur the distrust of members of the larger society and alienate themselves from those not in the military. Living in a military community, especially one as closed as the American Army community in Germany, involved many clashes with this premise of separation of domains. We have already examined several such fusions and their resulting stresses. Chapter 5, "Living with the Army," and Chapter 8, "If You Can't Control Your Family," detailed the fusion of family and work, a fusion sufficiently total that in practice participants felt that "the family is in the Army." This fusion of family and work troubled both soldiers and spouses greatly. Chapter 10, "Living in a Fishbowl," traced the many painful consequences of the fusion of community with work and work evaluation.

In this section, I want to highlight the explicitness of the fusion premise in the Army corporate culture and the intensity of the emotional alienation among soldiers and spouses that results from its application outside the Army's functional domain of training. A conversation between SSG Frank Barnes, his wife, Meg, and their friends, Mack (also a sergeant) and Donna Chalmers, illustrated the issues:

> "I don't like to be threatened," Meg fumed. "Like Community [Command]: first thing they will tell me is if I don't straighten up my act they gonna put me off-post. Take my ID card. And they will get my husband into trouble. This dispute might have been someone else's fault. And they slap me with: If I don't shut up, they telling me they got all the power and control, and I'm wrong. I don't like that at all. They tell me where my dog has to piss and shit."
> "They got rules for everything," Mack offered.
> "They are not restrictions, they are threats," Meg argued, and looking at her husband, asked, "What do you think?"
> "I never thought about it," Frank replied.
> "It is not this bad in the States," Meg asserted. "There, your home is your home."

Community functions merged with military work precisely because the military work organization controlled so much of the community organization. The tight fusion affected even the ability of community members to invite rational changes. Frank and Meg discussed with Mack and his wife the consequences of trying to reform the operating hours at the community's Child Development Center, so that working mothers could more easily get back and forth to their jobs at the large military service center forty-five to seventy-five minutes' drive away, depending on traffic. "I think it is going to be a long time coming before there is any change," said Meg with resignation. "I can't petition against the day care. I just can't," Frank lamented. Meg recognized his difficulty and added her own: "If I start petitioning, they are going to say, 'Sergeant Barnes, your wife is getting out of hand, and you had better get her under control or it is going to affect your career.'" There was an excited buzz of agreement among the two couples as Frank continued, "Child care, and so on, is a community responsibility. It revolves to the community commander. By right, it shouldn't go to the soldier's unit commander. When there is a conflict of interest between the [community] facility and the dependents, it shouldn't go to the unit." Meg's inability to "petition" the community regarding family services without the command structure of the unit threatening her husband that his wife was "getting out of hand" represented the clear fusion of unit, family, and community, and, according to American culture, constituted an infringement on the culturally expected separation of domains. The Army had a right to run training with contrastive premises, but not family or community.

Dispersion of Power versus Concentration of Power

When the contrast between the American premise of atomization and the military premise of unity is applied to issues of power, one gets a premise outcome closely related to separation versus fusion of domains. Americans distrust the concentration of power. To avoid concentrations of power, they create multiple single-purpose institutions, each with a single specific power or responsibility and a separate staff. The single-purpose institutions are then set against each other in a system of checks and balances. Such a system is inherently slow to react and predisposed to protect the status quo. But it liberates the individual from exposure to the risks of concentrated power.

Militaries, by contrast, must be able to act and react quickly, and thus they must concentrate power. If the American way of handling power in the civil domain were incorporated into the military system, one would have a prescription for military disaster that could put the whole society at risk. Any successful military, including the U.S. Army, must respond quickly to external pressures. It can do so precisely because it is nondemocratic and has highly concentrated access to power and decision making. As I showed in Chapter 4, "Danger Forward, Sir!," Americans tolerate these differences within military organizations because they believe them essential to the military's assigned task: to be ready to succeed in combat. But the differences in conceptual view nevertheless lead to the social alienation and distancing of career military personnel and their families and community from nonmilitary families and their communities.[6] Americans handle their resulting unease with the military by ensuring that soldier training and behavior rigorously inculcate the idea that soldiers of all ranks must obey the law—both civilian law and the laws of warfare—and submit to civilian authority. Military leadership is subject to elected civilian political control through the presidency. These requirements serve as checks and balances on the military's ability to concentrate power inappropriately or misuse the various ways in which the institution is permitted to deviate from the central principles of American culture. In sum, concentration of power under a single commander is a focused extension and synthesis of the premises of unity, hierarchy, and obedience, given the environment of violence.

Freedom of Choice versus Control

The idea of control stands closely related to the premise of obedience. Whether a permutation of obedience or a separate premise, the climate of restriction and control within the Army contrasts sharply with the climate of freedom perceived as the American's ideal and right. One aspect of the American right of free choice is a belief that government ought to be limited in the exercise of control over its citizens. The problem is that the military, to be combat functional, is based on a premise of strict control over its personnel, and this premise tends to permeate its entire institutional culture—imbuing family and community with the flavor of control. Thus, Meg Barnes and Donna Chalmers expressed their sense of irritation over the extensions of military premises into community life.

> "You're no longer American citizens living under the good old USA Constitution. You live under USAREUR laws and regulations," Meg complained.
> "How different are they from the USA?" My question was not very clear and Meg seemed to interpret it as a request to compare family and community life in the United States with that in Germany.
> "They are protecting you so you don't get in trouble with the Germans," Meg elaborated. "They build this fence around you, and they try to protect you so much that they limit your freedoms: 'By the way, we are sending your husband to Germany but don't give them [your German neighbors] a pack of cigarettes, even if they are your friends.'"
> Donna jumped into the fray, adding, "And tell your wife, 'Don't open her mouth or she will catch it.' She will catch it through him."
> "Would they do this in the States?" I asked.
> "What can they do? You're already home," Meg asserted. "And if they kick you out of quarters, you can just get an apartment."

Americans feel they are free if they can choose from among several alternatives in any given class of objects or activities. Such choice is especially important in several crucial areas: occupation, financial and medical services, and residence, to name a few. Thus, freedom, choice, and individual autonomy expected in the American environment contrasted with restriction, control, and group cohesion lived in the Army environment in Germany.

To Americans, one of the factors crucial to defining one's person, character, or prestige in society is occupation, and choosing one's job or career seems fundamental to well-being. According to SSG Alan Evanson, young soldiers felt they had rights that the military considered privileges the Army could grant or withhold. I asked him just how much freedom of choice he felt was still a right, even under military circumstances. He immediately mentioned occupation: "They need to be free to choose their job, as far as what profession they want to do in the military. That is very advantageous. If they don't choose, they will not be very satisfied. They need some choice as to what job they want to do." Evanson went on to name some other topics of interest regarding choice.

> This is a big one, my main complaint today: I feel they should have a choice as to what to do with their—[He paused and started again.] I feel the Army has too much control over their financial [matters]. We had no choice: the soldiers had no choice in banks. A lot of the soldiers had no input. Decisions were made way over them. It affects morale. I come back from the field—no checks still. I haven't received the teller card. That scares me. That to me is shades of *1984*. In the United States, [it is] a free society, but here you do not have an input, it is decisions made so far above, and yet it directly affects you.

One would hardly think that limited bank choice would be considered "shades of *1984*." But money is a core symbol in American culture and a passport to much that represents freedom. Thus, to have money limited, controlled, or not reliably provided may indeed be seen as shades of *1984*. SSG Evanson continued, "In the area of medical benefits, maybe they should have some choice of medical facilities," a matter treated extensively in Chapter 7, "The System Is Totally Screwed to Hell." It is enough to remember that lack of choice in medical access was a substantial concern for many. The soldier concluded with a general summary: "Basically, I think that there is too much contracting going on without any of the soldier's input." Essentially, the military operated in Germany by arranging contracts in which a provider guaranteed to deliver a particular negotiated service on the installations designated in the contract. From the soldier's point of view, there seemed to be little "soldier's input," because "the decision is made so far above." With no input, the soldier felt no control and no choice. To take one's business elsewhere seemed impossible to most because they did not understand German language or culture. One could not even complain, because complainers were looked down on and that could affect careers.

Choice of job assignment and of place of residence, matters of considerable importance to Americans, are further implementations of the core value of freedom of choice. Within the Army, however, job assignment is often made regardless of one's preferences, and place of residence is assigned. Mr. Trevor Foote, the Grossberg community regional social work supervisor, commented on this loss. "Within the system, where they send the people anywhere without asking them where they want to go, it is hard. Some of the wives just get tired of moving. When the military says they have to move, they have to move. It is hard. Some want their families to have one school for teenagers." Though all understood that career advancement drove the pattern of frequent moves, this knowledge did not eliminate the stress of compromised values.

When a soldier arrived at a military community, he or she often had no choice regarding government housing. If any were available, the soldier had to reside in the next available apartment within their categories of rank and family size. Although most families accepted this situation, some felt coerced. CPT Glen Cooper, of Richberg Kaserne said, "In the States, you go where you want, and no problems. Here, we are all stuffed together." Again, Mr. Foote observed, "The old Army treated soldiers and their family as property. It is easier to deal with property—you can just give commands: 'This is what I want you to do.' In the Navy they told me, 'If the Navy wanted me to have a wife, they would have put her in my sea bag.'

The Army has changed. They have high values placed on the family, but we haven't changed the system to be able to take care of that." Many a conversation about the aggravations of Army family life ended with a similar, the oft-repeated, sentence, "If the Army wanted you to have a wife [or family], they would have issued you one." Although the Army has improved the quality of family life by adding services and conveniences, as evidenced by the extensive community facilities and services it built in Germany in the 1980s and continued to build in the 1990s, it has not yet dealt with the deeper issues of contrastive premises raised in this chapter that fundamentally affect the morale of soldiers and family members.

Thus far, I have explored how basic premises and their permutations have helped define and create the largest organizational structures of the military. The same premises also work at other levels. I should like now to change the analytical focus from society writ large to the more micro processes, in this case the ways individuals connect to each other.

CONNECTING INDIVIDUALS THROUGH PREMISES

The premise contrasts I examine in this section have a clear impact on the ways individuals connect to each other. Put differently, the deep premises of unity, hierarchy, and obedience have resulted in a different pattern of social interconnection within the military than that produced by America's atomization, equality, and freedom of choice. I begin with the notion of responsibility as it relates to atomization and unity.

Individual and Self-Responsibility versus Responsibility for Others

Chapter 8, "If You Can't Control Your Family," provided numerous quotes demonstrating the prevailing distrust that resulted from the practice of controlling the spouse through the soldier. Not only did such control penetrate and disrupt the family and run counter to the premise of separate domains of family and work, the practice violated the general premise of individual or self-responsibility. As Terry Walsh put it, "In the States, they don't ask me for my husband's social security number. That is a big issue, the control." The Damon family complained that because they played their stereo late one Friday night, neighbors called the MPs who came to their home and told Sally Damon, "If it happens again, it is gonna be on your husband," and "If it comes down on the blotter report two or three times, he will get an Article 15 [an administrative punishment]." Sally went on to emphasize that the cultural premise of individual responsibility seemed to have been violated. Obviously irritated and upset, she blurted out:

> "I can go kill somebody, or beat the heck out of somebody and my husband is going to get in trouble for it!"
> "Why does that bother you?" I probed for her view of the obvious contradiction, wondering if she would think me daft.

"If I'm a bad person and he is a good person, he shouldn't be punished for my actions."

"Why not?" Again, I needed her logic, not mine, even though what she said made sense to me.

"Because *I* did it. *I* should be the one that is punished. They should make *me* do extra community action, or something, but they shouldn't take rank away from *him*. He didn't do it, and he worked so hard for the rank. In the civilian world, if a wife goes and does something, she has the bad record. In the Army, they don't care if it is the wife or the kid or whatever, but the enlisted person is going to get the heat."

Frances Orton, the statistician for the MP headquarters and wife of a senior non-commissioned officer, complained, "My discipline goes to his unit. He has to sign for my driver's license. If I get in trouble, the commander can yell at him—that he has to be responsible for his dependents. You have to think about that for a while!" She then went on to describe a case she knew regarding a female soldier and her dependent male spouse. She explained that a spouse "falls under" a soldier's commander, regardless of the sex of either. This soldier's husband was getting into some kind of trouble and a sergeant suggested to the soldier-wife that she control her husband.

> She [the soldier being rebuked] suggested maybe the commander could talk to his mother [presumably in the States, presumably by phone, and obviously said sarcastically], that maybe *she* [his mother] had control over him. Somehow it doesn't make sense that the commander goes and yells at the sponsor when you're the one that did it. You're in a traffic accident, and she is the sponsor, your commander yells at her for your traffic accident. It kind of defeats the purpose. Then she has to come and yell at you.

The degree to which the family became fused with the Army system was demonstrated in this woman's comment that a dependent husband "falls under" the female soldier's company commander. Recall the soldier whose wife set fire to their apartment while he was in the field. His description focused on individual responsibility: "I can't be responsible for a human being that I can't control." Moreover, he complained that "they bar me from enlistment for something from family matters," thus violating the expected separation of domains. Ultimately, these instances of responsibility for others and the collapsing of domains were permutations of the root premises of unity and hierarchy.

Independence versus Subordination

Closely related to the idea of individual responsibility and self-control is the cultural ideal of independence. Terry Walsh was an experienced critical care nurse. Married to a corporal, she seemed bored as well as frustrated that her nursing experience was not only going to waste, but that her nursing skills would atrophy and become invalid with time. She could not find nursing employment, and she had to quit volunteering at the community medical clinic because the clinic's liability insurance would not cover her. Pointing out that there were programs that keep two military spouses together in assignments, I asked, "Why not join the Army as a commissioned nurse?"

"Not in the Army! I don't want to have someone tell me that I'm going to work nights. No one will tell me that I'm going to be in the psych ward. I just can't envision me in the service."

"What repels you?" I asked.

"My independence: nobody is going to tell me what shift to work, how to dress, what therapy to work in, that you can or can not go in clubs, what I can or can't do. A colonel comes on the floor. He might be Dr. Twit, or he might be a brilliant physician. But the fact that he is colonel comes first. In civilian life, if I don't like the situation, I quit. But the Army doesn't make it that easy."

From the symbols of John Wayne, Clint Eastwood, or Rambo to the economic struggles of the entrepreneur seeking self-employment, the cultural ideal of independence has flourished in American society, though it sharply contradicts the institutionally perceived military need for subordination. Once again, subordination is a transformation of hierarchy and perhaps even of unity, whereas independence is a variant of individualism, both contained within atomization and closely related to freedom of choice. And just as these premises affect the larger construction of society or the character of relationships, they also condition particular behaviors.

ORIENTING BEHAVIOR WITH PREMISES

I shall now focus on a set of premises that may be seen clearly to affect patterns of behavior, recognizing that they also affect the constitution of society and the ways people interrelate. If one orients behavior by applying the premises of atomization, endurance, obedience, and readiness for violence, one gets a rather different behavioral outcome in any specific situation than would be the case were one to use the more generally applicable American premises. First, I explore privacy and its security implications for the individual and for the institution.

Individual Privacy versus Institutional Security

A post office that generally does not open letters, a phone system that generally cannot be tapped, a right for one's family to be exempt from search without probable cause—even an expectation that parents will knock on their children's bedroom door—these are specific manifestations of the premise of privacy within American culture. The Army scrupulously abided by the *legal* requirements of privacy, but, as we have seen, it breached the *culture* of privacy in many subtle ways. Routing information about the family through the company, for instance, violated the fundamental cultural premise of privacy and breached the premise of separation of domains.

In American culture, an institution must have a compelling reason to justify surveillance, given the general premise of privacy. Justifications for limiting privacy in the Army revolved around the mission, to include the need for safety and the need to prevent breaches of intelligence security. I asked 1LT Larry McDugal, then an acting company commander, why the military should be interested in or concerned about family or private life matters. He said, "It is important because it does affect his job. If he is running a ten-ton truck and he is an alcoholic, you should be concerned. The guys are handling classified materials, and you want to know if he is [deeply] in debt and is going to sell the stuff to the Russians."

In its need to know who could be a security risk, however, the Army often went too far. It did not stick to its chartered domain, spilling over into the surveillance of family and community. 1LT McDugal continued:

> "But there are a lot of piddly things. Like his kids in school. A lot of people get out [of the Army] because the Army does delve too deep in private affairs."
>
> "What is private?" I repeated his words to invite elaboration with minimum intrusion.
>
> "Kids' performance and behavior in school. Library books. The thing that really aggravates me is all these little notices about library and kids in school. They come to the commander. There is so much of this that there is some flunky opening the stuff. By the time the commander opens the stuff, there are five or six people that know it, unless it is [marked] 'commander's eyes only.' They know all the trash on everybody—not only the commander, but this whole series of flunkies. There is nothing comparable to that in the States. The note from the library comes right to your house and you handle it."

When a fundamental premise such as privacy was unreasonably violated, it caused deterioration of morale. The linkage could be seen easily in the operation of the barracks, where maintaining separation of private and military life was particularly difficult for the single soldier. The Atwoods, who only months before had both been single residents in the barracks, offered the following comments:

> "The main point is: the barracks—that is supposed to be your home," Betty argued forcefully. "I guarantee that if you talk to anyone on the post that is in the barracks, they don't feel that it is their home."
>
> "Why?"
>
> "Because." Betty paused. "I understand about inspections. I understand about their rules. But they make it so that you cannot have any private life and you can't have any personal items. You can't make your room the way that you would like to have it."
>
> "Comfortable!" Jeff interjected.
>
> "That really kills the soldier's self-esteem and motivation," Betty summarized with finality.

The inability to implement privacy is thus said to "really kill . . . self-esteem and motivation," the essence of morale.

Obviously, people possessed different levels of tolerance for the violation of privacy, but the matter was of some concern to nearly all I interviewed. Without prompting on the subject of privacy, I asked Beth Hammond, whose father had been a marine as she grew up, how she felt the Army treated her and her husband, CPL Ron Hammond.

"I was raised with the military," Beth reflected, "but in the Marines. It's different here. They [the Army] get into your personal life a lot."

"In the Army you don't have no personal life," Ron mirrored.

"How do you feel about that?" I probed.

"I don't like it at all," Ron responded with irritation. "That is one of my biggest dislikes about the Army. You have no privacy, no private life at all. How would you like it if your boss said, 'Pee in this cup'—and not over in a corner—but actually watched you pee in the cup? Or to go in your room any time he wants to. They go in your room any time they want to. And God forbid if you have too many civilian clothes: they will tell you to box them up. Or if you have a television and stereo, they may say, 'You got too many things in your room.' But it is supposed to be your home!"

Violations of privacy indeed undermined morale. Finally, it is worth pointing out that a violation of privacy was almost always, simultaneously, a failure to maintain separation of domains and infringed on the premise of individualism. Put differently, privacy, like these other premises, is a specific manifestation of atomization; privacy defines the boundaries between the atomic entities—the individuals—and gives them security. Individual privacy subverts group unity just as group unity nullifies individual privacy.

Fairness and the Value of the Individual versus Institutional Needs

Americans feel that equality and fairness should exist between individuals as well as between individuals and institutions. Within the Army, though, the premise of control and lack of options combined with the attitudes of occasionally demoralized service providers to create an atmosphere in which individuals often felt they were not treated fairly. Pay foul-ups, for example, which took time to clear the bureaucracy, were a particular point of frustration. Said Terry Walsh, "We [the government] owe you money; we will take our time. But if *we* [the soldier or family member] owe *them* money, they will have our skins. That is the government attitude"

Fairness issues emerged in the way housing allowances were allocated. Married soldiers received a housing allowance that increased with rank. It was intended to cover the cost of quarters and utilities. If one found quarters on the economy that were more expensive than the allowance, one paid the difference. In the case of on-post housing, however, the entire allowance was absorbed because quarters were issued in lieu of the allowance. Government quarters, by law, had to have sufficient bedrooms to accommodate age and gender separations among one's children. So a junior-ranking person with several children received a substantially larger apartment than persons of higher rank with fewer children in residence, yet the junior signed over a much smaller housing allowance amount. Of this practice, 1SG Enrique Gomez complained, "I don't know how you feel about this, but I'm an E8. I live in a two bedroom [apartment]. I pay x dollars because the government pays it. You got an E4 living there. He's got a four bedroom and he pays less than me. I don't think that is fair. Would you want to live in a house [where] you're paying $400 for less rooms [and] next door, he has a four bedroom, and yet he is paying $200?" These may seem like small irritations, but they grated against fundamental American assumptions about how economics, seniority, and free market systems ought, "in fairness," to run.

Convenience, Accessibility, and Comfort versus "Toughing It Out"

Americans organize much of their commercial activities so as to maximize convenience. The difference between the convenience expected as a member of American society and the inconvenience that existed in the U.S. Army community in Germany was a source of stress. Thus, CPT Peter Lawson complained, "I am so accustomed to 3:00 A.M. stores. You have to cope with no twenty-four-hour discount stores. Army has an extremely difficult task to bring as much of America as they can to Germany. The biggest adjustment is to deal with inconvenience." People complained about such things as not having laundry facilities handy (even though they were open twenty-four hours a day on-post) or the inability to find a particularly desired food. These circumstances conflicted with the core American values of convenience, accessibility, and freedom of choice.

Although no one in the Army would say that peacetime military life *ought* to be inconvenient, all would say that war is not convenient and that one has to be willing to suffer privation to prevail in combat. A combat army needs a premise of inurement to suffering or it cannot function. Corresponding to this, we have seen previously that one should not be a "complainer," a "sniveler," a "whiner," or a "crybaby." In a corporate culture that must be able to endure suffering to survive, convenience and comfort are secondary. The morale difficulty emerged when the Army's operating premise of "be tough," "suck it up," and "don't complain" carried over into community and family domains to discourage complaints and to increase tolerance of unnecessary suffering in a domain where unnecessary suffering was culturally inappropriate.

Logical Consistency and Utility versus Contradiction and Waste

Americans expect government agencies to do things for rational reasons and to obtain helpful results. They expect procedures to be consistent, noncontradictory, and, ideally, efficient and utilitarian. Although the Army shared these same values, complex military activities did not always work out quite rationally. Within the military, the hierarchy of command, urgency of the mission, desire to avoid embarrassment, and the existence of value systems that could justify alternative decisions in terms of either American or Army principles led to a complex, pressurized organization beset with internal contradictions. These incongruities created a kind of irrational inconsistency and often resulted in waste—all of which a soldier had to tolerate in the interest of a speedy accomplishment of mission. Obviously, the primary capability of the Army was to wage war—a necessary but wasteful and illogical task. In warfare, readiness is always more important than efficiency. The priority of readiness may explain the Army's insensitivity to issues of waste even during peacetime.

As an example of a contradiction, Mr. Stanley, the acting DCC of Middleberg, pointed out, "We provide everything. Yet we say, 'Don't be a barracks rat. Get out there and learn about the country.'" Sometimes the complexity of the structures and the competing needs of the system created difficulty and contradiction. For example, soldiers needed to take care of certain official tasks and clear up problems such as inaccurate pay, lost documents, or housing office matters. To avoid having soldiers randomly decide when to take time off from unit work, communities throughout Germany gave the soldiers a specified time off, one afternoon a week, for doing such tasks. An irksome contradiction arose because soldiers staffed many of the essential services. If these soldiers took time off to handle their own chores, many of the locations providing essential services were left unstaffed. Thus, other soldiers could not resolve their problems. MAJ Rodney Kimball described the irrationality of this "Duty First" time off: "One of the greatest follies is Duty First. The idea is to do things that are needed. But now the clinics are closed in the [Duty First] afternoon. Everybody is [out] on Duty First [time], so the only thing you can do for yourself is go to the commissary or PX. It is a goddamn farce." Having raised the topic of irrationality, he proceeded without pausing to the contradictions and frustrations of making a medical appointment: "You can't get through on the phone and you're not allowed to go in person. You end up 'do-looping.'[7] It's 'Catch-22'. You have to conduct business during duty hours. That gives the soldier a choice—either go AWOL [absent without leave] or not get the services. It is very difficult." SGT Ian Warnock evidenced frustration with inconsistent logic and waste in the units.

> "Some of the stuff we do don't make any sense. I'm in infantry. We have to pull maintenance on the vehicles. We spend three days cleaning it so you can eat off of it and only one day fixing what is wrong with it."
>
> "Why is that a problem?" I asked. (One always looks dumb when asking someone to be explicit about shared but implicit cultural assumptions.)
>
> "What good is being clean if it don't run? And the first time you take it out and drive it five miles, it is going to be just as dirty as if you had not touched it."

SGT Warnock had a sense of his unit's real mission and a desire not to waste his time on meaningless activity. In this case an additional feature intruded and led to further deviation from the real mission. The practice of inspection and the premises of hierarchy and obedience led to pleasing a supervisor's notion of the appearance of readiness rather than to ensuring practical combat readiness. An inappropriately demanding officer who controlled the fate of subordinate careers thus pushed the behavior of the unit away from what its soldiers understood were its real goals.

Clearly, several basic American premises and their associated permutations contrasted with Army premises and their variants. These differing premises led to differing perceptual settings when it came time to make decisions regarding any given circumstance. Repeated over and over, by many different individuals, in distinctive circumstances, the premise differences led to differences in behavioral patterns and styles. The distinctive styles confirmed in the minds of the participants that they lived their lives within two differing cultures—the one American and normal, the other military and deviant. The deviation was tolerable, however, because it was backed by a functionally legitimate reason, creating thereby a corporate culture that was both specific and limited.

THE ARMY AS A CORPORATE CULTURE

Specialized military premises guided the decisions of leaders and soldiers. Through their behavior, the premises or principles shaped the patterns and expectations of the Army institution. Through them, leaders and followers had created a corporate culture—a mode of thinking and a mode of acting deemed requisite to success in the peacetime tasks of being ready for war.

The mode of thought was actively taught in formal schools and made explicit in training manuals. Appendix A of *FM 100-5, Operations*, "the Army's keystone warfighting manual," for example, contains the "Principles of War," of which I treat only the second, third, and fifth principles, as enumerated in *FM 100-5*.[8]

The second principle of war, "offensive," is expressed as "Seize, retain, and exploit the initiative."[9] A commander must make decisions faster than his or her opponent, thereby forcing the other to react. The decisions made do not have to be the very best. If they are made faster than the enemy can assess them and react, one gains "the initiative, maintains freedom of action and achieves results."[10] The commander who achieves this is able to "impose his will on the enemy, set the terms and select the place of confrontation or battle, exploit vulnerabilities and react to rapidly changing situations and unexpected developments. No matter what the level, the side that retains the initiative through offensive action forces the foe to react rather than to act."[11] Here, speed of decision making, decisiveness, boldness, and implied central authority are conditions for "seizing" initiative. All this implies decision-making responsibility that is concentrated and nondemocratic. When applied outside the domain of military training—for example, to family or community affairs—the legitimacy of the premises and of the leaders are called into question. The soldiers become alienated because domains of socially responsible action have been violated, invaded by an inappropriate ideology of premises contrary to American culture.

According to the third principle, "mass,"

Superior combat power must be concentrated at the decisive place and time in order to achieve decisive results. This superiority results from the proper combination of the elements of combat power at a place and a time and in a manner of the commander's choosing in order to retain the initiative. The massing of forces, together with proper application of the other principles of war, may enable numerically inferior forces to achieve decisive campaign and battle outcomes.[12]

One sees here the concentration of forces, the concentration of power, and the unification of command. Violence must be focused and directed at one commander's attention point. Note that the elaborations of each principle are issued as instructional commands in the active voice.

The fifth principle is "unity of command." Thus, "For every objective, ensure unity of effort under one responsible commander."[13]

This principle ensures that all efforts are focused on a common goal. . . . The coordination of these forces requires unity of effort. . . . In both the operational and tactical dimensions, it is axiomatic that the employment of military forces in a manner that develops their full combat power requires unity of command. Unity of command . . . is . . . best achieved by vesting a single commander with the requisite authority to direct and to coordinate all forces employed in pursuit of a common goal.[14]

Both senior leaders and junior troops believed these principles essential to survival in modern battle. The principles had a logic vis-à-vis the expected environment and assigned task. They seemed to be correct. But it was not even necessary that they be correct—only that they were believed to be correct—to establish the institution's peculiar corporate culture. The point is that the culturally anticipated environment and the tasks assigned by the nation to the institution drove the deviations that had arisen between Army corporate culture and general American culture. The cultural deviations and the structure of practice occasioned by the premise differences led to the human alienation experienced by these American soldiers and their family members.

THE NATURE OF ALIENATION IN THE ARMY COMMUNITY

When taken together, the contradictions between the general American cultural premises and those specific Army premises designed to keep its members ready for combat led to an institutionalized way of life that was quite different from the American experience. The Army way of life felt "foreign" to soldiers and family members required to live it. The "foreignness" derived either from the fact that specific Army practices were sometimes evaluated with the more basic general cultural premises or from the fact that specific, combat-essential premises appropriate to the military context were used in family or community domains where, according to American culture, they were inappropriate.

Frustrated over these differences, soldiers or spouses sometimes used words such as "Marxist," "communist," or "totalitarian" to depict the Army's contrast with their idealized American concepts. For example, Kim Farley, the director of

ACS at Richberg said, "The military is a Marxist organization. The very things we are here to defend and fight against are exactly what we do in the Army to run it." CPL Hank Walsh similarly reflected, "The Army is a dictatorship." His wife, Terry, mused in response, "I understand it needs to be that way. And Hank likes it. But it's not for me." Interestingly, the "I understand it needs to be that way" indicated a recognition that the institution's premises had to deviate from the core culture's premises to accomplish the institution's chartered function. "I see the Army in some ways as being very socialistic or communistic, coming down and saying, 'I will control your life. I will control what you are gonna do,'" said one unidentified person I bumped into. CPT Bill Olsen blurted, "The Army is fascist, but the [American] people are democratic. I have got to be a dictator." He went on to explain how even though the entire community had participated in winning a substantial award from USAREUR for conserving electricity, neither the soldiers nor spouses had a significant say in how the prize money was to be used, "even though the wives saved the money." 1LT Russ Masterson, working as battalion personnel officer, answered my question as to whether or not he would stay in for a career of twenty years thus:

> I don't know if we are going to make a career of it. I come home to a house that the Army has said we have to live with. I have to live with those I am told to live with. I have to go to the field for weeks on end, and when I do, I am paid less for going. I am living in a situation where the Supreme Court says I do not have the same rights as a citizen. I am in a state of confinement: the battalion commander can pull my pass privileges, and they have the right to. While I understand that from the point of view of military necessity—you have to do this with the people we are dealing with—it is in such opposition to the nature of our free society.

The quote suggests that the evident irritation and the demoralization arose from the disjunction between the American cultural premise of freedom and the Army's daily practices arising from extension of the military's contrary premises beyond the boundaries necessary for readiness and warfare. Thus, although the Army is certainly pro-American, it is in some regards quite un-American. How can this be? How can the larger American system have a subsystem—an institution within it—that is so contradictory to the whole? The answer revolves around the interaction of general cultural premises with specifically tasked institutions that must accomplish a goal in a particular environment. Where the assigned tasks cannot be accomplished employing the general cultural premises, divergent institutional premises will be acceptable.

The conflict is endemic, but it is not irreconcilable. Soldiers and many spouses—those spouses who have been with the Army awhile and have tried to comprehend it—understand that combat and readiness for combat require a different mode of thought and a different style of action than ordinary life. For example, Terry Walsh's, "I understand it needs to be that way," or 1LT Masterson's "I understand . . . from the point of view of military necessity" show clear appreciation of the difference allowed by functional necessity. Soldiers and spouses were willing to abide by and employ the contradictory premises and practices when the deviating premises and practices were applied strictly within the Army's military activities. That was tolerable, certainly understandable, though perhaps not always comfortable, and not the slightest bit alienating.

Fundamental alienation, a feeling of enormous resentment, occurred under three conditions. First, soldiers and spouses felt alienated when the Army's specialized premises were applied outside the domain of the Army's combat responsibility. Here alienation arose from a violation of separation of domains. Thus, soldiers and spouses resented the invasion and militarization of family and community life that Americans felt should be separate domains. Second, soldiers and spouses felt alienated when specific Army practices defeated, impeded, or disrupted the larger goals of military mission safety and readiness. Thus, soldiers detested the toadying reports based on inaccurate self-protective information that led to orders from "higher" that bore little relation to soldier or mission needs. Junior troops and NCOs often despised officers, thinking them book-learned but ignorant, because their orders so often seemed out of sync with the on-the-ground reality. Third, soldiers and spouses felt alienated when the control features of the Army unnecessarily invaded their private and family time. No one complained about necessary and efficient invasion of family time; indeed, soldiers and spouses were quite willing to sacrifice for "real missions." But they hated seeing their sacrifices wasted, and they bitterly resented seeing Army inefficiencies being made up for by capturing family and private time via the obligation to obey and the twenty-four hour commitment.

CONCLUSION

The Army institutionalized principles that concentrated power, centralized control, and fused domains to provide those conditions that were held essential to its purpose: readiness for combat. The elements of combat success—maneuver, firepower, protection, leadership, initiative, agility, depth, synchronization, speed, concentration, mass, unity of command, and surprise, among others—were coordinated by fusing the separate components of Army organization, such as infantry, armor, artillery, medical support, communications, intelligence, transportation, supply systems, food services, maintenance, police, legal council, and more under the responsibility of a single commander. The Army's premises and consequent practices contrasted sharply with the generally applicable American premises and resultant practices, yet the differences were tolerated as a culturally understood functional necessity for readiness training and success in combat.

In this chapter, we have explored how the differences between basic American cultural principles and the essential institutional principles followed by the Army created conflicts for soldiers and their family members. Members of the community—soldiers, spouses, and their children—had to reconcile two quite opposite paradigms for action. They experienced conflict and felt alienated when military corporate-culture premises were used outside of military mission situations, primarily when used to interfere in the domains of family and community, which they held to be properly separate. The differences between American core culture and the

Army's functional requirements had additional consequences, for they resulted in the perception that the Army was un-American, and therefore "probably closest to a socialist system," as MAJ Waters suggested in the epigraph beginning this chapter. I argue that much of the pain and alienation experienced by members of the community derived from the extension of the specialized Army premises of unity and control beyond the management of military activities to the management of family and community affairs, domains that most of the military community's residents, as enculturated Americans, felt ought to be separate and run by American cultural premises. This fact accounts for the endemic state of deteriorated morale and alienation in Army communities in Germany and, I would suggest, throughout the Army.

Once one understands that the Army's premises and practices *must be different* from American premises and practices and that those differences are *felt to be legitimate* in the eyes of all participants—soldiers, spouses, and American citizens—*if they are strictly contained within the domain of the military mission*, the way is opened for providing structures that could significantly reduce the alienation of soldiers and spouses from the Army. Moreover, the same structures would diminish the alienation and distrust that American citizens often feel toward their military institutions and personnel. In the next chapter, I will briefly suggest the outlines of some practical remedies. The military reader deserves the outlines of some practical solutions, and the practical solutions, briefly presented, will clarify and summarize my arguments about the processes of alienation in the military community. Moreover, practical suggestions imply the possibility that the theory or interpretation on which they are based may be tested, a matter of some importance to the discipline of anthropology.

NOTES

1. Gary Witherspoon, *Dynamic Symmetry and Holistic Asymmetry in Navajo and Western Art and Cosmology* (New York: Peter Lang Publishers, 1995).

2. Here I follow such thinkers as Clifford Geertz, "Thick Description, Toward an Interpretive Theory of Culture," *The Interpretation of Cultures: Selected Essays* (New York: Basic Books, 1973): 3–30; David Schneider, "Notes Toward a Theory of Culture," in *Meaning in Anthropology*, ed. Keith H. Basso and Henry A. Selby (Albuquerque: University of New Mexico Press, 1976): 197–220; and Gary Witherspoon, *Dynamic Symmetry*, among others. I focus on premises—logical propositions about the nature of values and the universe—and posit that a well-formed premise will contain both a subject and a predicate, thus constituting a specification of meaning about something. Material and visual symbols are also important, for they define the boundaries of social groups that communicate with each other versus those with whom they compete. With regard to symbols, I am interested in the root meanings or propositions that symbols communicate, not the shape of the symbols themselves. Nevertheless, I recognize that through the human inclination to imitate, the physical shape of some symbols shows us the acceptable shapes of the behavioral patterns or of the material outcomes that would effectively satisfy the seemingly conflicting directions implied by multiple premises. As such, symbols constitute an important facet of the communication of culture.

3. Emile Durkheim, *The Rules of Sociological Method* (New York: The Free Press, 1964).

4. See especially Witherspoon, *Dynamic Symmetry*.

5. A debate emerges in U.S. policy circles as to whether organizations based on unity—armies and their nation states—can be attacked effectively by less organized, atomized fields of individuals sharing key premises, through terrorism.

6. Charles H. Coates and Roland J. Pellegrin, *Military Sociology: A Study of American Military Institutions and Military Life* (College Park, MD: The Social Science Press, 1965), for example, discuss the separation and distrust that has long existed between military personnel and families living in their enclosed communities and the larger civil society.

7. In FORTRAN computer programming, lines of code in the form of "do xyz" can order the computer register to go to a particular line of code and execute its instruction. If a line of a do-instruction orders the computer register back to a previous do-instruction in the (non-branching) path that led to the current statement, you get an infinite loop, called a "do-loop," in which the computer "runs" in the same closed logical circle until shut down by time limits.

8. Department of the Army, "Preface," *FM 100-5, Operations* (Washington, DC: Department of the Army, May 1986): i, 173–177. FM stands for Field Manual.

9. Department of the Army, *FM 100-5*, 173.

10. Ibid., 174.

11. Ibid., 174.

12. Ibid., 174.

13. Ibid., 175.

14. Ibid., 175–176.

Conclusion

To bring closure to this study of the soldiers and families who lived in the American Army communities of Cold War Germany, I must consider three matters. First, unmarried soldiers usually left the American military community in Germany after a tour of eighteen months, while married soldiers and their families usually left after a three-year tour. I will briefly consider some of the issues they faced in the departure process, remembering that the community remains stable even as personnel rotate in and out of it constantly. Second, I must lay out what has happened to the military communities and their residents since the end of my active fieldwork there. They have, in fact, experienced a substantial "drawdown" (withdrawal of troops from Germany) and a major change of mission. Finally, I consider the implications we may draw from this study. In a word, what are the benefits of this study and to whom? Here, I speak to three audiences: soldiers of all ranks, military families, and military community leaders; the American public; and the social science research community.

CLOSING A TOUR: PCS STATESIDE

Well before the end of a three-year tour, a family needed to decide where they might like to spend the next segment of their military lives. Although the needs of the Army always came first, the soldier could consult with career managers in "Personnel" and apply for positions based on career enhancement or residential preference.

Most eagerly anticipated their PCS, or permanent change of station, back to the States, many soldiers and spouses literally counting the days. Most military families departed from government quarters, a relatively easy operation. They had to receive orders, schedule packers, make travel arrangements, and clean their apartment. In the past, such cleaning was "inspected" by military personnel. In military life, inspections were a primary means of control and perceived harassment. Older couples remembered something akin to a reign of terror of last minute chores to "clear quarters" according to military inspection standards. During the time of my study, however, the Army had hired contract cleaners to do the detailed cleaning of rooms and appliances after the family had departed. The family simply had to leave their quarters "trash free and broom clean." The few military families still on the economy when they left Germany had to clean and, usually by contract, repaint or apply new wallpaper to their apartment. This was a standard provision of the German rental lease. Americans who used the military lease papers provided by the Housing Referral Office usually escaped this requirement, having paid for it in advance by being charged a monthly rental above the German market rate.[1] Given the anticipated relief and deep symbolic value attached to the "return home" to the States, such last-minute inconveniences were tolerated.

What could not be tolerated easily, however, was delay or uncertainty in the process of returning to "shopper's heaven," "the good ol' USA." Yet delay and uncertainty in the return process were commonplace. Sometimes, changes in government policy forced the imposition of either a mandatory extension or an early end of one's stay in Germany. The unexpectedness of such changes was especially unnerving. For example, because of an order designed to save the government money in the 1987 fiscal year, which ended September 30, many military families scheduled to depart during the summer were required to remain in Germany until after October 1, so that their moving expenses could be charged to the new fiscal year. For a family with children, this fragmented the school year in a way parents felt was extremely detrimental. Soldiers who would have ended their service in the Army in September or October were required to take earlier releases, again to reduce wage expenses in 1987. This created an environment of considerable uncertainty and a feeling that the Army was exploiting the indentured status of its personnel. And all suffered from the fact that a delay was announced but no one was told how long the delays would last or who would be affected for sure. In an interview for the *Stars and Stripes,* Karen Erickson, a command sergeant major, reflected, "I hope we won't need any more overseas tour extensions, but, even if we do, it's not the extensions that upset soldiers, it's the not knowing how that extension will affect them. They don't know until the last minute. If you tell them up front, they can deal with it. But when you don't, they don't know what to do with their family, school, etc. Soldiers can and will accept things if they are not played with."[2]

A clear statement of the deleterious impact of uncertainty came from two Air Force couples, who jointly signed a letter to the *Stars and Stripes,* stating:

We are trying to plan ahead for our next PCS move. Some of our plans include such things as buying and selling houses, family finances, and relocation of school-

age children. . . . Please set the record straight! The uncertainty is far worse than the answer we'd least like to hear.
— Staff Sgt. and Mrs. David G. Sabatini
— Tech. Sgt. and Mrs. Stuart M. Moylan
RAF Bentwaters, England[3]

Congressional budget cutting had made even the apparently simple tasks of transferring to a new post or exiting the Army unpredictable. The delays gave the appearance that the Army cared less for the soldiers than for its budgets. As SGT Larry Bracken remarked, "It kills me the *Army* can drop the contract, but if *we* wanted out, they'd say 'stay.' They're not considering the family; they are considering the budget." The opinion was widely reflected in *Stars and Stripes* letters to the editor:

It seems to me that the Army is just postponing the inevitable and we, the families, are paying the high interest rates in terms of personal disappointments and lowered morale, so that somewhere, *on paper*, the expense of moving our families back Stateside will not appear until the next fiscal year.
— Name withheld
Mainz, Germany[4]

We find here an example of the Army's institutional needs being placed above individual needs, when the American cultural premises generally suggest that the individual is to be protected more than the institution.

The final details of departing from Germany were fairly straightforward. The family spent a few days in the government transient hotel or in a nearby *gasthaus* while the soldier completed the paperwork required for "out-processing." Then they flew to their next PCS, which for most, meant a return to the States.

That brought to a close an individual's residence in the U.S. Army community in Germany. But larger social processes were at work, and shortly after I departed the field, world events led to the shutdown of many whole communities. We need to look at that process to get both closure and currency in this study.

CLOSING COMMUNITIES: THE CHANGING AMERICAN MILITARY PRESENCE IN GERMANY—1989–1999

Since the end of my fieldwork in Germany, June 30, 1988, much has changed, resulting in a substantial "drawdown" in U.S. forces in Germany and in the closure of many military communities. Here I outline that process and detail its implications for Middleberg, Richberg, and other communities where I studied.

Dismantling Cold War Communities

The end of the Cold War fundamentally altered the U.S. Army presence in Germany in the 1990s. *Perestroika,* the restructuring begun by Mikhail Gorbachev, the breakup of the Warsaw Pact, the splintering of the Soviet Union, the reunification of Germany, and the withdrawal of Soviet troops from former East Germany (completed by 1994) and from all the Warsaw Pact nations along German's border reduced Cold War tensions and risks. This reduction in risk precipitated massive U.S. troop withdrawals from Europe and led to the closure and return to Germany of more than 500 properties, many of them significant installations.

The first installation closings, closings that had been "rumored for weeks," were officially announced Monday, January 29, 1990. Twelve overseas installations and thirty-five U.S. bases were to be closed.[5] Although none of the installations belonged to the U.S. Army, and only one was in Germany, the task of restructuring the American military presence in Europe had begun in earnest. On September 19, 1990, the *Stars and Stripes* listed 150 overseas installations to be phased out. "The majority of the sites . . . are small facilities such as communications stations, family housing areas and barracks," but complete shutdown was the fate for a major air base Spain and for two air stations and two Army communities in Germany.[6] In addition, four of Grossberg's seven subcommunities were slated for closure, including Sudberg, Central Barracks, and Welby General Hospital. All units of Middleberg's forward brigade that had been stationed in Newberg would be moved, for Newberg, also, would be closed entirely.

Reaction to U.S. troop reductions in Germany was mixed. Leaders of the smaller German communities lobbied to keep their nearby American facilities filled with American military. The leaders of larger German cities hungered for the space, facilities, extra housing, and noise reduction. American military family reaction to the closures ranged from exasperation at the chaos that was induced in one's personal life to complete indifference. The *Stars and Stripes* printed no letters suggesting a sense of loss from the closures or a sense of attachment to Germany. Life went on with a certain touch of surrealism. New schools opened and huge construction projects continued in several communities on the "hit list" because there was not enough specific information to stop construction. One community had just completed $175 million of maintenance, repairs, upgrading, and new construction, all to be abandoned. American military families throughout Germany probably felt like the school principal who said that "she doesn't have a clue what the future holds [and] . . . 'I don't think anybody knows.'"[7] Day after day, *Stars and Stripes* articles and letters evinced little remorse. Soldiers and families simply moved on to the next task.[8]

Soldiers and spouses experienced imploding communities, indefinitely deployed partners, drawdown of troops, increasing threat of terrorism, and, by 1990, the risks of war in the Persian Gulf—the stress levels must have been astonishing in the military communities. Yet spouses coped and helped each other. The chain of concern and a shared community of anxiety brought spouses together. For example, the *Stars and Stripes* reported that "Lee Penman became what she calls the 'self-imposed' commander of her husband's unit Wednesday night." Her husband's unit had deployed to Saudi Arabia, and Penman

> plans to head up what she describes as the "chain of concern." . . . "I just want to make sure that we watch out for everybody who's left," said Penman, a soft-spoken

19-year Army wife. She said she also wants to ensure that those [mostly female spouses] left behind are "taken care of and that you don't have to worry that someone's going to forget them." . . . Under her command, open hearts, arms, minds and phone lines will be mandatory. No. 2 in the chain of concern is Betsy Dusdenbostel, whose husband, Maj. Warren Dusdenbostel, is the unit's executive officer. . . . She said her responsibilities include teaching those left behind "that they can depend on each other if they need any help." [9]

Dusdenbostel further reflected that "It would be nice to go home to Pennsylvania for a while during Desert Shield. . . . 'But our family is here—the other wives and the other families.'" [10] The chain of concern to assist the "Army family" was effective and operational—and precisely parallel to the chain of command.

On October 2, 1990, the *Stars and Stripes* announced the deactivation of the Berlin Brigade, with component units to be withdrawn starting in March 1991 and finishing in concert with the completion of the Soviet withdrawal from East Berlin, planned for 1994.[11] Checkpoint Alpha on the Berlin Corridor autobahn closed. The more famous Checkpoint Charlie had already closed when the East Germans opened the wall and removed their border guards in November 1989.

In the October 3, 1990, headline, "Reunited Germans Celebrate," each word boldly spanned the page.[12] U.S. service members could now travel freely in former East Germany, though the remaining Soviet military installations stayed off-limits. The united Parliament of Germany voted on October 5, 1990, to formally end Allied powers, privileges, and controls in Berlin, the last remaining enclave of World War II occupation status.[13]

The drawdown continued and additional base closings were announced in a total of seventeen distinct press releases.[14] Indeed, base-closing announcements became so routine that *Stars and Stripes* twice failed to print the latest Pentagon Base Realignment and Closing Office list of newly announced European post shutdowns. It was, in a sense, no longer worthy news. After the first dozen, announcements became shorter and perfunctory, eliciting little comment. Statistics tell the outlines of the story, a kind of CliffsNotes version shorn of the many individual joys and heartaches of the process. Prior to January 1, 1990, the United States Army in Germany occupied 774 definable installation properties, large and small. By October 24, 1994, 535 had been vacated and returned to Germany. Ten new properties were acquired in the adjustment process, leaving the U.S. military with 249 installations. In the United Kingdom, 5 out of 6 were returned, in Turkey 5 out of 5, in the Netherlands 5 out of 12, in Italy 6 of 12, in Greece 8 of 8, in France 24 of 24.[15] Army troop strength in Germany had dropped from 213,000 in mid-1992 to 65,000 by October 1995[16] and had further declined to 62,000 by late 1999.[17]

The Fates of Middleberg and Richberg

Statistics and newspaper articles do not convey the emotion of the drawdown. During the summer of 1991, I had an opportunity to visit Middleberg Barracks and Richberg Kaserne. Time was short and I was able to spend only a few hours in each. I found both communities under a cloud of uncertainty regarding their futures. Middleberg was gearing down. Its troops had been sent to the Persian Gulf, but its families remained in Germany. Middleberg's rear detachment leaders understood that the entire military community might soon be closed. Similarly, Richberg's combat units had been sent to the Persian Gulf in 1990. Richberg's rear detachment leaders, however, thought the *kaserne* had a new lease on life because there might be a Special Forces tenant unit assigned to Richberg that would keep it open. Even so, the mood of people in both locations was desultory.

In the summer of 1994, I again visited both communities briefly. Richberg Kaserne had indeed received a Special Forces unit as a new tenant. Surprisingly, gate guard and entry procedures were much relaxed compared with 1986–1988. However, a few hours of casual discussion with soldiers and family members suggested the major sources of family stress had not changed at all, except that family problems were intensified by the increased tempo of post-Cold War deployments that particularly affected this elite Special Forces unit. Middleberg, by contrast, had been completely vacated, shut down, and returned to the Germans, the main installation an empty ghost town. A fence divided off a few of Middleberg's buildings that had been pressed into service to process and house East European refugees. The German gate guard refused my request to enter any portion of the installation. From my view through the gate, the rest of Middleberg looked empty and desolate. Driving around the perimeter and peering through the fence at various locations, I confirmed that except for the portion of the barracks area used for housing refugees, Middleberg was empty, devoid of activity, its buildings empty shells beginning to show signs of deterioration, its grounds gone to weeds now knee-high. Just outside the fence, the former complex of Middleberg military family housing (i.e., government quarters) had been turned over to the Federal Republic, its apartments leased to German families. Likewise, Newberg, Sudberg, and Welby General Hospital and its community compound had been vacated and turned over to the Germans. Most of Central Barracks had also been returned. Only General Barracks remained a center of command and military community activity.

Changing Missions

On November 19, 1990, world leaders signed a treaty ending the four-decade era of Cold War tension. One may take this moment as the end of an era, an era during which the risk of surprise attack in Europe had been constant and during which NATO had focused on the NATO/Warsaw Pact frontier in a Cold War mission.[18] It was, at the same time, the beginning of a new era, an era in which NATO would use Europe as a platform from which to launch forces intended to solve problems outside of NATO.

Indeed, the mission of American soldiers in Germany changed completely.[19] Soldiers no longer patrolled the frontier with what had been East Germany or Czechoslovakia, training for immediate response to Warsaw Pact invasion. Indeed, the Warsaw Pact had ceased to exist and the Polish and Czech borders were deemed risk free, the two countries under consideration for inclusion in NATO. Rather, USAREUR soldiers trained for deployment outside NATO as peacemakers or peacekeepers.

The end of the Cold War, however, by no means signaled a reduction in soldier workload. On the contrary, the *Army Times* reported that "mission tempo"— the rate of outside-NATO deployment—had increased dramatically. During the main Cold War period, from 1948 to 1989, a total of 11,851 Army troops were involved in twenty-nine deployments outside NATO, an average of 410 troops per deployment, 0.63 deployments per year, and (on average) 258 troops on deployment sometime during a year.[20] During 1990 and 1991, operations Desert Shield and Desert Storm deployed 75,000 U.S. troops from Europe and about 40,000 "pieces of equipment."[21] Between the end of Desert Storm in February 1991 and the end of 1995, a period of nearly four years, a total of 24,027 USAREUR troops participated in sixty-six deployments, an average rate of 364 troops per deployment, 13.8 deployments per year, and 5,841 troops deployed per year.[22] The increased tempo in the post-Gulf War period is plain enough, just given these figures. But the real impact of the difference must be weighed against the fact that from 1948 to 1989, the 258 soldiers (on average) who deployed each year did so from a force of some 200,000 soldiers. Since 1989, the troop base had been declining rapidly to the October 1995 level of approximately 65,000 troops. Thus, some twenty-one times the number of deployments per year of some twenty-two times the number of troops per year were being taken from a pool of soldiers that had averaged half the size and had now declined to one-third of its former size. If the current deployment rate continues, the foreign deployment workload per American soldier in Germany may be some sixty times greater than during the Cold War period. A recent calculation by USAREUR suggested that in a three-year tour to Germany, armored battalion troops would spend 29 percent of their time away from their home installation, mechanized infantry battalion troops would spend 43 percent of their three years away, and personnel in a brigade headquarters would spend 53 percent of their time in training or on deployment, away from their home station and families.[23]

Ominously, the increased tempo of troop deployment outside Germany is likely to continue. This change will intensify stresses on the families, making the recommendations that emerged from this study even more apropos. Moreover, the postwar instabilities brought on by the end of two-power polarization, combined with the reduction in force brought on by budget cuts, have resulted in U.S.-based units acquiring rapid deployment responsibilities, going on increased alert, and being deployed more frequently. The deployment of Stateside troops to Haiti, Somalia, and Panama exemplify this trend. Although the economic separation and social isolation described in Chapter 9, "Little America," is not so great within the United States, the similarities are considerable. Active-duty Army families posted in the United States, as well as Reserve Army and National Guard families, will increasingly sense their kinship of forward deployment responsibility with the American Army families of late Cold War Germany.[24]

The Reproduction of Garrison Culture

With 62,000 soldiers remaining in Germany, some 30,000 to 35,000 families still live in military communities even more scattered and isolated than before. In Germany, the thirty-nine Army communities of the Cold War period were consolidated into fourteen BASOPS (Base Operations), roughly comparable to a complex supercommunity like Grossberg under the old system, with its constituent subcommunities. Each supercommunity covered an area geographically larger than that formerly covered by the Grossberg Military Community, an area that had overwhelmed community management during the Cold War period. The old military community cadre became the new BSB—Base Support Battalion. Thus, the formal structure of the post-Cold War Army community in Germany has stayed similar to that of the most complex and problem ridden of the 1980s supercommunities. In addition to this similarity of social structure, the same corporate-cultural principles—unity, endurance, obedience, hierarchy, and readiness—remain the basis for evaluating decisions to be made. Only the surface or outward mission of the Army in Europe—defending against a Soviet threat—has changed, not the underlying corporate-cultural principles needed to operate in an environment of threat, surprise, and violence. Nor has the tendency to fuse domains and confuse the boundaries between military, family, and community changed. In part, this fusion persists because the cultural disparity between military craft and American tradition is not well understood. So even in the new, outwardly changed post-Cold War world, a garrison culture replete with the pain of undermined hope continues to reproduce itself. Yet it need not be that way. If military leaders, common soldiers, and ordinary citizens had a better understanding of the underlying cultural and structural tensions, and if they changed a few key structures and practices to facilitate better information flow, more predictability, and sharper separation of domains, soldiers and spouses would feel their hopes less compromised.

Another study is needed to document both the changes and the continuities in the reproduction of garrison culture under the supposedly new community organization, with its overarching Area Support Group, its BASOPS, and its Base Support Battalions. I suspect we will find much old wine in newly named bottles, and if my analysis is correct, one can predict some trends. First, one can predict that the structural difficulties, personal alienation, and frustration that the leaders and members of subcommunities such as Richberg experienced within the complex Grossberg Military Community will become the norm, for the Base Support Battalion structure has now been generalized to all the American military communities. Each BASOPS area of responsibility is so large that the major installations within it will become subcommunities, competing with each other. Second, the post-Cold War American military communities are smaller in population and more widely dispersed. Yet its families are more concentrated in on-post housing than during the Cold War. The residents will either have to connect better to off-post nonmilitary recreation and social interaction or they will become more isolated, more judgmental, and therefore more unhappy than what I reported for 1986–1988. Third, the radically increased frequency of deployment would seem to imply trouble in the future for families and forebodes reduced retention. If the mission remains clearly understandable and acceptable to the on-the-ground soldier, however, the pace can be sustained for a while, perhaps quite a while, because sacrifice is tolerable if it is not wasted. At some point, however, issues of fairness will emerge from within the American cultural roots of these soldiers and someone else will have to do more. More ominous, however, is the possibility that the legitimacy of the mission tempo either won't be communicated or can't be communicated. At such point, a kind of Vietnam-style demoralization of soldiers and families might easily race through the scattered, overworked communities. If such failure of clarity or purpose were to occur, soldiers and their families might strive for relief, and if not relief, then release, being unable to sense the value of their sacrifices. Unfortunately, given the extraordinary costs to train soldiers in the current technology of war readiness and to keep them safer by keeping them technologically ahead of soldiers in other armies, failure to retain highly-skilled soldiers could result in additional human losses in future combat.

THE BROADER IMPLICATIONS—2001 AND BEYOND

So, where has our journey into the lives of these warrior families taken us? In the introduction, I suggested that the exploration should garner us insights of value to three groups of people.

First, I proposed that the soldiers and their spouses might benefit from the information. Indeed, I asserted that the Army's attempts at improving quality of life for married personnel were ineffective because the programs' executives did not understand the sources of discontent within the military. With improved knowledge of the structure, culture, and feedback organization of the system, leaders, as custodians of the institution, and soldiers and spouses, as participants in the institution, could make better decisions. If they better understood the *structures* and *practices* that led to human pain and institutional corruption, I suggested they could take steps toward appropriate change. Second, I proposed that ordinary nonmilitary Americans also could benefit from a knowledge of the military. Americans could be better citizens by understanding their military more thoroughly. They would be less subject to what scholars have recently identified as a civilian-military gap in cultural understanding, a gap that implies that citizens do not understand the culture and constraints of their military compatriots and that soldiers may not share the fundamental premises of their civilian overseers. In addition, I suggested that an understanding of military life, a life of intense occupational stress and contest between family and work, might shed light not only on the families of other high-stress job holders—police, fire personnel, medical practitioners— but also on the nature of all family life, this because the analysis of the extreme case clarifies issues not easily seen in the more fuzzy circumstances of ordinary life. Finally, I proposed that an analysis of human behavior in the pressured circumstances lived by the military community tribe would help social scientists—and anthropologists in particular—to see some issues of theory more clearly. In a word, anthropologists could help Army leaders overcome the alienation they experienced in the military institution. Conversely, by participating in a study of themselves, soldiers and spouses could help anthropologists overcome a certain misdirection and consequent alienation that anthropologists have experienced within their own discipline.

To see if I have accomplished these tasks, I must briefly review the high points of the ethnography.

Life in a Warrior Community: A Review

The soldiers and spouses I interviewed were hopeful and idealistic. They believed in the principles of American life, and they felt that they contributed to that American life by placing themselves at risk to defend it. They did so for a variety of reasons. Among them, they appreciated the material benefits that exceeded the expectations of high school graduates raised in working-class or impoverished circumstances. Most of them seized the opportunities for personal development that were placed before them. Those who stuck with it made themselves solidly middle class through time. Soldiers and spouses derived much personal satisfaction from forging a sense of community, from making racial equality work better in the Army than they had ever seen it work elsewhere, and from working at a job that mattered because they defended their country and helped one another to grow. Because the job mattered, they felt patriotic and fulfilled; because they felt patriotic, the job mattered and was fulfilling.

Soldiers and spouses lived their individual lives within four systems of social obligation and expectation. First, they lived in families. Second, they lived within military communities from which they received their social support and their physical provisioning. Third, they interacted with Army units, for in every household lived at least one obligated soldier. Fourth, they found themselves engulfed in German culture and society, a culture they did not know and to which they did not have significant access. Every institution in which they had previously participated was enveloped in the gossamer cocoon of American cultural experience and expectation. In Germany, however, soldiers and spouses did not find the American culture that they had grown up with and known so intimately. That foreignness led to a life of isolation, to the creation of an enclave society. The level of threat on the Soviet frontier conferred a degree of intensity to the demands made by the leaders. Together, isolation and intensity made forward deployment significantly more stressful than what most soldiers had experienced in their military service in the States. Being in a foreign country on the hair-trigger frontier of the Cold War isolated and intensified the lives of these warrior-Americans.

The Army brought young soldier families into this intense, demanding setting, and pushed most of them into the task of finding housing in the German community. The mostly new young soldiers and their spouses were not skilled in dealing with foreign settings. Moreover, they did not feel that they were given much support, they did not have much time, and housing was in short supply. In the rush to get settled, some made poor housing choices. The consequences of these choices lingered, for the shortage of time or the shortage of money resulting from their housing decisions circled back to hurt them in their units. The many pains of entry established a mind-set: that life in the Army in Germany was a bad assignment. Soldiers and spouses proceeded to interpret the rest of their assignment through this negative filter. That attitude, of course, drew down upon them a negative reaction from their leaders, and thus a spiral of morale deterioration began within days of their arrival.

The Army had a job to get done, by no means an easy one. The Soviet threat was massive, immediate, and pressing. That made the work demanding and unpredictable. Beyond that, multiple systems of culture, law, and military regulation had to be followed. Moreover, military properties were much smaller in Germany than in the States, forcing soldiers to leave their home installations frequently to train. Military and political leaders feared any incident—on or off duty—that might sour German-American relations. Finally, the soldiers tasked with these complex burdens for the most part lacked the language skills to interact adequately and confidently with those Germans who could help them. All these considerations greatly increased the complexity and intensity of the work, making it more subject to breakdown. The increased probability of breakdown, the soldier's obligation twenty-four hours a day, the practice of random alerts to test the system's readiness, and the various time cycles of different duty rosters led to considerable unpredictability in the workday, which had further repercussions for the family. Moreover, the structure of the career evaluation reporting system allowed leaders to make uncontrollable work demands of their soldiers.

The ability of the chain of command to make demands and the nearness, intensity, and reality of the threat led to constant demand overload. Sensitivity to any wish coming from higher in the chain of command easily led to mission distortion—demanding the unnecessary. Soldiers who would have felt their personal sacrifices were worthwhile had their activities contributed clearly to the "real mission"—training for defense of the frontier—felt themselves coerced, extorted, and alienated by demands that deviated from training for combat readiness.

The processes of command, control, reporting, and punishment injected fear into the system, which led to a suppression of feedback and to a distortion of reporting that further undermined the integrity of units. Officers appeared stupid because they made decisions based on inaccurate reports. Junior troops began to protect themselves through subtle resistance. Unable to communicate safely through words, the junior troops began to communicate in increasingly destructive forms of behavior, and the leaders began to tighten the exercise of control in a feedback process that induced more resistance by the weak. Again the feedback systems amplified the expression of inappropriate behavior, and morale suffered further.

In a variety of ways, unit activities penetrated the family systems of married soldiers. Long days, unpredictable hours, the complexity of the work, the ever present demand for readiness in the face of threat, and the ability of leaders to impose their demands through the obligation to obey and the threat of repercussions from Officer Evaluation Reports or Enlisted Evaluation Reports led to an infringement on family time and to an absolute unpredictability of time use.

Military families, like American families in general, based themselves on trust; constantly confirmed trust was a core symbol of family existence. Yet the unpredictability of Army demands immobilized the process by which families planned activities and developed trust. Indeed, family and Army fought for allegiance, for time, and for trust. Unless a soldier were willing to leave the Army, however, the Army had the more powerful mechanisms for enforcing its demands. The family took second place.

In recompense for the demands made and the isolation experienced, the Army provided a series of community supports to its families: child care, housing, a post exchange, a commissary, other shopping, and a variety of recreational services. But the support system did not work very well. The needed supports were in too short supply or use of the services could inadvertently get the user in trouble. Thus, soldiers and spouses felt the Army and its leaders to be in breach of contract, for their supports sometimes hurt. Again, they felt alienated, especially when required to use a service, such as child care, that was controlled yet in short supply or not structured to meet their needs. They felt caught in a contradiction, for if they made other arrangements, they got in trouble, and if they used what was available, they also got in trouble because they would, at some point, be late or make some other error, forcing the system to report them to the line of commanders who judged their or their spouses' careers.

The sense of breach was most intense in the medical system. The medical system symbolized the Army's intent to "take care of its own" after it put them in harm's way. In Germany, the military medical system attempted to care for the family members of its soldiers because using the German system was judged too difficult. Yet few additional medical assets were provided for the hugely increased dependent population to be served. This led to understaffing, absurd appointment procedures, delays in service, staff discourtesy, and client belligerence. Other complexities led to added bureaucracy, lost records, inefficiencies, and breaches of confidentiality. The process of using the medical system—the core symbol that the Army cared—gave some the strong feeling that the Army did not care at all. Delays or deferrals of needed care led to compounded medical problems. Soldiers and spouses felt trapped in a system with no alternatives, and they felt betrayed by military medicine because of the dangers its delivery system created. The sense of betrayal led to heightened alienation throughout the community.

Family members were not simply disrupted by the activities of the military. Rather, families were partially absorbed into the Army by the Army's fear of embarrassment and by the increased control and accountability that Germany required of NATO members by treaty. In the overseas context, American civil and criminal law did not apply to the control of family members. German legal authorities wanted little to do with American behavior that did not affect German citizens. In the legal vacuum, the Army exercised the regulatory control of family members that it could, and applied informal pressures on the careers of its obligated soldiers to induce the soldiers to control them further. The increased need for control, however, breached the culturally expected separation of the family and the military domains. In Germany, families were "in" the Army. The fusion of domains led to a range of unintended consequences that were deleterious to family, to the military units, and to the community in general. Among the effects, spouses expressed feelings of lost identity, dependency, a weakening of family discipline, and a militarization of interactions within the family. Units suffered, too, for they experienced lost work time, inadequate information flows, and attrition of personnel. Above all, the practice of controlling the family through threats to the soldier's career made the family a burden and a risk rather than a place of support or refuge.

Soldiers and spouses found themselves isolated into enclave communities. They were separated from Germany by the practicalities of different currencies, different languages and cultures, and different systems of vacation, store hours, and even transportation. At the same time, they were drawn together by subsidized prices, shared language, and comforting common symbols within the military community. Families experienced culture shock, turned inward, and isolated themselves, saying they hated Germany.

Once turned inward and isolated, and subjected to the military regimen of security surveillance, some families adopted the military ethic of reporting by reporting on one another. Sometimes they turned in anonymous reports. Sometimes they surreptitiously fueled gossip in the community. Especially in the housing areas, where building coordinators, chains of command, and chains of concern intersected with close residential living, the practice of surveillance and reporting fused the family area to the work area and subverted the development of trust in the military community. The failure of trust, the fusion of domains, and the effort to achieve "zero defects" led to a variety of personal behaviors designed to insulate the soldier and spouse from observation. Families withdrew, avoided therapy, tolerated injustice, hid behind facades, and grew cautious and conservative. They resented the hypocrisy of volunteer efforts, fostered gossip, trusted few in the community, and had few friends. Ultimately, they felt violated by the sense of breached confidentiality, loss of parental control, and loss of privacy. They grew to hate life in the stairwell—much as they had hated the first year of their assignment when forced to live in the German villages. They felt coerced and at risk, pushed by the force of social structures that made career success contingent on OERs and EERs that potentially evaluated whether their family and community behavior was supportive. Family responsibilities added to demand overload. Soldiers were distracted from their military mission as they sought to keep family members out of trouble. Leaders were diverted from mission planning as they dealt with the family issues of their soldiers. Soldiers and spouses grew to distrust and even loathe the unit leaders as they worked out their lives in communities laced with fear and alienation.

Of course, soldiers and spouses tried take a break from the isolated, densely interconnected military communities. The modes for taking a break, however, were thwarted by the fact that the military ran the recreation system available to the soldiers on-post. Finding little in the way of legitimate breaks, some soldiers sought to forge an escape through behavior that often became self-destructive. Withdrawal, alcohol abuse, marital friction and separation, subversion of the Army, or severance from the service all had their undesirable costs to the military and their negative impacts on morale in the units and among families in the community.

The desire to escape the military was fueled by more than the pressures of military work, the isolation of the families in a community, and the Army's fusion of the domains of work, family, and community in an atmosphere of pervasive surveillance and judgment. The need to escape was also impelled by a desire to lessen the contradictions between the logic of military life and the premises of American life. To be sure, combat survival requires premises at variance with the root beliefs of American democracy. The Army could legitimately have and use variant—even opposite—premises, provided their use was confined to legitimate mission circumstances. But the Army's fusion of domains caused military premises and practices to be extended into the family and community domains, where they replaced the ordinary American cultural premises that would have been expected in family and community decision making. Forced to live their lives quite at variance with the principles they felt should apply in family and community affairs, the soldiers and spouses sensed that the military had violated its cultural contract. They became, as a result, the backbone of an army of alienation.

This study of the military community invites us to think about its broader implications. In the words of Lévi-Strauss, a study of the U.S. Army is, I believe, "good to think with."[25] If indeed knowledge gives power, then just as surely, knowledge confers responsibility. To the extent that our knowledge grants increased understanding of the sources of human alienation and anguish, then we have a responsibility to try to use that knowledge to reduce the distress.

Implications for Soldiers, Spouses, and Leaders in the Military Community

As I conclude this book, I can deal only briefly with the largest issues that disrupt the lives of soldiers and their spouses living in forward deployment. Nevertheless, several issues and strategies of remediation stand out. I have suggested at several points that certain structures and practices lie at the heart of much current pain and anxiety in the military. I will, therefore, make some specific suggestions, but these suggestions are intended only as examples of what might be done. The Army is indeed a changing organization within a changing society, and some of the specific examples may no longer fit so exactly as they might have in the past. Therefore, it is important to keep in mind the principles that justify the suggested alterations; by employing the principles, the leader can modify these suggestions, adapting them to current local realities. Here are a few possibilities and the principles on which they are based. All would be actions initiated by leaders in the Army. For convenience, I divide them into *unit actions*, which must be initiated within the tactical unit chains of command, and *community actions*, which must be authorized and implemented by corps-level community leaders and their staffs. In reality, the two lines intertwine along the chain of command and merge most clearly at the brigade/division/community commander level and at the corps commander level.

Unit Chain of Command Actions. A variety of measures could be taken within the chain of command to ameliorate some of the conditions described above. Among them,

- **Change the structure of officer and enlisted career evaluation.** At a deep level, much of the corruption of military leadership was driven by the capricious rating system. One's "rater" or commander, and one's "senior rater" (often the rater's rater) held an inordinate amount of influence over how one might be viewed by a promotion board held years later. This diverted leaders from their assessment of real mission to their sense of what raters wanted. That power corrupted the flow of accurate information in the system.

  In spite of recent changes in the OER and EER forms, a new evaluation system is needed still. An improved system must suppress inflation and the capriciousness of wording. Inflation could be suppressed by taking advantage of the fact that an officer evaluates three to five people of the same subordinate rank and task. One could use a computer-scored ranking form in which the rater simply marks a bubble as to which subordinate is the best performer and which the worst performer (out of x many being ranked on this occasion) for each issue Army leaders think important.

  Such an approach would eliminate inflation and capriciousness of wording, but it would not deal with the corruptions caused by the fact that ratings of a leader come only from above. The Army needs, simultaneously, ratings from peers and from subordinates.[26] The combination of evaluation from three directions would give promotion boards much better evidence from which to decide which leader should be kept and which leader removed if the Army is to accomplish its goals of being ready for combat, retaining good soldiers, and improving unit and community morale.

- **Consolidate duty rosters and place units "on call" for one week per month.** The military leaders need to eliminate or reduce those practices that most disrupt the family. Part of the problem of disruption would be taken care of by transformations in the OER and the EER, for the suggestions I have made would tend to focus leadership decisions on the core mission. But certain practices, like the duty roster, remain especially disruptive. Among the possibilities, one might be able to combine multiple duty rosters so that weekends are not savaged by the random cycles of one's name on many rosters. Given increased computer capabilities, such a scheduling system should be possible within an organization as technologically oriented as the Army. One might also consider using the segmentary nature of Army organization to place one segment of each unit on call for everything, for one week per month. This would approximate the rotating call schedule of a physician's office. One week would be totally disrupted, but the fact would be known well in advance, whereas three or four successive weeks (depending on the number of segments in a given unit) would be completely stabilized.

- **Stabilize the duty day.** Easy to say, hard to do under the current structure and practice. In addition to the current or proposed top-down rating system, the

OER and the EER processes should require all *subordinates* to fill out a form with a line item such as "my current supervisor rarely lets the garrison duty day be extended for *nonessential* tasks (mark the boxes: agree strongly, agree, no opinion, disagree, disagree strongly)." Were such a requirement made, computer read, and posted statistically to one's permanent file, the garrison duty day would stabilize very quickly.

- **Make community leadership a career-enhancing assignment.** The feeling that community command drew its personnel from those passed over or cast off by the combat arms undermined trust in the community command system. To overcome that perception, the Army should make community command a valid secondary career specialty for officers and senior enlisted, and it should have the empty leadership slots filled by competitive board selection.[27]

Community Support Actions. Other actions that would improve conditions within the military community can be taken by leaders within the community chain of command. These should include,

- **Separate domains.** Much of the grief experienced by soldiers and their spouses spun off from the problems of inadequate domain separation. American culture posits a separation of domains. The practice disperses power and facilitates individualism through atomization. Soldiers felt the Army was at perfect liberty to use alternate premises within the military institution, and they recognized that specialized military premises (and the resulting practices) would be necessarily different from their American cultural experience. But they still wanted a separation of the military from the nonmilitary aspects or domains of their lives.

  To achieve greater separation, leaders should route family communications and family discipline through the DCC rather than through the company commander. Essentially, the Army needs to pay the additional costs of message transmission so that family matters do not flow through the company commanders. In addition, the Army needs to strengthen the legal and regulatory basis of the deputy community commander's office to deal with family behavior independently of the unit chain of command, so that the DCC can operate without contaminating the chain of command's perception of the soldier. Once the regulatory basis of family interaction with the military was strengthened, DCCs, or their designates, could handle family matters without the corrosive practice of manipulating the family through threats to the soldier's career. Finally, a wide range of nonmilitary community functions might be run on more democratic principles through an elected community administrator whose decisions would be subject to veto by the DCC in cases where military mission might be affected.

- **Facilitate soldier-to-family communication.** The Army needs to provide more modes of communication to help soldiers and families adjust to the day-to-day and hour-to-hour schedule changes. At the time I did this study, that seemed to mean authorizing brief private use of government phones, making

German pay phones available in each building, and installing additional phone lines to each installation, especially to the medical and dental clinics. Today, the possibilities for communication have widened considerably. E-mail messages, cell phones, pagers, and Web pages with message capacity all could help families be less surprised by the inevitable disruptions of Army work.

- **Make spouses legal adults in the military community.** The Army needs to create a legal or regulatory structure and a computer accounting system that allows spouses to sign for (and be held responsible for) family and community support resources. To not do so crushes important principles that surround adulthood, gender, and independence.

- **Train soldiers and spouses in community leadership issues.** The Army should recognize the fact of "pillow talk" and the disruptions it creates. It needs to train its leaders and their spouses on how to keep confidentiality even as they pass generic information to each other about the state of soldiers and their families. Such a move would not only deal with the sense of many leaders that they are not prepared to deal with family issues, it would also help secure the appropriate lines of separation between the domains of unit and family. Training might help spouses become much more skilled family support group resources.

- **Make German medical systems accessible.** A variety of measures could be taken to make German medical systems more available to spouses. Selected German doctors could be given fellowships for study in the United States in return for agreements that they would then serve military families in village clinics or more central hospitals. One could also place bilingual liaison nurses in key German medical facilities, a practice that would increase the sense of freedom of choice and reduce the sense of entrapment with regard to medical and mental therapy services.[28]

- **Make German society and culture more accessible.** The military community would be less isolated and the fusion of domains would be less intense if soldiers had more access to the surrounding German society and culture. One way to help accomplish that would be to hire a German recreation specialist at each installation to help connect soldiers and spouses to the wide variety of German sports, hobby, recreation, and skills clubs and facilities in the surrounding communities.

Soldiers and spouses would also feel less isolated if they could speak German better. Part of the problem was that when most families arrived, they were pushed out to residences in German villages. The on-post evening-school classes became inaccessible. By the time they acquired on-post housing, the obvious need for learning German had ended. One solution might be to give newly arrived families highest priority for government housing so that they could have access to the on-post German language and culture orientation classes for a year, prior to being moved into off-post residences.[29] Although this solution would cost more and might entail difficulties with German lease length, it would be decidedly more humane to the new arrivers and would reduce entry shock.

Ideally, a broad range of actions would be implemented simultaneously by leaders in both unit and community chains of command.

Implications for Citizens

I hope that this study will increase the understanding, compassion, trust, and tolerance that American and German citizens have toward members of the military communities in Germany. Indeed, if this book in any way contributes to the improvement of living conditions and work environment in the military, or to increasing the levels of understanding and tolerance between military citizens and ordinary citizens, then I, as one of those ordinary citizens, will be pleased to have played a small part.

Strive to Understand the Military. In the twenty-first century, Americans very likely will ask U.S. military personnel to take on the task of being a major player in a world police force. We should more thoroughly understand such an important institution and its vital taskings. Military actions in the late twentieth century—in Grenada, Panama, the Persian Gulf, Somalia, Rwanda, Bosnia, and Kosovo—suggest that the U.S. Army will take on a major post-Cold War role to protect humanitarian efforts, keep the peace between ethnic rivals, and subdue international thuggery. Globalization of transportation, communication, and markets has made the world a single interconnected village. Yet the village, so recently thrown together, is just beginning to figure out its laws and has not yet acquired a police force. The U.S. Army and the other U.S. and NATO military services seem likely to be tasked with international police functions while the world community builds new structures. It would seem most appropriate for the citizens of a country to understand their military well before and while sending them to such new tasks.

Reach Out. Military life is not easy. It is conflicted. Soldiers and spouses need alternative outlets. Over many years, soldier communities have been quite separated from and distrusted by the general American populace. In the media, soldiers are often portrayed in highly negative terms.

This study shows that married soldiers, to the contrary, are thoroughly American—patriotic, goal-directed, and sensitive to and aware of the ways their Army unit, family, and community lives get distorted by the practices of military life. To be sure, the Army will always be distinctive because the requirements of the combat environment will make it so. But that distinctiveness can be contained within military mission situations. After the mission, soldiers and their spouses need to be embraced by the surrounding community in which they live, whether German or American. A wide range of social contacts would help soldiers and spouses stay more composed, given the stress of the military life. Such contact would help them escape safely from, and buffer the effects of, too much fusion of domains and too much isolation within the military community. Civilians of both the United States and Germany, and any other country in which U.S. soldiers are stationed, need to voluntarily reach out in friendship to soldiers and spouses of all races and ranks.

Maintain Attractive Pay and Benefits. The diplomatic and technological aspects of modern warfare require educated, intelligent, highly skilled, well-balanced individuals. The American citizen would hardly want any other kind of person to handle such potent weapons or engage in such diplomatically sensitive tasks. As citizens, we should want to ensure that the best stay in. If pay scales and working conditions deteriorate too much relative to civilian work, however, the best (which is to say, those with options) get out. American citizens need to understand their military well enough both to appreciate them, thereby adding to the quality of their lives, and to be sure that soldiers' pay and benefits stay well within the norms of technical and managerial middle-class pay scales.

Learn from the Military Experience. There are two ways the civilian citizen can learn from the Army family experience. First, one can fruitfully discover something about how people experience the interaction of work and family in a number of occupations that have characteristics similar to the military. Here I speak of police, fire personnel, and medical service providers, among others. Each of these has characteristics similar to the military: around-the-clock duty, odd hours, insistently demanding occupational requirements, and consequent penetration and disruption of the family. Perhaps the most research has been done on the interaction of the family with police work. Christina Maslach and Susan Jackson, for example, approach the issues in "Burned-Out Cops and their Families."[30] Maslach and Jackson found that psychological factors created more stress than the physical dangers. Thus, "ambiguity and conflicting values surrounding the job, the responsibility for other people's lives and their well-being, the long hours of inactivity mixed with unpredictable crises, the frustrating encounters with . . . police administration, the negative public image of cops in general . . . are often more debilitating than the physical hazards."[31] Their interviews revealed that "it is almost impossible for policemen to avoid bringing work attitudes home when they leave the station." Moreover, "a cop is always a cop, even when off-duty," for he is "expected to respond appropriately to any emergency or crisis situation, even when in civilian clothes."[32] Finally, they note "the policeman's unusual working hours, which can disrupt family routines and minimize his contact with his wife and children."[33] All of these features we saw displayed in the work-family interaction within the Army family. The result is, in Maslach and Jackson's terms, "burnout," perhaps akin to what I have labeled the soldier's alienation from his work experience. And, like the soldiers and military families who become distant from civilian society, Maslach and Jackson report that police especially, and their families to a degree, become estranged from society at large, mirroring the separation between civil and military communities and people reported in the military family and community literature.[34] Maslach and Jackson report the existence of police unit spouse support groups, not unlike the family support groups and chain of concern in the military. Significantly, the male police officers do not use the support system, except through the support of other officers in bars, because it would be a "sign of weakness," holding that "if you need it, you're unfit for this line of work."[35]

More recently, the House of Representatives Select Committee on Children, Youth, and Families held hearings on the interaction of police stress and family well-being. The testimony of a police department psychologist found that single-parent officers "struggle to provide adequate child care . . . while working rotating shifts," and that in "all police families, shift work disrupts family life, as when the officer is unavailable on holidays, for family special events or is called to court on a day off."[36] Beyond shift work, the deeper problem is "one of unpredictability, crises, and emergency response, [which] generally communicates to the police family that the job must take priority over their needs."[37] As a result, "it is not unusual . . . for police family members to experience loneliness and alienation and to develop resentment for the pervasive influence that a career in law enforcement assumes over their lives."[38] A female former police officer testified that "when a life-threatening situation occurs, many officers find themselves in a situation where the spouse demands that they choose between their job or the spouse. Unfortunately, due to the sense of brotherhood on the force and the increased friction and feeling of isolation with the family, many officers choose the job." Given the stresses of police work, several testified to the importance of counseling for police officers and their families. Confidentiality, however, was stressed as essential, and the danger of information flowing to judging supervisors was implicit in such statements as, "[C]ounseling programs that are offered for police officers and families that are confidential in nature are very important in dealing with stress. In many organizations officers are given a letter or number identification and are entitled to unlimited visits with counselors without the fear of feedback to the administration or supervisors."[39] On a more positive side, and like the soldiers and families in Germany who made contact outside the Army community, she noted that "Families that successfully cope with police stress do so by breaking the cycle of isolation by becoming involved in the community outside police work. This involvement may be with a church that gives the family a sense of inner peace and a source of strength to count on for support. Involvement in community groups . . . helps break down the barriers between officers and the rest of the community."[40] In a similar vein, a professor of family studies found that "officers who claim that other officers were their best friends and only associated with other officers were the ones that were higher on burnout. Those officers who diversified their social network were the ones that had lower burnout. So the social network and the tightly-knit organization also needs to be examined in the context of the burnout process."[41]

According to Judi Marshall, nurses likewise feel conflicted between work and family. Erratic hours, the intensity of work, decisions, and emotions when dealing with the sick and dying, and the disparity between caring and the requirements of paperwork management all take their toll.[42] Thus, employees and families engaged in these and no doubt other high-stress occupations can learn from the Army experience.

But it is not just high-stress occupations. There is a modest amount of every facet of the Army experience hidden in the less intense work-family interaction of all of us. Take me, for example—a university professor. The university professor's life would not seem one of undue stress. Provided we meet our classes, there is, on the surface, enormous flexibility. But research competence is a never ending commitment, and it is easy to subvert family time with research demands taken home to be finished. In the very task of trying to finish this book, I have disrupted family and caused stress by commandeering hundreds of evenings, and many dozens of weekends and vacations. In this sense, I argue that the processes raised to a boil by the intensity of Army life are in fact simmering in the background of many, if not all, family-work interactions. It is just that we do not pay attention to that which is not so clear because it is not so intense. We can all learn from the Army, assess our lives, and do a little bit better. I certainly can, and I hope that I will.

Finally, I submit that it is not just members of the military community, or even average citizens—myself included—who can learn from the Army. Social scientists, including anthropologists (another community to which I belong), can also benefit from the study of the military. To show how this is so, I first touch on some concepts being argued amongst sociologists of the military. Then I explore a few concepts used more broadly in the examination of our common humanity.

Implications for the Sociology of the Military

Four concepts often associated with military studies seem particularly relevant in the light of this study. First is the concept of the military as a greedy institution, pioneered by Lewis Coser and applied by Mady Segal with particular force to the analysis of the military family. Second is Goffman's idea of the total institution. Third is a discussion about whether the military remains a profession or has become simply an occupation. Fourth is a debate about what is called the civil-military gap, the idea that civilians and military personnel less and less often share a common culture of mutual understanding.

On Greedy Institutions. In 1986, Mady Segal, following the work of Lewis Coser, published an article that suggested the Army and the family were "greedy institutions," simultaneously competing for the time and allegiance of the soldiers they shared.[43] It is worth contrasting Coser's concept of the greedy institution with the more anthropological concept of status contradiction or status incompatibility. For Coser, "greedy institutions . . . seek exclusive and undivided loyalty and they attempt to reduce the claims of competing rules and status positions on those they wish to encompass within their boundaries. Their demands on the person are omnivorous."[44] In the status contradiction perspective, the individual finds himself or herself in two relationships, each with obligations that are at once both inescapable and irreconcilable. In the classic example, the son-in-law (in the matrilineal social system) avoids his mother-in-law because they each have interests in the same woman—wife of one, daughter of the other. The wife/daughter cannot simultaneously fulfill both sets of obligations, and avoidance between the two reduces the possibility of simultaneously applying both sets of demands. If avoidance is not sufficient to reduce the conflict, mutual accusations of witchcraft are likely to express the feelings of distrust resulting from the structural contradictions inherent in the relationship.

There is certainly structural conflict and structural tension in the relation between unit and family in the Army, each having legitimate claims on the soldier. In the military case, however, the concept of greed is particularly useful because it connotes varying degrees of intensity and competition in the conflict. In the Army case, the perception of intense Soviet threat increased the drivenness of the Army's claim on the soldier, amplifying the tension to much higher levels than that experienced by soldiers in the States. Thus, although structural contradiction is present, greediness better portrays the fact that the external threat situation can heighten the intensity of the conflict, skewing it to increasingly favor the Army's demands over the family's demands on the soldier. Greediness is woefully imprecise, but it does portray the wide range of differences in intensity of demand that structural contradiction does not.

On Total Institutions. Erving Goffman defines the total institution as "a place of residence and work where a large number of like-situated individuals, cut off from the wider society for an appreciable period of time, together lead an enclosed, formally administered round of life."[45] By this definition, the military barracks is virtually a type case exemplification of the total institution. Likewise, government quarters in the overseas military community fits the definition for both the soldiers and their families. In Chapter 9, "Little America," I showed the considerable degree of their isolation, and in various chapters, I detailed aspects of the formal administration and control of their lives.

Goffman goes on to contrast civil society with the total institution: "A basic arrangement of modern society is that the individual tends to sleep, play, and work in different places, with different co-participants, under different authorities, and without an over-all rational plan. The central feature of total institutions can be described as a breakdown of the barriers ordinarily separating these three spheres of life."[46] Indeed, work, domestic life, and play are conjoined in the overseas garrison community, enacted in the same space, shared by the same participants, and subsumed under a single command authority that metes out punishment.

Goffman talks of the "similarities" of total institutions that "obtrude so glaringly and persistently that we have a right to suspect that there is good functional reasons for these features being present."[47] Throughout Goffman's work, the fundamental issues within total institutions concern inculcating control and infusing into the institution's adherents an ideology and a set of practices at variance with those of the encompassing world. In the Army's case, the variant ideology and practices are thought to have favorable consequences for survival in combat. Thus, Goffman asserts, "It is characteristic of inmates that they come to the institution with a 'presenting culture' . . . derived from a 'home world'—a way of life and a round of activities taken for granted until the point of admission to the institution."[48] One comes to the total institution with a culture. The dynamic relation between the total institution and the encompassing culture is seen through their structural opposition.

The full meaning for the inmate of being "in" or "on the inside" does not exist apart from the special meaning to him of "getting out" or "getting on the outside." In this sense, total institutions do not really look for cultural victory. They create and sustain a particular kind of tension between the home world and the institutional world and use this persistent tension as strategic leverage in the management of men.[49]

Goffman details the structures and practices of control and of inculcation of an institutionally specific ideology. In the Army, soldiers believe that their acquired ideology and behavioral practices will lead to combat readiness and therefore survival in combat. Given that today's Army is composed of volunteers who strongly embrace the surrounding American culture—Goffman's "presenting" culture—any Army practice that does not feel American must make sense in terms of preparation for combat. If the logic is too obscure, or if the practice is merely coerced by the obligation to obey but unrelated to the goal of readiness for combat, then soldiers and their families will not likely tolerate the deviation without feeling demoralized and alienated.

On the Institutional/Occupational Debate in the Military. In a series of papers, Charles Moskos and others have discussed whether the American military is being transformed from an institutional framework toward an occupational framework. By definition, when an individual operates within an institutional framework, she or he orients toward the rules, the traditions, and the structure of the organization, feeling herself or himself a professional within the institution, thereby maintaining it. Conversely, when one orients toward the occupational aspect, one becomes concerned with such matters as appropriate or increased pay and improved working conditions. Essentially, such an individual orients toward the military as though it were just another commodity on the market, and one acts as a self-interested individualist. The professional, by contrast, is willing to advance the legitimate goals of the institution even if in order to do so self-gain must be sacrificed.[50]

In this framework, where did these soldiers and families of Cold War Germany fit? Essentially I must give an impressionistic answer, for it was not a question that I asked myself while doing research. In retrospect, I found both institutional and occupational orientations held simultaneously. People expressed the market orientation at various times, often comparing their salaries mournfully with better paid but less significant jobs of the "civilian world." Hence the soldier who is "on call death" but makes less "than the guy who fixes your toilet." I also found the institutional orientation: pride in the organization and appreciation for the way it helped one to get "squared away" by submission to the ceaseless application of rules and inspections, and a willingness to sacrifice for the larger good if the sacrifice was not wasted. Yet the debate misses something, and I would like to get at that something through the circuitous route of examining an Israeli kibbutz.

In a penetrating study of Kibbutz Timem, T.M.S. Evans (1995) examines how this particular kibbutz, through time, grew in population and went through a process of occupational differentiation. The process led to a call for secret ballots.

Secret ballots, however, contradicted the "traditional" procedure of collective discussion followed by open vote within the public community meeting. Factionalism grew. Tempers flared. Was the organization going to move toward market rationalization? Or would it try to hold the course of structure and authority? Essentially, the kibbutz faced the institutional/occupational dilemma. The participants—or the elders, at any rate—reconceptualized the move to market rationality as a cleavage between generations, and they mobilized the biblical accounts so as to symbolically press for the youngers to submit to their elders.

Out of the close analysis of a limited set of behaviors, however, Evans drew an interesting conclusion regarding the human condition. His material suggested that all human action is suspended between the ever-competing claims of the individual (in this case the differentiated free market) and the societal (in this case the authority structure and the continued existence of this particular kibbutz). Indeed, precisely because they cannot escape the dilemma of balancing both individual and societal interests, humans have choice. Finally, he concludes, the essence of morality is to position one's choices so as to cultivate societal interests and not let them wither.

Let us now return to the Army. If Evans is correct, the soldier will always be suspended between the institutional pole, with its emphasis on societal issues, and the occupational, with its emphasis on individual circumstance. What I find interesting about the soldiers and their families in Germany is the implication of their alienation. Alienation implies disgruntlement, in this case disgruntlement because their labors were often appropriated against their will by being wasted. But waste implies a knowledge of some alternative better end. In the case of these soldiers, they knew it was mission readiness. In short, their alienation was not evidence of their abandonment of institutional values. It was, rather, an emotional response rooted in their absolute possession of professional values and their sense of betrayal by the practices of the institution that did not carry them closer to their image of those values. Soldier alienation evinced a profoundly moral commitment to the larger values of the organization. Their existential despair often hovered around cases where coercive aspects of the obligation to obey orders forced them to do tasks they felt were not "real mission" and therefore not ethical deviations from the "presenting" American culture. Forced by the obligation to obey orders, they felt alienated when they had to perform tasks that protected or advanced the interests of some individual, "whims" at the occupational/individual level rather than "needs" at the institutional/societal level. Thus, soldier and family alienation constituted an emotional response to ethical betrayal occasionally forced down the system by its potentially coercive structures. Most of the soldiers were professionals, institutionally oriented and ethically motivated even in their moments of most profound despair.

On the Civil-Military Gap. Recent scholarship on the military has suggested that civilian citizens do not adequately understand the military because, with the elimination of the draft, there is no longer a large segment of the American population that has had experience in the military. This lack of knowledge creates a danger to the society. Civilian leaders, for example, may be tempted to use the national instruments of force in ways that cannot succeed.

Concomitantly, the argument is made that continued separation between civil and military society leads to a military caste that acquires its own culture. Adding to the castelike condition, the institution often recruits the children of its senior leaders or former members, or it recruits youth socialized in violence-infested sectors of society, thereby taking in those already accustomed to violence as a way of life. The result, it is feared, leads to the evolution of a military that is isolated, potentially self-serving, and deviant from mainstream American democratic values.

The evidence of this case does not bear on the issue of civilian incomprehension of the military. That may well be a problem. This study does, however, suggest that the creation of a self-serving warrior-caste with radically different values from the originating culture is simply not the case. In Germany, soldiers of all ranks, both genders, and all races understood the reason for military cultural deviation from the American norm, and they fully understood and accepted the American norms. Moreover, they understood that each set of values should be compartmentalized into different domains of activity, and they resented violation of the expected compartmentalization. In a word, American soldiers in Germany were thoroughly American. The "dangerous soldier caste" facet of the supposed civil-military gap simply did not exist.

The notions of civilian-military gap and institution versus occupation are social concepts that apply almost exclusively to the study of the military. The ideas of greedy institution and total institution are more broadly applicable but are, nevertheless, particularly appropriate for the analysis of military institutions. In all four cases, this study of the U.S. Army communities in Germany reflects on the nature of the concepts and leads us to them to some degree. The study of the Army also leads us to examine other concepts, concepts even more central to anthropology and the social sciences in general. Among them, I focus here on the ideas of surveillance and control advanced by Foucault, the legitimacy of postmodernism as a perspective in the social sciences, the concept of alienation propounded by Marx, the nature of resistance explored by Scott, and the crisis of representation in anthropology as developed by Marcus and Fischer. To these fundamental social science issues I now turn.

Implications for Core Concepts in the Social Sciences

On Control Through Surveillance. In *Discipline and Punish*, sociologist Michel Foucault describes prison architecture to illustrate a point about behavioral conservatism in a human community. According to Foucault, when people believe they can be observed, and therefore might be observed at any time, and when they believe they might be punished for any infraction discovered, they adopt a self-monitored conservative mode of behavior. Indeed, they become tradition-oriented. Foucault exemplifies the principle using the architectural drawings of Jeremy Bentham, a jurist, philosopher, and key figure in the rise of nineteenth-century utilitarianism, who conceived of a circular prison in which guards in a central tower could observe all actions at any time of inmates in every cell, the cells being stacked in rings around the observation tower. By contrast, the observers—the guards in the central tower—could not be seen by the inmates. Thus, an inmate was conscious of always being subject to the possibility of observation. Hence, Bentham called it a Panopticon. Punishment then flowed from the central tower as infractions were observed. In Foucault's theory, the possibility of continuous observation built into the architecture led inmates to adopt internal controls of their own behavior, an internalized tradition of the acceptable, so as to avoid punishment.[51]

In ordinary life, such tradition orientation arises from the continuous observation and correction implicit in the face-to-face society, where little is hidden from the view or judgment of others in the community. The military community's version of the Panopticon—"living in a fishbowl"—derives from close association in fused housing and work domains, where any member of the community *might* interpret one's unusual behavior in a negative way and report it to the officers responsible for judgment. The Army community takes on prisonlike attributes similar to Bentham's Panopticon, with military community members themselves becoming the all-observing guards of each other. As a result, they develop in themselves a cautiousness regarding their public and private behavior. They come to behave in institutionalized ways, and these new patterns quickly become thought of as traditional. Through adherence to tradition, one avoids standing out and one avoids being criticized. The potential for both observation and discipline regarding any aspect of their lives leads to a feeling of imprisonment and gives rise to expressions of a need for escape. I have suggested that this desire for escape arises because the American premises of freedom clash with the local institutional practice of continuous observation and severe judgment.

With no disrespect to Foucault's elegant analysis, however, one must note that his ideas regarding surveillance were largely anticipated in Goffman's writings on the total institution. Moreover, anthropologists have known for more than seventy years that totally open mutual knowledge of one another's activities in the face-to-face village society, combined with the threat of gossip and witchcraft accusation, leads to a distinct cultural conservatism. In many societies, such as the Sisala and the Lugbara tribes of Africa, the most efficient and ceaseless of all observers are the deceased ancestors, who watch their descendants' behavior from their unseen spiritual vantage point and mete out punishments of disease and misfortune for any infraction or disrespect.[52]

Military communities, like many face-to-face village settings around the world, exemplify slightly less intense versions of the processes that Foucault intuits for the prison setting. As Giddens points out, people monitor themselves and one another, judging each other's behavior.[53] We anticipate the reactions of others to our potential behavior. The real or imagined possibilities of others' reactions become the objective structures that condition cultural learning. As a result, culture becomes substantially shared and codified at the same time.

On Postmodernism. One tenet of postmodernism seems to argue that people of diverse ethnic, racial, or gender backgrounds do not share a culture and do not interpret events at all similarly. This study of the Army, by contrast, suggests that Americans of all walks of life substantially share a culture, having absorbed or had inscribed into their minds a set of root premises or dispositions that orient their lives.[54] Yet Americans appear to think and act with considerable distinctiveness, and that appearance of distinctiveness needs explanation. First, Americans occupy distinctive social positions and combinations of positions. Second, the social institutions they participate in may require them to adopt alternative premises for those institutions. Behavioral and even ideological differences between individuals arise when people in different institutions or in different positions within an institution adapt or try to synthesize the requisite premises, responsibilities, and interests of their multiple positions. In the game of life, agents must divine ways to handle the essential compromises entailed by the fact that each person has multiple social roles in diverse institutions.[55] They find different ways to try to achieve a compromise, and some are more skilled than others at creating a synthesis. When the local structures make it impossible to "play the game" so as to accumulate specific symbols representing achievement of the larger social values, discontent or alienation sets in. There is a third component of American distinctiveness propelled not by the happenstance of positional differences but by the active creation of American culture. Americans cultivate the ideas that individual distinctiveness is good and that change is desirable. These two premises fuel the self-deceptive external appearance of individuated culture when in fact the participants are all playing the same cultural game by all trying to appear different within an accepted style.

The Army case leads one to conclude that the postmodern concept that each individual has a different culture and that no cultural view has priority or primary authenticity is a social science enshrining of the American cultural premise of differentiated, free individuals. By contrast, all residents in the Army community in Germany, regardless of rank, gender, or race, shared essentially the same concepts of the nature of life in the military milieu and expressed adherence to the same overarching American cultural values. Their language differed in the precise symbols chosen to express their experience. Their emotions differed as to how intensely they reacted to the perplexities of their society. Each focused on different aspects of the nature of the system, and none laid it out completely or in an orderly, analytical way as I have tried to do in this book. Yet they each had all the concepts.

To be sure, different individuals adapted with differing degrees of skill in conceiving and dealing with the problems. Some sampled the German environment, whereas others withdrew to become "barracks rats" in American ghettos. Some resorted to drinking, some engaged in resistance through other forms of behavior, and still others went shopping, traveled, or volunteered in community service. Some played the scene skillfully indeed, and some blundered blindly. Nevertheless, they shared a common experience and intuited its root implications. All played the game, or gave up on the game, according to their feel for it. The variations in how they played the game no doubt resulted in part from differences of personal history or personality. But the participants agreed on the basic nature and value of the family, on the nature of unit and mission, on the essential premises of American culture, on the difficulties created by living a military life while maintaining a family orientation, and on the frustration of trying to abide by American premises on the one hand and military expectations on the other while living isolated within a foreign social and cultural system.

Indeed, the complexities and contradictions between unit, family, community, American culture, and German society and culture made it particularly difficult to get a "feel for the game."[56] Any particular "feel" or style for playing the game of "life in Little America" was likely to betray the player in one or another of the institutions or domains. If one played by American premises, one was battered in the Army institution. If one played by Army strategies and premises, one was battered in the family or community domains and alienated by the difference between "Army" and "American." If one both played American and tried escape, one was battered by encounters with German expectations or the German "feel" for a different game. If one tried to avoid battery from encounters with ill-understood German expectations, isolation within the American military community led to its own set of strictures and controls, and such limitations conflicted with American cultural expectations of freedom and choice. Those who both understood the complexities of the system intuitively and could switch the style or feel with which they played in each institution fared the best. Thus, the most successful members of the military community were like pentathletes, compartmentalizers who could play several games at an exceptionally high skill level and switch easily between the differing sports. Whether skilled at the play or not, however, all soldiers and spouses sought to adapt fundamentally to the same structure: the contradictory and judgmental fusion of unit, family, community, and American culture set within the German environment.

The Army case draws one away from the nihilism of postmodernism toward the position of Bourdieu: that most people in a region share substantially a *habitus* or culture because they have had to deal with the harsh realities of similar encounters with objective structures.[57] The most objective structure of all, of course, is the potential of death doled out by the conditions of modern annihilation combat. These conditions have been imagined in various ways—even glorified in nationalisms and religious belief—throughout history. From time to time, however, the imaginations get corrected by the culture-constraining fury of war's outbreak. Those cultures whose armies can keep their institutional culture most closely tuned to the reality of war—rather than distort it in nationalisms, deify it in myth, or dilute it with accommodations to the patterns of the larger culture—will likely survive longer.

On Alienation. Any study of the Army will encounter behavior that resonates with the idea of alienation. My experience with soldiers and military families has pushed me to the conclusion that in Army society, alienation ("loss of morale") derives primarily from the misuse of institutions relative to shared expectations about the goals of those institutions. Thus, alienation is related to the interplay and misplay of institutions. Leaders, as agents and custodians of an institution, must decide the uses of power. Subordinates will judge a leader's decisions in the light of their shared culture.

Of course, alienation is not a new concept. For Marx, alienation occurs when the products of a worker's labors are "appropriated" to the benefit of owners. The worker experiences both a physical loss and a psychological decoupling from society that results from having been coerced. The processes rest on class differentiation and power arrangements that make workers easily exploitable.

One sees in military society a resonance between the class aspects of the officer/enlisted distinction in the military community and Marx's view of the class structure and class antagonisms existing between bourgeois and proletariat. Officers constitute a senior management level, and control soldiers through the non-commissioned officers. Marx would suggest that one look primarily at the specific organization of the means of production and the broad social relations of the mode of production for the foundations of social process. In a Marxian analysis, officers correspond to bourgeois managers of a capitalist enterprise, for in the eyes of the enlisted troops, officers do no real work. Rather, they make decisions about the use of the resources, they appropriate and allocate the labor of the enlisted workers, and they decide the retention or forced severance of the "proletarians," the junior troops. Moreover, officers—according to the enlisted—definitely reserve for themselves all privilege while they restrict the enlisted personnel and extract obeisance of them. The perceptions of these enlisted persons are largely correct, for the structure of the system indeed enables officers to coerce labor and respect from their juniors. Nevertheless, there are limitations to the view.

In the first place, the structure of the rank hierarchy extracts significant managerial labor out of the officers, just as it regularly extracts herculean physical labor out of the enlisted. In the second place, officers exercise control over the junior enlisted through the NCO Corps, who are also enlisted. On both these counts, Marx's two-class division is considerably blurred, though some modern Marxisms admit more complex class structures than Marx postulated.

Marx expected control by the owning class to lead to class antagonism. By contrast, I have shown that when Army leaders were doing what they were supposed to be doing, there was a great deal of ideological agreement and compatibility between the officer and enlisted segments. The members of both sectors willingly worked hard to cooperate in the common task. Alienation disappeared. According to Marx, however, officers and enlisted should have radically divergent class interests, with the officers exploiting the enlisted and the enlisted thoroughly alienated and even revolutionary. Thus, Marx's approach to the sources of class conflict and the alienation of laborer does not reconcile with these data on the U.S. Army.

As an alternative, I suggest that divergence between an institution's goals and the overarching society's general ideology, combined with the limiting concept of what that institution's chartered focus is, are more important factors than class structure, domination, and labor appropriation if we are to understand the genesis of alienation.[58]

On Resistance. In *Weapons of the Weak* and in *Domination and the Arts of Resistance,* James C. Scott analyzes peasant social systems in which an elite extracts or coerces labor and product from a subordinate laboring class. By definition, this condition is domination. According to Scott, such domination is achieved through the elaboration of a "public transcript," the open, elite-justifying rituals and expectations that affirm the rightness and actuality of elite control. In the process of appropriating peasant labor and product, however, the elites inevitably offend, humiliate, denigrate, and coerce their subordinates. Out of this process of humiliation, Scott asserts, there develops a reaction in which people begin to resist the ordinary conditions of domination. The peasants subject the elites to work slowdowns, shamming, sabotage, feigned ignorance, and acted incompetence. These and other devices create a self-preserving cultural space for the masses.

The behavior of soldiers in the U.S. Army, however, casts doubt on the inevitability of resistance when under domination. Enlisted soldiers certainly live and work under a state of domination. Yet the enlisted participate wholeheartedly and willingly when the Army engages in activities that fulfill its understood goals or charter (mission, to the soldiers), and when the institution (through its agents) does not undermine the capacity of other valid institutions, such as the family, to operate according to cultural expectations.

The Army case thus clarifies the conditions in which resistance to the official project occurs. In the Army, officers and the enlisted subordinates largely share their understandings of both the core American general premise system and the special premises, institutional goals, and domain limitations of the Army. Agreement between officers and enlisted soldiers is virtually complete when the Army is led within institutional boundaries so as to accomplish institutional tasks or goals. Resistance occurs

1. when particular leaders seem to subvert the Army institution and use it as a vehicle for self aggrandizement or self-protection,
2. when the special premises of the Army institution are used to guide behavior outside the Army's socially authorized activities, or
3. when the institution's coercive sanctions demand types or quantities of behavior that undermine the functioning of other legitimate institutions, such as the family.

The Army experience suggests that resistance is created not by domination per se, as Scott seems to imply, but by domination subverted by its use outside its institutional license or domain. Although not viewed this way by Scott, most of the examples of resistance in *Weapons of the Weak* and *Domination and the Arts of Resistance* can be reinterpreted from the perspective that resistance arises from the violation of a shared expectation in the overarching culture regarding the limits of authority and domination within particular social structures, rather than from the pure existence or exercise of authority or domination. Thus, contrary to Scott's assertion that all forms of labor extraction produce resistance, the Army case suggests that authority and its associated domination are culturally legitimate and do not generate resistance if three conditions are met:

1. that the forms of domination within the institution are deemed essential to the survival of the society, and

2. that the institution (through the actions of its participants) remains focused on its charter, maintaining authority and domination strictly within the socially agreed-upon activities defined by the institution's charter, and

3. that the institution does not make such excessive demands that other legitimate institutions are incapacitated.

These conditions are difficult to fulfill in the Army because individual leaders are varied, and someone will likely corrupt the institution, diverting it to illicit, self-serving ends. Alternatively, leaders may use the Army's demand orientation to make excessive, disruptive demands when circumstances clearly do not warrant such effort. In summary, whenever institutional excess is unfettered, self-protective resistance in the interest of survival will indeed appear the human norm, not because hierarchy elicited resistance, but because one institution's excess contradicted and blocked the operation of other legitimate institutions. Institutional excess induces the outwardly weak to protest, and where such communication is suppressed, the weak will resist more subversively. But resistance is not so certain a result as Scott suggests. Indeed, these Army data suggest that alienation and resistance are more closely attuned to the misappropriation or misuse of institutions than to the confiscation of labor (Marx) or the existence of humiliation while under domination (Scott).

On the Reproduction of Culture. Anthony Giddens argues persuasively that much of social behavior in complex society is patterned, understandable response to the accumulated product of unintended consequences.[59]   Among U.S. troops stationed in Germany, anger, withdrawn behavior, and passing inaccurate information up the system seem to exemplify his propositions. In a wide variety of ways, soldiers and spouses reacted to what they felt was inappropriate surveillance and overweening judgment with self-protective behavior that inadvertently drew down upon them further judgment and surveillance. Neither the leaders nor the members of the community got what they intended through their behavior. Rather, cycles of leadership control and personal negativity reproduced each other in multiple layers, so that most participants in the community were drawn into the sticky web that reproduced—indeed amplified—the distress-producing components of the system. At the heart of this self-reproduction lay the OER and EER processes. These two practices oriented those who wished to preserve their careers upward, toward superiors' wishes, rather than downward, toward soldier needs and mission realities. Facing an environment of capricious judgment, radical fusion of domains, the isolation of the American community within Germany, penetration and disruption of the family by duty rosters, and intense pressure from the nearby Soviet threat and from pushy orders, soldiers and spouses tended to react in ways that amplified their isolation and alienation, thereby replicating in themselves the low morale and defensive response patterns that they so detested in others. Thus, unintended consequences have had a profound power to shape further behavior in cycles of structuration that created what Bourdieu might call increasingly objective structures—social relations and social conditions that pressed all the harder on the individual.

On Functionalism, Agency, and Change. Giddens's rejection of the functional integration of society is of course correct. Societies are not holistically integrated, not even in the "classic" (and, I would add, purified) studies of early functionalist anthropologists. Conflict, contradiction, and competition seep into even the most sanitized structural-functional studies. Nevertheless, as Giddens would agree, people understand that there are goals, both individual and sometimes institutional. They make decisions to acquire symbols that state they have arrived at those goals and values. People act as empowered agents within institutional positions to organize and attract or coerce others to help them arrive at goals. They do not always get what they want, for situations are complex and their decisions may have been wrongheaded, or the reaction of others may get in the way of accomplishment, and the ever present unintended consequences frustrate the best-laid plans. But people try, and as custodians of institutions they try, monitor, adjust, and retry. Thus, to react to holistic system-level functionalism by throwing out all functional behavior (which Giddens does not do, but which seems to be the trend in anthropology) seems in error.[60] The central argument of this book, encapsulated in Chapter 4, "Danger Forward, Sir!," is that the socially assigned task—function, if you will—of the Army institution is to be ready to win in combat. In the light of its historical experience of combat (and with allowances for anticipated changes), Army leaders and soldiers have created and tried to monitor an institutional culture that its leaders feel will operate as successfully as possible in what they imagine the combat environment will be like. This corporate or institutional culture inculcates obedience to orders, quick decision making in nondemocratic hierarchical social structures, subordination of the individual to the higher merit of the unit, and uniformity and interchangeability of its human capital, among other attributes.

Thus, there is a thread of ecological functionalism in my presentation that cannot be ignored. The perception of the environment (violent competitive chaos) in which one can survive only by quick communal response drives much of Army organization, culture, and practice. In this, Karl Marx and Julian Steward were right: The organization of production, the cultural presuppositions, and the practices of society must provide for survival within the environment, an environment that includes terrain, resources, technology, population, and climate, as well as the competition and constraint provided by other social and cultural groupings. Were it not for the extremity of risk and the clarity of the Army's function in the coiled, ready, trip-wire outpost frontiers of Germany, I might have missed this ecological aspect of all societal life.

The structural arrangements that implement that readiness, unfortunately, have several unanticipated consequences. For example, duty rosters, created to ensure fair distribution of tasks, in fact disrupt one's private or family life because there are so many duties on differing cycle lengths that one cannot predict when one will be able to plan family time. Likewise, the evaluation system, created to find and keep the best personnel, distorts the flow of information and leadership decisions, creating out of many small distorted decisions a system that appears irrational to many of its soldiers at lower and middle ranks. The whole undermines morale, and that drives out some of the best personnel. What does one make of this theoretically?

In the first place, though Bronislaw Malinowski has been much disparaged for his theories of functionalism, the basic concept of institution—an organization dedicated to a socially recognized charter or task—cannot be abandoned. However bumbling or misdirected their attempts, leaders of institutions try to achieve their institutions' chartered goals. Leaders in this regard act, ideally, as custodians. Malinowski and Radcliffe-Brown were both seriously wrong in their notion that social institutions and practices were essentially harmonious, that practices invariably or even usually led to desired outcomes or produced cohesion, and that societies had needs. This overly cohesive, picture-perfect view of small-scale society has been justly out of favor for many years, beaten down by the detail of Manchester school conflict analyses, the manifest tensions of colonial and capitalist society, and the patently obvious facts of radical change and considerable disorganization in the actual behavior of people in societies of every size.

At the leading edge of modern social analysis, Anthony Giddens has rightly attacked the change-challenged paradigm of structural-functionalism, arguing that only individuals are goal-oriented and that a society's functional orientation is a chimera.[61] I think the Army case, however, amply and clearly shows that the present-day analytical rejection of Malinowski and Radcliffe-Brown caused by the obvious excesses of the heyday of structural-functionalism has in fact been an overreaction. Somewhere midway between the pluperfect rigidity of the functionally integrated society as healthy organism and the total chaos of the unanticipated outcomes of individual self-interest stands a reflexive middle ground where individuals act as custodial agents of, and participants in, organizations, and where they make decisions in terms of an organization, their understanding of its needs, and their conceptions of its goals. In the midst of what Giddens rightly points out as the enormous clutter and drag of unanticipated consequences, individuals recursively and reflexively examine both their own behavior and that of their associates, comparing the overall patterns of outcome with their conceptions of what ought to be or their intuitions of what might be better. No matter the undeniable messiness of unanticipated consequences, functionally oriented behavior by institutional custodians—patterns of choice made for and on behalf of the welfare of the institution and the society at large—this concept is alive and well in Army leadership. And the cycles of alienation which I have detailed likewise presuppose that individuals evaluate their experience against expected ideals and functionally respond to enhance or preserve such values as they can. Thus, the concept of institutional and individual functional evaluation—goal orientation, if you will—needs to be repatriated to the social sciences if its practitioners wish to provide an interpretation of society that resembles the reality of humans acting as agents that, from time to time, evaluate their actions and those of others in terms of socially given goals.

Moreover, people acquire the essence of choice because they engage in daily-changing fields of social interaction within multiple institutions that produce complex, interacting, unpredictable and therefore unanticipated consequences. People must react—play by their "feel for the game," in Bourdieu's phrase—choice makers always.[62] Indeed, the essence of morality and agency arises out of the relation between the multiple pulls of individual, institutional, and surrounding-culture values. The task of morality and the path to social respect of the community consist of making choices that sufficiently sustain the conflicting and even oppositional goals and values of the multiple conflicting institutions.[63]

As they work through the obstacles of unanticipated consequences, sometimes challenging and changing them, sometimes accommodating to them, soldiers and spouses activate change through their own pursuit of a functional—which is to say, more acceptable—outcome. Given societal imperfection due to unintended consequences (among other things), functional logic is, then, an agent of change. Though the old concept of the harmonious, tightly self-maintaining, functionally integrated society did indeed inhibit an examination of change, one need not throw out functionalism to helpfully interpret change. One does need, however, to make functionalism agent-centered, focused on individuals both as individuals and as custodians of institutions in empowered positions of control. Indeed, the irony is that change emerges from the process of choice precisely because individuals, as custodians of institutions and as selves, must weave through the partial chaos of unanticipated consequences, bearing in mind (and sometimes evaluating and rejecting) chartered purpose, to reformat accepted practices, and to reconstitute organizational schemes if these are intuited to be obstacles to the overarching, chartered, legitimate goals.

In short, structure, culture, ecology, function, agency, choice, and change are all tightly interwoven and fully implicated in the daily lives of soldiers and their families. No analysis can afford to be without any of the traditional arrows in the anthropological quiver if it is to adequately hit the mark of portraying humanity.

On the Crisis of Representation. In *Anthropology as Cultural Critique*, George Marcus and Michael Fischer suggest anthropology is experiencing a "crisis of representation." Granted, it is impossible to describe fully or accurately the complexities of another way of life or to understand completely the daily practices, decision-making strategies, and local context of any given individual. The issue is, how best to present or represent a field experience such as it was. The older models of presentation have clear problems (given our current totemic concerns), so the younger practitioners of the discipline consequently are experimenting with a broad range of forms or styles of write-up. How can we as anthropologists present and represent the peoples with whom we have interacted? How do we convey their interaction, what is the nature of that interaction, and how do we give an account of the changes induced by our presence as researchers? How do we describe the subjective feel of the field experience? The questions reveal deep insecurities about the legitimacy of the anthropological enterprise. Marcus and Fischer analyze new experiments in ethnographic writing style, but they do not settle on any particular approach as likely to sustain superior results.[64]

The crises of representation has been fueled by postmodernism's premise that an authoritative interpretation cannot exist.[65] In the absence of any ability to speak with authenticity for or about any other people, one postmodernist trend—reflexive anthropology—concludes we can at least know and write about ourselves. In this view, all we can know for sure is the nature of our own feelings resulting from the challenges inherent in interacting with people bearing another culture. Should we not then simply write about the nature of our own experience and engage in increasingly reflexive anthropology?[66] Emphatically, no! The soldiers and spouses and the military and civilian community leaders who shared their views with me expected more than my ruminations about the day-to-day events and my feelings of the encounter. They wanted to know how to fix things so they or their replacements would not feel so conflicted. Nevertheless, under the influence of reflexive postmodernist thought, our discipline is moving rapidly toward a sophisticated transformation of the travelogue. From Marco Polo's *Travels* to Tocqueville's *Democracy in America* to James Michener's *Iberia: Spanish Travels and Reflections*, wonderful books based on travels and long residence have given us insight into the lives of various peoples. Postmodern ethnologies indeed have added readable, insightful, thought-provoking books that enrich our understanding of the human experience.[67]

But something is missing. There is still a crisis in the discipline of anthropology. Indeed, the crisis is caused precisely because, under the influence of postmodernism, we have lost faith in the possibility of authority and have therefore abandoned the task of evaluation. Thus the "crisis of *representation*" posited by Marcus and Fischer is a misnomer. The concept diverts our attention from the underlying problem. To use a Marxian turn of phrase, the crisis of representation is a false consciousness. The core problem in anthropology is not a failure of *representation*, a failure to determine what topics to describe or what writing style to use. The core problem is, rather, a failure to judge. In a word, the core problem is an acute crisis of *evaluation*.

The process proceeds roughly like this: First we adopt a theory regarding the ethnographic other, primarily because some facet of the other is construed to represent or cause us to reflect on an aspect of our own social predicament or anxiety. Later, when we become bored with a theory's repeated use in ethnographies, we focus on some shortcoming of social theory (easy to find, given the richness of social complexity) vis-à-vis our perceptions of our own society. Meanwhile, we proceed to adopt some new theory that has been generated and becomes generally accepted among the anthropologists of a particular culture area, largely because of its totemic resonance to a more current dilemma or angst emerging from within the society originating the theory. The older theory is relegated, eventually, to a cluttered corner of anthropological history because it did not address well the current angst or issue. The cycle is interpretive and largely a humanistic exercise in cultural narcissism.

I agree with Geertz, nevertheless, that anthropology must be decidedly interpretive and humanistic. Indeed, it can hardly be otherwise. I would suggest, however, that one way we can try to escape the conundrum that theory and ethnography are cultural reproductions of our own anxieties is to try to test the merits of our interpretations. Theories or even specific interpretations of society have implications.

Implications ought to be tested. In saying this, I follow Karl Popper substantially, recognizing that many shortcomings in his work have become clear over the years.[68] Nevertheless, we must find ways to test or evaluate the relative merits of interpretations or they will remain but thought-provoking totems. We must find ways to determine when theories need modification. And, after suggesting modifications or alternatives, we must seek opportunities to test the changes. The refiner's forge for theory will have to be built upon the fires of experiment. In saying this, I suspect—and therefore submit—that anthropology must approximate the use of experiment. To do so, we will probably have to make changes in a social milieu while taking careful account of the before-situation and the after-result.

Of course there are problems with the idea, and the most dedicated interpretivists will mock the suggestion. Indeed, they will say, "How can one use the model of 'hard' science when much of 'hard' science is also a cultural reproduction of the premises of our society?" Rather than be discouraged, we should be heartened by the fact that the hard sciences are like the social sciences, in that they are both culturally rooted. The difference is that the "hard" sciences have used a set of methods whereby they could comparatively test the relative fit between two theories and the evidences of their utility in or fit with the surrounding world, in spite of the wide range of social and cultural factors that often override and make the process less than efficient and straightforward. That is, the hard sciences have been able to comparatively rate the productive yield of their theories. As a result, chemistry has moved from alchemy to the computerized manufacture of designer compounds. Physics has moved from an earth-centered universe to a vastly different cosmology, plumbed by spacecraft. Even the messy sciences—climatology, biology, and geology—become increasingly predictive. In every case, the current theories, although culturally rooted, have been refined, transformed, and held or discarded based, eventually, on utility of predictions. The combination of more successful use or prediction, larger span of explanation, and comparative simplicity tends to drive out the competitors, though the process can be much slowed by social factors, such as hierarchical control by a self-defensive don ensconced in a major university or grant-giving agency.

Again, the interpretivists might ask, "How can the relatively simple experiments of the physical sciences be used as a model when social situations are orders of magnitude more complex?" Physics and chemistry experiments may have been simple fifty or 100 years ago, but today in biology, immunology, space science, human physiology, global weather, and other fields, theories about systems of enormous complexity are regularly tested, through numerous trials and careful statistical analysis. The results are never perfect explanations, but a given theory can be shown to predict better, be more elegant, and embrace more phenomena than its competitors. Something rather similar—an evaluative process—is needed in anthropology to clear the clutter of competing ideological theories that are quasi-religiously embraced. An "experimental moment" is indeed needed, as Marcus and Fischer suggest.[69] Their solution of experimenting with differing modes of both theory and style of writing, although absolutely necessary, is, nevertheless, insufficient. What is needed, rather, is a way to winnow theories, and that will take experiments in applied social change.

Applied social change, however, raises issues of ethics in human experiments. We do not believe we need to acquire permission of the elements to mix them in controlled experiments. We do believe we need the permission of humans. Herein lies the advantage of client-centered applied anthropology. The request and the subsequent co-participation between analyst and group served makes the endeavor ethical.

I submit that social theories indeed can be tested ethically and that it is easiest to do so if the testing is done in the context of *client-requested applied anthropology*, such as this study. In client-requested applied anthropology, a client or class of clients is dissatisfied with a situation and asks for an assessment of the problem and a recommendation of what can be done about it. Admittedly, societies are complex and are obviously composed of multiple participants. Thus, one anthropologist's client might be another group's social antagonist. Some ethical judgment regarding such cases will no doubt be needed from time to time, especially if the client has superordinate control over some other group's resources. In general, however, it is possible to use a theory to identify the likely sources of collectively experienced pain or frustration built into a system. From this theory-suffused description, one then extrapolates a set of recommended changes that seem likely (according to the theory) to bring a reasonable improvement to the widest range of participants possible. For example, as a result of client requests, I have been able to study U.S. Army communities in Germany; describe the interaction of work, marriage, community, and culture (as I have done in Chapters 4 through 12); frame a theory as to the sources of soldier and family member discontent or alienation (in this chapter); and extrapolate from the theory and description several concrete recommendations for changes in Army community structure and process.

But the task is not complete. To test any theory convincingly, this one included, one must measure the impact of the recommendations derived from the theory. To do so, several steps must be taken that follow the fieldwork, analysis, and recommendations for change. First, one must arrange to administer a standardized or repeatable "instrument" to the people requesting the changes. Regarding such an instrument, social scientists must agree that it measures quantitatively some aspect of human well-being or relative discontent, or some working proxy of a people's sense of well-being or discontent. I recognize many problems in the task of measurement and in the nature of what is measured, and therefore speak here only of trying to find a reasonable proxy for well-being. Nevertheless, the well-being of the population must be assessed in a pretest before the suggested changes are instituted. Second, with proper consent and mutual consultation between the analysts and the members of the community contemplating change, one must then implement the changes suggested by the theory if agreed to by the clients. Finally, one must arrange for the readministration of the same measure of well-being after the changes have had time to have their effect and after sufficient time has passed so that the "Hawthorne Effect"—a group's tendency to feel "well-being" if it is being paid attention to, regardless of the nature of the changes—has had a chance to dissipate. Waiting for the Hawthorne Effect to dissipate is relatively easy in the Army, because the rate of personnel turnover gives a nearly complete population replacement every three years. In just one year, the newly arrived "minors" become adults embarking on their second year, and the second-year adults become elders embarking on their third year. The third-year elders become ghosts as they depart the community at the beginning of a fourth year. At that point, virtually no one but civilian support staff remains from the period when the changes were introduced. The new arrivals to the community will experience the changes as a natural state of affairs rather than as an experimental state in which one is being "paid attention to."

For example, if the strength of the approach taken in this book is to be evaluated, one would organize a pretest of the well-being of the soldiers and family members in several American military communities in Germany. Military leaders would then discuss with the community members the recommendations presented earlier in this chapter and implement as many of them as possible. The communities could be paired, so that each pair was as similar as possible in its military units and activities. For each pair, changes would be made in one of the communities, whereas the other would be maintained unchanged for a period of time as a control group. Finally, there would be a retest of both the changed and control communities. If this is done, the theory undergirding the suggested changes could be partially evaluated.

Just what would be tested or evaluated if the above procedure were followed with regard to my work in Germany? First, one would test the merit of separating premises into layers of general cultural premises and specific institutional premises. Second, one would test the notion that institutions have premise deviations tuned to the functional requirements of accomplishing their institutional charter. In short, one would test the legitimacy of reviving the much maligned concept of chartered functionality, repatriating it to the anthropological conversation or casting it out as a productive analytical tool. Third, one would test the utility of reintegrating ecological analysis with cultural and social structural perspectives. And fourth, one would test these rather non-Marxian ideas of the psychological consequences of internal premise contradiction and institutionalized role conflict. All of these propositions have been demanded, in my view, by the Army community data. Although I am the first to admit I have not presented a tight or explicit theory, the suggestions for change have been driven by these basic perspectives. By testing the actual consequences of the proposed changes, we would directly judge the overarching approach, and the process certainly would set a worthwhile standard for testing the consequences of other qualitative theories.

Should such an evaluation procedure turn out to be effective and bring about test-based confirmations or rejections of theory repeatedly, applied anthropology would likely shift from its current position at the periphery of the academic discipline to the theoretical center, as applied anthropology would be the only component of sociocultural anthropology able to submit theories to tested refutation and reformation, problematic though this idea is.

My colleague John Clark, in personal communication, points out that applied anthropology may well have an advantage of providing a context for testing theory. But this would constitute a decided advantage only if there were no other valid way to test theory or evaluate ethnography. Of course there are other criteria for the comparative evaluation of theory. These include internal coherence, simplicity, comprehensiveness, and the stimulation of fruitful new concepts, among other attributes. Such criteria may well help considerably. Indeed, Giddens uses an implicit notion of comprehensiveness (the theory covers more phenomena) when he critiques structural-functionalism for its failure to include obvious data regarding the experience of individual agency. Nevertheless, the history of anthropology seems to suggest that the perception of coherence, simplicity, and comprehensiveness is easily influenced by our interest in creating self-explanatory totemism. These ancillary criteria of good theory are so qualitative that their relative presence or absence can be misconstrued easily.

At another level of analysis, the postmodernists will think me naive to the point of being daft in suggesting the possibility of testing something so fickle as theory in an environment as complex as society. After all, "Post-modernists . . . no longer make a distinction between what is happening and its interpretation. There is no Real World with which different theories can be compared to find out if they are correct."[70] But I suspect testing can be done, and the military is a particularly likely place to be able to succeed precisely because it is segmental (fractal, repetitive) in the anthropological sense, and therefore presents paired units at every level of its structure, available as test group and control. Moreover, I am not worried in the slightest by the postmodernists' denial of the "Real World" or their having given up on the distinction between fact and fiction. Warfare would restore their belief in such distinctions and realities, as would an examination of their behavior were one of their representatives to try to walk across a busy freeway. In either case, reality will soon intrude if the cultural assumptions are not reasonably accurate.

Why, one might ask, must the process of social theory testing entail applied, intrusive, change-oriented anthropology? Can not other styles of anthropological inquiry study a situation and offer legitimate insight without the need for intrusion by change? To be sure, many of the approaches that have been used in anthropology have offered significant insights. Lacking persuasive forms of evaluation, however, we remain stuck in the vortex of totemism. Does the insight feel profound because it speaks to our anxieties, or because the theory really works? Only a careful test can discern the difference.

THE RECIPROCITY OF ESCAPE FROM ALIENATION

Any community that engages in the process of being analyzed anthropologically, tested with implemented change, and reinvestigated enters a cycle of reciprocal exchange with the community of anthropologists. For example, my experience observing and thinking about the American military communities in Germany has changed me, enticing me to a more complex repatriation of the founding ideas of anthropology. It has forced me to see that culture, structure, function, agency, and environment are mutually essential to understanding the human condition generally and to describing the specific processes that have made discontentment structurally endemic in U.S. Army communities. Because I have benefited from what the Army community has taught me, I owe a reciprocal exchange. Ideally, this description and analysis will provide both a set of principles and a hint of the kinds of changes that members of the Army community might evaluate, modify, and choose to implement. If the recommended changes are made and *if the communities in which the changes are made are compared through adequate pre- and post-testing to similar communities where no changes were made,* the military community acquires a robust set of principles with which to evaluate further increments of self-change. Conversely, the anthropological community acquires a setting and a robust approach to reforming its own concepts of structure, culture, agency, and behavioral process. One hopes that the Army community—or any other community that enters the process—will be changed in ways it would have wanted but seemed unable to accomplish by itself, by understanding better how to structure unit, family, and community interaction so as to enhance both mission effectiveness and the population's sense of well-being. Conversely, if the "before the change" and "after the change" conditions and perceptions are carefully documented both qualitatively and quantitatively (though, for test purposes, quantitative measures are now more important), then the structural process of change that the Army community wants for itself will simultaneously facilitate a process of theoretical change in the community of anthropologists. The change that will come to anthropology is, similarly, a change that anthropologists want but seem unable to accomplish by themselves. They must refine theory and develop a community of agreement based on a way to evaluate their representations. This requires the anthropologist to interact intensely with an interested, honest, willing community. That certainly has been the case with these soldiers, their families, and the community leaders in Germany. The two communities may thus enter a relationship of organic reciprocity, for each community provides the other with the understanding that it needs to change the structures that have made its own discontent endemic. Indeed, only out of such reciprocity can the members of either community hope to discover the culturally camouflaged sources of their own alienation.

NOTES

1. Most Americans knew they were charged more for renting an apartment than a German would have been charged for the same facility, though few knew the reason. Most felt that the higher rents gave evidence of German dislike of and discrimination toward Americans, conditions to be tolerated silently to avoid offense in the host country.

2. *Stars and Stripes* (hereafter *S&S*), 2 August 1987, 15.

3. *S&S*, 18 October 1986, 11. The two couples issued the letter jointly.

4. *S&S*, 26 May 1987, 11.

5. Chuck Vinch, "35 U.S. bases, 12 abroad due to close," *S&S*, 30 January 1990, 1. Note that the *Stars and Stripes* switched its headline capitalization style to lowercase except for proper nouns.

6. Chuck Vinch, "Here's the hit list; Pentagon names 150 sites set to close," *S&S*, 19 September 1990, 1, 9.

7. Jimi Jones, "Closure worries leave schools up in the air," *S&S*, 20 September 1990, 2; "Communities react to news they're on Pentagon hit list," *S&S*, 20 September 1990, 3.

8. Rosemary Sawyer, "For some, there are few qualms about going home," *S&S*, 21 September 1990, 3.

9. Gary Pomeroy, "Chain of concern links families left behind by gulf-bound GIs," *S&S*, 21 September 1990, 9.

10. Ibid., 9.

11. Ken Clauson, "Berlin Comd [Command] deactivated," *S&S*, 2 October 1990, 1; Ken Clauson, "End of the road for Checkpoint Alpha, Tiny, remote post closes 44 years of allied history," *S&S*, 2 October 1990, 9.

12. "Reunited Germans celebrate," *S&S*, 3 October 1990, 1.

13. "Bundestag formally ends Allies' rights," *S&S*, 6 October 1990, 1.

14. Unpublished computer list from the Base Realignment and Closing Office, the Pentagon, May 1996.

15. The information in this paragraph is a synthesis of unpublished documents supplied by the Base Realignment and Closing Office and the USAREUR Liaison Office, both in the Pentagon, through April 1996.

16. *Army Times*, 2 January 1995, 20, 41; USAREUR Liaison Office, the Pentagon, Washington DC.

17. United States Army Europe, *America's Army in Europe: On Point for the Nation*, occasional pamphlet, circa October 1999, 3.

18. "Leaders close 'previous age' by signing historic CFE [Conventional Forces in Europe] treaty," *S&S*, 20 November 1990, 1.

19. United States Army Europe, *U.S. Army Europe & 7th Army: 1996* (Heidelberg, Germany: Public Affairs Office, Headquarters, U.S. Army Europe, 1996): 11.

20. *Army Times*, 30 October 1995, 23, apparently based on data in United States Army Europe, *U.S. Army Europe & 7th Army: 1995*, 4–5.

21. *Army Times,* 30 October 1995, 23.

22. United States Army Europe, *U.S. Army Europe & 7th Army: 1995* (Heidelberg, Germany: Public Affairs Office, Headquarters, U.S. Army Europe, 1995): 4–5. This volume gives the figures as 11,851 soldiers deployed prior to 1989, with 21,883 soldiers deployed after 1989. *Army Times* may have used updated figures.

23. United States Army Europe, "Today's USAREUR," USAREUR briefing slides, CGSCAWC 5/11/95, slide 26. The slides were given to me by the Pentagon USAREUR Liaison Office, but are sublabeled as though created for or used by the Command and General Staff College system.

24. Donna Miles, "Upping the Tempo," *Soldiers* 50, no. 6 (June 1995): 14–17, reports high operating tempo within the United States, approaching 50 percent of soldier time spent away from home on training or deployment. The then outgoing Chief of Staff of the Army, General Gordon R. Sullivan, is summarized as saying, "[W]hile the Army has reduced its force by one-third its operational missions have increased a full 300 percent" (14). Referring to U.S.-based forces, Colonel Michael Starry, director of the Future Battle Directorate, TRADOC (Training and Doctrine Command) is summarized: "The Army's aim is to design units that can deploy anywhere from the United States within 48 to 72 hours, and be powerful enough to win the battle once on the ground" (Sean D. Naylor, "What the future holds . . .," *Army Times*, 17 March 1997, 20).

25. Claude Lévi-Strauss, *Totemism*, trans. Rodney Needham (Boston: Beacon Press, 1963): 89.

26. Larry Ingraham, "The OER Cudgel: Radical Surgery Needed," *Army*, November 1985: 55–56.

27. A recent interview suggests competitive board selection for BASOPS commander is now the case, and a definite improvement, but this does not mean that assignment to the position is considered "career enhancing." (Personal communication with a former BASOPS commander, October 1999, the Pentagon.)

28. The process of making German medical facilities more available had begun in the community of Middleberg in the closing month of my fieldwork. Just how the process may have continued I do not know.

29. This practice may already be in place in some areas. (Personal communication with a recent BASOPS commander, October 1999, the Pentagon.)

30. Christina Maslach and Susan E. Jackson, "Burned-Out Cops and Their Families," *Psychology Today* (May 1979): 59–62.

31. Ibid., 59.

32. Ibid., 61.

33. Ibid., 61.

34. On the separation of military from civilian citizenry, see Charles H. Coates and Roland J. Pellegrin. *Military Sociology: A Study of American Military Institutions and Military Life* (College Park, MD: The Social Science Press, 1965).

35. Maslach and Jackson, "Burned-Out Cops," 62.

36. Select Committee on Children, Youth, and Families, House of Representatives, *On the Front Lines: Police Stress and Family Well-Being* (Washington, DC: U.S. Government Printing Office, 1991): 15.

37. Ibid., 15.

38. Ibid., 19.

39. Ibid., 30.

40. Ibid., 29.

41. Ibid., 34.

42. Judi Marshall, "Stress Amongst Nurses," *White Collar and Professional Stress*, ed. Cary L. Cooper and Judi Marshall (New York: John Wiley and Sons, 1980): 19–59.

43. Mady Weschsler Segal, "The Military and the Family as Greedy Institutions," *Armed Forces and Society* 13, no. 1 (1986): 9–38.

44. Lewis A. Coser, *Greedy Institutions: Patterns of Undivided Commitment* (New York: The Free Press, 1974): 4.

45. Erving Goffman, *Asylums: Essays on the Social Situation of Mental Patients and Other Inmates* (Garden City, NY: Anchor Books, 1961): xiii.

46. Ibid., 5–6.

47. Ibid., 123–124.

48. Ibid., 12.

49. Ibid., 13.

50. Charles C. Moskos and Frank R. Wood, eds., *The Military: More than Just a Job?* (Washington, DC: Pergamon-Brassey's International Defense Publishers, 1988): 15–26.

51. Michel Foucault, *Discipline and Punish: The Birth of the Prison* (New York: Pantheon Books, 1977). See plates 3–7 following page 169, and pages 200–202.

52. My thanks to Eugene Mendonsa, personal communication, for reminding me that the ancestor spirits are continual observers of the human condition and reliable punishers of infraction. For ethnographic examples, see Eugene L. Mendonsa, *The Politics of Divination: A Processual View of Reactions to Illness and Deviance Among the Sisala of Northern Ghana* (Berkeley: University of California Press, 1982) and John Middleton, *Lugbara Religion; Ritual and Authority among an East African People* (London:

International African Institute by the Oxford University Press, 1964).

53. Anthony Giddens, *The Giddens Reader,* ed. Philip Cassell (Stanford, CA: Stanford University Press, 1993): 92–101.

54. There are, of course, some true cultural enclaves in American society. Among them, one might include the Hutterites, the Navajos, and sometimes, the senior generations of immigrants living in social ghettos. But authentic cultural enclaves are not as common as the American cultural premise of distinctiveness would have us believe. A cultural enclave must have fundamental general premise differences and not just institutional premise differences or differences in environmentally contingent procedures or concepts.

55. Such role conflict was long ago described by anthropologists on both sides of the Atlantic.

56. Pierre Bourdieu, *The Logic of Practice*, trans. Richard Nice (Stanford, CA: Stanford University Press, 1990).

57. Bourdieu, *The Logic of Practice.*

58. One might argue that the enlisted, in accepting their situation, have simply absorbed a false consciousness foisted upon them. This seems an inadequate approach for two reasons. First, it does not explain why soldiers disagree with officers in the cases that they do. Second, the attribution of false consciousness to that which does not fit one's theory makes the theory impossible to challenge with any ethnographic data.

59. Anthony Giddens, "Functionalism: après la lutte," *Studies in Social and Political Theory* (London: Hutchinson & Co., 1977): 123; Giddens, *Central Problems in Social Theory: Action, Structure and Contradiction in Social Analysis* (Berkeley, Los Angeles: University of California Press, 1979): 56 and throughout his work.

60. Giddens, "Functionalism," 123.

61. Anthony Giddens, *Central Problems,* 75–87; *The Giddens Reader*, ed. Philip Cassell, 89.

62. Pierre Bourdieu, *The Logic of Practice*, trans. Richard Nice (Stanford, CA: Stanford University Press, 1990).

63. Charles W. Nuckolls, *Culture: A Problem that Cannot be Solved* (Madison, WI: University of Wisconsin Press, 1998).

64. George E. Marcus and Michael M. J. Fischer, *Anthropology As Cultural Critique: An Experimental Moment in the Human Sciences* (Chicago: University of Chicago Press, 1986).

65. Pauline Marie Rosenau, *Post Modernism and the Social Sciences: Insights, Inroads, and Intrusions* (Princeton NJ: Princeton University Press, 1992).

66. Eugene Mendonsa, in personal communication, points out that under the assumptions of postmodernism, we cannot even know our own feelings, or at any rate, we cannot communicate them reliably to others and perhaps not even to ourselves, hence the irony of writing books to convey the feel of the field experience.

67. The primary thing "new" about reflexive anthropology is the term with which it is labeled and the openness with which it is practiced. Excellent studies in the mode of reflexive anthropology long predate the current fad. See, for example, Bronislaw Malinowski, introduction to *Argonauts of the Western Pacific* (New York: E. P. Dutton, 1961 [1922]). Evans-Pritchard and his thoughts and feelings stand central to the cross-cultural understanding of *Witchcraft, Oracles, and Magic Among the Azande* (Oxford: Oxford University Press, 1937). Laura Bohannan perhaps felt nervous about her reflexivity in *Return to Laughter: An Anthropological Novel* (Garden City, NY: Anchor Books, 1964) or perhaps she simply wanted to keep her personal feelings separate from her analytical craft. In any event, she published under a pseudonym: Elenore Smith Bowen. See also the reflexive classics of culturally contextualized humor, such as Richard Lee's "Eating

Christmas in the Kalahari" *Natural History* (December 1969): 14–22, 60–63, or Laura Bohannan's "Shakespeare in the Bush," *Natural History* (August/September 1966): 28–33.

68. Karl Popper, *The Logic of Scientific Discovery* (New York: Harper Torchbooks, 1959) and *Conjectures and Refutations: The Growth of Scientific Knowledge* (New York: Harper Torchbooks, 1963).

69. Marcus and Fischer, *Anthropology As Cultural Critique*, 40–44.

70. Karin Geuijen, Raven Diederick, and Jan de Wolf, introduction to *Post-Modernism and Anthropology: Theory and Practice*, ed. by Karin Geuijen, Raven Diederick, and Jan de Wolf (Assen, The Netherlands: Van Gorcum, 1995): ix–xxvi.

Appendix I: Acronyms

ACRONYM[1]	USE[2]	EXPANSION
1LT	E	First Lieutenant (O2)
1SG	E	First Sergeant (E8) (Not technically an official rank, but the term is so used for the position of senior company NCO)
2LT	E	Second Lieutenant (O1)
AAFES	W	Army Air Force Exchange System ['a-fēs] (procurement, management, and sales system for all nonsubsidized commercial products sold on-post for family or personal use)
ACS	L	Army Community Services
ADCO	W	Alcohol and Drug Control Officer ['adc ō]
ADFC	L	Assistant Division Forward Commander (ie., the division XO)
AIT	L	Advanced Individual Training
AVF	L	All Volunteer Force
AWOL	W or L	Absent Without Leave ['ā-wäl]
BASOPS	W	Base Operations ['bās-åps] (a unit equivalent to a super-sized military community and its subcommunities)
BDU	L	Battle Dress Uniform
BEQ	L	Bachelor Enlisted Quarters
BG	E	Brigadier General
BOQ	L	Bachelor Officer Quarters
BS	L	Bullshit
BSB	L	Base Support Battalion (the unit tasked with administering a community or subcommunity)

CDC	L	Child Development Center (on-post child care center)
CHAMPUS	W	Civilian Health and Medical Program of the Uniformed Services ['cham-pəs]
CMAA	?	Civilian Misconduct Action Authority
COB	L	Close of Business (the end of the workday)
COHORT	W	Cohesion, Operational Readiness, Training ['k ō-hōrt]
COL	E	Colonel (O6)
COLA	W	Cost of Living Allowance ['k ō-lə]
CONUS	W	Continental United States ['k ōn- əs]
CPL	E	Corporal (E4)
CPO	L	Civilian Personnel Office
CPT	E	Captain (O3)
CQ	L	Charge of Quarters, a person responsible for night watch duty in a building or area
CSM	E	Command Sergeant Major (E9)
CW2	E	Chief Warrant Officer Two
CW3	E	Chief Warrant Officer Three
CW4	E	Chief Warrant Officer Four
CYA	L	Cover Your Ass
DCC	L	Deputy Community Commander
DEH	L	Directorate of Engineering and Housing
DIO	L	Directorate of Industrial Operations
DM	L or E	Deutsche Mark (German currency unit)
DOD	E	Department of Defense
DODDS	W	Department of Defense Dependent Schools ['dä-dz]
DPCA	L	Directorate of Personnel and Community Affairs
DWI	L	Driving While Intoxicated
E1, E2, E3, . . . E9	L	Enlisted pay grades of increasing rank. See Table 2.2.
EDCO	W	Education Coordinating Officer ['ed-k ō]
EER	L	Enlisted Evaluation Report
EM	L	Enlisted Man/men
ET	L	European Theater
ETO	L	European Theater of Operations
EUCOM	W	European Command ['yü-käm]
FACMT	L	Family Action Case Management Team
FCC	L	Family Child Care (a military-certified home child care provider system)
FM	L	Field Manual
G1, G2, G3, G4	L	Correspond to S1, S2, S3, S4, but at the division rather than battalion level
GE	L	Germany
GEN	E	General (O10)
GI	L	Government Issue, a metonym for an American soldier
HQ	L	Headquarters
HRO	L	Housing Referral Office
IC	L	Installation Coordinator
ID	L	Identification
IG	L	Inspector General
JAG	W	Judge Advocate General [jaig] (the military's legal services department and officer-lawyers)

LTC	E	Lieutenant Colonel (O5)
LTG	E	Lieutenant General (O9)
M-16	L	The U.S. Army's standard issue infantry automatic rifle
MAJ	E	Major (O4)
MG	E	Major General (O8)
MG		Military Government
MI	L	Military Intelligence
MOS	L	Military Occupational Specialty
MP	L	Military Police
MSG	E	Master Sergeant (E8)
MW5	E	Master Warrant Officer Five
NATO	W	North Atlantic Treaty Organization ['nai-tō]
NBC	L	Nuclear, Biological, Chemical
NCO	L	Noncommissioned Officer (E5–E9)
NCOIC	L	Noncommissioned Officer In Charge
NEO	W	Noncombatant Evacuation Office ['nē- ō]
NTC	L	National Training Center
O1, O2, O3. . .O10	L	Officer pay grades of increasing rank. See Table 2.1.
OB-GYN	L	Obstetrics-Gynecology
OCONUS	W	Outside the CONtinental United States [ō-'k ōn- əs]
OCWC	L	Officers' and Civilian Wives' Club
OER	L	Officer Evaluation Report
OHA	L	Overseas Housing Allowance
OIC	L	Officer in Charge
OMGUS		Office of Military Government of the United States for Germany
P&N	L	Psychiatry and Neurology (clinic in military hospitals responsible for treatment of psychological, psychiatric, and neurological disorders)
PCS	L	Permanent Change of Station
PFC	E	Private First Class (E3)
POMS	W	Post-Operation Maintenance Services [päms]
PT	L	Physical Training
PTA	L	Parent-Teacher Association
PVT	E	Private (E1 and E2)
PX	L	Post Exchange (a military-operated department store)
RAF	L	Royal Air Force
RIF	W or L	Reduction in Force [rif]
ROTC	L or W	Reserve Officer Training Corps [' rät-s ē]
S&S		*Stars and Stripes* (newspaper abbreviation coined for this book)
S1	L	Staff officer in charge of personnel administration at battalion level
S2	L	Staff officer in charge of intelligence at battalion level
S3	L	Staff officer in charge of operations at battalion level
S4	L	Staff officer in charge of logistics at battalion level
SFC	E	Sergeant First Class (E7)
SGT	E	Sergeant (E5)
SOFA	W	Status of Forces Agreement ['s ō-fə]
SOP	L	Standing Operating Procedure

SP4	E	Specialist Fourth Class (E4), Specialist Four
SPO	W	Security, Plans, and Operations Division [spō, spōd]
SSG	E	Staff Sergeant (E6)
TDA	L	Table of Distribution and Allowances
TDY	L	Temporary Duty
TLA	L	Temporary Living Allowance
UCMJ	L	Uniform Code of Military Justice
USAFE		United States Air Force Europe
USAMRU-E	W	U.S. Army Medical Research Unit—Europe [yü-'sam-rü-' ē]
USAREUR	W	United States Army Europe ['yü-sər-ə]
USFET		Unites States Forces European Theater
VAT	W or L	Value-Added Tax [vat]
WD		War Department
WEU		Western European Union
WO1	L	Warrant Officer (One)
WRAIR	W	Walter Reed Army Institute of Research [rer]
WWII		World War II
XO	L	Executive Officer (second in command of a unit)

NOTES

1. To assist international readers, I have added a few nonmilitary acronyms that are now standard English.

2.   E = Used fully expanded.

L = Used by naming the letters in rapid succession.

W = Used as a word, with the acronym letters melded. Pronunciation provided [in brackets] following the expanded term, using diacritic symbols according to *Webster's Ninth New Collegiate Dictionary* (Springfield, MA: Merriam-Webster Inc., 1990): 42.

For acronyms from WWII, I leave the use column blank because I do not know for sure the common soldier's usage in speech.

Appendix II: Principal Consultants

Pseudo-surname	Rank*	Pseudo first names		Remarks	Community**	Sample***	Race
		Soldier	Spouse				
Anderson	Mr.	Ken		Middleberg DPCA	M	L	W
Anthony	CPT	Wade		company commander	R	L	W
Ashton	SGT	Rick	Cindy	met at party	N	S	W
Atwood	SP4 & SP4	Jeff	Betty	dual military couple	M	M	W
Baldwin	SFC	Arthur		platoon sergeant	R	L	
Barnes	SSG	Frank	Meg		R	G	B
Bateman	LTC	Keith		mech. infantry battalion commander	R	L	W
Bracken	SGT	Larry	Marla		M	G	W
Bramwell	Mr.	Steve		social worker	M	L	W
Brenton	CW3	Don	Kathy	wife was ACS volunteer coordinator	M	G	W
Brimley			Oprah	ACS financial adviser; married to an NCO	R	L	B
Buckley	MAJ	Eric		judge advocate, FACMT	M	L	W
Call	LTC	Douglas		DCC Sudberg	S	L	W

Carson	COL	Felix		Welby General Hospital manager	W	L/M	W
Chalmers	SGT	Mack	Donna	Friends of Barnes	R	S	B
Clifford	LTC	Manny		General Barracks clinic commnder	G	L/M	W
Cobb	SSG	Nate	Gwen		R	G	W
Cooper	CPT	Glen	Jane	Richberg dentist	R	G	W
Cornell	CPT	Darren		BN & community chaplain (Protestant)	R	L	W
Cutler	CSM	Barry		community CSM	R	L	W
Damon	SSG	Don	Sally		R	G	B
Davis	LTC	Nevin		regional dental commander	W	L/M	W
Donahue	SSG	Mary			R	L	
Doty	MAJ	Spencer		psychiatrist	W	L/M	W
Evanson	SSG	Alan		night watch	R	S	W
Farley			Kim	first ACS director	R	L	W
Farnsworth	PFC	Nolan		night watch, a medic	R	S	W
Farr	SFC	Darwin		platoon sergeant	R	L	
Felsted	SGT	Scott			M	G	
Finley	CPT	Andy		dental clinic commander	M	L	W

Surname	Rank	First	Name	Notes	C	L	W
Foote	Mr.	Trevor		Grossberg social work supervisor		L	W
Frazier	SFC	James			R	L	
Gomez	1SG	Enrique		first sergeant	R	L	H
Goodwin	COL	Lee		medical commander of Welby General	W	L/M	W
Granville	SGT	Edgar	Anne		M	M	B
Green	CPL	Winston			R	S	W
Green	1SG	Floyd			M	L	B
Griggs	Mrs.	Tanya		Army Family Services chief	M	L	W
Halverson	CPT	Earl			M	L	W
Hamilton	SGT&SGT		Carla	dual military couple	R	S	B/W
Hammond	CPL	Ron	Beth		N	S	
Hansen	CPL	Craig	Rebecca		M	E	W
Hatch	SSG	Gary			R-PV	H	
Hickman	1SG	Gerald		first sergeant	R	L	
Hill	SGT	John	Pam		S	S	W
Howard	CPL	Richard	Yvette		R	G	B
Ivie			Christina	second ACS director, wife of senior sgt.	R	L	B

Last	Rank	First	Spouse	Notes			
Jasper	SGT	Todd		night watch interview	R	S	B
Keele	COL	Wayne		chief Army psychiatrist in Germany	L	L/M	W
Kezerian	1SG	Grant			M	G	
Kimball	MAJ	Rodney	Elsie	brigade staff officer	M	M	W
Koford	SFC	Mike			R	L	
Lawson	CPT	Peter		JAG officer	R	L	W
Lincoln	Maj	Ralph	Shirley	company commander, then BN staff. Shirley was formerly a company commander	S	S	B
Lind			Deena	ACS director	M	L	W
Mantock	WO	Vance	Fay		M	M	W
Marshall	SFC	Brian			M	L	
Martinez	SFC	Ricardo	Julia	platoon sergeant	M	G	H
Masterson	1LT	Russ			N	L	W
McCormick	CW3	Bill	Gretchen	Gretchen was from Germany.	M	G	W
McDonald	MSG	Oscar	Susan	former 1SG	R	G	B
McDugal	1LT	Larry	Lani		N	L	W

					R	E	B/W
McGregory	SGT	Sam	Jean				
Mercer	SP4	Stan	Chris		M	E	W
Morrow	MSG	Nick		in community command cadre	R	L	W
Newell	LTC	Max	Nancy	DCC	R	L	W
Norton	SGT	Adam	Barbara		R	G	W
Olsen	CPT	Bill		COHORT company commander,	M	L	W
Orton			Frances	statistician, MP station	G	L	W
Owens	1LT	Ivan			R	L	
Park	1LT	Calvin			R	L	
Parry	SFC	Kenneth		ACS NCO assistant	M	L	W
Parsons	COL	Bert		senior psychiatrist, Welby Gen. Hos.	W	L/M	W
Paul	1LT		Hilda	ACS jobs coordinator, wife of 1LT	M	L	W
Penrod	1SG	Ray			M	L	
Peterson	SFC	Zeke		platoon sergeant	M	G	W
Pile	SP4	Joe			R	S	W
Powell	1SG	Stewart			M	L	B
Quilter	1LT	Irving			N	L	W

Renquist	Mr.	Harvey		director of and counselor in Community Counseling Center, retired military	M	L	W
Robbins	CW3	Kevin		TMC physician's assistant	R	L	W
Rodgers	SSG	Victor	Ruth		R-PV	H	B
Roper	1SG	Evan			M	L	B
Salinas	SGT	Juan			M	E	H
Scott	MAJ	Quintin		chief chaplain, Grossberg region	C	L	W
Simmons	LTC	Clyde		social work commander	W	L/M	W
Sims			Linda	HRO volunteer, wife of senior sgt.	R	L	W
Smith	1LT	Curtis			M	L	W
Soto	CPT	Francisco		BN chaplain, and community chaplain, (Catholic)	R	L	H
Stanley	Mr.	Walter		acting DCC, then DCC's assistant. retired military	M	L	W
Stewart			Denise	deputy ACS director	R	L	
Strong	SSG	Jeremy	Claire		M	E	B
Tall	CPT	Patrick		deputy DCC	R	L	W

Tanner	SFC	Alex			R	L	
Taylor	MAJ	Matthew	Abigail		M	G	W
Thompson	CPL	Mike	Laura		M	E	W
Ulman	SGT	Shane		yard crew	R	S	W
Vinney	1LT	Hal			R	S	W
Vogel	Mr.	Carl		regional drug and alcohol head	W	L/M	W
Walsh	E4	Hank	Terry		M	E	W
Walters			Afton	ACS deputy director	R	L	
Warnock	SGT	Ian	Emma		M	S	W
Waters	MAJ	Tim			A	L	W
Watkins	BG	Nathan	Cynthia	wife of Middleberg's commanding general	M	L	W
Webster	SSG	Martin		night watch	R	S	
Wilde			Holly	ACS volunteer, wife of senior NCO	M	L	W
Williams	1SG	Omar			M	L	
Yardley			Nikole	BN commander's wife	M	S	W
Yates	CSM	Henry		Grossberg community CSM	C	L	B

				R	L	W
Zark	ILT	David				
Zeller		Victoria	officer's wife	C	S	W
Ziegler	SSG	Jane	female squad leader	M	L	B

* A "rank" of Mr. or Mrs. indicates that the person was a civilian employee of the Department of Defense, hired directly rather than as a "spouse [of military] hire." If rank is blank, the person interviewed is a "spouse hire," but I did not interview the employee's military spouse.

**
A = Alpenberg
C = Central Barracks, the administrative center of Grossberg Military Community
G = General Barracks
L = Lanstule Military Hospital, not a pseudonym
M = Middleberg Military Community
N = Newberg Military Community
R = Richberg Military Community
R-PV = Patriot Village , soldier serving at Richberg Barracks
S = Sudberg Military Community
W = Welby General Hospital, the central facility of Welby Military Community

***
G = From 5 percent random sample of persons living in on-post Government housing.
E = From attempt to interview all persons living in selected German villages at varying distances from Middleberg and Richberg.
S = "Snowball" sample. These are people I bumped into in the course of conducting fieldwork and living life in the military community. Often I did not know their names, and the interaction varied from several hours contact (rarely that long) to a few moments shared at a bus stop.
L = From deliberate effort to interview leaders of military units and civilian-staffed social support organizations.
M = Persons interviewed because they were frequent users of the medical system's resources.

311

Bibliography

Army Times. January 1994–December 1997. Springfield, VA: Army Times Publishing Company.

Base Realignment and Closing Office. Unpublished computer printout of base closings. Washington, DC: The Pentagon, 1996.

Bassford, Christopher. *The Spit Shine Syndrome.* Westport, CT: Greenwood Press, 1988.

Bellah, Robert, Richard Madsen, William M. Sullivan, Ann Swidler, and Steven M. Tipton. *Habits of the Heart: Individualism and Commitment in American Life.* New York: Harper & Row, 1985.

Bering, Henrik. *Outpost Berlin: The History of the American Military Forces in Berlin, 1945–1994.* Chicago: Edition Q, 1995.

Bohannan, Laura [Elenore Smith Bowen, pseud.]. *Return to Laughter: An Anthropological Novel.* Garden City, NY: Anchor Books, 1964 (1954).

———. "Shakespeare in the Bush." *Natural History* (August/September 1966): 28–33.

Bourdieu, Pierre. *The Logic of Practice.* Translated by Richard Nice. Stanford, CA: Stanford University Press, 1990.

Campbell, J. K. *Honour, Family, and Patronage.* New York: Oxford University Press, 1964.

Cincinnatus (pseud.). *Self-Destruction.* New York: Norton, 1981.

Coates, Charles H., and Roland J. Pellegrin. *Military Sociology: A Study of American Military Institutions and Military Life.* College Park, MD: The Social Science Press, 1965.

Coser, Lewis A. *Greedy Institutions: Patterns of Undivided Commitment.* New York: The Free Press, 1974.

Department of the Army. *Study on Military Professionalism.* Carlisle Barracks, PA: U.S. Army War College, 1970.

———. *FM 100-5, Operations.* Washington, DC: Department of the Army, May 1986.

Duke, Simon. *United States Military Forces and Installations in Europe.* Oxford: Oxford University Press / Stockholm International Peace Research Institute, 1989.

Durkheim, Emile. *The Rules of Sociological Method*. New York: The Free Press, 1964.

Epstein, Joshua M. *Conventional Force Reductions: A Dynamic Assessment*. Washington, DC: The Brookings Institution, 1990.

Evans-Pritchard, E. E. *Witchcraft, Oracles, and Magic Among the Azande*. Oxford: Oxford University Press, 1937.

Foster, George. "Peasant Society and the Image of the Limited Good." *American Anthropologist* 67 (1965): 293–315.

Foucault, Michel. *Discipline and Punish: The Birth of the Prison*. New York: Pantheon Books, 1977.

Gabriel, Richard A., and Paul L. Savage. *Crisis in Command*. New York: Hill & Wang, 1978.

Garrett, James M. *The Tenuous Balance: Conventional Forces in Central Europe*. Boulder, CO: Westview Press, 1989.

Geertz, Clifford. "Thick Description: Toward an Interpretive Theory of Culture." In *The Interpretation of Cultures: Selected Essays*, 3–30. New York: Basic Books, 1973.

German Bundestag. *Questions on German History*. Bonn: German Bundestag Press, 1984.

Geuijen, Karin, Raven Diederick, and Jan de Wolf. Introduction to *Post-Modernism and Anthropology: Theory and Practice*, ix–xxvi. Edited by Karin Geuijen, Raven Diederick, and Jan de Wolf. Assen, The Netherlands: Van Gorcum, 1995.

Giddens, Anthony. "Functionalism: après la lutte." In *Studies in Social and Political Theory*. London: Hutchinson & Co., 1977.

———. *Central Problems in Social Theory: Action, Structure and Contradiction in Social Analysis*. London: Macmillan Publishers, Ltd., 1979.

———. *The Giddens Reader*. Edited by Philip Cassell. Stanford, CA: Stanford University Press, 1993.

Goffman, Erving. *Asylums: Essays on the Social Situation of Mental Patients and Other Inmates*. Garden City, NY: Anchor Books, 1961.

Gravois, Martha. "Military Families in Germany, 1946–1986: Why They Came and Why They Stay." *Parameters: Journal of the U.S. Army War College* 16 (4): 57–67.

Hackworth, David. *About Face*. New York: Simon & Schuster, 1989.

Hauser, William L. *America's Army in Crisis*. Baltimore: Johns Hopkins University Press, 1973.

Holmes, Thomas H., and Richard H. Rahe. "Social Readjustment Rating Scale." *Journal of Psychosomatic Research* 11 (1967): 213–218.

Ingraham, Larry. *The Boys in the Barracks: Observations on American Military Life*. Philadelphia: Institute for the Study of Human Issues, 1984.

———. "The OER Cudgel: Radical Surgery Needed." *Army* (November 1985): 54–56.

———. "Fear and Loathing in the Baracks—And the Heart of Leadership." *Parameters: Journal of the U.S. Army War College* (December 1988): 75–80.

Kirkland, Faris R. "Assessing COHORT." *Army* 40, no. 5 (May 1990): 44–50.

Kirkland, Faris R., and Pearl Katz. "Combat Readiness and the Army Family." *Military Review* 69, no. 4 (April 1989): 63–74.

Kitfield, James. *Prodigal Soldiers*. New York: Simon & Schuster, 1995.

Lee, Richard Borshay. "Eating Christmas in the Kalahari." *Natural History* (December 1969): 14–22, 60–63.

Lévi-Strauss, Claude. *Totemism*. Translated by Rodney Needham. Boston: Beacon Press, 1963.

Lewis, Charlene S. "COHORT Life OCONUS: A Report to the New Manning System." In David H. Marlowe et. al., eds., *New Manning System Evaluation Report No. 2.,* Appendix F. Washington DC: Walter Reed Army Institute of Research, 1986.

———. "The Financial Status of 100 Families Beginning an Overseas Tour: An Initial Analysis of Data Collected on the Government Rental Housing Program." Heidelberg, Germany: U.S. Army Medical Research Unit—Europe, HQ, 7th Medical Command, APO NY 09102-4428, 1987.

———. "Families and Finances in Europe: Final Evaluation of the Government Rental Housing Program—Phase I." Heidelberg, Germany: U.S. Army Medical Research Unit—Europe, HQ, 7th Medical Command, APO NY 09102-4428, 1988.

Loeffke, Bernard, Brigadier General. "Values for Infantry Leaders." *Infantry* 76, no. 5 (September/October, 1986): 11–12.

Luvaas, Jay. *Dear Miss Em: General Eichelbergers's War in the Pacific 1942–1943.* Westport, CT: Greenwood Press, 1973.

Malinowski, Bronislaw. *Argonauts of the Western Pacific: An Account of Native Enterprise and Adventure in the Archipelagoes of Melanesian New Guinea.* New York: E. P. Dutton, 1961 (1922).

Mallonee, Richard D. II. *The Naked Flagpole: Battle for Bataan.* San Rafael, CA: Presidio Press, 1980.

Marcus, George E., and Michael M. J. Fischer. *Anthropology As Cultural Critique: An Experimental Moment in the Human Sciences.* Chicago: University of Chicago Press, 1986.

Marlowe, David H., Faris R. Kirkland, Theodore P. Furukawa, Joel M. Teitelbaum, Larry H. Ingraham, and Bruce T. Caine. *Unit Manning System Field Evaluation,* Technical Report No. 5. Washington, DC: Walter Reed Army Institute of Research, 1987.

Marshall, Judi. "Stress Amongst Nurses." In *White Collar and Professional Stress,* edited by Cary L. Cooper and Judi Marshall, 19–59. New York: John Wiley and Sons, 1980.

Maslach, Christina, and Susan E. Jackson. "Burned-Out Cops and Their Families." *Psychology Today* (May 1979): 59–62.

Mendonsa, Eugene L. *The Politics of Divination: A Processual View of Reactions to Illness and Deviance Among the Sisala of Northern Ghana.* Berkeley: University of California Press, 1982.

Merritt, Anna J., and Richard J. Merritt. *Public Opinion in Semisovereign Germany.* Urbana: University of Illinois Press, 1980.

Michener, James. *Iberia: Spanish Travels and Reflections.* New York: Random House, 1968.

Middleton, John. *Lugbara Religion; Ritual and Authority among an East African People.* London: International African Institute by the Oxford University Press, 1964.

Miles, Donna, "Upping the Tempo." *Soldiers* 50, no. 6 (June 1995): 14–17

Mogahadam, L. Z. "The Reciprocal Nature of Work and Family: Perception of the Work-Family Interface and Its Impact on Army Reenlistment Behavior." Ph.D. diss., University of Maryland, Department of Sociology, 1989.

Morrison, Peter A., Georges Vernez, David W. Grissmer, and Kevin F. McCarthy. *Families in the Army: Looking Ahead.* R-3691-A. Santa Monica, CA: Arroyo Center, Rand Corporation, 1989.

Moskos, Charles C., and John Sibley Butler. *All That We Can Be: Black Leadership and Racial Integration the Army Way.* New York: Basic Books, 1996.

Moskos, Charles C. and Frank R. Wood, eds. *The Military: More than Just a Job?* Washington: Pergamon Brassey's International Defense Publishers, 1988.

NATO Information Service. *NATO and the Warsaw Pact: Force Comparisons.* Brussels: NATO Information Service, 1984.

Nelson, Daniel J. *A History of U.S. Military Forces in Germany.* Boulder, CO: Westview Press, 1987.

Newman, Aubrey "Red" (Major General, retired). *Follow Me: The Human Element in Leadership.* Novato, CA: Presidio Press, 1981.

North Atlantic Treaty Organization. "North Atlantic Treaty, Status of Forces Agreement." In *United States Treaties and Other International Agreements,* vol. 4, pt. 2. (TIAS 2846, pages 1792–1829.) Washington, DC: United States Government Printing Office, 1953.

Nuckolls, Charles W. *Culture: A Problem that Cannot be Solved.* Madison: University of Wisconsin Press, 1998.

O'Connor, Robert. *Buffalo Soldiers.* New York: Vintage Books, 1994.

Office of the Assistant Secretary of Defense. *Family Status and Initial Term of Service.* Vol. 2 of 4 vols. Washington, DC: Office of the Assistant Secretary of Defense, 1993.

———. *Population Representation in the Military Services: Fiscal Year 1994.* Washington, DC: Office of the Assistant Secretary of Defense, 1995.

Popper, Karl. *The Logic of Scientific Discovery.* New York: Harper Torchbooks, 1959.

———. *Conjectures and Refutations: The Growth of Scientific Knowledge.* New York: Harper Torchbooks, 1963.

Rosen, Leora N., Linda Z. Moghadam, and Mark A. Vaitkus, "The Military Family's Influence on Soldiers' Personal Morale: A Path Analytic Model," *Military Psychology* 1, no. 4 (1989): 201–213.

Rosenau, Pauline Marie. *Post Modernism and the Social Sciences: Insights, Inroads, and Intrusions.* Princeton NJ: Princeton University Press, 1992.

Rothberg, Joseph M., Robert J. Ursano, and Harry C. Holloway, "Suicide in the United States Army," *Psychiatric Annals* 17 (August 1987): 545–548.

Schneider, David M. *American Kinship: A Cultural Account.* Englewood Cliffs, NJ: Prentice-Hall, 1968.

———. "Notes Toward a Theory of Culture." In *Meaning in Anthropology.* Edited by Keith H. Basso and Henry A. Selby, 197–220. Albuquerque: University of New Mexico Press, 1976.

Scott, James C. *Weapons of the Weak: Everyday Forms of Peasant Resistance.* New Haven, CT: Yale University Press, 1985.

———. *Domination and the Arts of Resistance: Hidden Transcripts.* New Haven, CT: Yale University Press, 1990.

Segal, Mady Wechsler. "The Military and the Family as Greedy Institutions." *Armed Forces and Society* 13, no. 1 (1986): 9–38.

Select Committee on Children, Youth, and Families, House of Representatives. *On the Front Lines: Police Stress and Family Well-Being.* Washington, DC: U.S. Government Printing Office, 1991.

Stars and Stripes. 1 May 1945–December 1997. German edition.

Tocqueville, Alexis de. *Democracy in America.* Edited by J. P. Mayer. Translated by George Lawrence. Garden City, NY: Anchor Books, Doubleday & Company, 1969.

United States Army Europe. *Community and Deputy Community Commanders Handbook.* USAREUR Pamphlet 10-20. Heidelberg, Germany: Headquarters, USAREUR and Seventh Army, APO NY 09403, 1 August 1986.

———. *U.S. Army Europe & 7th Army: 1995.* Heidelberg, Germany: Public Affairs Office, Headquarters, U.S. Army Europe, 1995.

————. *U.S. Army Europe & 7th Army: 1996.* Heidelberg, Germany: Public Affairs Office, Headquarters, U.S. Army Europe, 1996.

————. *America's Army in Europe: On Point for the Nation.* Occasional pamphlet, circa October 1999, 3.

Varenne, Herve. *Americans Together: Structured Diversity in a Midwestern Town.* New York: Teachers College Press, 1977.

Vernez, Georges, and Gail L. Zellman. *Families and Mission: A Review of the Effects of Family Factors on Army Attrition, Retention, and Readiness*, N-2624-A. Santa Monica, CA: Rand Corporation, August 1987.

Washington Post. September 12–20, 1971, March 26, 1985.

Webster's Ninth New Collegiate Dictionary. Springfield, MA: Merriam-Webster Inc., 1990.

Witherspoon, Gary. *Dynamic Symmetry and Holistic Asymmetry in Navajo and Western Art and Cosmology.* American Indian Series, Vol. 5. New York: Peter Lang Publishing, 1995.

Wolf, Charlotte. *Garrison Community: A Study of an Overseas American Military Colony.* Westport, CT: Greenwood Publishing, 1969.

Index

About the Author

JOHN P. HAWKINS is Professor of Anthropology at Brigham Young University. He is also a lieutenant colonel in the Medical Service Corps of the United States Army Reserve (retired as of August 2000) and has been a research associate of the Department of Military Psychiatry (now called Soldier and Family Studies), Division of Neuropsychiatry, Walter Reed Army Institute of Research since 1981.